# SPECTRUM®

# Grade 3

Published by Spectrum®
an imprint of Carson-Dellosa Publishing
Greensboro, NC

Spectrum®
An imprint of Carson-Dellosa Publishing LLC
P.O. Box 35665
Greensboro, NC 27425  USA

ISBN 978-1-4838-1322-6

02-154151120

# Table of Contents Grade 3

## Math

## Language Arts

**Chapter 1:** Grammar

**Chapter 2:** Mechanics

## Reading

# SPECTRUM®

# Math

# Chapter 1

## Lesson 1.1 Adding through 20

addend     3  ⟶  Find the **3**-row.
addend  + 8  ⟶  Find the **8**-column.
_____
sum      11  ⟵  The sum is named where the 3-row and the 8-column meet.

**8-column**
**Addend**

| +  | 0 | 1  | 2  | 3  | 4  | 5  | 6  | 7  | 8  | 9  |
|----|---|----|----|----|----|----|----|----|----|----|
| 0  | 0 | 1  | 2  | 3  | 4  | 5  | 6  | 7  | 8  | 9  |
| 1  | 1 | 2  | 3  | 4  | 5  | 6  | 7  | 8  | 9  | 10 |
| 2  | 2 | 3  | 4  | 5  | 6  | 7  | 8  | 9  | 10 | 11 |
| 3  | 3 | 4  | 5  | 6  | 7  | 8  | 9  | 10 | 11 | 12 |
| 4  | 4 | 5  | 6  | 7  | 8  | 9  | 10 | 11 | 12 | 13 |
| 5  | 5 | 6  | 7  | 8  | 9  | 10 | 11 | 12 | 13 | 14 |
| 6  | 6 | 7  | 8  | 9  | 10 | 11 | 12 | 13 | 14 | 15 |
| 7  | 7 | 8  | 9  | 10 | 11 | 12 | 13 | 14 | 15 | 16 |
| 8  | 8 | 9  | 10 | 11 | 12 | 13 | 14 | 15 | 16 | 17 |
| 9  | 9 | 10 | 11 | 12 | 13 | 14 | 15 | 16 | 17 | 18 |

**3-row**

**Addend**

---

Add.

|     | a | b | c | d | e | f |
|-----|---|---|---|---|---|---|
| **1.** | 2<br>+3<br>5 | 7<br>+9 | 2<br>+5 | 1<br>+7 | 0<br>+3 | 9<br>+5 |
| **2.** | 7<br>+2 | 3<br>+3 | 9<br>+0 | 6<br>+5 | 0<br>+7 | 8<br>+5 |
| **3.** | 4<br>+3 | 2<br>+9 | 7<br>+7 | 5<br>+6 | 5<br>+9 | 0<br>+6 |
| **4.** | 0<br>+0 | 8<br>+3 | 8<br>+6 | 6<br>+1 | 5<br>+3 | 4<br>+8 |
| **5.** | 5<br>+2 | 3<br>+1 | 2<br>+4 | 8<br>+2 | 8<br>+8 | 3<br>+6 |
| **6.** | 10<br>+10 | 15<br>+ 0 | 13<br>+ 7 | 6<br>+9 | 9<br>+9 | 5<br>+7 |

# Lesson 1.2 Subtracting through 20

**7-column**

minuend     1 2  ⟶  Find the **12** in
subtrahend − 7  ⟶  the **7**-column.

difference     5  ⟵  The difference is the number at the end of the row.

| − | 0 | 1 | 2 | 3 | 4 | 5 | 6 | 7 | 8 | 9 |
|---|---|---|---|---|---|---|---|---|---|---|
| 0 | 0 | 1 | 2 | 3 | 4 | 5 | 6 | 7 | 8 | 9 |
| 1 | 1 | 2 | 3 | 4 | 5 | 6 | 7 | 8 | 9 | 10 |
| 2 | 2 | 3 | 4 | 5 | 6 | 7 | 8 | 9 | 10 | 11 |
| 3 | 3 | 4 | 5 | 6 | 7 | 8 | 9 | 10 | 11 | 12 |
| 4 | 4 | 5 | 6 | 7 | 8 | 9 | 10 | 11 | 12 | 13 |
| 5 | 5 | 6 | 7 | 8 | 9 | 10 | 11 | 12 | 13 | 14 |
| 6 | 6 | 7 | 8 | 9 | 10 | 11 | 12 | 13 | 14 | 15 |
| 7 | 7 | 8 | 9 | 10 | 11 | 12 | 13 | 14 | 15 | 16 |
| 8 | 8 | 9 | 10 | 11 | 12 | 13 | 14 | 15 | 16 | 17 |
| 9 | 9 | 10 | 11 | 12 | 13 | 14 | 15 | 16 | 17 | 18 |

Subtract.

| | a | b | c | d | e | f |
|---|---|---|---|---|---|---|
| **1.** | 7 −2 | 6 −0 | 5 −4 | 11 − 6 | 16 − 9 | 13 − 8 |
| | 5 | | | | | |
| **2.** | 6 −3 | 9 −6 | 5 −2 | 8 −0 | 18 − 9 | 9 −7 |
| **3.** | 7 −2 | 3 −0 | 8 −2 | 7 −4 | 10 − 3 | 9 −2 |
| **4.** | 14 − 3 | 3 −2 | 19 − 3 | 13 − 5 | 13 − 8 | 17 − 4 |
| **5.** | 12 − 5 | 6 −4 | 1 −0 | 12 − 3 | 10 − 6 | 11 − 5 |
| **6.** | 3 −1 | 20 − 3 | 9 −1 | 5 −1 | 8 −7 | 14 − 8 |

# Lesson 1.3 Adding 2-Digit Numbers (no renaming)

First, add the ones.    Then, add the tens.

```
  4 3              4 3              4 3     addend
+ 2 2            + 2 2            + 2 2     addend
_____          _____          _____
                     5              6 5     sum
```

```
  2 2     addend
+ 1 6     addend
_____
  3 8     sum
```
↑ ↑  --- First, add the ones.
     --- Then, add the tens.

Add.

|  | a | b | c | d | e | f |
|---|---|---|---|---|---|---|
| **1.** | 2 3<br>+ 1 6<br>—<br>3 9 | 1 1<br>+ 2 2 | 2 0<br>+ 1 0 | 1 6<br>+ 1 2 | 7 3<br>+ 1 5 | 6 3<br>+ 1 3 |
| **2.** | 1 0<br>+ 1 7 | 1 8<br>+ 3 0 | 1 3<br>+ 1 4 | 3 2<br>+ 5 1 | 8 1<br>+ 1 1 | 3 4<br>+ 2 1 |
| **3.** | 1 4<br>+ 1 2 | 3 4<br>+ 1 3 | 4 1<br>+ 1 8 | 3 0<br>+ 5 0 | 2 7<br>+ 5 0 | 2 2<br>+ 2 2 |
| **4.** | 1 8<br>+ 4 1 | 1 3<br>+ 4 2 | 1 2<br>+ 4 4 | 3 1<br>+ 1 7 | 2 7<br>+ 4 2 | 3 1<br>+ 3 8 |
| **5.** | 1 3<br>+ 1 4 | 1 5<br>+ 4 3 | 2 3<br>+ 4 2 | 2 2<br>+ 7 1 | 3 7<br>+ 6 0 | 3 5<br>+ 2 3 |
| **6.** | 1 0<br>+ 4 3 | 7 3<br>+ 2 0 | 8 6<br>+ 1 3 | 5 2<br>+ 1 3 | 4 2<br>+ 2 6 | 3 2<br>+ 4 5 |

# Lesson 1.4 Subtracting 2-Digit Numbers (no renaming)

First, subtract the ones.    Then, subtract the tens.

| 3 6 | 3 6 | 3 6 | minuend |
|---|---|---|---|
| − 2 3 | − 2 3 | − 2 3 | subtrahend |
| | 3 | 1 3 | difference |

Subtract.

|  | a | b | c | d | e | f |
|---|---|---|---|---|---|---|
| 1. | 23<br>−12<br>15 | 86<br>−22 | 93<br>−71 | 30<br>−10 | 92<br>−11 | 48<br>−16 |
| 2. | 62<br>−10 | 83<br>−13 | 65<br>−44 | 54<br>−12 | 37<br>−25 | 88<br>−32 |
| 3. | 86<br>−45 | 92<br>−70 | 89<br>−62 | 75<br>−62 | 88<br>−44 | 90<br>−60 |
| 4. | 82<br>−41 | 57<br>−36 | 35<br>−23 | 65<br>−43 | 81<br>−60 | 42<br>−30 |
| 5. | 60<br>−30 | 46<br>−25 | 92<br>−81 | 86<br>−32 | 57<br>−36 | 29<br>−13 |
| 6. | 25<br>−15 | 28<br>−12 | 36<br>−13 | 46<br>−15 | 75<br>−14 | 64<br>−23 |

# Lesson 1.5 Adding 2-Digit Numbers (with renaming)

Add the ones.
Rename 12 as 10 + 2.

Add the tens.

$$
\begin{array}{r} 37 \\ +25 \\ \hline \end{array}
$$

$$
\begin{array}{r} 7 \\ +\ 5 \\ \hline 12 \ \text{or}\ 10+2 \end{array}
$$

$$
\begin{array}{r} \overset{1}{3}7 \\ +25 \\ \hline 2 \end{array}
$$

$$
\begin{array}{r} \overset{1}{3}7 \\ +25 \\ \hline 62 \end{array}
$$

addend
addend

sum

Add.

|  | a | b | c | d | e | f |
|---|---|---|---|---|---|---|
| **1.** | 23 +18 | 76 +15 | 13 +77 | 36 +16 | 19 +62 | 29 +19 |
|  | 41 |  |  |  |  |  |
| **2.** | 27 +36 | 52 +39 | 36 +28 | 30 +50 | 56 +27 | 59 +13 |
| **3.** | 54 +27 | 53 +28 | 28 +17 | 13 +19 | 39 +17 | 56 +14 |
| **4.** | 62 +19 | 27 +18 | 26 +55 | 18 +13 | 72 +18 | 37 +17 |
| **5.** | 23 +57 | 29 +16 | 25 +16 | 38 +14 | 26 +28 | 76 +15 |
| **6.** | 29 +17 | 34 +27 | 43 +27 | 25 +26 | 48 +12 | 45 +46 |

# Lesson 1.6 Subtracting 2-Digit Numbers (with renaming)

|  | Subtract the ones. Rename 52 as "4 tens and 12 ones." | Subtract the ones. | Subtract the tens. |  |
|---|---|---|---|---|
| $\begin{array}{r} 52 \\ -19 \\ \hline \end{array}$ | $\begin{array}{r} \overset{4\ 12}{\cancel{5}\cancel{2}} \\ -19 \\ \hline \end{array}$ | $\begin{array}{r} \overset{4\ 12}{\cancel{5}\cancel{2}} \\ -19 \\ \hline 3 \end{array}$ | $\begin{array}{r} \overset{4\ 12}{\cancel{5}\cancel{2}} \\ -19 \\ \hline 33 \end{array}$ | minuend<br>subtrahend<br>difference |

Subtract.

|  | a | b | c | d | e | f |
|---|---|---|---|---|---|---|
| 1. | $\begin{array}{r} 30 \\ -22 \\ \hline 8 \end{array}$ | $\begin{array}{r} 22 \\ -19 \\ \hline \end{array}$ | $\begin{array}{r} 53 \\ -28 \\ \hline \end{array}$ | $\begin{array}{r} 41 \\ -27 \\ \hline \end{array}$ | $\begin{array}{r} 92 \\ -56 \\ \hline \end{array}$ | $\begin{array}{r} 86 \\ -27 \\ \hline \end{array}$ |
| 2. | $\begin{array}{r} 83 \\ -66 \\ \hline \end{array}$ | $\begin{array}{r} 62 \\ -56 \\ \hline \end{array}$ | $\begin{array}{r} 51 \\ -17 \\ \hline \end{array}$ | $\begin{array}{r} 34 \\ -15 \\ \hline \end{array}$ | $\begin{array}{r} 46 \\ -29 \\ \hline \end{array}$ | $\begin{array}{r} 57 \\ -38 \\ \hline \end{array}$ |
| 3. | $\begin{array}{r} 72 \\ -37 \\ \hline \end{array}$ | $\begin{array}{r} 82 \\ -67 \\ \hline \end{array}$ | $\begin{array}{r} 64 \\ -18 \\ \hline \end{array}$ | $\begin{array}{r} 86 \\ -57 \\ \hline \end{array}$ | $\begin{array}{r} 41 \\ -16 \\ \hline \end{array}$ | $\begin{array}{r} 53 \\ -29 \\ \hline \end{array}$ |
| 4. | $\begin{array}{r} 24 \\ -17 \\ \hline \end{array}$ | $\begin{array}{r} 60 \\ -20 \\ \hline \end{array}$ | $\begin{array}{r} 86 \\ -27 \\ \hline \end{array}$ | $\begin{array}{r} 93 \\ -26 \\ \hline \end{array}$ | $\begin{array}{r} 52 \\ -17 \\ \hline \end{array}$ | $\begin{array}{r} 47 \\ -28 \\ \hline \end{array}$ |
| 5. | $\begin{array}{r} 86 \\ -38 \\ \hline \end{array}$ | $\begin{array}{r} 45 \\ -18 \\ \hline \end{array}$ | $\begin{array}{r} 42 \\ -19 \\ \hline \end{array}$ | $\begin{array}{r} 96 \\ -39 \\ \hline \end{array}$ | $\begin{array}{r} 63 \\ -27 \\ \hline \end{array}$ | $\begin{array}{r} 87 \\ -68 \\ \hline \end{array}$ |
| 6. | $\begin{array}{r} 53 \\ -17 \\ \hline \end{array}$ | $\begin{array}{r} 92 \\ -45 \\ \hline \end{array}$ | $\begin{array}{r} 86 \\ -18 \\ \hline \end{array}$ | $\begin{array}{r} 72 \\ -17 \\ \hline \end{array}$ | $\begin{array}{r} 63 \\ -45 \\ \hline \end{array}$ | $\begin{array}{r} 52 \\ -13 \\ \hline \end{array}$ |

## Lesson 1.7 Adding Three Numbers

Add the ones.                                          Add the tens.

```
  2 3      3                          1          1
  4 7      7        1 0             2 3        2 3    addend
+ 1 6    + 6      +   6             4 7        4 7    addend
                  ─────           + 1 6      + 1 6    addend
                  1 6  or 10 + 6     6        ─────
                                             8 6      sum
```

Add.

|     | a | b | c | d | e | f |
|-----|---|---|---|---|---|---|
| **1.** | 1 3<br>2 6<br>+ 4 5<br>──────<br>8 4 | 7<br>2 9<br>+ 5 6 | 1 6<br>2 3<br>+ 2 5 | 2 7<br>7<br>+ 3 4 | 6<br>1 3<br>+ 2 9 | 1 0<br>3 0<br>+ 5 0 |
| **2.** | 2 2<br>3 1<br>+ 4 5 | 1 9<br>2 1<br>+ 3 2 | 2 9<br>1 6<br>+ 1 5 | 1 3<br>1 5<br>+ 2 5 | 4 2<br>2 1<br>+ 8 | 2 6<br>2 3<br>+ 3 5 |
| **3.** | 1 1<br>3 0<br>+ 4 2 | 2 7<br>1 6<br>+ 9 | 4<br>7<br>+ 8 | 3 4<br>1 6<br>+ 4 1 | 1 6<br>2 3<br>+ 3 5 | 2 9<br>3 1<br>+ 2 5 |
| **4.** | 8 2<br>5<br>+ 9 | 3 3<br>4 7<br>+ 1 2 | 8 6<br>5<br>+ 2 | 1 8<br>3 2<br>+ 1 6 | 4 6<br>2 9<br>+ 1 6 | 5 3<br>2 1<br>+ 1 5 |
| **5.** | 6 6<br>2 1<br>+ 8 | 4 7<br>1 3<br>+ 8 | 2 2<br>4 1<br>+ 2 8 | 2 3<br>1 5<br>+ 1 7 | 1 8<br>1 6<br>+ 2 4 | 2 3<br>3 5<br>+ 1 7 |

# Chapter 2

## Lesson 2.1 Adding 2-Digit Numbers

Add the ones.

Add the tens.

$$
\begin{array}{r}
75 \\
+66 \\
\hline
\end{array}
\qquad
\begin{array}{r}
\overset{1}{7}5 \\
+66 \\
\hline
1
\end{array}
\qquad
\begin{array}{r}
\overset{1}{7}5 \\
+\phantom{0}66 \\
\hline
141
\end{array}
\quad
\begin{array}{l}
\text{addend} \\
\text{addend} \\
\text{sum}
\end{array}
$$

$5 + 6 = 11$

Add.

| | a | b | c | d | e | f |
|---|---|---|---|---|---|---|
| **1.** | 23 +95 = 118 | 17 +86 | 90 +50 | 72 +46 | 87 +23 | 97 +65 |
| **2.** | 19 +75 | 26 +93 | 47 +58 | 54 +59 | 64 +94 | 87 +27 |
| **3.** | 23 +79 | 38 +81 | 75 +86 | 23 +92 | 86 +41 | 39 +82 |
| **4.** | 43 +71 | 65 +39 | 37 +82 | 19 +83 | 43 +62 | 75 +95 |
| **5.** | 60 +40 | 20 +87 | 23 +97 | 26 +85 | 94 +45 | 23 +63 |
| **6.** | 67 +72 | 95 +92 | 83 +67 | 49 +69 | 27 +99 | 82 +57 |

# Lesson 2.2 Subtracting 2 Digits from 3 Digits

| Subtract the ones. | To subtract the tens, rename the 1 hundred and 2 tens as "12 tens." | Subtract the tens. | |
|---|---|---|---|

$$\begin{array}{r} 125 \\ -\phantom{0}84 \\ \hline \end{array} \qquad \begin{array}{r} 125 \\ -\phantom{0}84 \\ \hline \phantom{00}1 \end{array} \qquad \begin{array}{r} ^{12}\not{1}\not{2}5 \\ -\phantom{0}84 \\ \hline \phantom{00}1 \end{array} \qquad \begin{array}{r} ^{12}\not{1}\not{2}5 \\ -\phantom{0}84 \\ \hline \phantom{0}41 \end{array}$$

minuend
subtrahend
difference

Subtract.

|     | a | b | c | d | e | f |
|-----|-----|-----|-----|-----|-----|-----|
| 1.  | 173<br>− 33<br>**140** | 121<br>− 60 | 195<br>− 44 | 122<br>− 11 | 147<br>− 53 | 182<br>− 90 |
| 2.  | 143<br>− 62 | 180<br>− 70 | 119<br>− 15 | 123<br>− 12 | 186<br>− 65 | 187<br>− 42 |
| 3.  | 154<br>− 13 | 127<br>− 83 | 187<br>− 67 | 135<br>− 42 | 115<br>− 24 | 171<br>− 60 |
| 4.  | 132<br>− 51 | 177<br>− 43 | 192<br>− 71 | 186<br>− 92 | 134<br>− 72 | 125<br>− 45 |
| 5.  | 129<br>− 86 | 176<br>− 75 | 120<br>− 40 | 194<br>− 53 | 189<br>− 62 | 134<br>− 42 |
| 6.  | 165<br>− 51 | 167<br>− 45 | 150<br>− 30 | 157<br>− 63 | 149<br>− 61 | 139<br>− 62 |
| 7.  | 175<br>− 82 | 167<br>− 43 | 133<br>− 41 | 148<br>− 78 | 165<br>− 43 | 128<br>− 57 |

# Lesson 2.2 Subtracting 2 Digits from 3 Digits

| Rename 5 tens and 3 ones as "4 tens and 13 ones." | | Subtract the ones. | Rename 1 hundred and 4 tens as "14 tens." | Subtract the tens. |
|---|---|---|---|---|

$$
\begin{array}{r} 153 \\ -\ 65 \\ \hline \end{array}
\qquad
\begin{array}{r} {}^{4\ 13} \\ 1\,\cancel{5}\,\cancel{3} \\ -\ 65 \\ \hline \end{array}
\qquad
\begin{array}{r} {}^{4\ 13} \\ 1\,\cancel{5}\,\cancel{3} \\ -\ 65 \\ \hline 8 \end{array}
\qquad
\begin{array}{r} {}^{14\,13} \\ 1\,\cancel{5}\,\cancel{3} \\ -\ 65 \\ \hline 8 \end{array}
\qquad
\begin{array}{r} {}^{14\,13} \\ 1\,\cancel{5}\,\cancel{3} \\ -\ 65 \\ \hline 88 \end{array}
$$

minuend
subtrahend
difference

Subtract.

|  | a | b | c | d | e | f |
|---|---|---|---|---|---|---|
| 1. | 162 − 73 = 89 | 175 − 97 | 182 − 94 | 103 − 17 | 116 − 39 | 127 − 88 |
| 2. | 174 − 95 | 147 − 68 | 132 − 65 | 115 − 49 | 107 − 39 | 181 − 95 |
| 3. | 101 − 75 | 100 − 92 | 127 − 79 | 133 − 44 | 142 − 73 | 135 − 47 |
| 4. | 141 − 63 | 137 − 79 | 142 − 73 | 153 − 67 | 155 − 96 | 164 − 88 |
| 5. | 100 − 72 | 106 − 48 | 117 − 88 | 124 − 66 | 163 − 89 | 180 − 93 |
| 6. | 172 − 87 | 161 − 92 | 145 − 66 | 132 − 57 | 130 − 43 | 120 − 62 |
| 7. | 164 − 85 | 152 − 63 | 144 − 87 | 157 − 69 | 123 − 45 | 174 − 87 |

# Lesson 2.3 Adding 3-Digit Numbers

|  | Add the ones. | Add the tens. | Add the hundreds. |
|---|---|---|---|
| 755<br>+469 | 7 5̇ 5<br>+469<br>―――<br>4 | 7̇ 5̇ 5<br>+469<br>―――<br>2 4 | 7̇ 5̇ 5<br>+ 469<br>―――<br>1 2 2 4 |

Add.

|  | a | b | c | d | e | f |
|---|---|---|---|---|---|---|
| 1. | 123<br>+562<br>――<br>685 | 982<br>+171 | 342<br>+591 | 782<br>+341 | 123<br>+321 | 681<br>+975 |
| 2. | 862<br>+313 | 900<br>+130 | 720<br>+850 | 931<br>+111 | 823<br>+457 | 547<br>+321 |
| 3. | 861<br>+421 | 862<br>+139 | 431<br>+250 | 782<br>+191 | 751<br>+605 | 871<br>+323 |
| 4. | 791<br>+191 | 144<br>+800 | 192<br>+175 | 257<br>+147 | 203<br>+211 | 541<br>+693 |
| 5. | 705<br>+719 | 641<br>+209 | 873<br>+505 | 700<br>+650 | 105<br>+341 | 450<br>+362 |
| 6. | 593<br>+741 | 861<br>+209 | 735<br>+145 | 820<br>+431 | 738<br>+387 | 719<br>+120 |
| 7. | 153<br>+312 | 712<br>+210 | 619<br>+715 | 205<br>+316 | 153<br>+814 | 613<br>+261 |

NAME _____

# Lesson 2.4 Subtracting 3-Digit Numbers

Rename 2 tens and
1 one as "1 ten and
11 ones." Then,
subtract the ones.

Rename 6 hundreds and
1 ten as "5 hundreds and
11 tens." Then, subtract
the tens.

Subtract the
hundreds.

```
  6 2 1        6 2̷ 1̷        5̷ 2̷ 1̷        5̷ 2̷ 1̷   minuend
- 2 5 9      - 2 5 9      - 2 5 9      - 2 5 9   subtrahend
  ___          ___          ___          ___
                 2           6 2          3 6 2   difference
```

Subtract.

|  | a | b | c | d | e | f |
|---|---|---|---|---|---|---|
| 1. | 321 −109 | 745 −152 | 639 −150 | 830 −710 | 626 −146 | 457 −309 |
|  | 212 | | | | | |
| 2. | 729 −321 | 657 −451 | 386 −107 | 411 −305 | 486 −109 | 311 −121 |
| 3. | 983 −652 | 971 −572 | 876 −357 | 549 −360 | 721 −144 | 958 −637 |
| 4. | 256 −142 | 347 −139 | 725 −196 | 863 −692 | 980 −532 | 720 −500 |
| 5. | 543 −457 | 762 −135 | 132 −107 | 921 −571 | 631 −545 | 982 −144 |
| 6. | 531 −250 | 720 −371 | 582 −357 | 793 −457 | 612 −483 | 592 −107 |

# Lesson 2.5 Thinking Subtraction for Addition

To check

215 + 109 = 324,

subtract 109 from 324.

$$\begin{array}{r} 215 \\ +109 \\ \hline 324 \\ -109 \\ \hline 215 \end{array}$$

These should be the same.

---

Add. Check each answer.

|     | a | b | c | d | e | f |
|-----|---|---|---|---|---|---|
| 1. | $\begin{array}{r} 157 \\ +212 \\ \hline 369 \\ -212 \\ \hline 157 \end{array}$ | $\begin{array}{r} 719 \\ +182 \\ \hline \end{array}$ | $\begin{array}{r} 312 \\ +105 \\ \hline \end{array}$ | $\begin{array}{r} 213 \\ +519 \\ \hline \end{array}$ | $\begin{array}{r} 306 \\ +215 \\ \hline \end{array}$ | $\begin{array}{r} 120 \\ +170 \\ \hline \end{array}$ |
| 2. | $\begin{array}{r} 710 \\ +398 \\ \hline \end{array}$ | $\begin{array}{r} 357 \\ +249 \\ \hline \end{array}$ | $\begin{array}{r} 712 \\ +363 \\ \hline \end{array}$ | $\begin{array}{r} 714 \\ +291 \\ \hline \end{array}$ | $\begin{array}{r} 312 \\ +\ 85 \\ \hline \end{array}$ | $\begin{array}{r} 419 \\ +\ 57 \\ \hline \end{array}$ |
| 3. | $\begin{array}{r} 300 \\ +547 \\ \hline \end{array}$ | $\begin{array}{r} 591 \\ +120 \\ \hline \end{array}$ | $\begin{array}{r} 612 \\ +319 \\ \hline \end{array}$ | $\begin{array}{r} 425 \\ +125 \\ \hline \end{array}$ | $\begin{array}{r} 411 \\ +120 \\ \hline \end{array}$ | $\begin{array}{r} 247 \\ +259 \\ \hline \end{array}$ |
| 4. | $\begin{array}{r} 863 \\ +192 \\ \hline \end{array}$ | $\begin{array}{r} 459 \\ +130 \\ \hline \end{array}$ | $\begin{array}{r} 603 \\ +209 \\ \hline \end{array}$ | $\begin{array}{r} 711 \\ +191 \\ \hline \end{array}$ | $\begin{array}{r} 252 \\ +130 \\ \hline \end{array}$ | $\begin{array}{r} 412 \\ +283 \\ \hline \end{array}$ |

# **Lesson 2.6** Thinking Addition for Subtraction

To check

982 − 657 = 325,

add 657 to 325.

```
    982  ←- - - -┐
   -657          │
   ────          │
    325   These should be the same.
   +657          │
   ────          │
    982  ←- - - -┘
```

---

Subtract. Check each answer.

|     | **a** | **b** | **c** | **d** | **e** | **f** |
|-----|-------|-------|-------|-------|-------|-------|
| **1.** | 720 | 321 | 125 | 983 | 456 | 442 |
|     | −150 | − 83 | − 92 | −657 | −291 | −220 |
|     | 570 |       |       |       |       |       |
|     | +150 |       |       |       |       |       |
|     | 720 |       |       |       |       |       |

|     | **a** | **b** | **c** | **d** | **e** | **f** |
|-----|-------|-------|-------|-------|-------|-------|
| **2.** | 300 | 119 | 423 | 259 | 592 | 708 |
|     | −179 | −104 | −197 | −147 | −463 | −412 |

|     | **a** | **b** | **c** | **d** | **e** | **f** |
|-----|-------|-------|-------|-------|-------|-------|
| **3.** | 519 | 540 | 192 | 710 | 683 | 712 |
|     | −120 | −320 | − 86 | −447 | −419 | −307 |

|     | **a** | **b** | **c** | **d** | **e** | **f** |
|-----|-------|-------|-------|-------|-------|-------|
| **4.** | 719 | 919 | 687 | 912 | 542 | 728 |
|     | −532 | −457 | −250 | −609 | −327 | −530 |

# Chapter 3

## Lesson 3.1 Adding 3 or More Numbers (1- and 2-digit)

| Add the ones. | | Add the tens. |
|---|---|---|

```
    4 5          5                          →   4 5        4 5
    6 2          2  ⟍    7                      6 2        6 2
  + 9 4        + 4     + 4                    + 9 4      +  9 4
  _____       ___     ___                    _____      _____
                       1 1  or 10 + 1            1        2 0 1
```

---

Add.

|  | a | b | c | d | e | f |
|---|---|---|---|---|---|---|
| **1.** | 3<br>6<br>+9<br>___<br>1 8 | 7<br>5<br>+8 | 6<br>1 2<br>+1 3 | 8<br>1 7<br>+1 9 | 1 2<br>3 2<br>+5 3 | 8<br>6<br>+2 |
| **2.** | 1 7<br>9 3<br>+2 3 | 1 6<br>4 5<br>+9 2 | 8 2<br>1 8<br>+2 3 | 7<br>1 9<br>+5 7 | 2 2<br>8 6<br>+3 4 | 5 0<br>4 0<br>+6 0 |
| **3.** | 8 6<br>9 3<br>+7 2 | 2 3<br>3 5<br>+6 2 | 1 8<br>3 5<br>+6 7 | 8 6<br>5 4<br>+8 3 | 3 2<br>4 9<br>+7 6 | 1 3<br>1 9<br>+2 3 |
| **4.** | 2 5<br>6 6<br>+7 2 | 8 1<br>1 9<br>+8 3 | 5 3<br>4 2<br>+9 3 | 1 3<br>1 2<br>+1 4 | 1 0<br>2 0<br>+9 0 | 8 2<br>7 6<br>+5 4 |
| **5.** | 8 6<br>5 4<br>3 2<br>+5 2 | 9 2<br>1 0<br>5 3<br>+4 7 | 8 1<br>7 1<br>3 6<br>+2 7 | 1 2<br>1 8<br>2 4<br>+1 9 | 9 3<br>4 8<br>1 3<br>+2 7 | 4 1<br>8 6<br>5 3<br>+2 2 |

NAME _____

# Lesson 3.2 Adding 3 or More Numbers (3-digit)

|  | Add the ones. | Add the tens. | Add the hundreds. |
|---|---|---|---|
| 231<br>457<br>+625 | 231<br>457<br>+625<br>——<br>3 | 231<br>457<br>+625<br>——<br>13 | 231<br>457<br>+ 625<br>——<br>1313 |

Add.

|  | a | b | c | d | e | f |
|---|---|---|---|---|---|---|
| **1.** | 522<br>367<br>+151<br>——<br>1040 | 868<br>321<br>+405 | 150<br>200<br>+300 | 701<br>231<br>+862 | 986<br>105<br>+525 | 129<br>318<br>+467 |
| **2.** | 803<br>623<br>+186 | 545<br>309<br>+119 | 868<br>740<br>+809 | 132<br>195<br>+118 | 200<br>300<br>+600 | 180<br>240<br>+303 |
| **3.** | 861<br>757<br>+409 | 863<br>404<br>+891 | 731<br>356<br>+402 | 865<br>591<br>+217 | 238<br>405<br>+596 | 898<br>777<br>+192 |
| **4.** | 341<br>127<br>+192 | 864<br>425<br>+323 | 127<br>291<br>+867 | 205<br>876<br>+198 | 712<br>490<br>+600 | 750<br>400<br>+203 |
| **5.** | 591<br>603<br>907<br>+432 | 862<br>191<br>183<br>+251 | 892<br>645<br>320<br>+123 | 132<br>169<br>119<br>+105 | 323<br>309<br>452<br>+690 | 712<br>613<br>518<br>+437 |

# Lesson 3.2 Problem Solving

Solve each problem.

1. Joe earned 135 dollars during his first week of work. He earned 213 dollars during his second week of work. He earned 159 dollars during his third week of work. How much money did Joe earn during the three weeks that he worked?

   Joe earned _____ dollars during his first week.

   Joe earned _____ dollars during his second week.

   Joe earned _____ dollars during his third week.

   Joe earned _____ dollars for all 3 weeks of work.

2. On the first floor of a 3-story apartment building, there are 186 apartments occupied. On the second floor, there are 175 apartments occupied. On the third floor, there are 182 apartments occupied. How many apartments are occupied in all?

   There are _____ apartments occupied on the first floor.

   There are _____ apartments occupied on the second floor.

   There are _____ apartments occupied on the third floor.

   There are _____ apartments occupied in all.

3. The following numbers of students attend four different schools: 543, 692, 487, and 603. How many students attend all four schools?

   _____ students attend all four schools.

4. In a book, chapter 1 has 112 pages and chapter 2 has 119 pages. Chapter 3 has 103 pages and chapter 4 has 108 pages. How many pages are in the book?

   There are _____ pages in the book.

**1.**

**2.**

**3.**

**4.**

# Lesson 3.3 Adding 4-Digit Numbers

| | Add the ones. | Add the tens. | Add the hundreds. | Add the thousands. |
|---|---|---|---|---|
| 3746<br>+5899 | ¹<br>3746<br>+5899<br>5 | ¹¹<br>3746<br>+5899<br>45 | ¹¹¹<br>3746<br>+5899<br>645 | ¹¹¹<br>3746<br>+5899<br>9645 |

Add.

|  | a | b | c | d | e | f |
|---|---|---|---|---|---|---|
| **1.** | 7865<br>+1192<br>9057 | 8654<br>+1219 | 4320<br>+3069 | 3543<br>+3921 | 4293<br>+5176 | 6405<br>+3398 |
| **2.** | 1982<br>+1782 | 7083<br>+2907 | 4325<br>+4986 | 6057<br>+1239 | 8761<br>+1032 | 2305<br>+5747 |
| **3.** | 3050<br>+4707 | 6932<br>+2349 | 5437<br>+2968 | 1718<br>+2347 | 7923<br>+1250 | 4523<br>+3962 |
| **4.** | 5431<br>+2989 | 7986<br>+1479 | 1119<br>+2459 | 7239<br>+1635 | 2450<br>+7267 | 6527<br>+2985 |
| **5.** | 5431<br>+1982 | 7986<br>+1246 | 1543<br>+3989 | 7121<br>+1923 | 8763<br>+1005 | 4321<br>+2387 |
| **6.** | 5450<br>+1987 | 4733<br>+2576 | 3981<br>+2877 | 6986<br>+2928 | 7181<br>+2111 | 7900<br>+2005 |

# Lesson 3.3 Problem Solving

Solve each problem.

**1.** Two local high schools have 1,523 students and 1,695 students. How many students are there at both high schools together?

One high school has _____ students.

The other high school has _____ students.

There are a total of _____ students at both high schools.

**2.** Monica started at an elevation of 1,200 feet for her hiking trip. She hiked up the mountain for 1,320 feet in elevation. How high did she hike?

Monica started at _____ feet in elevation.

She hiked _____ feet in elevation.

She hiked up to an elevation of _____ feet.

**3.** Steve has a coin worth 1,050 dollars. He has another coin worth 1,072 dollars. How much are both coins worth?

Both coins are worth _____ dollars.

**4.** Roy ran 1,100 yards as a running back during his junior year of high school. During his senior year of high school, he ran 1,500 yards as a running back. How many yards did he run in both years combined?

Roy ran a total of _____ yards for both his junior and senior year of high school.

**1.**

**2.**

**3.**

**4.**

# Lesson 3.4 Subtracting to 4 Digits

| Subtract the ones. | Rename 4 hundreds and 3 tens as "3 hundreds and 13 tens." Subtract the tens. | Rename 5 thousands and 3 hundreds as "4 thousands and 13 hundreds." Subtract the hundreds. | Subtract the thousands. |
|---|---|---|---|

$$\begin{array}{r} 5437 \\ -1592 \\ \hline \end{array} \qquad \begin{array}{r} 5437 \\ -1592 \\ \hline 5 \end{array} \qquad \begin{array}{r} 5\overset{3\ 13}{\cancel{4}\cancel{3}}7 \\ -1592 \\ \hline 45 \end{array} \qquad \begin{array}{r} \overset{13}{\underset{4\ \cancel{3}\ 13}{\cancel{5}\cancel{4}\cancel{3}}}7 \\ -1592 \\ \hline 845 \end{array} \qquad \begin{array}{r} \overset{13}{\underset{4\ \cancel{3}\ 13}{\cancel{5}\cancel{4}\cancel{3}}}7 \\ -1592 \\ \hline 3845 \end{array}$$

Subtract.

|    | a | b | c | d | e |
|----|-----|-----|-----|-----|-----|
| 1. | 9865 −2382 | 7528 − 792 | 8654 −3993 | 1925 − 183 | 1876 − 982 |
|    | 7483 | | | | |
| 2. | 5473 −3591 | 8762 − 682 | 7945 − 963 | 8654 − 772 | 7846 −3974 |
| 3. | 6932 −2840 | 1389 − 794 | 2545 − 963 | 7863 −2572 | 8121 − 640 |
| 4. | 7865 − 974 | 3456 − 661 | 7982 − 490 | 8163 −4670 | 4325 −1534 |
| 5. | 9876 − 985 | 8716 −5823 | 5432 −3651 | 3287 − 395 | 7805 − 164 |
| 6. | 5439 − 767 | 4321 − 841 | 7865 − 974 | 7976 −4682 | 5439 − 866 |

# Lesson 3.4 Problem Solving

**SHOW YOUR WORK**

Solve each problem.

1. There are 2,532 students at the school. 1,341 are girls. How many are boys?

   There are _____ students.

   There are _____ girls.

   There are _____ boys.

2. In 2013, the average rent for a house was 1,250 dollars per month. In 1944, the average rent for a house was 495 dollars per month. How much higher was the rent in 2013 than in 1944?

   Rent in 2013 was _____ dollars per month.

   Rent in 1944 was _____ dollars per month.

   Rent in 2013 was _____ dollars per month higher than in 1944.

3. In the year 1986, Mrs. Olveras turned 103 years old. In what year was she born?

   In the year _____,

   Mrs. Olveras turned _____ years old.

   Mrs. Olveras was born in _____.

4. In the year 1996, Mr. Smith's car was considered a classic. The car was made in 1942. How old is Mr. Smith's car?

   Mr. Smith's car is _____ years old.

5. Kayla wants to visit her grandmother who lives 2,583 miles away. The airplane will only take her 2,392 miles toward her destination. Kayla needs to rent a car to drive the remaining miles. How many miles does Kayla need to drive?

   Kayla would need to drive _____ miles.

**1.**

**2.**

**3.**

**4.**     **5.**

# Lesson 3.5 Rounding

The steps for rounding are:

1) Look at the digit one place to the right of the digit you wish to round.
2) If the digit is less than 5, leave the digit in the rounding place as it is, and change the digits to the right of the rounding place to zero.
3) If the digit is 5 or greater, add 1 to the digit in the rounding place, and change the digits to the right of the rounding place to zero.

Round 5,432 to the nearest hundred. 4 is in the hundreds place. Look at the 3. Do not change the 4. 5,432 rounded to the nearest hundred is 5,400.

Round each number to the nearest ten.

|  | a | b | c | d |
|---|---|---|---|---|
| **1.** | 963 ___960___ | 154 _____ | 186 _____ | 4,031 _____ |
| **2.** | 125 ___130___ | 3,452 _____ | 8,657 _____ | 7,987 _____ |

Round each number to the nearest hundred.

|  | a | b | c | d |
|---|---|---|---|---|
| **3.** | 8,765 _____ | 986 _____ | 3,250 _____ | 7,913 _____ |
| **4.** | 507 _____ | 1,349 _____ | 842 _____ | 4,370 _____ |

Round each number to the place named.

|  | a | b | c | d |
|---|---|---|---|---|
| **5.** | 8,576 hundreds | 1,930 hundreds | 364 tens | 1,543 tens |
|  | _____ | _____ | _____ | _____ |
| **6.** | 1,886 hundreds | 765 tens | 863 hundreds | 86 tens |
|  | _____ | _____ | _____ | _____ |
| **7.** | 451 tens | 8,713 tens | 472 hundreds | 5,325 tens |
|  | _____ | _____ | _____ | _____ |
| **8.** | 3,651 hundreds | 123 tens | 486 tens | 2,356 hundreds |
|  | _____ | _____ | _____ | _____ |

# Lesson 3.5 Rounding

Round each number to the place named.

|  | a | b | c | d |
|---|---|---|---|---|
| **1.** | 543 <br> tens | 867 <br> hundreds | 479 <br> tens | 962 <br> tens |
| **2.** | 5,678 <br> hundreds | 9,654 <br> tens | 4,432 <br> hundreds | 1,605 <br> tens |
| **3.** | 592 <br> hundreds | 86 <br> tens | 5,432 <br> hundreds | 981 <br> tens |
| **4.** | 4,932 <br> tens | 9,651 <br> hundreds | 596 <br> hundreds | 720 <br> hundreds |
| **5.** | 1,081 <br> hundreds | 7,090 <br> tens | 7,446 <br> tens | 1,143 <br> tens |
| **6.** | 4,599 <br> tens | 3,923 <br> hundreds | 5,103 <br> tens | 638 <br> hundreds |
| **7.** | 85 <br> tens | 963 <br> tens | 7,732 <br> hundreds | 541 <br> tens |
| **8.** | 326 <br> hundreds | 717 <br> tens | 148 <br> tens | 823 <br> hundreds |

# Lesson 3.6 Estimating Addition

Round each number to the highest place value the numbers have in common.
Then, add from right to left.

$$
\begin{array}{r}
194 \longrightarrow 190 \\
+\ 76 \longrightarrow +\ 80 \\
\hline
270
\end{array}
\qquad
\begin{array}{r}
203 \longrightarrow 200 \\
+196 \longrightarrow +200 \\
\hline
400
\end{array}
$$

The highest place value for 194 and 76 is the tens place. Round 194 and 76 to the tens place. Add.

The highest place value for 203 and 196 is the hundreds place. Round 203 and 196 to the hundreds place. Add.

Estimate each sum.

|     | a | | b | c | d |
|-----|------|------|------|------|------|
| **1.** | 25<br>+36 | 30<br>+40<br>—<br>70 | 23<br>+14 | 57<br>+51 | 42<br>+92 |
| **2.** | 92<br>+51 | | 131<br>+ 42 | 165<br>+ 92 | 147<br>+ 97 |
| **3.** | 147<br>+362 | 100<br>+400<br>—<br>500 | 175<br>+302 | 457<br>+603 | 543<br>+261 |
| **4.** | 1132<br>+ 432 | | 1250<br>+ 347 | 5786<br>+ 432 | 4679<br>+ 578 |
| **5.** | 1562<br>+3492 | 2000<br>+3000<br>—<br>5000 | 6054<br>+6542 | 3541<br>+7987 | 2795<br>+2454 |

# Lesson 3.6 Problem Solving

Solve each problem by using estimation.

**1.** Kirima read 534 pages last week and 352 pages this week. About how many pages did Kirima read?

Kirima read about _____ pages.

**1.**

**2.** Tim has 13 dollars. James has 15 dollars. About how many dollars do they have together?

Tim and James have about _____ dollars together.

**2.**

**3.** Mr. Hwan had 532 dollars in his savings account before he made a deposit of 259 dollars. About how much money does he have in his savings account now?

Mr. Hwan has about _____ dollars in his savings account now.

**3.**

**4.** Mrs. Luna is 43 years old. Mrs. Turner is 52 years old. Mrs. Rockwell is 39 years old. About how much is their combined age?

Their combined age is about _____ years.

**4.**

**5.** Marla bought 4 boards at the home center. The boards were 86, 103, 152, and 161 inches long. About how many inches of boards did Marla buy?

Marla bought about _____ inches of boards.

**5.**

# Lesson 3.7 Estimating Subtraction

Round each number to the highest place value the numbers have in common. Then, subtract from right to left.

$$
\begin{array}{r}
236 \longrightarrow 240 \\
- \ 49 \longrightarrow - \ 50 \\
\hline
190
\end{array}
\qquad
\begin{array}{r}
396 \longrightarrow 400 \\
-287 \longrightarrow -300 \\
\hline
100
\end{array}
$$

The highest place value for 236 and 49 is the tens place. Round 236 and 49 to the tens place. Subtract.

The highest place value for 396 and 287 is the hundreds place. Round 396 and 287 to the hundreds place. Subtract.

Estimate each difference.

|  | a |  | b | c | d |
|---|---|---|---|---|---|
| **1.** | 56<br>−43 | 60<br>−40<br>20 | 49<br>−12 | 72<br>−61 | 80<br>−45 |
| **2.** | 451<br>− 72 |  | 986<br>− 59 | 760<br>− 32 | 542<br>− 57 |
| **3.** | 543<br>−290 | 500<br>−300<br>200 | 943<br>−457 | 547<br>−249 | 686<br>−162 |
| **4.** | 1543<br>− 661 |  | 3247<br>− 843 | 4560<br>− 493 | 7631<br>− 647 |
| **5.** | 8798<br>−4453 | 9000<br>−4000<br>5000 | 9476<br>−2652 | 7345<br>−6443 | 9432<br>−1486 |

# Lesson 3.7 Problem Solving

Solve each problem by using estimation.

1. Fred had 39 dollars. He gave 23 dollars to Kim. About how much money does Fred have left?

   Fred has about _____ dollars left.

2. There are 186 apartments in an apartment building. 92 are not rented. About how many apartments are rented?

   There are about _____ rented apartments.

3. Sue wants to buy a bicycle for 560 dollars. She has 430 dollars. About how much more money does she need to buy the bicycle?

   Sue needs about _____ more dollars to buy the bicycle.

4. At the theater, 98 adult tickets were sold. If 210 tickets were sold, about how many children's tickets were sold?

   About _____ children's tickets were sold.

5. Kelly bought a roll of cloth 197 inches long. She cut 85 inches off the roll to use in a project. About how many inches did she have left on the roll?

   Kelly had about _____ inches left on the roll:

1.

2.

3.

4.

5.

# Chapter 4

## Lesson 4.1 Understanding Multiplication

two times seven
$$2 \times 7 \text{ means } 7 + 7$$

$$
\begin{array}{r}
7 \\
\times\ 2 \\
\hline
14
\end{array}
\begin{array}{l}
\text{factor} \\
\text{factor} \\
\text{product}
\end{array}
\qquad
\begin{array}{r}
7 \\
+\ 7 \\
\hline
14
\end{array}
$$

five times three
$$5 \times 3 \text{ means } 5 + 5 + 5$$

$$
\begin{array}{r}
5 \\
\times\ 3 \\
\hline
15
\end{array}
\begin{array}{l}
\text{factor} \\
\text{factor} \\
\text{product}
\end{array}
\qquad
\begin{array}{r}
5 \\
5 \\
+\ 5 \\
\hline
15
\end{array}
$$

Multiply. Write the corresponding addition problem next to each multiplication problem.

|  | a | b | c | d | e |
|---|---|---|---|---|---|
| **1.** | $\begin{array}{r}3\\ \times 2\\ \hline 6\end{array}$  $\begin{array}{r}3\\ +3\\ \hline 6\end{array}$ | $\begin{array}{r}7\\ \times 2\\ \hline\end{array}$ | $\begin{array}{r}6\\ \times 2\\ \hline\end{array}$ | $\begin{array}{r}9\\ \times 2\\ \hline\end{array}$ | $\begin{array}{r}8\\ \times 2\\ \hline\end{array}$ |
| **2.** | $\begin{array}{r}2\\ \times 2\\ \hline\end{array}$ | $\begin{array}{r}1\\ \times 2\\ \hline\end{array}$ | $\begin{array}{r}5\\ \times 3\\ \hline\end{array}$ | $\begin{array}{r}6\\ \times 3\\ \hline\end{array}$ | $\begin{array}{r}3\\ \times 3\\ \hline\end{array}$ |
| **3.** | $\begin{array}{r}2\\ \times 3\\ \hline\end{array}$ | $\begin{array}{r}1\\ \times 3\\ \hline\end{array}$ | $\begin{array}{r}4\\ \times 3\\ \hline\end{array}$ | $\begin{array}{r}7\\ \times 3\\ \hline\end{array}$ | $\begin{array}{r}2\\ \times 4\\ \hline\end{array}$ |
| **4.** | $\begin{array}{r}4\\ \times 4\\ \hline\end{array}$ | $\begin{array}{r}1\\ \times 4\\ \hline\end{array}$ | $\begin{array}{r}5\\ \times 4\\ \hline\end{array}$ | $\begin{array}{r}9\\ \times 4\\ \hline\end{array}$ | $\begin{array}{r}8\\ \times 4\\ \hline\end{array}$ |
| **5.** | $\begin{array}{r}3\\ \times 4\\ \hline\end{array}$ | $\begin{array}{r}4\\ \times 2\\ \hline\end{array}$ | $\begin{array}{r}5\\ \times 2\\ \hline\end{array}$ | $\begin{array}{r}8\\ \times 3\\ \hline\end{array}$ | $\begin{array}{r}9\\ \times 3\\ \hline\end{array}$ |
| **6.** | $\begin{array}{r}6\\ \times 4\\ \hline\end{array}$ | $\begin{array}{r}7\\ \times 4\\ \hline\end{array}$ | $\begin{array}{r}3\\ \times 2\\ \hline\end{array}$ | $\begin{array}{r}7\\ \times 3\\ \hline\end{array}$ | $\begin{array}{r}9\\ \times 2\\ \hline\end{array}$ |

# Lesson 4.2 Multiplying through 5 × 5

| | | | |
|---|---|---|---|
| factor | 3 | → | Find the **3**-row. |
| factor | × 5 | → | Find the **5**-column. |
| product | 1 5 | ← | The product is named where the 3-row and the 5-column meet. |

**5-column** ↓

| x | 0 | 1 | 2 | 3 | 4 | 5 |
|---|---|---|---|---|---|---|
| 0 | 0 | 0 | 0 | 0 | 0 | 0 |
| 1 | 0 | 1 | 2 | 3 | 4 | 5 |
| 2 | 0 | 2 | 4 | 6 | 8 | 10 |
| 3 | 0 | 3 | 6 | 9 | 12 | 15 |
| 4 | 0 | 4 | 8 | 12 | 16 | 20 |
| 5 | 0 | 5 | 10 | 15 | 20 | 25 |

**3-row**

Multiply.

|  | a | b | c | d | e | f |
|---|---|---|---|---|---|---|
| **1.** | 2<br>×5<br>10 | 5<br>×3 | 1<br>×3 | 1<br>×4 | 3<br>×4 | 5<br>×2 |
| **2.** | 0<br>×5 | 1<br>×1 | 3<br>×5 | 2<br>×2 | 0<br>×3 | 4<br>×3 |
| **3.** | 4<br>×4 | 5<br>×2 | 4<br>×5 | 2<br>×3 | 5<br>×5 | 5<br>×0 |
| **4.** | 4<br>×2 | 0<br>×0 | 3<br>×3 | 4<br>×4 | 3<br>×2 | 1<br>×2 |
| **5.** | 0<br>×2 | 3<br>×3 | 2<br>×4 | 4<br>×0 | 3<br>×2 | 5<br>×4 |
| **6.** | 5<br>×1 | 2<br>×0 | 3<br>×1 | 5<br>×5 | 1<br>×0 | 2<br>×4 |

# Lesson 4.3 Problem Solving

**SHOW YOUR WORK**

Solve each problem.

1. Ian has 4 bags. He puts 5 marbles in each bag. How many marbles are there in all?

   Ian has _____ bags.

   Each bag has _____ marbles.

   There are _____ marbles in all.

2. Jennifer jumped over 3 rocks. She jumped over each rock 2 times. How many times did she jump in all?

   There are _____ rocks.

   Jennifer jumped over each rock _____ times.

   She jumped _____ times in all.

   **2.**

3. There are 4 pots of flowers. There are 2 flowers in each pot. How many flowers are there in all?

   There are _____ pots.

   Each pot has _____ flowers.

   There are _____ flowers in all.

   **3.**

Write a word problem to fit each number sentence. Solve.

4. $5 \times 1 =$ _____

5. $3 \times 4 =$ _____

# Lesson 4.4 Multiplying through 5 x 9

|     | 7-column |
| --- | --- |

factor      3 ⟶ Find the **3**-row.
factor    × 7 ⟶ Find the **7**-column.
product    2 1 ⟵ The product is
named where the
3-row and the
7-column meet.

**3-row**

| x | 0 | 1 | 2 | 3 | 4 | 5 | 6 | 7 | 8 | 9 |
|---|---|---|---|---|---|---|---|---|---|---|
| 0 | 0 | 0 | 0 | 0 | 0 | 0 | 0 | 0 | 0 | 0 |
| 1 | 0 | 1 | 2 | 3 | 4 | 5 | 6 | 7 | 8 | 9 |
| 2 | 0 | 2 | 4 | 6 | 8 | 10 | 12 | 14 | 16 | 18 |
| 3 | 0 | 3 | 6 | 9 | 12 | 15 | 18 | 21 | 24 | 27 |
| 4 | 0 | 4 | 8 | 12 | 16 | 20 | 24 | 28 | 32 | 36 |
| 5 | 0 | 5 | 10 | 15 | 20 | 25 | 30 | 35 | 40 | 45 |
| 6 | 0 | 6 | 12 | 18 | 24 | 30 |  |  |  |  |
| 7 | 0 | 7 | 14 | 21 | 28 | 35 |  |  |  |  |
| 8 | 0 | 8 | 16 | 24 | 32 | 40 |  |  |  |  |
| 9 | 0 | 9 | 18 | 27 | 36 | 45 |  |  |  |  |

Multiply.

| | a | b | c | d | e | f |
|---|---|---|---|---|---|---|
| **1.** | 5<br>×0<br>0 | 3<br>×9 | 6<br>×5 | 1<br>×4 | 5<br>×1 | 6<br>×3 |
| **2.** | 9<br>×2 | 8<br>×5 | 5<br>×8 | 0<br>×0 | 2<br>×9 | 3<br>×4 |
| **3.** | 4<br>×6 | 7<br>×3 | 6<br>×1 | 7<br>×2 | 3<br>×5 | 4<br>×1 |
| **4.** | 6<br>×2 | 5<br>×5 | 9<br>×1 | 2<br>×4 | 3<br>×7 | 7<br>×0 |
| **5.** | 0<br>×9 | 3<br>×6 | 7<br>×5 | 5<br>×6 | 3<br>×2 | 4<br>×2 |
| **6.** | 7<br>×4 | 3<br>×3 | 1<br>×9 | 2<br>×7 | 0<br>×6 | 1<br>×3 |

## Lesson 4.5 Multiplying through 9 x 9

**8-column**

| x | 0 | 1 | 2 | 3 | 4 | 5 | 6 | 7 | 8 | 9 |
|---|---|---|---|---|---|---|---|---|---|---|
| 0 | 0 | 0 | 0 | 0 | 0 | 0 | 0 | 0 | 0 | 0 |
| 1 | 0 | 1 | 2 | 3 | 4 | 5 | 6 | 7 | 8 | 9 |
| 2 | 0 | 2 | 4 | 6 | 8 | 10 | 12 | 14 | 16 | 18 |
| 3 | 0 | 3 | 6 | 9 | 12 | 15 | 18 | 21 | 24 | 27 |
| 4 | 0 | 4 | 8 | 12 | 16 | 20 | 24 | 28 | 32 | 36 |
| 5 | 0 | 5 | 10 | 15 | 20 | 25 | 30 | 35 | 40 | 45 |
| 6 | 0 | 6 | 12 | 18 | 24 | 30 | 36 | 42 | 48 | 54 |
| 7 | 0 | 7 | 14 | 21 | 28 | 35 | 42 | 49 | 56 | 63 |
| 8 | 0 | 8 | 16 | 24 | 32 | 40 | 48 | 56 | 64 | 72 |
| 9 | 0 | 9 | 18 | 27 | 36 | 45 | 54 | 63 | 72 | 81 |

factor   6 ⟶ Find the **6**-row.
factor × 8 ⟶ Find the **8**-column.
product   48 ⟵ The product is named where the 6-row and the 8-column meet.

**6-row**

Multiply.

|  | a | b | c | d | e | f |
|---|---|---|---|---|---|---|
| **1.** | 3 ×9 = 27 | 7 ×6 | 5 ×4 | 7 ×9 | 8 ×6 | 5 ×0 |
| **2.** | 4 ×3 | 8 ×5 | 4 ×9 | 3 ×0 | 5 ×7 | 2 ×9 |
| **3.** | 5 ×1 | 4 ×6 | 8 ×2 | 6 ×8 | 4 ×0 | 0 ×9 |
| **4.** | 3 ×1 | 6 ×4 | 9 ×2 | 3 ×4 | 6 ×3 | 5 ×6 |
| **5.** | 3 ×8 | 3 ×6 | 7 ×6 | 9 ×9 | 8 ×4 | 5 ×3 |
| **6.** | 2 ×6 | 8 ×8 | 9 ×3 | 7 ×4 | 8 ×0 | 7 ×7 |

# Lesson 4.6 Problem Solving

Solve each problem.

1. Steven wants to buy 6 pieces of bubblegum. Each piece costs 5 cents. How much will he have to pay for the bubblegum?

   Steven wants to buy _____ pieces of bubblegum.

   One piece of bubblegum costs _____ cents.

   Steven will have to pay _____ cents total.

2. There are 7 girls on stage. Each girl is holding 9 flowers. How many flowers are there in all?

   There are _____ girls.

   Each girl is holding _____ flowers.

   There are _____ flowers in all.

3. There are 4 rows of desks. There are 8 desks in each row. How many desks are there in all?

   There are _____ rows of desks.

   There are _____ desks in each row.

   There are _____ desks in all.

1.

2.

3.

Write a word problem to fit each number sentence. Solve.

4. $7 \times 5 =$ _____

5. $4 \times 9 =$ _____

# **Lesson 4.7** Multiplying by Multiples of 10

|  | Multiply 0 ones by 4. | Multiply 7 tens by 4. |
|---|---|---|
| 70<br>× 4<br>———— | 70<br>× 4<br>————<br>0 | 70<br>× 4<br>————<br>2 8 0 |

Multiply.

|  | **a** | **b** | **c** | **d** | **e** | **f** |
|---|---|---|---|---|---|---|
| **1.** | 30<br>× 3<br>————<br>9 0 | 20<br>× 1<br>———— | 1 0<br>× 9<br>———— | 60<br>× 4<br>———— | 80<br>× 2<br>———— | 70<br>× 7<br>———— |
| **2.** | 40<br>× 5<br>———— | 50<br>× 8<br>———— | 90<br>× 6<br>———— | 40<br>× 2<br>———— | 80<br>× 5<br>———— | 60<br>× 8<br>———— |
| **3.** | 90<br>× 2<br>———— | 1 0<br>× 5<br>———— | 20<br>× 7<br>———— | 50<br>× 3<br>———— | 70<br>× 3<br>———— | 30<br>× 5<br>———— |
| **4.** | 20<br>× 4<br>———— | 1 0<br>× 3<br>———— | 90<br>× 4<br>———— | 70<br>× 9<br>———— | 60<br>× 2<br>———— | 50<br>× 5<br>———— |

# Lesson 4.7 Multiplying by Multiples of 10

Multiply.

|  | a | b | c | d | e | f |
|---|---|---|---|---|---|---|
| 1. | 20 × 5 | 50 × 3 | 10 × 3 | 10 × 4 | 30 × 4 | 50 × 2 |
|  | 100 |  |  |  |  |  |
| 2. | 30 × 5 | 10 × 4 | 30 × 6 | 20 × 2 | 70 × 3 | 40 × 3 |
| 3. | 40 × 4 | 80 × 2 | 40 × 6 | 20 × 7 | 50 × 6 | 50 × 5 |
| 4. | 40 × 8 | 90 × 0 | 70 × 5 | 40 × 9 | 30 × 2 | 10 × 8 |
| 5. | 70 × 2 | 30 × 8 | 20 × 9 | 60 × 5 | 80 × 6 | 80 × 4 |
| 6. | 50 × 9 | 90 × 7 | 30 × 1 | 90 × 5 | 70 × 0 | 20 × 8 |
| 7. | 90 × 2 | 70 × 8 | 60 × 9 | 70 × 7 | 80 × 8 | 80 × 3 |
| 8. | 50 × 7 | 90 × 9 | 30 × 9 | 90 × 4 | 80 × 7 | 30 × 7 |

# Lesson 4.8 Problem Solving

SHOW YOUR WORK

Solve each problem.

**1.** Gary read 3 books with 60 pages each. How many pages did he read in all?

There are _____ pages in each book.

Gary read _____ books.

Gary read _____ pages in all.

**2.** There are 4 classes at a school. Each class has 20 students. How many students are at the school?

There are _____ students in each class.

There are _____ classes.

There are _____ students in the school.

**3.** Yolanda used up 4 rolls of stickers. If each roll has 30 stickers, how many stickers did she use in all?

Each roll has _____ stickers.

Yolanda used _____ rolls.

Yolanda used a total of _____ stickers.

**4.** During a game, 2 teams play against each other. There are 10 players on the field for each team. How many players are on the field during the game?

There are _____ players on the field.

**5.** There are 10 apples in each basket. If Mary buys 6 baskets, how many apples does she have?

Mary has _____ apples.

**1.**

**2.**

**3.**

**4.**          **5.**

NAME _____

# Lesson 4.9 Two-Step Problem Solving SHOW YOUR WORK

Make a mental computation first. Then, solve the problem.

The PE teacher gave each team 6 basketballs and 6 tennis balls. If there were 5 teams, how many total balls did the PE teacher give out?

Each team gets 6 of each type of ball. I know that 6 times 5 is 30, so that is 30 basketballs and 30 tennis balls. Then, I can add the balls together, and 30 plus 30 is 60. So, there are 60 balls in all.

$$\begin{array}{r} 6 \\ \times\ 5 \\ \hline 30 \end{array} \qquad \begin{array}{r} 30 \\ +30 \\ \hline 60 \end{array}$$

Mental Computation: 60

1. Eight girls and 5 boys each have a button collection. Each girl has 8 buttons in her collection, and each boy has 4 buttons in his collection. How many buttons altogether do the boys and girls have?

   Mental Computation: _____

   The boys and girls have _____ buttons altogether.

   1.

2. There are 2 rows of 5 computers in each office. If there are 7 offices in the building, how many computers are in the building altogether?

   Mental Computation: _____

   There are _____ computers in the building.

   2.

3. Kayla bought 5 bags of dried mango slices. Each bag has 7 slices. How many mango slices does Kayla have left over after she gives away 10 slices?

   Mental Computation: _____

   Kayla has _____ mango slices left.

   3.

4. Jin bought 7 boxes of Mixed Mints and 4 boxes of Fudge Crunchies. Each Mixed Mints box has 10 cookies and each Fudge Crunchies box has 7. How many cookies does Jin have altogether?

   Mental Computation: _____

   Jin has _____ cookies altogether.

   4.

# Chapter 5

## Lesson 5.1 Understanding Division

$\overline{)\phantom{xx}}$ means divide.

$$\begin{array}{r} 6 \\ 3{\overline{)1\,8}} \end{array}$$

divisor $\longrightarrow$ $3{\overline{)1\,8}}$ $\quad$ 6 $\leftarrow$ quotient
$\quad\quad\quad\quad\quad\quad\quad\quad\quad$ dividend

$3{\overline{)1\,8}}$ is read "18 divided by 3 is equal to 6."

$4{\overline{)1\,2}}$ is read "12 divided by 4 is equal to 3."

In $4{\overline{)1\,2}}$, the divisor is 4, the dividend is 12, and the quotient is 3.

$\div$ also means divide.

$$10 \div 2 = 5$$

dividend   divisor   quotient

$10 \div 2 = 5$ is read "10 divided by 2 is equal to 5."

$6 \div 3 = 2$ is read "6 divided by 3 is equal to 2."

In $6 \div 3 = 2$, the divisor is 3, the dividend is 6, and the quotient is 2.

---

Complete each sentence.

1. $6{\overline{)1\,2}}$ is read "_12_ divided by 6 is equal to _2_."

2. $8{\overline{)2\,4}}$ is read "___ divided by 8 is equal to ___."

3. $4{\overline{)3\,6}}$ is read "___ divided by 4 is equal to ___."

4. In $4{\overline{)8}}$, the divisor is ___, the dividend is ___, and the quotient is ___.

5. In $7{\overline{)3\,5}}$, the divisor is ___, the dividend is ___, and the quotient is ___.

6. $20 \div 5 = 4$ is read "___ divided by 5 is equal to ___."

7. $27 \div 9 = 3$ is read "___ divided by 9 is equal to ___."

8. $6 \div 2 = 3$ is read "___ divided by 2 is equal to ___."

9. In $15 \div 3 = 5$, the divisor is ___, the dividend is ___, and the quotient is ___.

10. In $14 \div 2 = 7$, the divisor is ___, the dividend is ___, and the quotient is ___.

## Lesson 5.1 Understanding Division

8 △ in all.
4 △ in each group.
How many groups?

8 ÷ 4 = 2

There are 2 groups.

△△△△
△△△△

8 △ in all.
2 groups of △.
How many △ in each group?

8 ÷ 2 = 4

There are 4 in each group.

Check by multiplication: quotient × divisor = dividend.

$2 \times 4 = 8$          $4 \times 2 = 8$

---

Complete the following.

**a**

**b**

**1.** 12 ☐ in all.

3 ☐ in each group.

How many groups?

12 ÷ 3 = __4__

There are __4__ groups.

Check: __4 × 3 = 12__

☐☐☐
☐☐☐
☐☐☐
☐☐☐

12 ☐ in all.

4 groups of ☐.

How many in each group?

12 ÷ 4 = _____

There are _____ ☐ in each group.

Check: _____

**2.** 20 As in all.

_____ As in each group.

How many groups?

20 ÷ 4 = _____

There are _____ groups.

Check: _____

AAAA
AAAA
AAAA
AAAA
AAAA

20 As in all.

_____ groups of As.

How many in each group?

20 ÷ 5 = _____

There are _____ As in each group.

Check: _____

**3.** _____ Fs in all.

_____ Fs in each group.

How many groups?

12 ÷ 2 = _____

There are _____ groups.

Check: _____

FF
FF
FF
FF
FF
FF
FF

_____ Fs in all.

_____ groups of Fs.

How many in each group?

12 ÷ 6 = _____

There are _____ Fs in each group.

Check: _____

NAME _____

# Lesson 5.2 Dividing through 27 ÷ 3

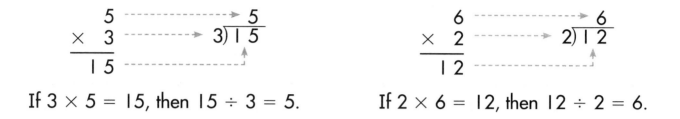

If 3 × 5 = 15, then 15 ÷ 3 = 5.   If 2 × 6 = 12, then 12 ÷ 2 = 6.

Divide. Under each division problem, write the corresponding multiplication problem.

|   | a | b | c | d | e |
|---|---|---|---|---|---|

**1.** $3\overline{)6}$ (2 above) | $2\overline{)14}$ | $1\overline{)5}$ | $2\overline{)4}$ | $1\overline{)4}$

3 × 2 = 6

**2.** $3\overline{)27}$ | $1\overline{)3}$ | $2\overline{)18}$ | $1\overline{)7}$ | $3\overline{)21}$

**3.** $3\overline{)12}$ | $2\overline{)16}$ | $1\overline{)5}$ | $3\overline{)18}$ | $2\overline{)10}$

**4.** $1\overline{)6}$ | $1\overline{)8}$ | $2\overline{)8}$ | $1\overline{)2}$ | $1\overline{)1}$

**5.** $3\overline{)24}$ | $3\overline{)9}$ | $1\overline{)9}$ | $2\overline{)6}$ | $2\overline{)2}$

# Lesson 5.3 Dividing through 54 ÷ 6

$$\begin{array}{r} 5 \\ \times\ 4 \\ \hline 20 \end{array} \longrightarrow \begin{array}{r} 5 \\ 4\overline{)20} \end{array} \qquad\qquad \begin{array}{r} 8 \\ \times\ 6 \\ \hline 48 \end{array} \longrightarrow \begin{array}{r} 8 \\ 6\overline{)48} \end{array}$$

If $4 \times 5 = 20$, then $20 \div 4 = 5$.      If $6 \times 8 = 48$, then $48 \div 6 = 8$.

Divide. Under each division problem write the corresponding multiplication problem.

|  | a | b | c | d | e |
|---|---|---|---|---|---|
| **1.** | $6\overline{)54}$   9 | $3\overline{)27}$ | $6\overline{)48}$ | $5\overline{)25}$ | $4\overline{)36}$ |
|  | $6 \times 9 = 54$ |  |  |  |  |
| **2.** | $5\overline{)30}$ | $4\overline{)24}$ | $4\overline{)32}$ | $4\overline{)16}$ | $4\overline{)20}$ |

Divide.

|  | a | b | c | d | e |
|---|---|---|---|---|---|
| **3.** | $6\overline{)36}$ | $4\overline{)28}$ | $5\overline{)35}$ | $6\overline{)24}$ | $3\overline{)21}$ |
| **4.** | $5\overline{)45}$ | $6\overline{)12}$ | $5\overline{)40}$ | $3\overline{)24}$ | $6\overline{)18}$ |
| **5.** | $3\overline{)12}$ | $2\overline{)16}$ | $4\overline{)12}$ | $2\overline{)18}$ | $3\overline{)9}$ |
| **6.** | $5\overline{)15}$ | $6\overline{)42}$ | $3\overline{)18}$ | $6\overline{)6}$ | $3\overline{)27}$ |

# Lesson 5.3 Problem Solving

Solve each problem.

**1.** There are 24 hours in a day. If the day is divided into 6 equal time segments, how many hours will be in each time segment?

There are _____ hours.

There are _____ time segments.

There are _____ hours in each time segment.

**2.** There are 30 desks in the classroom. There are 6 desks in each row. How many rows of desks are there?

There are _____ desks.

There are _____ desks in each row.

There are _____ rows of desks.

**3.** Mr. Villa handed out 42 papers to 6 students. Each student received the same number of papers. How many papers did each student receive?

Mr. Villa handed out _____ papers.

There are _____ students.

Each student received _____ papers.

**4.** There are 12 months in a year. There are 4 seasons in a year. If each season has an equal number of months, how many months are in each season?

There are _____ months in each season.

**5.** Bianca has 48 roses. She has 6 vases. Bianca wants to put an equal number of roses in each vase. How many roses will Bianca put in each vase?

Bianca will put _____ roses in each vase.

**1.**

**2.**

**3.**

**4.**       **5.**

# Lesson 5.4 Dividing through 81 ÷ 9

$$\begin{array}{r} 6 \\ \times\ 9 \\ \hline 54 \end{array} \quad\longrightarrow\quad \begin{array}{r} 6 \\ 9\overline{)54} \end{array}$$

If $9 \times 6 = 54$, then $54 \div 9 = 6$.

$$\begin{array}{r} 9 \\ \times\ 7 \\ \hline 63 \end{array} \quad\longrightarrow\quad \begin{array}{r} 9 \\ 7\overline{)63} \end{array}$$

If $7 \times 9 = 63$, then $63 \div 7 = 9$.

Divide. Under each division problem write the corresponding multiplication problem.

|  | a | b | c | d | e |
|---|---|---|---|---|---|
| **1.** | $7\overline{)7}$  $\ \ ^1$  $7 \times 1 = 7$ | $6\overline{)24}$ | $8\overline{)56}$ | $6\overline{)30}$ | $8\overline{)64}$ |
| **2.** | $6\overline{)12}$ | $7\overline{)35}$ | $8\overline{)24}$ | $7\overline{)28}$ | $6\overline{)36}$ |

Divide.

|  | a | b | c | d | e |
|---|---|---|---|---|---|
| **3.** | $9\overline{)63}$ | $9\overline{)81}$ | $7\overline{)56}$ | $5\overline{)35}$ | $8\overline{)24}$ |
| **4.** | $9\overline{)18}$ | $7\overline{)14}$ | $7\overline{)21}$ | $8\overline{)48}$ | $9\overline{)45}$ |
| **5.** | $7\overline{)49}$ | $8\overline{)16}$ | $9\overline{)27}$ | $9\overline{)9}$ | $7\overline{)42}$ |
| **6.** | $9\overline{)27}$ | $9\overline{)54}$ | $8\overline{)8}$ | $6\overline{)54}$ | $8\overline{)40}$ |

# Lesson 5.4 Problem Solving

**SHOW YOUR WORK**

Solve each problem.

1. Spencer wants to save 72 dollars. How many weeks will it take Spencer to save 72 dollars if he saves 9 dollars each week?

   Spencer wants to save _____ dollars.

   He saves _____ dollars each week.

   It will take Spencer _____ weeks to save 72 dollars.

2. Ms. Jefferson worked 40 hours this week. She worked 8 hours each day. How many days did she work this week?

   Ms. Jefferson worked _____ hours this week.

   She worked _____ hours each day.

   She worked _____ days this week.

3. There are 16 football players on the field. If there are 8 players on each team, how many teams are on the field?

   There are _____ football players on the field.

   There are _____ players on each team.

   There are _____ teams on the field.

4. Mrs. Daniels ordered 63 tables and 7 chairs for a banquet. Each table will have the same number of chairs. How many chairs will be at each table?

   There will be _____ chairs at each table.

**1.**

**2.**

**3.**

**4.**

NAME _____

# Lesson 5.5 Division Practice

Divide.

|     | a | b | c | d | e |
|-----|-----|-----|-----|-----|-----|
| **1.** | 5)25 | 4)16 | 7)21 | 9)81 | 6)18 |
| **2.** | 6)54 | 3)27 | 9)72 | 7)49 | 5)5 |
| **3.** | 3)24 | 4)28 | 9)36 | 2)14 | 1)9 |
| **4.** | 3)6 | 8)16 | 7)35 | 5)15 | 3)9 |
| **5.** | 7)42 | 9)45 | 2)2 | 7)63 | 2)6 |
| **6.** | 5)20 | 2)18 | 8)32 | 4)24 | 8)72 |
| **7.** | 1)1 | 8)64 | 6)36 | 5)45 | 2)16 |
| **8.** | 8)48 | 3)15 | 3)21 | 9)54 | 1)5 |
| **9.** | 8)24 | 7)28 | 4)36 | 7)14 | 9)9 |
| **10.** | 5)35 | 6)42 | 5)45 | 1)2 | 9)63 |

# Lesson 5.6 Division and Multiplication Practice

Divide or multiply.

|  | a | b | c | d | e | f |
|---|---|---|---|---|---|---|
| 1. | 3)6 | 9)18 | 4)36 | 6)54 | 3)27 | 2)4 |
| 2. | 8)40 | 3)18 | 2)6 | 3)9 | 2)16 | 5)20 |
| 3. | 4)32 | 9)27 | 2)8 | 1)7 | 5)5 | 9)54 |
| 4. | 7)42 | 6)12 | 9)81 | 4)4 | 6)24 | 2)10 |

| 5. | 50 × 2 | 30 × 2 | 40 × 8 | 20 × 1 | 10 × 5 | 90 × 3 |
|---|---|---|---|---|---|---|
| 6. | 7 ×6 | 60 × 5 | 80 × 5 | 30 × 3 | 70 × 4 | 40 × 2 |
| 7. | 10 × 6 | 10 × 7 | 70 × 5 | 60 × 8 | 90 × 2 | 9 ×2 |
| 8. | 50 × 8 | 40 × 7 | 20 × 7 | 80 × 2 | 40 × 5 | 30 × 9 |

## Lesson 5.7 Problem Solving

**SHOW YOUR WORK**

Make a mental computation first. Then, solve the problem.

In 4 days, Paige saw a total of 32 skydivers. In 4 more days she saw another total of 32 skydivers. If she saw the same number of skydivers each day, how many skydivers did Paige see in one day?

*I know 30 plus 30 is 60, and 2 plus 2 is 4, so 32 plus 32 is 64. There are 8 total days, so I need to divide 64 by 8. I know 8 times 8 is 64, so 64 divided by 8 is 8.*

$$\begin{array}{r} 32 \\ +32 \\ \hline 64 \end{array} \qquad \begin{array}{r} 4 \\ +4 \\ \hline 8 \end{array} \qquad \begin{array}{r} 8 \\ 8\overline{)64} \end{array}$$

Mental Computation: 8

---

**1.** Emma has 50 photos in one box and 10 photos in another. She wants to put an equal number of photos on each of the 10 pages of her album. How many photos should Emma put on each page?

Mental Computation: _____

Emma should put _____ pictures on each page.

**1.**

**2.** A group of 10 third graders are making cardboard penguins. Each student needs 1 cardboard tube, 2 wiggle eyes, and 1 piece of construction paper. How many items do all 10 third graders need?

Mental Computation: _____

All 10 third graders need _____ items for the penguin project.

**2.**

**3.** Greg has 91 erasers, and Janelle gives him 8 more. Greg gives each of his 9 friends an equal number of erasers. How many erasers does each friend get?

Mental Computation: _____

Each friend gets _____ erasers.

**3.**

**4.** There were 21 skiers waiting in line for the ski lift. Three skiers can sit on each seat on the lift. How many seats are needed for all of the skiers?

Mental Computation: _____

_____ seats are needed for all of the skiers.

**4.**

# Chapter 6

## Lesson 6.1 Parts of a Whole

A fraction is a number for part of a whole.

$\dfrac{1}{4}$ ← numerator    (part of the whole)
   ← denominator  (parts in all)

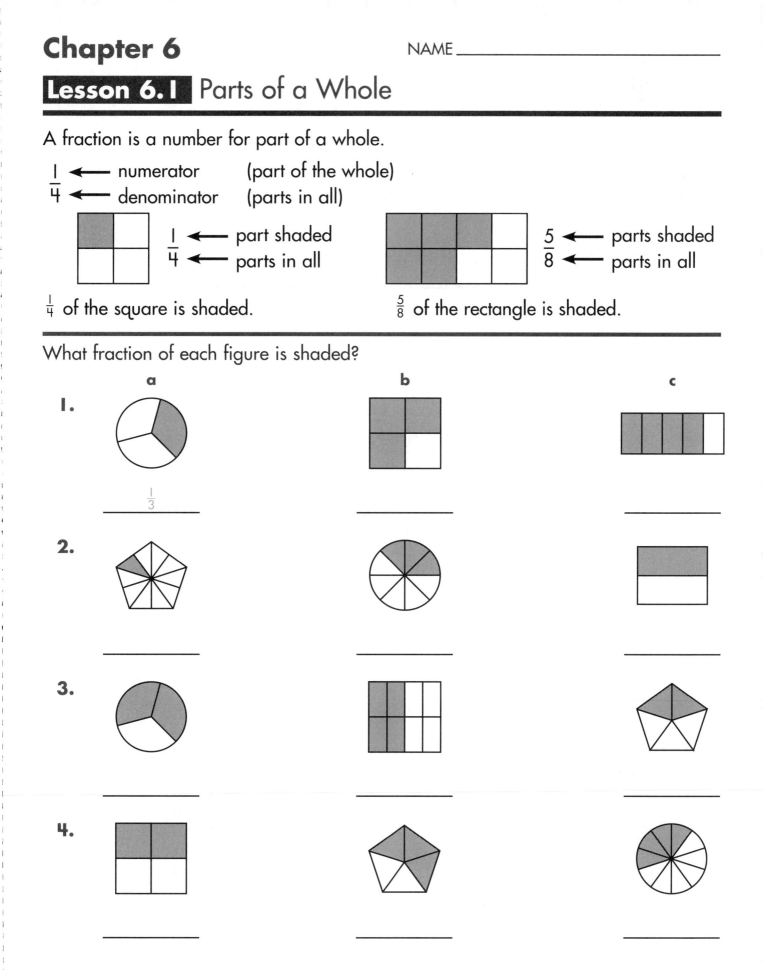

$\dfrac{1}{4}$ ← part shaded
   ← parts in all

$\dfrac{5}{8}$ ← parts shaded
   ← parts in all

$\frac{1}{4}$ of the square is shaded.        $\frac{5}{8}$ of the rectangle is shaded.

What fraction of each figure is shaded?

|  | a | b | c |
|---|---|---|---|
| 1. | $\frac{1}{3}$ | | |
| 2. | | | |
| 3. | | | |
| 4. | | | |

# Lesson 6.2 Parts of a Set

A fraction is a number for part of a set.

$\frac{1}{2}$ ← numerator (part of the set)

← denominator (parts in all the set)

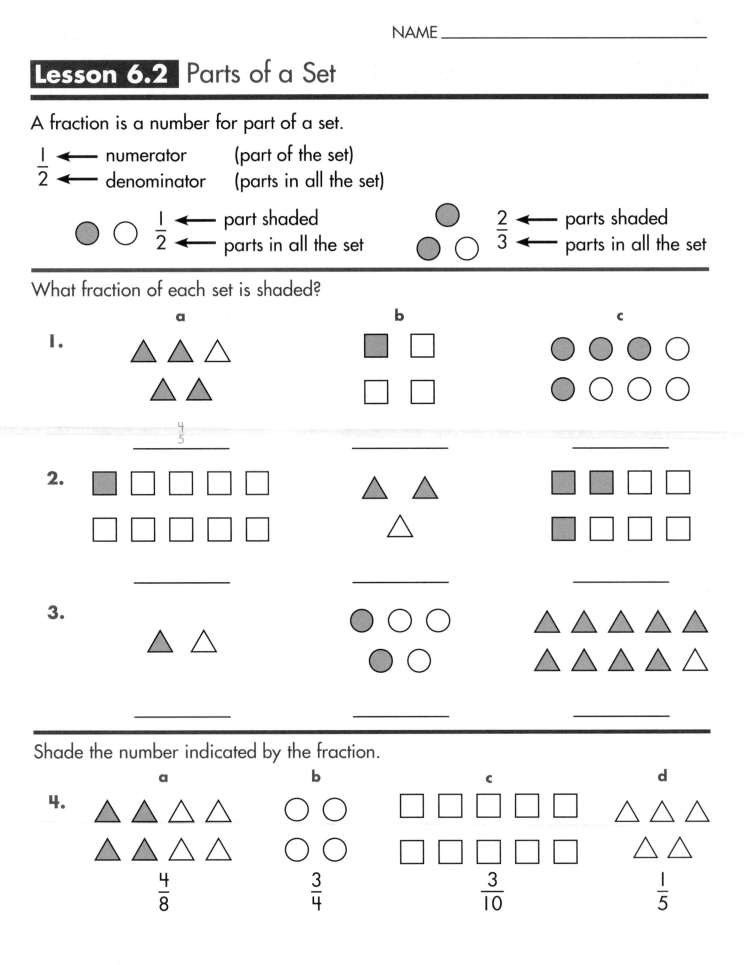

○ ○ $\frac{1}{2}$ ← part shaded
← parts in all the set

$\frac{2}{3}$ ← parts shaded
← parts in all the set

---

What fraction of each set is shaded?

|  | a | b | c |
|---|---|---|---|
| **1.** | △ △ △  △ △ | ■ □  □ □ | ● ● ● ○  ● ○ ○ ○ |
|  | $\frac{4}{5}$ | _____ | _____ |
| **2.** | ■ □ □ □ □  □ □ □ □ □ | △ △  △ | ■ ■ □ □  ■ □ □ □ |
|  | _____ | _____ | _____ |
| **3.** |  △ △ | ● ○ ○  ● ○ | △ △ △ △ △  △ △ △ △ △ |
|  | _____ | _____ | _____ |

---

Shade the number indicated by the fraction.

|  | a | b | c | d |
|---|---|---|---|---|
| **4.** | △ △ △ △  △ △ △ △ | ○ ○  ○ ○ | □ □ □ □ □  □ □ □ □ □ | △ △ △  △ △ |
|  | $\frac{4}{8}$ | $\frac{3}{4}$ | $\frac{3}{10}$ | $\frac{1}{5}$ |

# Lesson 6.3 Comparing Fractions

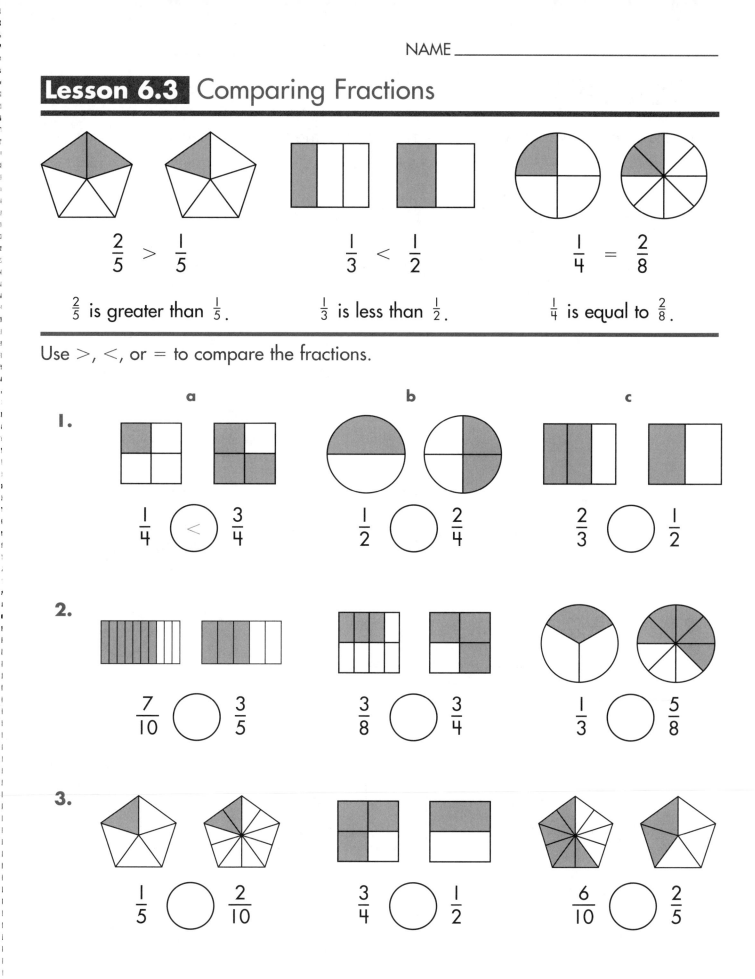

$\frac{2}{5} > \frac{1}{5}$

$\frac{1}{3} < \frac{1}{2}$

$\frac{1}{4} = \frac{2}{8}$

$\frac{2}{5}$ is greater than $\frac{1}{5}$.      $\frac{1}{3}$ is less than $\frac{1}{2}$.      $\frac{1}{4}$ is equal to $\frac{2}{8}$.

Use >, <, or = to compare the fractions.

|  | a | b | c |
|---|---|---|---|
| 1. | $\frac{1}{4}$ ◯< $\frac{3}{4}$ | $\frac{1}{2}$ ◯ $\frac{2}{4}$ | $\frac{2}{3}$ ◯ $\frac{1}{2}$ |
| 2. | $\frac{7}{10}$ ◯ $\frac{3}{5}$ | $\frac{3}{8}$ ◯ $\frac{3}{4}$ | $\frac{1}{3}$ ◯ $\frac{5}{8}$ |
| 3. | $\frac{1}{5}$ ◯ $\frac{2}{10}$ | $\frac{3}{4}$ ◯ $\frac{1}{2}$ | $\frac{6}{10}$ ◯ $\frac{2}{5}$ |

# Lesson 6.3 Comparing Fractions

What fraction of each figure is shaded? Compare the fractions. Use >, <, or =.

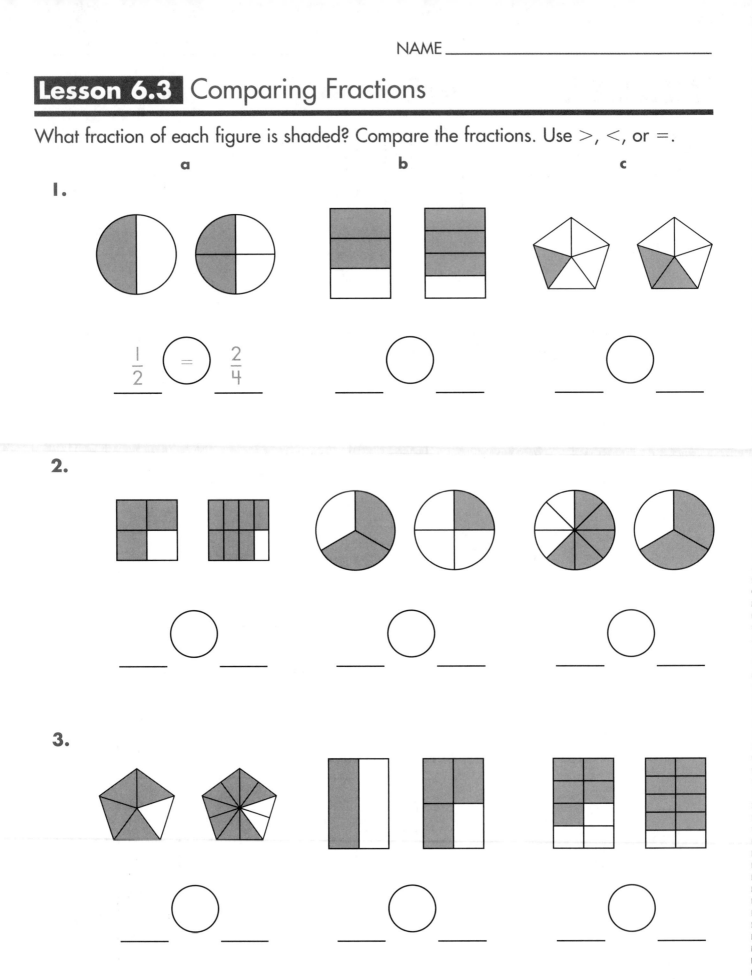

## Lesson 6.4 Fractions on a Number Line

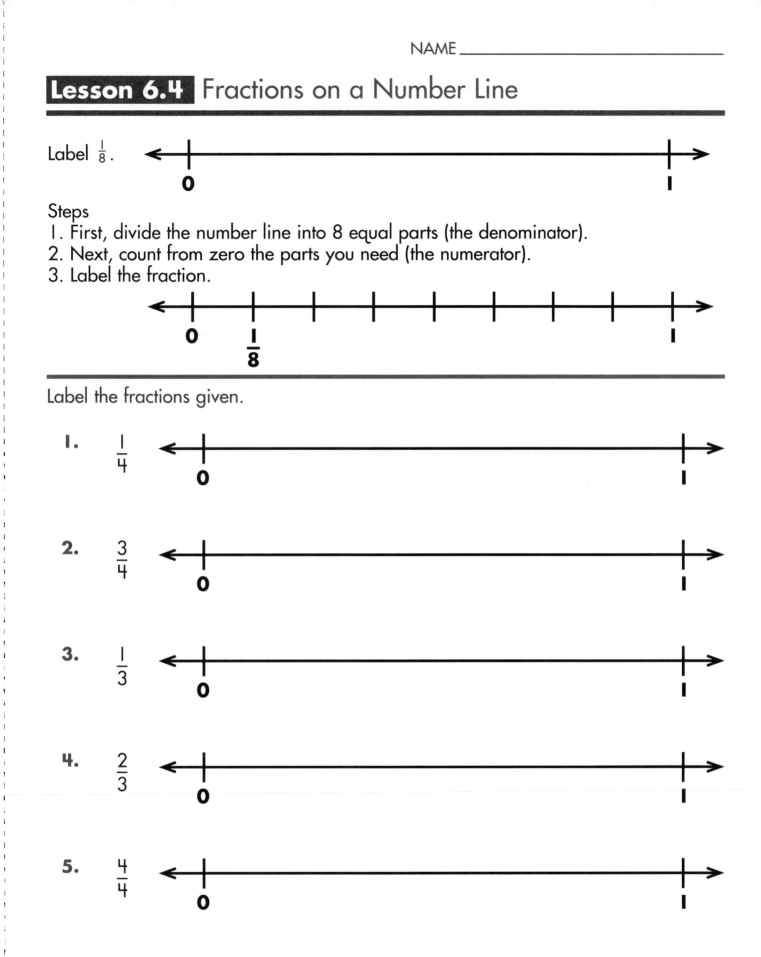

Label $\frac{1}{8}$.

Steps
1. First, divide the number line into 8 equal parts (the denominator).
2. Next, count from zero the parts you need (the numerator).
3. Label the fraction.

Label the fractions given.

1. $\frac{1}{4}$

2. $\frac{3}{4}$

3. $\frac{1}{3}$

4. $\frac{2}{3}$

5. $\frac{4}{4}$

# Lesson 6.5 Equivalent Fractions on a Number Line

The fractions $\frac{2}{4}$ and $\frac{1}{2}$ are equivalent because they are at the same spot on the number line.

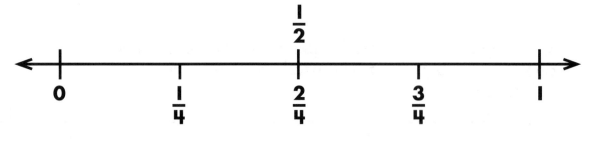

---

Answer the questions based on the number lines.

1. Are the fractions $\frac{1}{8}$ and $\frac{1}{4}$ equivalent? _____

   Name 2 other fractions that are equivalent. _____ _____

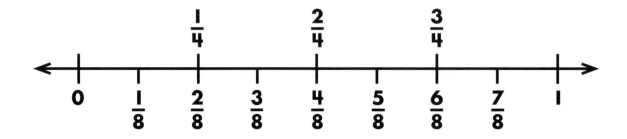

2. Are the fractions $\frac{1}{6}$ and $\frac{2}{3}$ equivalent? _____

   Name 2 other fractions that are equivalent. _____ _____

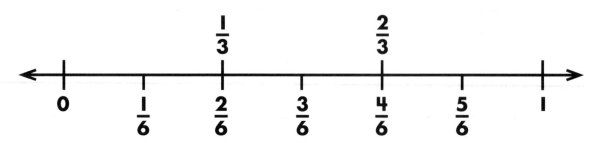

## Lesson 6.6 Whole Numbers as Fractions

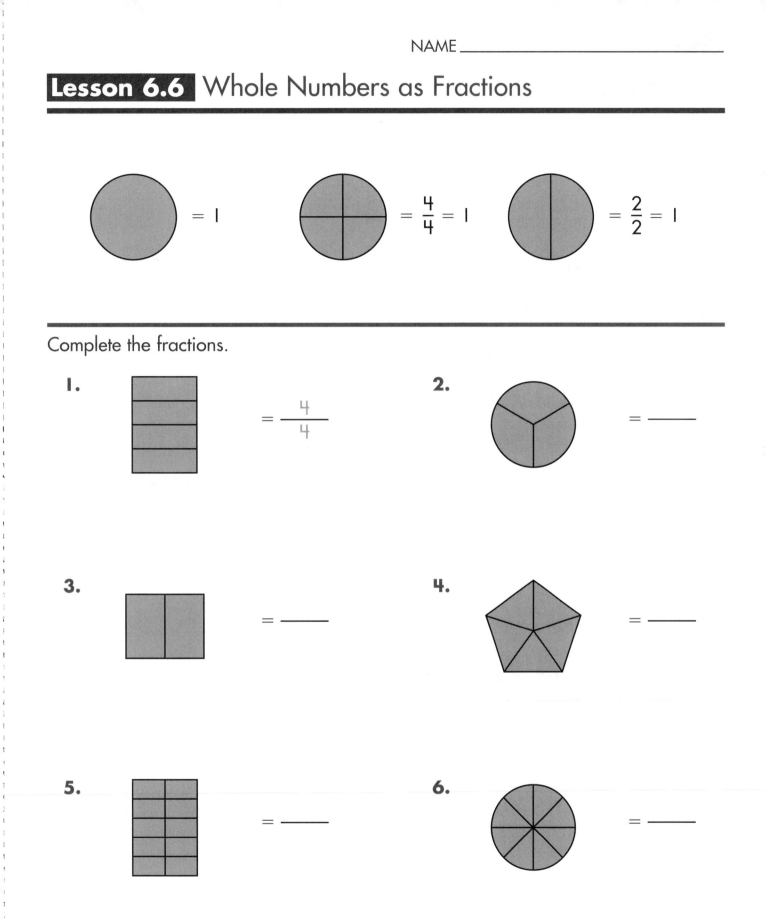

Complete the fractions.

1. $= \dfrac{4}{4}$

2. $= \underline{\hspace{1cm}}$

3. $= \underline{\hspace{1cm}}$

4. $= \underline{\hspace{1cm}}$

5. $= \underline{\hspace{1cm}}$

6. $= \underline{\hspace{1cm}}$

# Chapter 7

## Lesson 7.1 Measuring Volume and Mass

Answer each question.

**1.** A refrigerator weighs about:    90 grams    90 kilograms    9 kilograms

**2.** A wading pool holds about:    500 grams    500 liters    5,000 liters

**3.** A small dog weighs about:    15 grams    50 grams    5,000 grams

**4.** A nail weighs about:    1 gram    10 grams    100 grams

Solve.

**5.** Emily's bag of fruit weighs 32 ounces. Jason's bag of fruit weighs 14 ounces. How many ounces do Emily and Jason's bags weigh altogether?

Emily and Jason's bags of fruit weigh _____ ounces altogether.

**6.** Vince brought 4 quarts of juice for the party. Jose brought 6 quarts of juice for the party. How many more quarts of juice did Jose bring than Vince?

Jose brought _____ more quarts of juice than Vince.

**7.** Jim had 18 gallons of paint to paint his entire house. He only used 11 gallons. How many gallons of paint does Jim have left?

Jim has _____ gallons of paint left.

**8.** Inez weighed 3 kilograms when she was born. Now she weighs 13 kilograms. How much weight did Inez gain since she was born?

Inez gained _____ kilograms since she was born.

# Lesson 7.1 Measuring Volume and Mass

Answer each question.

| | | | |
|---|---|---|---|
| **1.** A dump truck can hold about: | 1 liter | 10 liters | 1,000 liters |
| **2.** A butterfly weighs about: | 100 grams | 1 gram | 10 grams |
| **3.** A juice bottle can hold about: | 2 liters | 200 liters | 2,000 liters |
| **4.** A chicken can weigh: | 7 grams | 70 grams | 700 grams |

Solve.

**5.** A carton contains 2 liters of juice. If there are 18 cartons of juice, how many liters of juice are there?

There are _____ liters of juice.

**6.** A saltshaker holds 5 grams of salt. If there are 20 saltshakers in the restaurant, how many grams of salt are in the restaurant?

There are _____ grams of salt in the restaurant.

**7.** Clarissa has 6 plants in her house. Each plant weighs 4 kilograms. How many kilograms do the plants weigh altogether?

Clarissa's plants weigh _____ kilograms altogether.

**8.** Danny caught a fish that was 15 pounds. Ashley caught a fish that was 20 pounds. How many more pounds does Ashley's fish weigh than Danny's fish?

Ashley's fish weighs _____ pounds more than Danny's fish.

NAME _____

## Lesson 7.2 Drawing Picture Graphs

A **picture graph** uses symbols to represent data.

The key tells you the value of each symbol on the picture graph.

Use the frequency table to complete the graph.

**Students' Hair Color**

| Brown | 웃 웃 웃 웃 웃 웃 웃 |
|-------|-------------------|
| Black | 웃 웃 웃 웃 웃 |
| Blonde | 웃 웃 웃 웃 웃 ʒ |
| Red | 웃 ʒ |

Key: 웃 = 2 students

**Frequency Table**

| Brown | |||| |||| |||| |
|-------|-----------------|
| Black | |||| |||| |
| Blonde | |||| |||| | |
| Red | ||| |

How many students have red hair?

Each stick figure represents two students.

Count by twos when counting the stick figures in the row labeled "red." Add 1 to the sum for the half stick figure.

____3____ students have red hair.

---

Complete the picture graph. Answer the question.

**Flowers In My Garden**

| | |
|---|---|
| | |
| | |
| | |

Key: 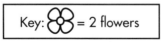 = 2 flowers

**Frequency Table**

| Daisies | |||| ||| |
|---------|----------|
| Roses | |||| |
| Sunflowers | || |

How many total flowers are in the garden? _____

NAME _____

## Lesson 7.3 Drawing Bar Graphs

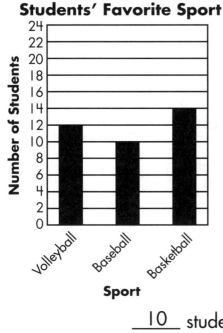

**Students' Favorite Sport**

A **bar graph** uses rectangular bars to represent data.

Use the frequency table to complete the graph.

How many students chose baseball as their favorite sport?

Find the bar labeled baseball.

Follow the top of the bar to the scale at the left.

This value represents the number of students whose favorite sport is baseball.

**Frequency Table**

| Volleyball | 12 |
| Baseball | 10 |
| Basketball | 14 |

___10___ students chose baseball as their favorite sport.

Complete the bar graph. Answer the question.

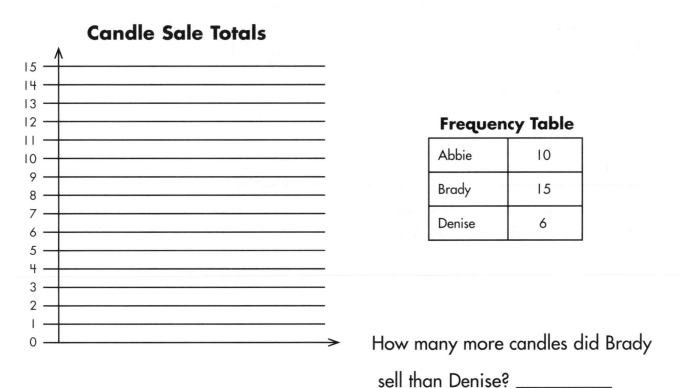

**Candle Sale Totals**

**Frequency Table**

| Abbie | 10 |
| Brady | 15 |
| Denise | 6 |

How many more candles did Brady

sell than Denise? _____

Spectrum Grade 3
63

## Lesson 7.4 Gathering Data to Draw a Line Plot

Use a ruler to measure the length of each object.

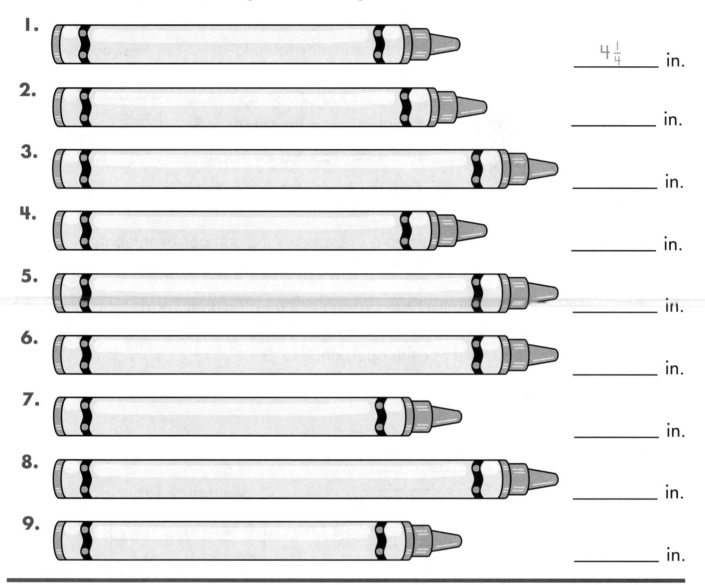

1. _____ $4\frac{1}{4}$ _____ in.

2. _____ in.

3. _____ in.

4. _____ in.

5. _____ in.

6. _____ in.

7. _____ in.

8. _____ in.

9. _____ in.

Use the information above to fill in the line plot.

10.

**Crayons Used in the Classroom**

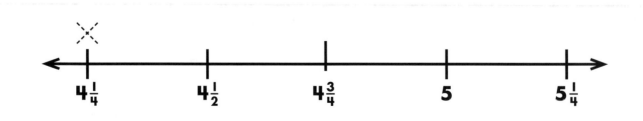

## Lesson 7.4  Gathering Data to Draw a Line Plot

Use a ruler to measure the length of each object.

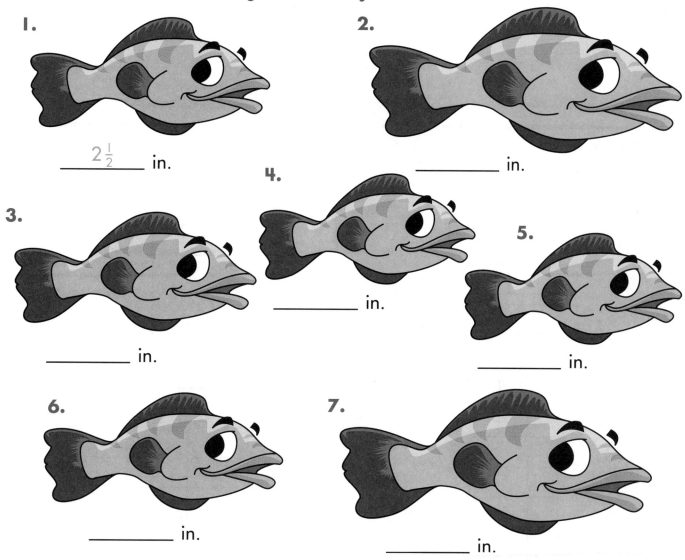

**1.**

_____2 ½_____ in.

**2.**

_____ in.

**3.**

_____ in.

**4.**

_____ in.

**5.**

_____ in.

**6.**

_____ in.

**7.**

_____ in.

Use the information above to fill in the line plot.

**8.**

**Fish in the Pond**

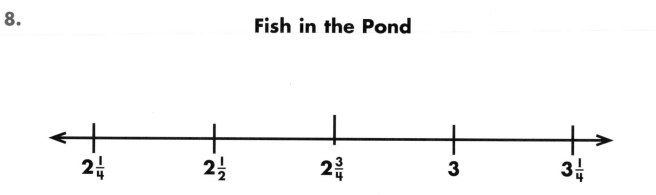

$2\frac{1}{4}$   $2\frac{1}{2}$   $2\frac{3}{4}$   $3$   $3\frac{1}{4}$

# Lesson 7.5 Finding Area with Unit Squares

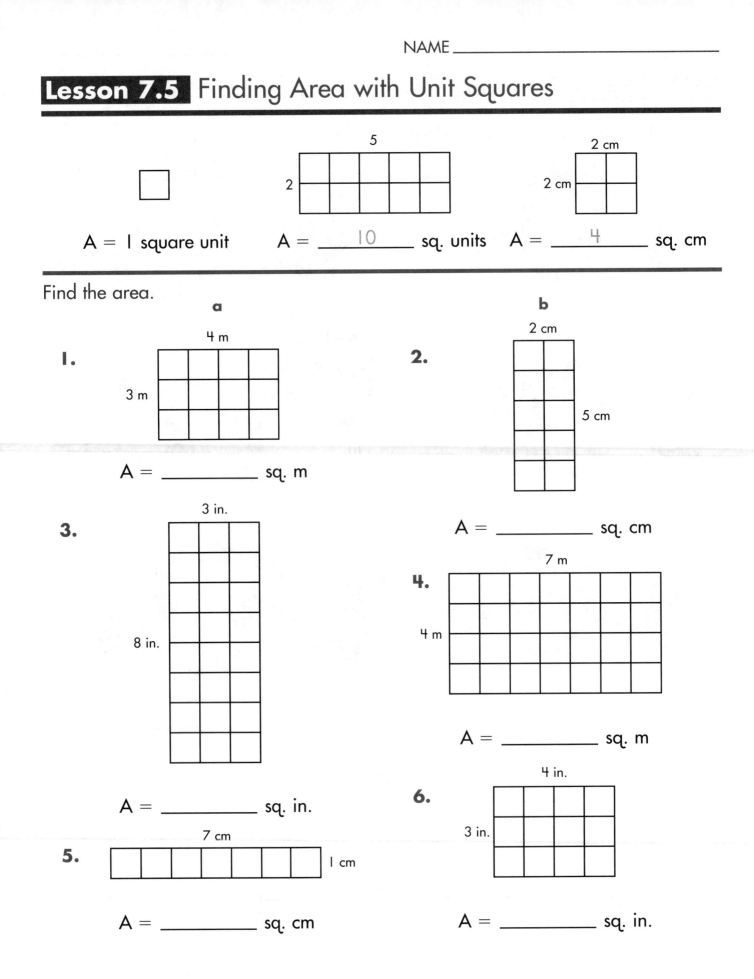

A = 1 square unit      A = ___10___ sq. units      A = ___4___ sq. cm

Find the area.

**a**

**b**

**1.**    4 m

3 m

A = _____ sq. m

**2.**    2 cm

5 cm

A = _____ sq. cm

**3.**    3 in.

8 in.

A = _____ sq. in.

**4.**    7 m

4 m

A = _____ sq. m

**5.**    7 cm

1 cm

A = _____ sq. cm

**6.**    4 in.

3 in.

A = _____ sq. in.

## Lesson 7.5  Finding Area with Unit Squares

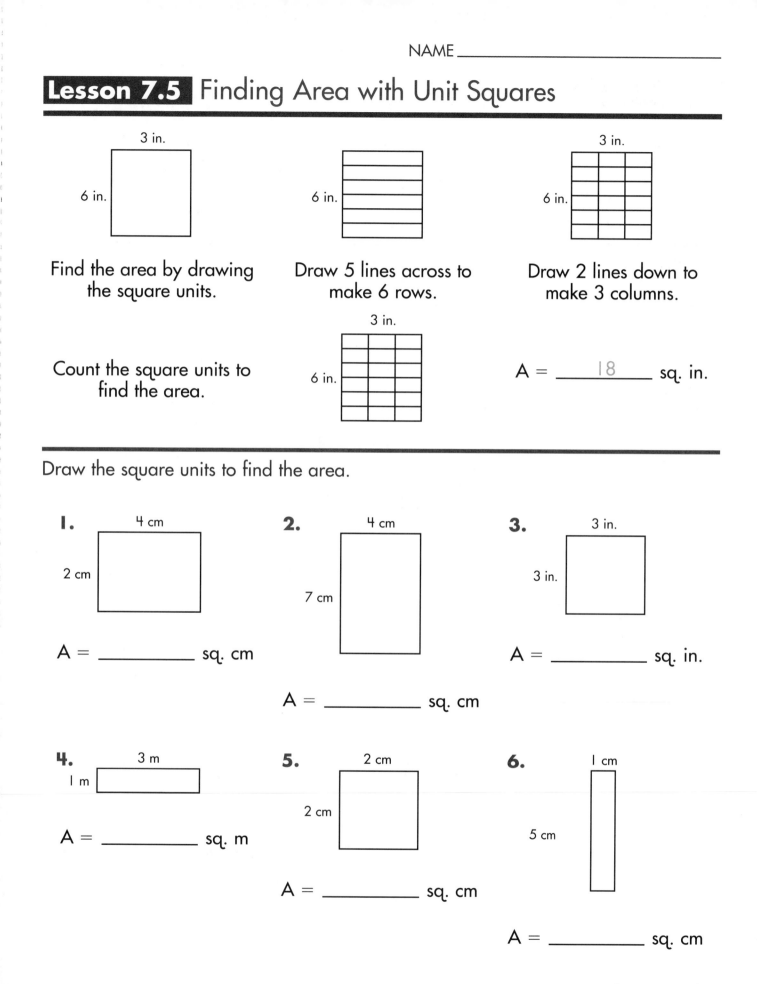

3 in.

6 in.

Find the area by drawing the square units.

Count the square units to find the area.

Draw 5 lines across to make 6 rows.

6 in.

3 in.

6 in.

Draw 2 lines down to make 3 columns.

3 in.

6 in.

A = _____18_____ sq. in.

___

Draw the square units to find the area.

**1.**  4 cm

2 cm

A = _____ sq. cm

**2.**  4 cm

7 cm

A = _____ sq. cm

**3.**  3 in.

3 in.

A = _____ sq. in.

**4.**  3 m

1 m

A = _____ sq. m

**5.**  2 cm

2 cm

A = _____ sq. cm

**6.**  1 cm

5 cm

A = _____ sq. cm

# Lesson 7.6 Measuring Area

To find the area of a square or rectangle, multiply length by width.

10 ft. × 2 ft. = 20 sq. ft.

The product is written as 20 square feet.

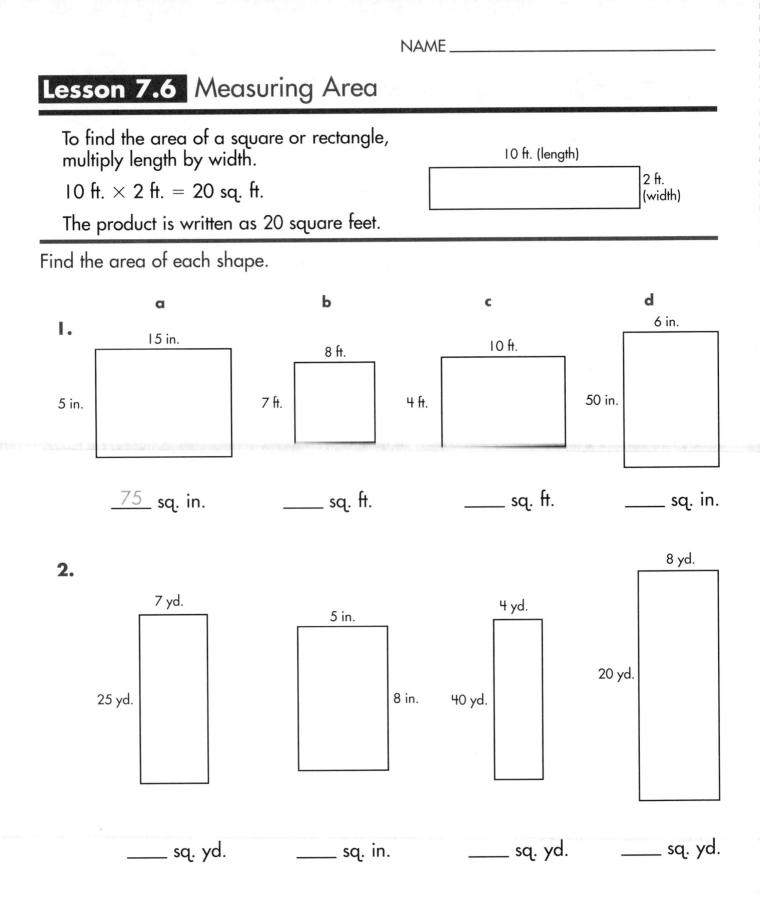

Find the area of each shape.

|   a   |   b   |   c   |   d   |
|-------|-------|-------|-------|

1.

a. 15 in. × 5 in. = __75__ sq. in.

b. 8 ft. × 7 ft. = _____ sq. ft.

c. 10 ft. × 4 ft. = _____ sq. ft.

d. 6 in. × 50 in. = _____ sq. in.

2.

a. 7 yd. × 25 yd. = _____ sq. yd.

b. 5 in. × 8 in. = _____ sq. in.

c. 4 yd. × 40 yd. = _____ sq. yd.

d. 8 yd. × 20 yd. = _____ sq. yd.

# Lesson 7.6 Measuring Area

Draw the square units.

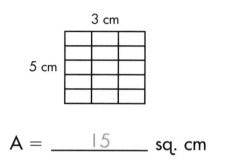

3 cm

5 cm

A = ___15___ sq. cm

Multiply to check your answer.

___5___ × ___3___ = ___15___

A = ___15___ sq. cm

---

Draw the square units. Then, multiply to check your answer.

**1.**

3 cm

8 cm

_____ × _____ = _____

A = _____ sq. cm

**2.**

2 in.

2 in.

_____ × _____ = _____

A = _____ sq. in.

**3.**

4 cm

1 cm

_____ × _____ = _____

A = _____ sq. cm

**4.**

9 in.

3 in.

_____ × _____ = _____

A = _____ sq. in.

# Lesson 7.7 Finding Area of Irregular Shapes

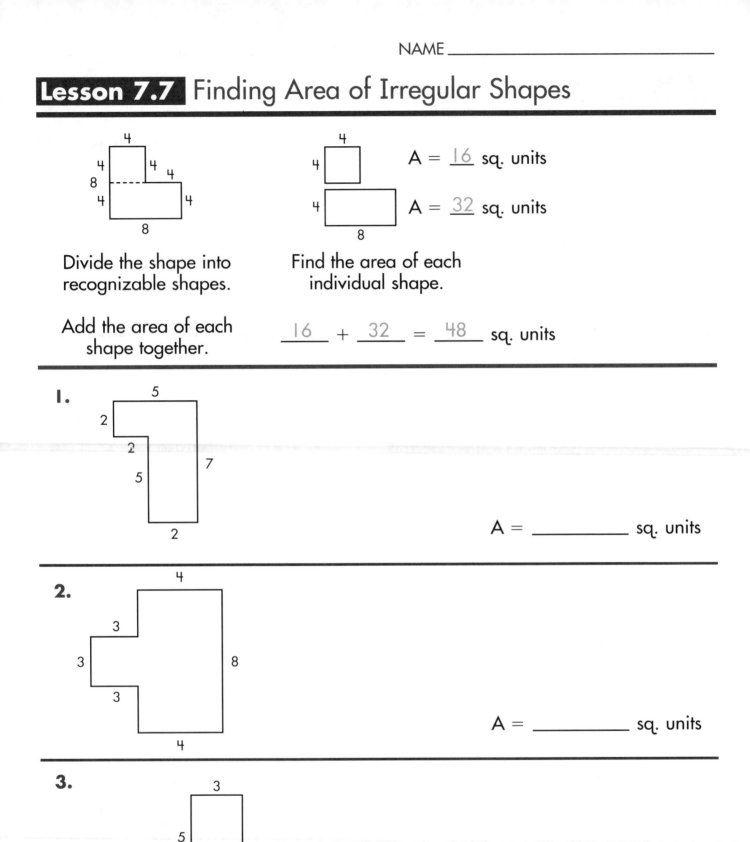

Divide the shape into recognizable shapes.

Find the area of each individual shape.

A = 16 sq. units

A = 32 sq. units

Add the area of each shape together.

16 + 32 = 48 sq. units

**1.**

A = _____ sq. units

**2.**

A = _____ sq. units

**3.**

A = _____ sq. units

# Lesson 7.8 Problem Solving

**SHOW YOUR WORK**

Solve.

1. The Garcia brothers are painting a wall in their living room. The wall measures 8 feet by 10 feet. What is the area of the wall?

   The area of the wall is _____ square feet.

2. Freda is putting carpet down in a room that measures 9 feet long by 10 feet wide. What is the area of the room?

   The area is _____ square feet.

3. The zoo is building a new hippo pool that will measure 50 feet by 9 feet. What is the area of the pool?

   The area is _____ square feet.

4. The Foster's deck was almost finished. Each side of the square deck was 9 feet long. What was the area of the deck?

   The area was _____ square feet.

5. The college donated land for a park. The land is 90 feet long and 9 feet wide. What is the area of the land?

   The area is _____ square feet.

6. Jill digs a flowerbed that is 8 meters long and 7 meters wide. What is the area of the flowerbed?

   The area is _____ square meters.

7. Emma wants to tile her kitchen floor. How many 1 foot square tiles will she need if her floor is 10 feet long by 9 feet wide?

   Emma will need _____ tiles.

1.

2.

3.

4.

5.

6.

7.

# Lesson 7.9 Measuring Perimeter

**Perimeter** is the distance around a shape.

To calculate perimeter, add together the lengths of all the sides.

Perimeter = 17 in. + 10 in. + 17 in. + 10 in.

Perimeter = 54 in.

Find the perimeter of each shape.

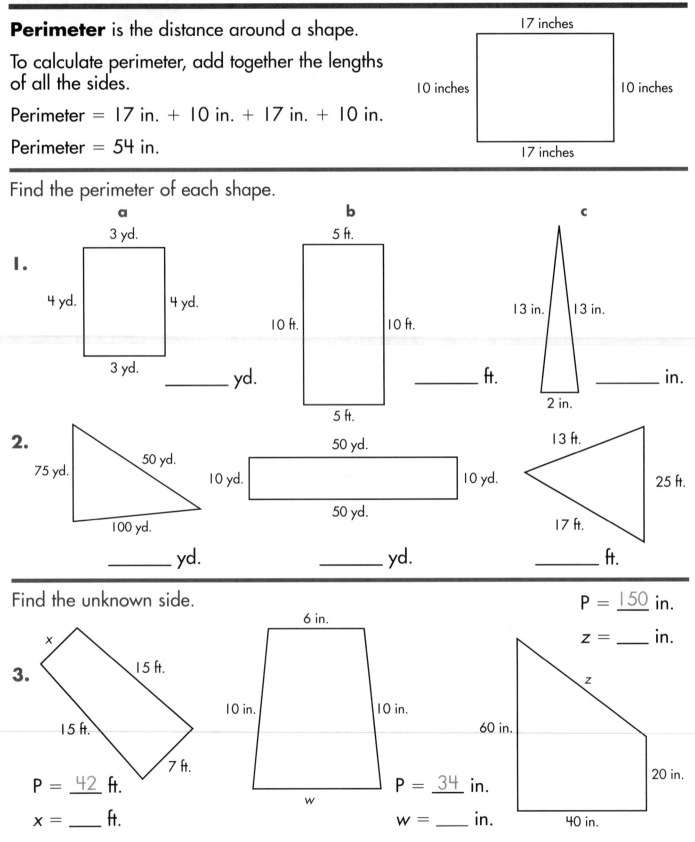

**a**

3 yd.

**1.**

4 yd.    4 yd.

3 yd.

_____ yd.

**b**

5 ft.

10 ft.    10 ft.

5 ft.

_____ ft.

**c**

13 in.    13 in.

2 in.

_____ in.

**2.**

75 yd.    50 yd.

100 yd.

_____ yd.

50 yd.

10 yd.    10 yd.

50 yd.

_____ yd.

13 ft.

25 ft.

17 ft.

_____ ft.

Find the unknown side.

**3.**

x

15 ft.

15 ft.

7 ft.

P = _42_ ft.

x = ___ ft.

6 in.

10 in.    10 in.

w

P = _34_ in.

w = ___ in.

P = _150_ in.

z = ___ in.

z

60 in.

20 in.

40 in.

# Lesson 7.9 Problem Solving

**SHOW YOUR WORK**

Solve.

1. The town of Yarmouth is planning a skateboard park and needs to know the perimeter of the park. The property measures 7 yards by 3 yards by 10 yards by 5 yards. What is the perimeter?

   The park's perimeter is _____ yards.

2. John cleared a vacant lot to plant a garden. The lot measured 35 by 15 feet. What is the perimeter of the garden lot?

   The perimeter of the lot is _____ feet.

3. Gabriel built a cage for his tropical birds. The cage measures 14 feet by 12 feet. What is the perimeter of the cage?

   The perimeter of the cage is _____ feet.

4. The length of the walking track is 103 feet and the width is 50 feet. What is the perimeter of the track?

   The perimeter is _____ feet.

5. Anna is buying trim to go around her rug. Her rug measures 54 inches by 42 inches. How many inches of trim will Anna need to buy?

   Anna will need to buy _____ inches of trim.

6. Natalie is putting a fence around her pool. Her pool is 10 feet by 8 feet. How many feet of fencing will Natalie need?

   Natalie will need _____ feet of fencing.

7. The rectangular third-grade classroom has a perimeter of 130 feet. If it is 25 feet wide, how many feet long is the classroom?

   The classroom is _____ feet long.

1.

2.

3.

4.

5.

6.

7.

# Chapter 8

NAME _____

## Lesson 8.1  Telling Time

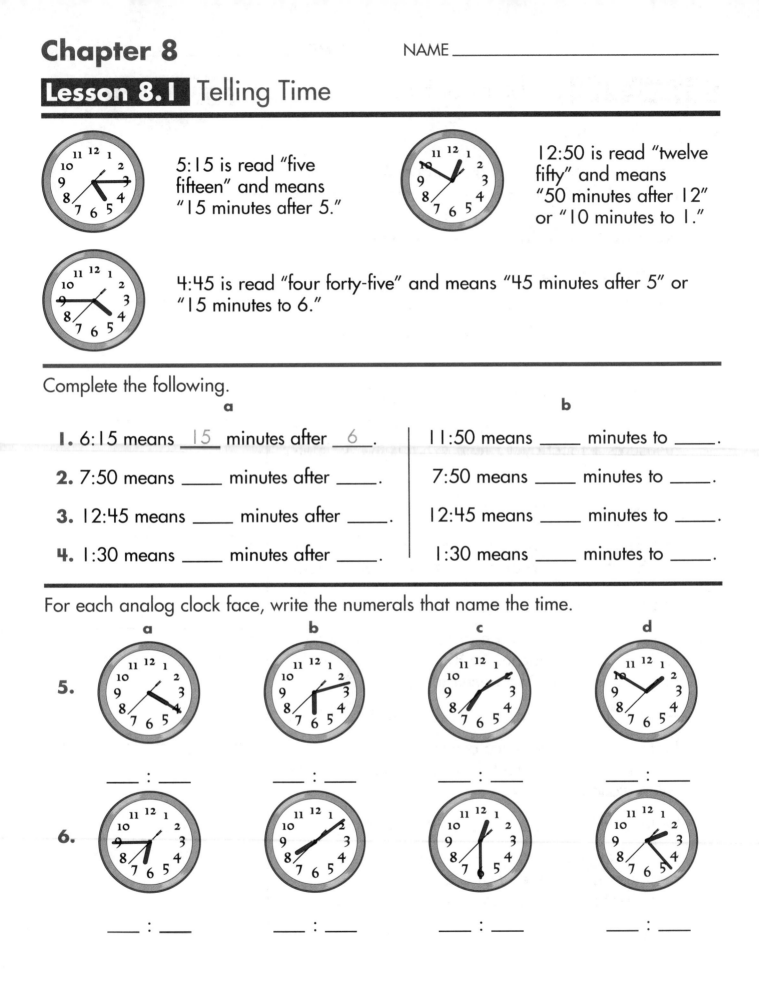

5:15 is read "five fifteen" and means "15 minutes after 5."

12:50 is read "twelve fifty" and means "50 minutes after 12" or "10 minutes to 1."

4:45 is read "four forty-five" and means "45 minutes after 5" or "15 minutes to 6."

Complete the following.

|  | a | b |
|---|---|---|
| **1.** | 6:15 means __15__ minutes after __6__. | 11:50 means ____ minutes to ____. |
| **2.** | 7:50 means ____ minutes after ____. | 7:50 means ____ minutes to ____. |
| **3.** | 12:45 means ____ minutes after ____. | 12:45 means ____ minutes to ____. |
| **4.** | 1:30 means ____ minutes after ____. | 1:30 means ____ minutes to ____. |

For each analog clock face, write the numerals that name the time.

|  | a | b | c | d |
|---|---|---|---|---|
| **5.** | ___ : ___ | ___ : ___ | ___ : ___ | ___ : ___ |
| **6.** | ___ : ___ | ___ : ___ | ___ : ___ | ___ : ___ |

## Lesson 8.1 Telling Time

6:41

The closest hour on an analog clock is determined by the hour hand (the short hand).

The closest half hour, quarter hour, and minute are determined by the minute hand (the long hand).

A half hour is at 30 minutes or 1 hour.

A quarter hour is at 15, 30, 45 minutes, or 1 hour.

What time is it to the nearest hour? ___7:00___, half hour? ___6:30___,

quarter hour? ___6:45___, minute? ___6:41___

---

Write the time to the nearest hour, half hour, quarter hour, or minute as indicated.

|   | **a** | **b** | **c** | **d** |
|---|---|---|---|---|
| | hour | half hour | quarter hour | minute |
| **1.** | ___ : ___ | ___ : ___ | ___ : ___ | ___ : ___ |
| | hour | half hour | quarter hour | minute |
| **2.** | ___ : ___ | ___ : ___ | ___ : ___ | ___ : ___ |

---

Draw the hands on the analog clock to express the time presented on the digital clock.

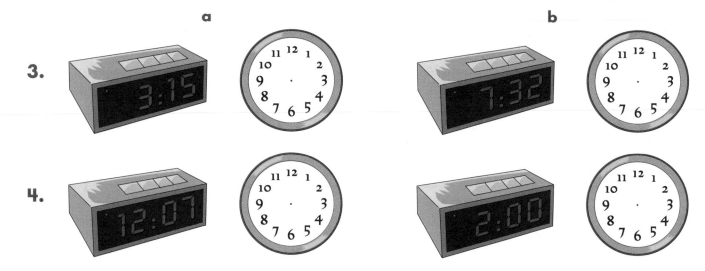

**a**

**b**

**3.** 3:15

**4.** 12:07

2:00

# Lesson 8.2  Time on a Number Line

Quinn gets up at 7:30 a.m. She leaves the house at 9:20 a.m. How much time passed between when she got up and left the house?

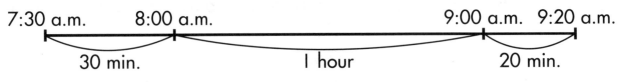

7:30 a.m.        8:00 a.m.                                        9:00 a.m.   9:20 a.m.

30 min.                              1 hour                      20 min.

First, find out how much time until the next hour.
Second, find out how much time passed since the previous hour.
Then, find out how much time passed between the next hour and the previous hour.
Last, add up the minutes and hours to find out the total time that has passed.

_____ 1 hour 50 minutes _____

---

Solve.

**1.** Alexa went to the bookstore at 5:45 p.m. She left the bookstore at 9:10 p.m. How long was Alexa at the bookstore?

_____

5:45 p.m.                                                                      9:10 p.m.

├──────────────────────────────────────────────┤

**2.** Hugo leaves for work at 7:45 a.m. He leaves work to go home at 4:15 p.m. How much time does Hugo spend at work?

_____

7:45 a.m.                                                                      4:15 p.m.

├──────────────────────────────────────────────┤

# Chapter 9

## Lesson 9.1 Plane Figures

A **plane figure** is a flat surface.

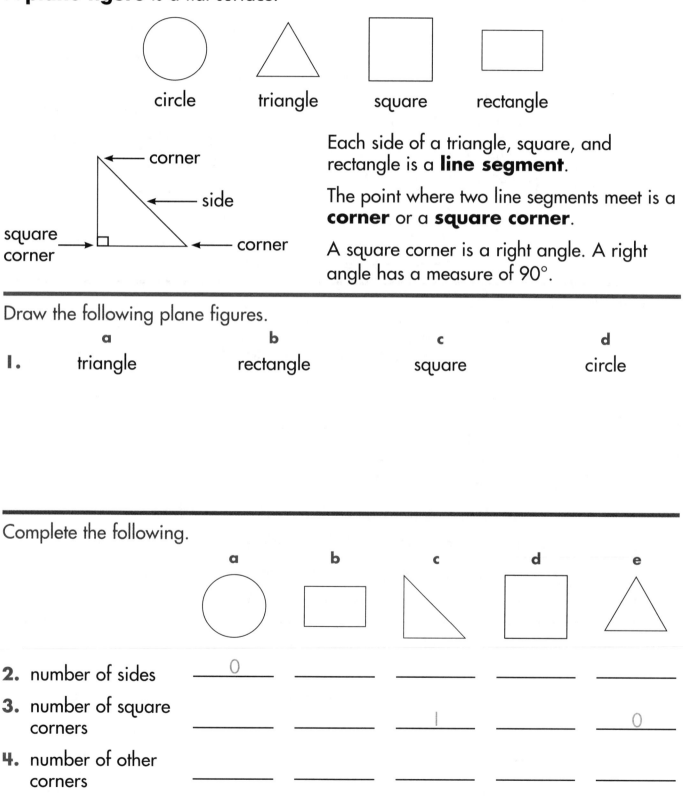

Each side of a triangle, square, and rectangle is a **line segment**.

The point where two line segments meet is a **corner** or a **square corner**.

A square corner is a right angle. A right angle has a measure of 90°.

Draw the following plane figures.

|  | a | b | c | d |
|---|---|---|---|---|
| **1.** | triangle | rectangle | square | circle |

Complete the following.

|  | a | b | c | d | e |
|---|---|---|---|---|---|
| **2.** number of sides | 0 | ___ | ___ | ___ | ___ |
| **3.** number of square corners | ___ | ___ | 1 | ___ | 0 |
| **4.** number of other corners | ___ | ___ | ___ | ___ | ___ |

# Lesson 9.2 Solid Figures

A **solid figure** is a three-dimensional object. Solid figures may be hollow or solid.

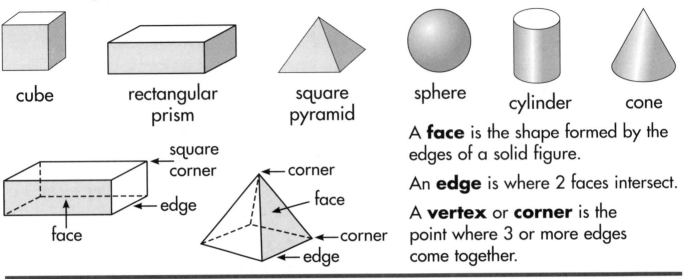

cube

rectangular prism

square pyramid

sphere

cylinder

cone

A **face** is the shape formed by the edges of a solid figure.

An **edge** is where 2 faces intersect.

A **vertex** or **corner** is the point where 3 or more edges come together.

Complete the table.

|  | Solid Figure | Number of Square Faces | Number of Rectangle Faces | Number of Triangle Faces |
|---|---|---|---|---|
| **1.** | cube |  |  | 0 |
| **2.** | rectangular prism |  |  |  |
| **3.** | square pyramid | 1 |  |  |

4. How many edges does a sphere have? _____ edges

5. How many edges does a square pyramid have? _____ edges

6. How many edges does a cube have? _____ edges

7. How many edges does a rectangular prism have? _____ edges

8. How many corners does a square pyramid have? _____ corners

Give a physical example of each of the following plane figures.

|  | **a** | **b** | **c** |
|---|---|---|---|
| **9.** | cube | rectangular prism | square pyramid |
|  | sugar cube | | |
| **10.** | sphere | cylinder | cone |

# Lesson 9.3 Classifying Quadrilaterals

**Quadrilaterals** are four-sided shapes. To be a quadrilateral, all four sides must be connected.

**Parallelograms** are quadrilaterals with two sets of parallel sides.

**Rectangles** are parallelograms with four right angles.

**Rhombuses** are parallelograms with four sides of equal length.

**Squares** are rectangles with four equal sides. They are also rhombuses with four right angles.

Circle the shapes named. Then, answer the question.

1. Circle the quadrilaterals.

2. Circle the parallelograms.

3. Circle the rectangles.

4. Circle the rhombuses.

5. Circle the squares.

6. Which of the shapes defined above fits into all five categories?

_____

# Lesson 9.4 Dividing Shapes

Halves = 2 equal pieces

Thirds = 3 equal pieces

Fourths = 4 equal pieces

Fifths = 5 equal pieces

and so on . . .

Divide this shape into thirds.

Label each third.

Divide each shape into the given amount of equal parts. Then, label each piece with the appropriate fraction.

1. halves

2. thirds

3. thirds

4. halves

5. fourths

6. fifths

7. halves

8. fourths

# Chapter 10

## Lesson 10.1  Number Patterns

A number pattern can be developed by addition or subtraction.

Complete this pattern by subtraction.

$25 - 5 = 20$    $20 - 5 = 15$    $15 - 5 = 10$    $10 - 5 = 5$    $5 - 5 = 0$

25          20          15          10          5          0

Complete the pattern by using addition or subtraction.

|  |  |  |  | a | b | c |
|---|---|---|---|---|---|---|
| 1. | 2 | 4 | 6 | 8 | 10 | 12 |
| 2. | 1 | 3 | 5 | ___ | ___ | ___ |
| 3. | 20 | 18 | 16 | ___ | ___ | ___ |
| 4. | 21 | 15 | 10 | ___ | ___ | ___ |
| 5. | 13 | 12 | 11 | ___ | ___ | ___ |
| 6. | 5 | 10 | 15 | ___ | ___ | ___ |
| 7. | 3 | 6 | 9 | ___ | ___ | ___ |
| 8. | 10 | 20 | 40 | ___ | ___ | ___ |
| 9. | 16 | 13 | 10 | ___ | ___ | ___ |
| 10. | 10 | 9 | 8 | ___ | ___ | ___ |

# Lesson 10.2 Number Sentences

A **number sentence** is an equation with numbers.

| **Identity Property** | **Commutative Property** |
|---|---|
| for addition:       $0 + 3 = 3$ | for addition:       $3 + 2 = 2 + 3$ |
| for multiplication: $1 \times 3 = 3$ | for multiplication: $4 \times 2 = 2 \times 4$ |

A number sentence can change its look but not change its value.

$3 + 5 = 8$ or $3 + 5 = 4 + 4$         $3 \times 8 = 24$ or $3 \times 8 = 6 \times 4$

---

Complete each number sentence.

|     | a | b | c | d |
|-----|---|---|---|---|
| **1.** | $0 + 4 = \boxed{4}$ | $0 + 6 = \square$ | $\square + 2 = 2$ | $\square + 7 = 7$ |
| **2.** | $1 \times 2 = \square$ | $1 \times 5 = \square$ | $\square \times 4 = 4$ | $\square \times 9 = 9$ |
| **3.** | $7 + 2 = \square + 7$ | $3 + 4 = \square + 3$ | $1 + 2 = 2 + \square$ | $\square + 5 = 5 + 4$ |
| **4.** | $5 \times 7 = 7 \times \square$ | $4 \times \square = 3 \times 4$ | $\square \times 3 = 3 \times 5$ | $9 \times 4 = \square \times 9$ |

---

Complete the following.

|     | a | b | c | d |
|-----|---|---|---|---|
| **5.** | $2 + 7 = 9$ or $2 + 7 = 5 + \boxed{4}$ | $5 + 7 = 12$ or $5 + 7 = 6 + \square$ | $4 + 3 = 7$ or $4 + 3 = 5 + \square$ | $6 + 9 = 15$ or $6 + 9 = 10 + \square$ |
| **6.** | $6 + 4 = 10$ or $6 + 4 = 5 + \square$ | $6 + 7 = 13$ or $6 + 7 = 8 + \square$ | $5 + 3 = 8$ or $5 + 3 = 6 + \square$ | $9 + 2 = 11$ or $9 + 2 = 5 + \square$ |
| **7.** | $5 \times 6 = 30$ or $5 \times 6 = 10 \times \square$ | $4 \times 3 = 12$ or $4 \times 3 = 2 \times \square$ | $6 \times 3 = 18$ or $6 \times 3 = 9 \times \square$ | $6 \times 2 = 12$ or $6 \times 2 = 4 \times \square$ |

## Lesson 10.2 Number Sentences

| **Associative Property** | **Distributive Property** |
|---|---|
| $(2 \times 3) \times 4 = c$ | $6 + 5 = 11$ |
| $2 \times 3 = 6$ | $11 \times 8 = (6 \times 8) + (5 \times 8)$ |
| $6 \times 4 = 24$ | $48 + 40 = 88$ |
| $c = 24$ | $11 \times 8 = 88$ |

Solve using the associative property.

|  | **a** | **b** |
|---|---|---|
| **1.** | $3 \times 5 \times 2 = d$ | $2 \times 9 \times 1 = h$ |
|  | _____ × _____ = _____ | _____ × _____ = _____ |
|  | _____ × _____ = _____ | _____ × _____ = _____ |
|  | $d = $ _____ | $h = $ _____ |
| **2.** | $4 \times 6 \times 2 = e$ | $7 \times 4 \times 2 = g$ |
|  | _____ × _____ = _____ | _____ × _____ = _____ |
|  | _____ × _____ = _____ | _____ × _____ = _____ |
|  | $e = $ _____ | $g = $ _____ |

Solve using the distributive property.

**3.** $12 \times 4 = (6 \times 4) + ($ _____ $\times 4)$      $14 \times 3 = (8 \times 3) + ($ _____ $\times 3)$

_____ + _____                             _____ + _____

$12 \times 4 = $ _____                     $14 \times 3 = $ _____

**4.** $19 \times 2 = (9 \times 2) + ($ _____ $\times 2)$      $16 \times 5 = (7 \times 5) + ($ _____ $\times 5)$

_____ + _____                             _____ + _____

$19 \times 2 = $ _____                     $16 \times 5 = $ _____

# SPECTRUM®

# Language Arts

# Chapter 1

## Lesson 1.1 Common and Proper Nouns

A **common noun** can be a person, place, or thing.

    *teacher* (person)                *museum* (place)

    *notebook* (thing)

A **proper noun** is a noun that names a specific person, place, or thing. Proper nouns are capitalized to show that they are important.

Here are some examples of common and proper nouns:

| Common nouns | Proper nouns |
|---|---|
| school | Hickory Hills Elementary School |
| zoo | Memphis Zoo |
| brother | Alexander |
| city | Tallahassee |
| day | Sunday |
| cat | Sasha |

## Complete It

Complete the sentences below with a noun from the box. If there is a **P** after the space, use a proper noun. If there is a **C** after the space, use a common noun.

| Walnut High School | Saturday | town |
|---|---|---|
| dog | Jordan Lake | brother |

1. Uncle Dale is taking me fishing at _____ (P).

2. We will leave early on _____ (P) morning.

3. My _____ (C), Kris, is coming with us.

4. Uncle Dale lives an hour away in a _____(C) called Rockvale.

5. He is a math teacher at _____ (P).

6. Uncle Dale's _____ (C), Patches, always comes fishing with us.

## Lesson 1.1 Common and Proper Nouns

### Identify It

Underline the nouns in the sentences below. The number in parentheses will tell you how many nouns there are. Above each noun, write **P** for *proper* or **C** for *common*.

1. Patches jumped into the rowboat. (2)

2. Kris and I put on our life jackets. (2)

3. Last August, we went to Griggs Lake. (2)

4. We stopped at Elmwood Historic Car Museum on the way home. (2)

5. We caught six fish on our trip. (2)

6. Uncle Dale cooked them on the grill. (2)

7. Mom made some coleslaw and potatoes. (3)

### Try It

1. Write a sentence using at least two common nouns. Circle the nouns.

_____

_____

2. Write a sentence using two proper nouns and one common noun. Circle the common noun. Underline the proper nouns.

_____

_____

# Lesson 1.2 Abstract Nouns

**Abstract nouns** are nouns that you can't experience with your five senses. They are feelings, concepts, and ideas. Some examples are *friendship*, *childhood*, *bravery*, *hope*, and *pride*.

## Identify It

Underline the abstract noun or nouns in each sentence below.

1. Maya's honesty is one of the reasons we are best friends.

2. Martin Luther King, Jr., wanted to change hate and injustice in the world.

3. Darius's patriotism is the reason he joined the army.

4. I love the delight on my sister's face on her birthday.

5. Your kindness will not be forgotten.

6. Benji felt great pride when his team won the championship.

7. What are your parents' best stories about their childhood?

8. It is important to me that you always tell the truth.

# Lesson 1.2 Abstract Nouns

## Complete It

Fill in each blank below with an abstract noun from the box.

| wisdom | liberty | freedom | knowledge |
|--------|---------|---------|-----------|
| courage | joy | kindness | |

1. Our country was founded on the ideas of _____ and _____ for all.

2. It took great _____ to rebuild after the hurricane.

3. Uncle Zane's _____ of birds amazes me.

4. The room was filled with _____ when Will found his lost puppy.

5. Neighbors showed us much _____ when my baby sister was born.

6. Grandpa has the _____ that comes with a long life.

## Try It

Write three sentences that use abstract nouns. You may use abstract nouns from the exercises or think of your own.

1. _____

2. _____

3. _____

# Lesson 1.3 Pronouns

A **pronoun** is a word that takes the place of a noun. Pronouns keep you from using the same noun or nouns over and over again.

Some pronouns take the place of a single person or thing: *I, me, you, he, she, him, her,* and *it.* Other pronouns take the place of plural nouns: *we, us, they,* and *them.*

In the examples below, pronouns take the place of the underlined nouns.

> The <u>grizzly bears</u> waded into the stream.
> *They* waded into the stream.
> <u>Molly</u> finished her report at noon.
> *She* finished her report at noon.
> Put <u>the bowl</u> on the table.
> Put *it* on the table.

## Identify It

Read the paragraphs below. Circle each pronoun. You should find 15 pronouns.

Sonja Henie was an amazing figure skater. She was born in Oslo, Norway, in 1912. When Sonja was only five years old, she won her first skating contest. It was the start of a great career. She was a world champion for ten years. People around the world became interested in skating. They followed the career of the talented young girl.

Sonja also wanted to be a movie star. She moved to Hollywood and began acting. She also performed in a traveling ice show. It was very popular. Huge crowds came to watch Sonja perform. They could not get enough of her. Sonja enjoyed her fame and the money it brought her. But her first and greatest love was always skating.

## Lesson 1.3 Pronouns

**Rewrite It**

Read the sentences below. Rewrite each sentence using a pronoun in place of the underlined noun or nouns.

Example: <u>David</u> kicked the ball toward the goal.

*He* kicked the ball toward the goal.

1. <u>Bryan and Anna</u> had their first skating lesson on Tuesday.

_____

2. <u>Bryan</u> had never skated before.

_____

3. <u>The ice</u> was slick and shiny.

_____

4. The teacher helped <u>Anna</u> tighten the skates.

_____

5. The teacher told <u>Bryan and Anna</u> that they did a great job.

_____

**Try It**

1. Think about the first time you tried something new. Write a sentence about your experience. Circle the pronoun.

_____

2. Write a sentence using the pronoun *he, she,* or *it.*

_____

## Lesson 1.4 Verbs

**Verbs** are often action words. They tell what happens in a sentence. Every sentence has a verb.

Ramon *put* on his running shoes. He *grabbed* his headphones. He *opened* the door and *took* a deep breath. Ramon *stretched* for a few minutes. Then, he *ran* down the street toward the park.

### Complete It

A verb is missing from each sentence below. Complete the sentences with verbs from the box.

| breathed | moved | attached | invented |
|----------|-------|----------|----------|
| gave | kept | carried | helped |

1. In 1819, August Siebe _____ the first diving suit.

2. The large helmet _____ to a leather and canvas suit.

3. Weights _____ divers stay underwater.

4. The divers underwater _____ air through hoses.

5. Later on, rubber suits _____ divers dry.

6. The invention of scuba gear _____ divers more freedom.

7. Divers _____ from place to place on their own.

8. They _____ their air with them.

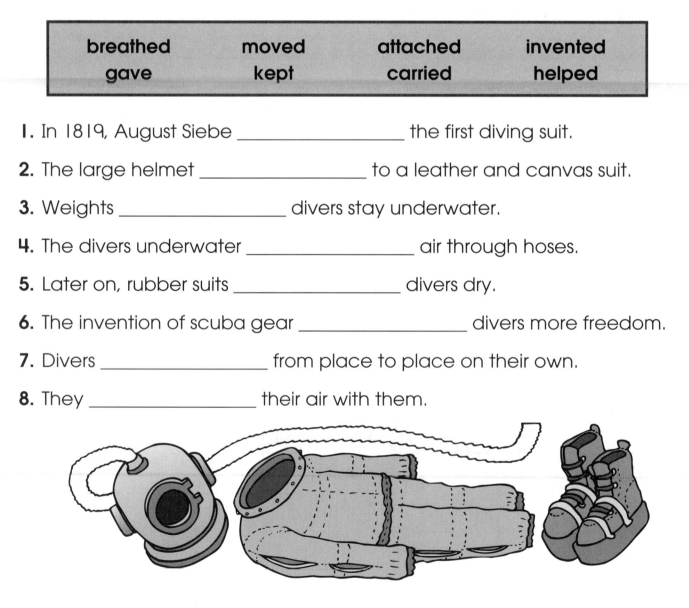

# Lesson 1.4 Verbs

**Identify It**

Circle the 10 action verbs in the paragraphs below.

Jacques Cousteau explored many of Earth's oceans. In 1950, he bought a ship called *Calypso*. On the *Calypso*, Jacques traveled to bodies of water around the world. He wrote many books and made many movies about his travels. He won prizes for some of his work. Jacques also invented things, like an underwater camera and the first scuba equipment.

Jacques Cousteau believed it was important to protect ocean life. He created a group called the *Cousteau Society*. More than 300,000 people belong to the Cousteau Society today.

**Try It**

1. Write a sentence about a place you would like to visit one day. Circle the verb.

   _____

   _____

   _____

2. Write a sentence about your favorite thing to do during the weekend. Circle the verb.

   _____

   _____

   _____

# **Lesson 1.5** Linking Verbs

A **linking verb** links the subject to the rest of the sentence. Linking verbs are not action words.

The verb *to be* is a linking verb. Some different forms of the verb *to be* are *is, am, are, was,* and *were.* Some other linking verbs are *become, feel,* and *seem.*

**Identify It**

Read the sentences below. Underline the linking verbs. Circle the action verbs. Some sentences may have more than one verb.

1. My grandmother is a marine biologist.

2. She studies undersea life.

3. She was always a good student.

4. She loved the ocean and animals as a child.

5. It was hard for her to become a scientist.

6. When she was young, some people felt women could not be good at science.

7. My grandma proved she was smart and hardworking.

8. One day, I might become a marine biologist myself.

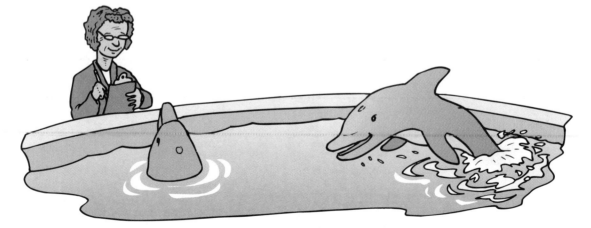

## Lesson 1.5 Linking Verbs

### Solve It

Use the linking verbs from the box to complete each sentence. Some may work for more than one sentence. Then, look for the linking verbs in the word search puzzle. Circle each word you find.

1. Today, my grandfather _____ a stage actor.

2. He first _____ a movie star at the age of 22.

3. He _____ lucky to have had such an amazing career.

4. I _____ going to see him in a Broadway play next week.

5. When my dad _____ little, he was in one of Grandpa's movies.

| feels | am | |
|-------|-----|--------|
| was | is | became |

| a | d | r | j | k | f | p |
|---|---|---|---|---|---|---|
| b | e | c | a | m | e | i |
| d | w | a | s | b | e | y |
| a | f | v | c | u | l | p |
| m | u | f | q | i | s | g |

### Try It

1. Write a sentence using a linking verb.

_____

_____

2. Write a sentence using a linking verb and an action verb.

_____

_____

# Lesson 1.6 Adjectives and Articles

**Adjectives** are words that describe. They give more information about nouns. Adjectives answer the questions *What kind?* and *How many?* They often come before the nouns they describe.

Fat raindrops bounced off the umbrella. (what kind of raindrops?)

Adjectives can also appear other places in the sentence. If you are not sure a word is an adjective, look for the noun you think it describes.

The robot was *helpful.*          The package is *huge!*

An **article** is a word that comes before a noun. *A, an,* and *the* are articles.

Use *the* to talk about a specific person, place, or thing.

*the* computer      *the* jacket      *the* bicycle      *the* starfish

Use *a* or *an* to talk about any person, place, or thing. If the noun begins with a consonant sound, use *a*. If it begins with a vowel sound, use *an*.

*a* wig      *a* bed      *an* apple      *an* envelope

## Complete It

Complete each item below with an adjective from the box.

| | | | | |
|---|---|---|---|---|
| shy | electric | prickly | warty | smelly |
| seven | skinny | tiny | howling | wrinkled |

1. the _____ porcupine

2. the _____ toad

3. the _____ eel

4. the gray, _____ elephant

5. the _____ hummingbird

6. the tall, _____ giraffe

7. the _____ skunk

8. the _____ deer

9. the _____ wolf

10. _____ flamingos

# Lesson 1.6 Adjectives and Articles

## Rewrite It

The sentences below do not give the reader much information. Rewrite the sentences. Add at least two adjectives to each sentence.

1. The dog barked at the squirrel as it ran up the tree.

   _____

   _____

2. The dolphin dove into the waves and swam toward the sunset.

   _____

   _____

## Proof It

Read the paragraph below. Circle the 20 articles you find. Six of the articles are incorrect. Cross them out, and write the correct articles above them.

A time capsule is a interesting way to communicate with people in a future. A time capsule is a group of items from the present time. An items tell something about a person, a place, or a moment in time. They are sealed in a container. A glass jar or the plastic box with a tight lid works well. Then, the capsule is buried or put in an safe place. An attached note should say when the capsule will be opened. Some capsules are opened in the year or in ten years. Others will stay buried or hidden for a thousand or even five thousand years!

# Lesson 1.7 Adverbs

**Adverbs** are words that describe verbs. Adverbs often answer the questions *When? Where?* or *How?*

She *joyfully* cheered for them.     *Joyfully* tells *how* she cheered.

*Yesterday*, I had a picnic.     *Yesterday* tells *when* I had a picnic.

Brady put the box *downstairs*.     *Downstairs* tells *where* Brady put the box.

Adverbs can also describe adjectives. They usually answer the question *How?*

Sierra was **too** late.     The sunset was **really** beautiful.

Adverbs can describe other adverbs, too.

Luke spoke **extremely** quietly.     Shawn **very** sadly said good-bye.

## Complete It

An adverb is missing from each sentence below. Choose the adverb from the box that best completes each sentence. Write it on the line. Then, circle the word the adverb describes.

| | | |
|---|---|---|
| loudly | brightly | often |
| beside | suddenly | completely |

1. Dylan sat _____ Amina at the school play.

2. The two friends _____ went to plays together.

3. The room was _____ dark.

4. _____, the curtain opened.

5. The scenery onstage was _____ painted.

6. The children said their lines _____ so that everyone could hear them.

# Lesson 1.7 Adverbs

**Solve It**

Read the sentences below. Find the adverb in each sentence. Write it on the lines after the sentence.

1. The prince slowly climbed Rapunzel's long hair.

   ___ ___ ___ ◯ ___ ___

2. Little Red Riding Hood safely returned home.

   ◯ ___ ___ ___ ___ ___

3. The wolf hid outside. ◯ ___ ___ ___ ___ ___ ___

4. Jack climbed down the beanstalk to escape the giant.

   ◯ ___ ___ ___

5. The cast proudly bowed at the end of the play.

   ___ ___ ◯ ___ ___ ___ ___

Write the circled letters from your answers on the lines below.

___ ___ ___ ___ ___

Unscramble the letters to find the missing word in the title of the play.

   Into the _____

**Try It**

Write two sentences about a fairy tale. Use an adverb from the box in each sentence. Circle the adverb. Then, underline the word the adverb describes.

| | | | |
|---|---|---|---|
| quickly | carefully | softly | completely |
| suddenly | gently | sadly | |

1. _____

2. _____

# Lesson 1.8 Conjunctions

A **conjunction** joins together words, phrases, and parts of sentences. The most common conjunctions are *and*, *or*, and *but*. Other conjunctions are *since*, *because*, *although*, *if*, *while*, *unless*, and *however*.

>     Chloe loves Brussels sprouts, *but* Haley won't eat them.
>     *Since* you play soccer, can you give me some tips?

## Complete It

Choose a conjunction to complete each sentence. Write it on the line.

  1. Do you want to play the violin _____ the piano? (or, but)

  2. Mr. Randall canceled Lucy's lesson _____ he had a cold. (unless, because)

  3. Let's play a duet at the recital _____ we can learn it in time. (while, if)

  4. Owen plays the drums, _____ Marcus plays the trombone. (and, or)

  5. Mrs. Klein likes to knit _____ Ezra practices singing. (however, while)

  6. Liam always practices his scales, _____ Alla never does. (but, if)

  7. Jade can buy a drum set, _____ her parents want her to help pay for it. (however, or)

  8. _____ Vikram's lesson is at 11:00, he often arrives at 10:30. (While, Although)

## Lesson 1.8 Conjunctions

**Rewrite It**

Combine each pair of sentences using a conjunction. There may be more than one correct answer for each item.

1. Jack wants to take violin lessons. His sister has been taking them for years.

   _____

   _____

2. Nora plays piano by ear. She can't read notes at all.

   _____

   _____

3. Dion enjoys listening to music. He doesn't play any instruments yet.

   _____

   _____

4. Mr. Santiago hums. He practices every afternoon.

   _____

   _____

**Try It**

Write a short paragraph about music. Use at least four conjunctions, and circle them.

_____

_____

_____

_____

# Lesson 1.9 Statements and Commands

A **statement** is a sentence that begins with a capital letter and ends with a period. A statement gives information.

    **D**iego will be 13 in April.      **S**udan is a country in Africa.

**Commands** are sentences that tell you to do something. Commands also begin with a capital letter and end with a period.

    **U**se the bright blue marker.      **C**hop the onions.

| Tip | Statements usually begin with a noun or a pronoun. Commands often begin with a verb. |
| --- | --- |

## Complete It

The statements below are missing periods. Add periods where they are needed. Circle each period you add so that it is easy to see.

                                             Monday, July 16

Dear Diary,

      On Saturday, Shi-Ann and I set up a lemonade stand  We made colorful signs to hang around the neighborhood  Dad helped us make cookies and chocolate pretzels  We wanted to make sure our customers would be thirsty

      At the store, we bought a tablecloth, cups, and napkins  Dad let us borrow some money to use in our change box  Once we opened for business, we had tons of customers  Shi-Ann and I had to keep making fresh lemonade all day

      We each made ten dollars from our lemonade stand  I had fun, but now I know that owning a business is a lot of work

# Lesson 1.9 Statements and Commands

## Identify It

Read the sentences below. If a sentence is a statement, write **S** in the space. If it is a command, write **C** in the space.

1. It is simple and fun to make your own lemonade. _____

2. Ask an adult to cut ten lemons in half. _____

3. Use a juicer to squeeze the juice from the lemons. _____

4. Mix the lemon juice with six cups of water. _____

5. The amount of sugar you add depends on how sweet you like your lemonade. _____

6. I use one cup of sugar. _____

7. Stir in the sugar until it dissolves. _____

8. Add some ice, and enjoy a glass of cool, refreshing lemonade. _____

## Try It

1. Write a command you might use to advertise a lemonade stand. Remember, a command usually begins with a verb.

   Example: Buy some cold, sweet lemonade today.

   _____

2. Write a statement about a business that you could start on your own.

   _____

## Lesson 1.10 Questions

**Questions** are sentences that ask something. When a person asks a question, he or she is looking for information. A question begins with a capital letter and ends with a question mark.

**W**ill you go to the party with me**?**
**W**hat is the weather like in Phoenix**?**

**Rewrite It**

Read each statement below. Then, rewrite it as a question.

Example: It was cold and rainy on Saturday.
<u>What was the weather like on Saturday?</u>

**1.** The largest frog in the world is called the Goliath frog.

_____

**2.** The skin of a toad feels dry and bumpy.

_____

**3.** Gliding leaf tree frogs can glide almost 50 feet in the air.

_____

**4.** The poison-dart frog lives in Colombia, South America.

_____

**5.** There are more than 4,000 species of frogs in the world.

_____

| Tip | Questions often begin with the words *who, what, where, when, how,* or *why.* |
|---|---|

# Lesson 1.10 Questions

**Proof It**

Read the following paragraphs. There are seven incorrect end marks. Cross out the mistakes. Then, write the correct end marks above them.

Have you ever heard someone say it was "raining frogs". You might have thought that it was just a figure of speech. But in rare cases, it has actually rained frogs? How could this happen. It sounds impossible. During a tornado or a powerful thunderstorm, water from a pond or lake can be sucked into the air. This includes anything that is in the water.

The storm continues to move? As it travels, it releases the water into the air. Does this mean that frogs and fish come raining down from the sky. Yes, this is exactly what happens.

Cases of strange things falling from the sky have been reported for many years? People have seen small frogs, fish, grasshoppers, and snails drop from the sky in places like France, India, Louisiana, and Kansas. Are animals the only things that get swept up by storms. No. In fact, in 1995, it rained soda cans in the Midwest.

**Try It**

1. Write a question you would like to ask a frog expert.

   _____

2. Write a question you would like to ask a weather expert.

   _____

## Lesson 1.11 Exclamations

**Exclamations** are sentences that show excitement or surprise. Exclamations begin with a capital letter and end with an exclamation point.

  **T**he Gold Nuggets won the championship**!**

  **W**e missed the bus**!**

Sometimes an exclamation can be a single word. Sometimes it can contain a command.

  Oops! Uh-oh! Watch out! Come back!

### Complete It

Read the advertisement below. Some of the end marks are missing. Write the correct end marks on the lines.

# Lesson 1.11 Exclamations

## Proof It

Read the sentences below. If the end mark is correct, make a check mark (✓) on the line. If the end mark is not correct, cross it out and write the correct end mark in the space.

1. Watch out. _____

2. Did you take the dog for a walk! _____

3. Luis is going to learn how to play the trumpet? _____

4. We won the game. _____

5. I lost my wallet? _____

6. How old is Ella. _____

7. My grandma had 16 brothers and sisters! _____

8. Harry wore a new suit to the wedding. _____

## Try It

Imagine that you were going on a jungle animal safari. Think of two exclamations you might make. Write them on the lines below.

Examples: Watch out for that big snake!

That leopard runs really fast!

_____

_____

# Lesson 1.12 Parts of a Sentence: Subject

The **subject** of a sentence is what a sentence is about. In a statement, the subject is usually found at the beginning of the sentence before the verb. A subject can be a single word or it can be several words.

*The entire team* cheered when the winning goal was scored.
*Irina* loves to eat oatmeal for breakfast.
*Brian Adams and Brian Rowley* are in the same class.
*Four raccoons, three chipmunks, and an opossum* live in my backyard.

**Identify It**

Underline the subject in each sentence below.

1. The Golden Gate Bridge is located in San Francisco, California.

2. The bridge was built in 1937.

3. It was the longest suspension bridge in the world until 1964.

4. A suspension bridge is a bridge that hangs from cables.

5. Joseph Strauss was the engineer who designed the amazing bridge.

6. The Verrazano Narrows Bridge and the Mackinac Bridge are two other famous bridges.

7. The bridge's orange color was chosen so that it would be easy to see on foggy days.

8. Many movies and TV shows have included views of the bridge.

9. You can walk or bike across the Golden Gate Bridge during the day.

# Lesson 1.12 Parts of a Sentence: Subject

## Complete It

Each sentence below is missing a subject. Find the subject in the box that best fits each sentence. Write the subject on the line.

| The Golden Gate Bridge | A statue of Joseph B. Strauss |
| People and cars | Maria |
| The cost to build the bridge | About nine million people |

1. _____ learned all about different kinds of bridges from her teacher.

2. _____ is 1.7 miles long.

3. _____ celebrates the famous engineer.

4. _____ visit the bridge every year.

5. _____ that travel north on the bridge do not have to pay a toll.

6. _____ was 27 million dollars.

## Try It

1. Write a sentence in which the subject is a person's name. Underline the subject.

   _____

2. Write a sentence in which the subject is more than one word. Underline the subject.

   _____

# Lesson 1.13 Parts of a Sentence: Predicate

A **predicate** tells what happens in a sentence. It tells what the subject is or does. The predicate always includes the verb. Finding the verb in a sentence can help you identify the predicate.

In the sentences below, the verbs are in bold type. The predicates are in italics.

Evelina **recycles** *all her cans and bottles.*
The seagull **soared** *above the stormy waters.*
Jermaine **took** *a picture of the dog with his camera.*

**Identify It**
Read the paragraph below. Underline the predicate in each sentence.

In the United States, April 22 is Earth Day. On Earth Day, people celebrate the planet Earth. They take the time to remember that the environment is fragile. The first Earth Day was held in 1970. About 20 million Americans celebrated that year. Today, more than 500 million people around the world take part in Earth Day activities.

On Earth Day, people learn about different types of pollution. They also learn what they can do to help save the planet. Many people recycle things. Paper, glass, and aluminum can be reused in new ways. Some groups plant trees to help keep the air clean. Others pick up litter in their parks and neighborhoods. For some caring people, every day is Earth Day!

# Lesson 1.13 Parts of a Sentence: Predicate

**Rewrite It**

One box below is filled with subjects. One box is filled with predicates. Draw a line to match each subject to a predicate. Then, write the complete sentences on the lines below. (There is more than one correct way to match the subjects and predicates.)

| Subjects | Predicates |
|---|---|
| Roma and Patrick | held an Earth Day 5K Run. |
| Alexis | cleaned up litter at McCoy Park. |
| Ms. Piazza's class | learned many ways to reuse newspapers. |
| My sister and I | donated ten dollars to a fund for endangered animals. |
| The students at Waxhill Elementary | planted eight small trees on Earth Day. |

1. _____

2. _____

3. _____

4. _____

5. _____

**Try It**

Write two sentences about something you can do every day to protect the planet. Underline the predicate in each sentence.

_____

_____

# Lesson 1.14 Sentence Fragments and Run-On Sentences

A sentence is a group of words that contains a complete thought or idea. All sentences have a subject and a predicate. Part of a sentence, or an incomplete sentence, is called a **sentence fragment**. Sentence fragments cannot stand alone.

Examples:  *Drove to the store.* (no subject)
*Because the sun.* (group of words)
*The girls on the porch.* (no predicate)

**Run-on sentences** are sentences that are too long. They are hard to follow, so they need to be split into two separate sentences. If the two sentences are about the same idea, they can be joined with a comma and a conjunction like *and* or *but*.

Clare likes cheese her brother Miles does not. (run-on)
Clare likes cheese. *Her* brother Miles does not. (split into two sentences)
Clare likes cheese, *but* her brother Miles does not. (combined with a comma and conjunction)

## Identify It

Read each item below. If it is a complete sentence, write **C** on the line. If it is a sentence fragment, write **F** on the line.

1. _____ Threw the ball.

2. _____ After Madeline made a basket.

3. _____ James scored a goal.

4. _____ Cheered, clapped, and yelled.

5. _____ The volleyball bounced off the net.

# Lesson 1.14 Sentence Fragments and Run-On Sentences

## Proof It

Read the paragraphs below. There are four run-on sentences. Make a slash (/) where you would break the run-on sentences into two sentences.

Example: The clown wore enormous shoes / he had a large, red nose.

There are many different breeds of dogs each one has a special personality. Basset hounds are often thought of as hunting dogs. They have long, floppy ears and wrinkly skin they can be loyal, friendly, and stubborn. Some people think their droopy eyes are sweet others think these hounds always look sad.

Cocker spaniels are good dogs for families. They are friendly and good with children they have beautiful, long silky ears. Cocker spaniels are usually tan or black in color.

## Try It

On a separate piece of paper, write two sentence fragments. Trade papers with a classmate. On the lines below, turn your classmate's fragments into complete sentences.

1. _____

2. _____

## Lesson 1.15 Combining Sentences: Subjects and Objects

Sometimes sentences that tell about the same thing can be combined. Then, the writer does not have to repeat words. Instead, the writer can combine two sentences into one by using the word *and*.

> Terrence likes popcorn.   Peter likes popcorn.
> Terrence *and* Peter like popcorn.

Because the subject (Terrence and Peter) is plural, the verb form has to change from *likes* to *like*.

In the example below, both sentences tell about what Jill read, so they can be combined.

> Jill read a new book.   Jill read a magazine.
> Jill read a new book *and* a magazine.

**Identify It**

Read each pair of sentences below. If the sentences tell about the same thing and can be combined with the word *and*, make a check mark (✓) on the line. If they tell about different things and cannot be combined, make an **X** on the line.

1. _____ Snakes are reptiles. Lizards are reptiles.

2. _____ Cheetahs are mammals. Toads are amphibians.

3. _____ The robin ate some berries. The robin ate a worm.

4. _____ Tarantulas are spiders. Black widows are spiders.

5. _____ The dolphin swam beside its baby. The whale headed for deeper waters.

## Lesson 1.15 Combining Sentences: Subjects and Objects

**Rewrite It**

Combine each pair of sentences below into one sentence. Write the new sentence on the line.

1. Bobcats live in the mountains of Virginia.
   Bears live in the mountains of Virginia.

   _____

2. The deer drinks from the stream. The coyote drinks from the stream.

   _____

3. The airplane startled the rabbit. The airplane startled the owl.

   _____

4. It is rare to spot mountain lions. It is rare to spot bald eagles.

   _____

5. Andy saw a deer at dusk. Andy saw a raccoon at dusk.

   _____

**Try It**

Write two sentences about wild animals you have seen. Then, combine your sentences into a single sentence.

Example:  I saw a wild turkey. I saw a woodpecker.
          I saw a wild turkey and a woodpecker.

_____

_____

# Lesson 1.16 Combining Sentences: Verbs

When two sentences tell about the same thing, they can sometimes be combined using the word *and*. The first two sentences below are about what Veronica did at breakfast, so they can be combined.

> Veronica ate some cereal. Veronica drank a glass of orange juice.
>
> Veronica ate some cereal *and* drank a glass of orange juice.

Some sentences can be combined using the word *or*. Use *or* if there are several choices about what might happen. In the example below, we do not know which choice Habib will make, so the word *or* is used.

> Habib might walk home. Habib might ride his bike home. Habib might run home.
>
> Habib might walk, ride his bike, *or* run home.

If you list several things in a row, place a comma after each one except the last.

## Complete It

Read the sentences below. Fill in each blank with the missing word.

1. Grandpa spread out the tent. Grandpa hammered the stakes.

   Grandpa spread out the tent _____ hammered the stakes.

2. Will might look for sticks. Will might cook dinner.

   Will might look for sticks _____ cook dinner.

3. Will put the pillows in the tent. Will unrolled the sleeping bags.

   Will put the pillows in the tent _____ unrolled the sleeping bags.

4. Grandpa and Will might make sandwiches. Grandpa and Will might grill hamburgers.

   Grandpa and Will might make sandwiches _____ grill hamburgers.

# Lesson 1.16 Combining Sentences: Verbs

**Rewrite It**

Combine each set of sentences below into one sentence. Write the new sentence on the line.

1. Grandpa stacked the wood. Grandpa found the matches. Grandpa lit the fire.

   _____

2. Grandpa toasted a marshmallow. Grandpa placed it between two graham crackers.

   _____

3. Will read in the tent with a flashlight. Will finished his book.

   _____

4. Grandpa and Will looked at the night sky. Grandpa and Will found the Big Dipper.

   _____

5. Next summer, they might sail down the coast. Next summer, they might go fishing.

   _____

**Try It**

1. Write two sentences that tell about things you do in the morning. Use a different verb in each sentence.

   _____

   _____

2. Now, combine the two sentences you wrote using the word *and*.

   _____

# Lesson 1.17 Combining Sentences: Adjectives

Sometimes, sentences can be combined.

The leaves are green. They are shiny. They are large.

The adjectives *green*, *shiny*, and *large* all describe *leaves*. The sentences can be combined into one by using the word *and*. Remember to use a comma after each adjective except the last.

The leaves are green, shiny, *and* large.

In the example below, only a comma is needed to combine the two sentences. Both sentences describe the jacket.

The red jacket is Amelia's favorite. The jacket is warm.

The warm, red jacket is Amelia's favorite.

## Identify It

Read each set of sentences below. If the adjectives describe the same thing, the sentences can be combined. Make a check mark (✓) on the line. If they describe different things, the sentences cannot be combined. Make an **X** on the line.

1. _____ The strawberries are red. They are juicy.

2. _____ The lemons are tart. The lemonade is sweet.

3. _____ I like wild blueberries. I like fresh blueberries.

4. _____ The grapes are ripe. They are dark purple. They are plump.

5. _____ The fuzzy kiwi is on the table. It is round.

6. _____ Oranges are tropical. Apples can be red, green, or yellow.

## Lesson 1.17 Combining Sentences: Adjectives

**Rewrite It**

Combine each set of sentences below into one
sentence. Write the new sentence on the line.

**1.** Cucumbers are long. They are thin. They are green.

_____

**2.** Sam grew some huge tomatoes in his garden. They were juicy.

_____

**3.** The rabbits seem to love Mom's lettuce. It is leafy.

_____

**4.** The seedlings are tiny. The seedlings are pale green.

_____

**5.** Rohan's peppers were small. They were spicy.

_____

**Try It**

**1.** Write two sentences that describe a piece of clothing you are wearing.
Use a different adjective in each sentence.

Example: I am wearing a new shirt. My shirt is striped.

_____

_____

**2.** Now, write a sentence that combines the two sentences you wrote.

Example: I am wearing a new, striped shirt.

_____

# Chapter 2

## Lesson 2.1  Capitalizing the First Word in a Sentence

The first word of a sentence always begins with a **capital letter**. A capital letter is a sign to the reader that a new sentence is starting.

*I* live on the third floor of the apartment building.

*Do* you like green beans?

*Here* comes the parade!

*Maya* grinned at Jeff.

**Proof It**

Read the paragraphs below. The first word of every sentence should be capitalized. To capitalize a letter, underline it three times (≡). Then, write the capital letter above it.

Example: <u>m</u>y sister taught me a new computer game.
        M

have you ever played golf? if you have, you know that it can be harder than it looks. golfer Michelle Wie makes it look pretty easy. that's because she can hit a golf ball more than 300 yards! at the age of 13, Michelle became the youngest winner ever of the Women's Amateur Public Links. she has even played on the famous men's golf tour, the PGA Tour. some people think that this amazing six-foot-tall golfer will be the next Tiger Woods.

# Lesson 2.1 Capitalizing the First Word in a Sentence

## Rewrite It

Rewrite each sentence below. Make sure your sentences begin with a capital letter.

1. michelle Wie's family is Korean.

   _____

2. she started beating her parents at golf when she was about eight.

   _____

3. today, Michelle plays regularly on the LPGA Tour.

   _____

4. *competitive* and *determined* are two words that describe Michelle.

   _____

5. david Leadbetter was Michelle's coach for years.

   _____

6. what kind of golfing records will Michelle set in the future?

   _____

## Try It

1. What sports do you like to play or watch? Begin your sentence with a capital letter.

   _____

2. What sports figure do you most admire? Begin your sentence with a capital letter.

   _____

# Lesson 2.2 Capitalizing Names and Titles

Capitalize the **specific names of people and pets**.

> My cousin *Umeko* moved here from Japan.
> We named the puppy *George*.

A **title** is a word that comes before a person's name. A title gives more information about who a person is. Titles that come before a name are capitalized.

> *Grandpa* Bruce                    *Aunt* Juliet
> *Captain* Albrecht                 *President* Abraham Lincoln
> *Senator* Barbara Boxer            *Judge* Naser

**Titles of respect** are also capitalized.

> *Mr.* Watterson        *Miss* Newton        *Mrs.* Cohen
> *Dr.* Gupta            *Ms.* Liang

| Tip | If a title is not used with a name, it is not capitalized. My *aunt* is funny. The *judge* was here. But, if a title is used as a name, it is capitalized. Tell *Mom* I am going to the park. *Grandpa* will fix the computer. |
|---|---|

## Complete It

Complete each sentence below with the words in parentheses ( ). Some of the words will need to be capitalized. Others will not.

1. Kelly took her dog, _____, for a walk to the park. (abby)

2. My school has a new _____. (principal)

3. On Tuesday, _____ is coming to visit. (grandma)

4. The best teacher I ever had was _____. (mr. butler)

5. The baby dolphin at the zoo is named _____. (michi)

# Lesson 2.2 Capitalizing Names and Titles

## Proof It

Read the letter below. There are ten mistakes. To capitalize a letter, underline it three times, and write the capital letter above it. To lowercase a letter (or change it from a capital letter to a small letter), make a slash through it. Then, write the small letter above it.

Example: Olivia and <u>m</u>att asked their G̶randma if she knew <u>m</u>r. Buckman.
(M above matt, g above Grandma, M above mr.)

April 12

Dear mayor Hendricks,

My name is annie Chun. My aunt and Uncle live near Pebblebrook Creek. When I visited them last week, we went wading. We were looking for rocks for a science project I am doing in mrs. sutton's class. We found the rocks, but we found many other things, too. For example, aunt Rose found several soda cans. Uncle Richard found some candy wrappers. Their dog, louie, discovered an old bottle. He thought it was a bone.

I would like to organize a cleanup of Pebblebrook Creek. I know the environment is important to you as the town Mayor. Can you help me organize this event? Maybe the next time my Aunt, uncle, Louie, and I go wading, we won't find anything but rocks.

Sincerely,

Annie chun

## Lesson 2.3 Capitalizing Place Names

The **names of specific places** always begin with a capital letter.

| | |
|---|---|
| *Madison, Wisconsin* | *Rocky Mountains* |
| *Italy* | *Liberty Avenue* |
| *Science Museum of Minnesota* | *Jupiter* |
| *Jones Middle School* | *Los Angeles Public Library* |

**Complete It**

Complete each sentence below with the word or words in parentheses ( ). Remember to capitalize the names of specific places.

1. There are many _____ (towns) across _____ (america) that have interesting names.

2. Have you ever heard of Okay, _____ (arkansas)?

3. Some towns are named after foods, like Avocado, California, and _____ (two egg), Florida.

4. Some names, like Chickasawhatchee and _____ (goochland) are fun to say.

5. A person from _____ (russia) might be surprised to find a town named Moscow in Vermont.

6. If you're on your way to visit _____ (mount rushmore), look for Igloo, South Dakota.

7. Would you like to go to _____ (boring elementary school) in Boring, Oregon?

| Tip | In the names of specific places, some words are not capitalized. All the important words begin with a capital letter. Small words, like *of*, *the*, *and*, and *a*, do not begin with a capital letter unless they are at the beginning of a sentence. |
|---|---|

# Lesson 2.3 Capitalizing Place Names

**Proof It**
Read the directions below. Capitalize the names of specific places. To capitalize a letter, underline it three times (≡), and write the capital letter above it.

- Take wilbur street to preston parkway, and turn left.

- Travel about two miles on preston parkway.

- You will pass montgomery library and the talbot recreation center.

- At the light, turn right onto solomon road.

- You will drive over haystack bridge and pass a gas station.

- children's playhouse is located on the west side of the street.

- The address is 1548 solomon road.

**Try It**
On the lines below, write your own set of directions from your home to a friend's house. Be sure to include street names and any landmarks like schools, libraries, parks, and so on.

_____

_____

_____

# Lesson 2.4 Capitalizing Dates and Holidays

The **days of the week** each begin with a capital letter.

Monday, Tuesday, Wednesday, Thursday, Friday, Saturday, Sunday

The **months of the year** are capitalized.

January, February, March, April, May, June, July,
August, September, October, November, December

The **names of holidays** are capitalized.

Memorial Day, Mother's Day,
Thanksgiving, Kwanzaa

## Complete It

Complete the sentences below with the name
of a day, month, or holiday. Remember to use
capital letters where needed.

1. I was born in the month of _____.

2. On _____, many people stay up until midnight to welcome the new year.

3. My favorite day of the week is _____.

4. On _____, Austin made a card for his dad and washed his dad's car.

5. _____ is the middle of the week.

6. In northern states, it often snows in _____.

7. The groundhog did not see his shadow on _____ this year.

8. Independence Day is on _____ 4th every year.

| Tip | The names of the seasons (*spring, summer, autumn,* and *winter*) are not capitalized unless they appear at the beginning of a sentence. |
|---|---|

# Lesson 2.4 Capitalizing Dates and Holidays

## Rewrite It

Rewrite the sentences below. Capitalize the names of days, months, and holidays.

1. presidents' day is on monday, february 21.

   _____

2. If the weather is nice, we will have a cookout on labor day.

   _____

3. thanksgiving day always falls on a thursday.

   _____

4. Ty gave a valentine to every person in his class on valentine's day.

   _____

5. Jessy is having a pool party on saturday, june 20.

   _____

## Try It

1. What is your favorite holiday? Why?

   _____

   _____

2. What is the coldest month of the year where you live? What is the warmest month?

   _____

   _____

## Lesson 2.5 Capitalizing Book, Movie, and Song Titles

The titles of books, movies, and songs are capitalized. Small words, like *of, the, and, in, to, a, an,* and *from,* do not begin with a capital letter unless they are the first or last word of a title.

| Books | Movies | Songs |
|---|---|---|
| Stuart Little | Epic | "Down by the Bay" |
| Ramona the Brave | The Secret Garden | "Pop Goes the Weasel" |
| A Light in the Attic | Jumanji | "When You Wish Upon a Star" |

**Rewrite It**

Rewrite the sentences below. Capitalize the names of books, movies, and song titles.

**1.** It took Shakhil only two days to read the book <u>how to eat fried worms</u>.

_____

**2.** Sara is sleeping over tonight, and we are going to watch <u>toy story 2</u>.

_____

**3.** The song "let it go" is from the movie frozen.

_____

**4.** I love the poems in Bruce Lansky's book <u>no more homework, no more tests</u>.

_____

**5.** Devon listened to the song "yellow submarine" on his mom's Beatles CD.

_____

## Lesson 2.5 Capitalizing Book, Movie, and Song Titles

**Proof It**

Read the sentences below. There are 24 words that should begin with a capital letter but do not. To capitalize a letter, underline it three times. Then, write the capital letter above it.

1. I love to sing "hakuna matata" from the Lion King because the words are fun to say.

2. Have you seen the old version or the new version of The parent trap?

3. Felipe borrowed the way things work by David Macaulay from the library.

4. If you watch Schoolhouse Rock, you can learn the song "conjunction junction."

5. Last week, Lottie read Freckle juice and Chocolate fever.

6. madeline is the name of a book and a movie.

7. Reading the great kapok tree by Lynne Cherry is a good way to learn about rain forests.

8. My little sister sings "shake your sillies out" every morning.

9. Paul and Tyler saw walking with dinosaurs three times in the movie theater!

**Try It**

1. Imagine that you were shipwrecked on a desert island. If you could bring only one book with you, what would it be?

_____

2. What is the funniest movie you have seen in the last year?

_____

## Lesson 2.6 Periods

A **period** is an end mark that follows a statement or a command.

      Put your bike in the garage.     Natalie has four brothers.

Periods are also used after initials. An **initial** is a letter that stands for a name.

      Darren *B.* Johnson   *P. L.* Travers   *J. P.* O'Bryan

The **days of the week** are often written as abbreviations, or in a shorter form. A period follows the abbreviation.

      Mon.  Tues.  Wed.  Thurs.  Fri.  Sat.  Sun.

The **months of the year** can also be abbreviated. May, June, and July are not abbreviated because their names are short.

      Jan.  Feb.  Mar.  Apr.  Aug.  Sept.  Oct.  Nov.  Dec.

**People's titles** are usually abbreviated when they come before a name.

      *Mrs.* = mistress   *Mr.* = mister   *Dr.* = doctor

**Types of streets** are written as abbreviations in addresses.

      *St.* = street    *Ave.* = avenue    *Dr.* = drive    *Ln.* = lane

      *Rd.* = road    *Blvd.* = boulevard    *Ct.* = court    *Cir.* = circle

## Match It

Write the letter of the correct abbreviation on the line.

1. _____ October 2      **a.** Oct. 2      **b.** Octob. 2

2. _____ John Fitzgerald Kennedy      **a.** John F Kennedy      **b.** John F. Kennedy

3. _____ Tuesday      **a.** Tu.      **b.** Tues.

4. _____ Chester Avenue      **a.** Chester Avn.      **b.** Chester Ave.

5. _____ December 19      **a.** Dec. 19      **b.** Dcmbr. 19

6. _____ Madison Anne Hall      **a.** Madison A Hall      **b.** Madison A. Hall

## Lesson 2.6 Periods

**Proof It**

Read the schedule below. Cross out words that can be written as abbreviations. Write the correct abbreviations above them.

| | |
|---|---|
| Monday, March 7 | Hot Potatoes concert at 422 Lakeshore Drive—7:00 |
| Thursday, April 14 | Cassie's dentist appointment with Doctor Phillips—10:00 |
| Friday, April 29 | Meeting with Mister Haddad—noon |
| Saturday, May 21 | Drop-off costumes at Mistress Jensen's house—1668 Dublin Lane |
| Tuesday, August 30 | Jimmy Ortega's birthday party—46 Brentwood Boulevard |
| Sunday, September 18 | Brunch with Mister Sato—11:00 |

**Try It**

1. Write a sentence about what you would do if someone gave you a hundred-dollar bill. End your sentence with a period.

_____

2. Ask three friends when their birthdays are. Write the dates on the line using abbreviations for the names of the months.

_____

**Tip**

Abbreviations for days, months, and types of streets are used only in addresses and casual writing. For example, you might abbreviate the name of a day or month in a calendar or a note. Do not use these abbreviations in the body of a letter, a report, or a story.

## Lesson 2.7 Question Marks

Use a **question mark** to end a sentence that asks a question.

Would you like some fruit punch**?**　　How many books did you read**?**

Where is Connor going**?**　　Can all birds fly**?**

**Complete It**

Read each answer below. Then, write the question that goes with the answer.

Example: **Q:** How tall is Mr. Stein? _____

**A:** Mr. Stein is six feet tall.

1. **Q:** _____

   **A:** Jupiter has at least 63 known moons.

2. **Q:** _____

   **A:** The sun is the largest body in the solar system.

3. **Q:** _____

   **A:** Mars is closer to the sun than Saturn.

4. **Q:** _____

   **A:** Galileo made his first telescope in 1608.

5. **Q:** _____

   **A:** Astronaut Shannon Lucid has spent more than 200 days in space.

6. **Q:** _____

   **A:** Mercury is the smallest planet.

# Lesson 2.7 Question Marks

**Proof It**

Read the paragraphs below. Cross out the six incorrect end marks. Add the correct end marks, and circle them.

Have you ever visited the Sleeping Bear Dunes. They are located along the shore of Lake Michigan. The enormous dunes, or sand hills, are more than 400 feet tall in places. Many people travel to Michigan every year to climb the dunes? Most visitors come in the summer, but some people come in the winter, instead. Why would they visit the icy shores of the lake in the winter. Sledding down the steep slopes can be a lot of fun!

Do you know where the dunes got their name. A Native American legend says that a mother bear lay on the beach to watch for her cubs after a fire. Over time, sand covered the bear? Some people still think they can see the shape of a bear sleeping on the beach. This is how the dunes came to be called the Sleeping Bear Dunes?

**Try It**

On the lines below, write a question you could ask a park ranger at Sleeping Bear Dunes National Lakeshore.

_____

_____

## Lesson 2.8 Exclamation Points

An **exclamation point** is used to end a sentence that is exciting or expresses strong feeling. Sometimes exclamation points are used to show surprise or fear.

That pan is hot!                                    Lindsay won first prize!

I can't believe you broke the chair!      There's a snake!

**Proof It**

Read the diary entry below. Five of the periods should be exclamation points. Find the five incorrect periods, and cross them out. Then, add exclamation points where they are needed.

Saturday, May 6

Dear Diary,

     Something interesting happened today. I am going to be in a movie. The movie <u>The Time Travelers</u> is being filmed in my town. My mom works at the library. The director was learning about the history of the town at the library. My mom helped the director find what she needed. The director saw my picture on my mom's desk. She asked my mom if I would be interested in a small part in the movie. Would I ever.

     I will have only two lines to say. Mom said she will help me memorize them. My scene will last about five minutes. Do you know what the best part is? I get to work with my favorite actor. I can't wait to start filming. Who knows? Maybe I'll be famous one day.

# Lesson 2.8 Exclamation Points

**Complete It**

The sentences below are missing end marks.
Add the correct end mark in the space
following each sentence. You should add
four periods, two question marks, and three
exclamation points.

1. Evan and Tanner have been jumping on
   the trampoline all morning___

2. Have you read the book <u>A Cricket in Times Square</u> ___

3. Kazuki's swimming lesson was cancelled___

4. Watch out___

5. Please clean your room before bedtime___

6. The Bradview Tigers won the championship___

7. Would you like cheese on your sandwich___

8. There's a huge spider in my bed___

9. Tereza traded stickers with her little brother___

**Try It**

1. Write a sentence that shows excitement. Your sentence should end
   with an exclamation point.

   _____

2. Write a sentence that shows fear. Your sentence should end with an
   exclamation point.

   _____

# Lesson 2.9 Commas with Dates, Cities, States, and Addresses

Commas are used in dates. They are used in between the day and the year.

March 4, 2006     September 22, 1750     June 1, 1991

Commas are also used in between the names of cities and states or cities and countries.

Portland, Oregon     Paris, France     Minneapolis, Minnesota

When the names of cities and states (or countries) are in the middle of a sentence, a comma goes after the state or country, too.

Bethany stopped in Burlington, Vermont, on her way home.

In an address, a comma is used between the city name and state abbreviation.

Richmond, VA     Juneau, AK

**Proof It**

Read the sentences below. Add commas by using this symbol (∧).

Example: The Rock and Roll Hall of Fame is in Cleveland∧Ohio.

1. Basketball star LeBron James was born on December 30 1984.

2. Sarah Hughes skated in the Winter Olympics in Salt Lake City Utah.

3. In 2004, Lance Armstrong traveled to Liege Belgium to ride in the Tour de France.

4. Olympic swimmer Michael Phelps was born in Baltimore Maryland in 1985.

| Tip | When only a month and year are given, do not separate them with a comma. August 1999     February 2014     December 1941 |
| --- | --- |

NAME _____

## Lesson 2.9 Commas with Dates, Cities, States, and Addresses

**Identify It**

There are two choices below for each item. Choose the correct version, and write the letter in the space.

1. _____ **a.** October, 12 1954          **b.** October 12, 1954

2. _____ **a.** Omaha, NE          **b.** Omaha NE

3. _____ **a.** August, 2007          **b.** August 2007

4. _____ **a.** January 24, 1936          **b.** January, 24, 1936

5. _____ **a.** Amarillo Texas          **b.** Amarillo, Texas

6. _____ **a.** September 30, 2015          **b.** September 30 2015,

7. _____ **a.** Nashville, Tennessee, is 284 miles from Shreveport, Louisiana.
        **b.** Nashville Tennessee, is 284 miles from Shreveport, Louisiana.

8. _____ **a.** The ship traveled from Crete, Greece, to the shores of Turkey.
        **b.** The ship traveled from Crete, Greece to the shores of Turkey.

**Try It**

Ask two people in your class or your family the questions below. Record their answers on the lines.

1. In what city and state were you born?

_____

_____

2. What is your birth date?

_____

_____

# Lesson 2.10 Commas in a Series

A **series** is a list of words. Use a comma after each word in a series except the last word.

> Ms. Pinckney asked Alonzo, Erica, and Charley to work on the project together.
>
> Dakota put a sandwich, an apple, and a granola bar in her lunchbox.
>
> Our neighbors have two dogs, three cats, seven chickens, and a goat.

## Proof It

Read the note below. Twelve commas are missing. Add commas where they are needed by using this symbol (∧).

Dear Dillon,

Please go to the store for me when you get home from school. Tonight we are going to make muffins for Grandad's birthday breakfast. We will need blueberries eggs sugar and lemon juice. I left some money on the kitchen table.

Ellie is going swimming with Rob Aliya Eve and Hunter. She will be home around 4:00. Please remind her to let the dog out hang up her swimsuit and start her homework.

I made a list of the things you said you will need for your science project. I put glue sand newspaper vinegar and baking soda on the list. Is anything missing? We can go shopping tomorrow afternoon.

See you in a couple of hours!

Love,

Mom

# Lesson 2.10 Commas in a Series

**Rewrite It**

The numbered sentences are missing commas. Rewrite each numbered sentence in the recipe, using commas where needed.

## Lemony Blueberry Muffins

1½ cups flour
½ cup yellow cornmeal
½ cup sugar
1½ teaspoons baking powder
½ teaspoon baking soda
¼ teaspoon salt

½ cup milk
½ cup plain yogurt
3 tablespoons oil
1 tablespoon lemon juice
1 egg
1 cup blueberries

*Always have an adult help you when you are cooking.

- (1) You will also need cooking spray a muffin tin a measuring cup two bowls a teaspoon a tablespoon and a wooden spoon.

_____

_____

_____

- Preheat the oven to 400°F. Spoon the flour into the measuring cup.
- (2) Combine the flour cornmeal sugar baking powder baking soda and salt.

_____

_____

- (3) In the other bowl, combine the milk yogurt oil lemon juice and egg.

_____

_____

- Add the wet mixture to the flour mixture. Stir until moist. Fold in the blueberries.
- Spoon the batter into the muffin tin. Bake at 400°F for 20 minutes.
- (4) Remove the muffins from the pan place them on a wire rack and let them cool.

_____

_____

## Lesson 2.11 Commas in Compound Sentences

A **simple sentence** tells about one complete thought. A **compound sentence** is made of two or more simple sentences. To form a compound sentence, use a comma and the conjunction *and, or,* or *but* to join the simple sentences.

In the examples below, the underlined parts of each compound sentence can stand alone as simple sentences. Notice that a comma follows the first simple sentence.

> <u>Sadie likes orange juice</u>, *but* <u>her brother prefers apple juice.</u>
> <u>Do you want to go to the zoo</u>, *or* <u>would you rather go to the art museum?</u>
> <u>Alejandro collects baseball cards</u>, *and* <u>Adam collects coins.</u>

### Identify It

Read each sentence below. If it is a simple sentence, write **S** on the line. If it is a compound sentence, write **C** on the line. Then, underline each simple sentence in the compound sentence.

1. _____ Have you noticed birds in your yard or your neighborhood?

2. _____ Feeding birds can be fun, and it can be educational.

3. _____ Some birds like birdseed, but others like suet, a type of fat.

4. _____ In the winter, many birds prefer fatty foods, like peanut butter.

5. _____ Bird food placed on the ground will attract birds, but it will also attract other animals.

6. _____ Squirrels are known for eating bird food and scaring birds away.

7. _____ Once birds notice that you are feeding them, they will come to visit often.

8. _____ Finches love thistle seed, and orioles love oranges.

# Lesson 2.11 Commas in Compound Sentences

**Proof It**

Read the paragraph below. Three commas are missing from compound sentences. Add each comma by using this symbol (∧).

If you have a plastic soda bottle, you can make your own bird feeder. With an adult's help, make two holes on opposite sides of the bottle and push a twig through each hole. Small birds can perch on the twig. Then, make several other holes in the bottle. The birds will be able to eat seeds from these holes. Tie some string around the neck of the bottle and hang it from a sturdy tree branch. Enjoy watching the birds from a window but don't forget to feed them.

**Try It**

1. Write a simple sentence about birds you have seen at a park or in your neighborhood.

   _____

   _____

2. Write a compound sentence about other city wildlife you have seen.

   _____

   _____

# Lesson 2.12 Punctuating Dialogue

The exact words a person says are called **dialogue**. One set of quotation marks is used before the first word of dialogue. A second set of quotation marks is used after the last word of dialogue.

"I love to sail."                              "Is the fruit ripe**?**"

If the dialogue does not end the sentence, put a comma (not a period) inside the quotation marks. The period belongs at the very end of the sentence.

"I love to sail," Chloe said.            "The fruit isn't ripe," said Geoff.

If the dialogue is a question and does not end the sentence, keep the question mark inside the quotation marks.

"Do you love sailing**?**" Chloe asked.

"Are the bananas ripe**?**" asked Geoff.

If part of the sentence comes before the dialogue, put a comma after that part of the sentence. The period at the end of the sentence belongs inside the quotation marks.

Chloe said, "I love to sail."            Geoff asked, "Is the fruit ripe**?**"

**Proof It**

Read each sentence below. If the sentence is correct, make a check mark on the line (✓). If it is not correct, make an **X** on the line. Then, use the proofreading marks in the box to show the changes.

| | |
|---|---|
| ∧ | = insert comma |
| ⊙ | = insert period |
| ⌄ | = insert quotation marks |

Example: __**X**__ Our suitcases are in the attic͢" said Dad⊙

I. _____ This summer, I am going to take Spanish lessons, said Mackenzie.

2. _____ "My family is driving all the way across the country in an RV,"
Ryan said.

3. _____ Nicolae said "I plan to go swimming at the lake every day

# Lesson 2.12 Punctuating Dialogue

**Rewrite It**

The sentences below are missing commas, periods, and quotation marks. Rewrite each sentence. Add punctuation marks where needed.

**1.** I have never been to a farm before replied Audrey

_____

**2.** Neither have I agreed Nicolae

_____

**3.** My grandparents have cows, horses, goats, and barn cats said Van

_____

**4.** He added I stay with them every summer, and there is always something to do

_____

**5.** I would love to learn how to ride a horse or milk a cow said Audrey

_____

**6.** Van grinned at Audrey and said My grandparents can always use an extra hand

_____

**Try It**

Ask two of your classmates what they plan to do next summer. Record their answers on the lines below. Remember to use quotation marks to show the exact words your classmates use.

**1.** _____

**2.** _____

## Lesson 2.13 Punctuating Titles

**Titles of books, movies, and plays** are underlined.

Lucas did a book report on <u>Two Heads Are Better Than One</u>.

The movie <u>Two Brothers</u> is an adventure about twin tiger cubs.

For Dionne's birthday, her family went to see the play <u>Peter Pan</u>.

**Titles of songs, poems, and stories** are set in quotation marks.

Judith Viorst wrote the poem "If I Were in Charge of the World."

The story "The Emperor's Clothes" is in my book of fairy tales.

My favorite song is "Bright Eyes" by Remy Zero.

### Complete It

Read each sentence below. Underline the titles of books, movies, and plays. Put quotation marks around the titles of songs, stories, and poems.

1. Before the first softball game of the season, we always sing Take Me Out to the Ballgame.

2. Scotty Smalls is the main character in the movie The Sandlot.

3. My favorite poem is Eletelephony by Laura E. Richards.

4. In the play Annie, Bridget McCabe had the lead role.

5. Laura Ingalls Wilder wrote Little House in the Big Woods.

6. The movie The Incredibles won an award for Best Animated Film.

7. When it was time for bed, Dad told me a story called Gregory and Grandpa's Wild Balloon Ride.

8. I memorized Edward Lear's poem The Owl and the Pussycat.

9. Singing the song Purple People Eater makes my sister laugh.

| Tip | Remember to place periods inside quotation marks if a title comes at the end of a sentence. |
|-----|---------------------------------------------------------------------------------------------|

# Lesson 2.13 Punctuating Titles

**Proof It**

Read the diary entry below. Find the titles, and underline them or place them in quotation marks. To add quotation marks, use this symbol (⌄).

Thursday, October 8

Dear Diary,

    I had a very busy week. On Monday, I went to the library after school. I worked on the story I am writing. It is called The Mystery of the Golden Toothbrush. I borrowed the books Summer of the Sea Serpent, Stone Fox, and Pink and Say. I am going to write a book report on one of them, but I haven't decided which one.

    On Wednesday, I recited two poems for Poetry Week. I chose The Shadow by Robert Louis Stevenson and Jellyfish Stew by Jack Prelutsky. After school, I tried out for the play The Princess and the Pea. I hope I land the role of the princess.

    On Friday night, Ankit and Kendra came over to watch some movies. We rented Antz and My Neighbor Totoro. Antz is Kendra's favorite movie. My parents made subs and popcorn for us. We had a lot of fun, but I'm glad this crazy week is over!

**Try It**

1. What is your favorite song? Write the title on the line.

_____

2. Think of an idea for a story you could write. Then, write two possible titles for your story on the lines below.

_____

_____

# Chapter 3

## Lesson 3.1 Subject-Verb Agreement: Adding **s** and **es**

The **subject** of a sentence tells who or what the sentence is about. When the subject is **singular**, it is only one person, place, or thing. When there is a singular subject, the verb ends with **s** or **es**.

Add **s** to most regular verbs that have a single subject.

> *The boat* sail**s** close to shore.　　　*The woman* water**s** the flower.

Add **es** to regular verbs that have a single subject and end in **sh**, **ch**, **s**, **x**, and **z**.

> *Gran* kiss**es** us good-bye.　　　*Jake* crunch**es** his cereal loudly.

When the subject is **plural**, it is more than one person, place, or thing. When the subject is plural, the verb does not end with **s** or **es**.

> *The kittens* sleep on the sofa.　　　*Zared and Nina* latch the gate.

### Proof It

Read the paragraph below. Underline the subjects. Find the verbs that do not agree with their subjects. Add or delete **s** or **es** from the verbs so that they agree with their subjects. Use this symbol (^) to add a letter or letters. Cross out letters that don't belong.

Mr. Ruskin wash his historic car on Saturdays. Aaron and Ali helps him. Mr. Ruskin sprays the old car with warm water. He scrub every inch of the car with a big sponge. The children polishes the windshield and the mirrors. They use clean, soft rags. Aaron wax the beautiful red car. It shine in the sunlight. He wishes to have a car just like his dad's one day. Mr. Ruskin take Aaron and Ali for a drive in the shiny car every Saturday afternoon. They buy ice-cream cones. Then, they walks in the park.

## Lesson 3.1 Subject-Verb Agreement: Adding **s** and **es**

**Complete It**

Read each sentence below. Then, read the pair of verbs in parentheses ( ). Choose the correct verb form. Write it on the line.

1. Emily and Mateo _____ a ball in the backyard. (toss, tosses)

2. The Jorgensons _____ their pumpkins every autumn. (harvest, harvests)

3. My little brother _____ his teeth with an electric toothbrush. (brush, brushes)

4. Britta _____ ten miles a day when she is in training for the race. (bike, bikes)

5. The blender _____ the ingredients. (mix, mixes)

6. The Guzmans _____ near a crystal-clear mountain lake every summer. (camp, camps)

7. The shaggy Irish setter _____ the ball each time I throw it. (catch, catches)

8. Aunt Celeste _____ about two hours away. (live, lives)

**Try It**

1. Write a sentence using one of the following verbs: *climb, skate, twirl, travel, race, point,* or *bake.* Underline the subject in your sentence, and circle the verb. Make sure that the subject and the verb agree.

_____

2. Write a sentence using one of the following verbs *push, crash, finish, pitch, watch, miss,* or *fix.* Underline the subject in your sentence, and circle the verb. Make sure that the subject and the verb agree.

_____

# Lesson 3.2 Irregular Verbs: *Am, Is, Are*

*Am, is,* and *are* are all different forms of the verb *to be.*

*Am* is used only with the subject *I.*

    *I **am** sleepy.   I **am** hungry.   I **am** under the bed.*

*Is* is used when the subject is singular.

    *Mickey **is** sixteen.   Annabelle **is** tall.   The beach **is** rocky.*

*Are* is used with the subject *you.*

    *You **are** very funny.   You **are** correct.   You **are** first in line.*

*Are* is also used when the subject is plural.

    *Haley Joel Osment and Dakota Fanning **are** actors.*
    *The boys **are** at home.*

**Rewrite It**

Rewrite each sentence below. If it has a plural subject, rewrite it with a single subject. If it has a single subject, rewrite it with a plural subject. Remember that the form of the verb must agree with the subject and verb.

Example: The salad dressing and the salad are on the table.
       The salad dressing is on the table.

**1.** Nissa and Toby are eight.

_____

**2.** The photograph is in an album.

_____

**3.** The CDs on the shelf are from the library.

_____

**4.** We are excited about traveling to Mexico.

_____

# Lesson 3.2 Irregular Verbs: *Am, Is, Are*

## Proof It

Read the paragraphs below. There are 11 mistakes with the verbs *am, is,* and *are.* Cross out each mistake. Then, write the correct form of the verb above it.

A topiary (*toe pee air ee*) are a kind of sculpture made from plants. Topiaries is cut to look like many different things. Some am shaped like animals. For example, a topiary can look like an elephant, a bear, a horse, or even a dinosaur. Other topiaries is trimmed to look like castles, cones, or mazes.

A topiary gardener are an artist. He or she can turn simple shrubs into beautiful sculptures. Boxwood, holly, bay laurel, and yew am some of the best plants to use for topiary. They is easy to train and to trim.

In May, I are going to visit the Green Animals Topiary Garden in Rhode Island. It am one of the oldest topiary gardens in the country. There am 80 pieces of topiary there! It are fun to imagine all the green animals coming to life and roaming the gardens.

## Try It

Write three sentences on the lines below. Use the verbs *am, is,* or *are* in each sentence.

_____

_____

_____

# Lesson 3.3 Irregular Verbs: *Has, Have*

*Has* and *have* are different forms of the verb *to have*.

*Have* is used when the subject is *I* or *you*.

    *I **have** a cold.*            *You **have** two brothers.*

*Have* is also used with plural subjects.

    *We **have** a book about dinosaurs.*

    *Roberto and Chiara **have** a baby sister.*

    *They **have** a yellow house.*     *Both cars **have** flat tires.*

*Has* is used when there is a single subject like *he, she,* or *it*.

    *She **has** blonde hair.*       *The librarian **has** a cheerful smile.*

    *A male deer **has** antlers.*

## Complete It

Complete each sentence below with the word *has* or *have*. Write the correct word in the space.

1. Gus and Emily _____ a shell collection.

2. A horse conch _____ a cone shape and can grow to be almost two feet long.

3. Shells _____ value when they are beautiful or rare.

4. The shapes of some shells _____ interesting names, like helmet, basket, lamp, frog, and trumpet.

5. Oysters and clams _____ shells that are hinged at the back.

6. Emily _____ a necklace made from polished pieces of shell.

7. Cowrie shells _____ been used as money on Indian and Pacific islands.

8. If Gus _____ more than one of a certain shell, he will trade it with other collectors.

# Lesson 3.3 Irregular Verbs: *Has, Have*

## Proof It

Read the letter below. There are eight mistakes with the verbs *have* and *has*. Cross out each incorrect verb. Then, write the correct form of the verb above it.

---

August 6, 2015

Dear Kyra,

How is life at home in Massachusetts? We are having a great time in Florida. Gus and I has 40 new shells to add to our collection! We has been busy searching the beaches here. Gus and I already has labels for our new shells. We don't want to forget their names by the time we get home.

Some shells still has animals living in them. We never collect those shells. Our parents has helped us look in rock crevices and tide pools. That is how we found a true tulip shell. It have a pretty peachy color and an interesting pattern.

I has a surprise to bring home for you. You has never seen a shell like this. I can't wait to see you. Wish you were here!

Your friend,

Emily

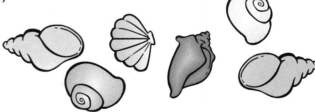

---

# Lesson 3.4 Forming the Past Tense by Adding ed

Verbs in the **present tense** tell about things that are happening right now. Verbs in the **past tense** tell about things that have already happened.

Add **ed** to a regular verb to change it to the past tense. If the verb already ends in **e**, just add **d**.

> The concert end**ed** at 9:00.     It snow**ed** 16 inches yesterday!
> Uncle Donny taste**d** the pudding.   The waitress smile**d** at the girl.

If a verb ends in **y**, change the **y** to **i** and add **ed**.

> We hur**ry** to catch the bus.      We hur**ried** to catch the bus.
> I d**ry** the laundry outside.       I d**ried** the laundry outside.

**Complete It**

Read the sentences below. Complete each sentence with the past tense of the verb in parentheses ( ).

1. Leonardo da Vinci _____ the mysterious *Mona Lisa*. (paint)

2. Women and children often _____ for artist Mary Cassatt. (pose)

3. The Impressionists _____ the world that not all paintings had to look realistic. (show)

4. Grandma Moses _____ to paint cheerful pictures of life in the country. (love)

5. Jackson Pollack, who made colorful paint-splattered paintings, _____ with Thomas Hart Benton. (study)

6. Vincent van Gogh _____ more than 800 oil paintings during his lifetime! (create)

7. Chinese artist Wang Yani _____ painting when she was only two. (start)

# Lesson 3.4 Forming the Past Tense by Adding ed

## Rewrite It

Read the sentences below. They are all in the present tense. Underline the verb in each sentence. Then, rewrite the sentences in the past tense.

1. Norman Rockwell lives from 1894 until 1978.

_____

2. Norman studies at the National Academy of Design in New York.

_____

3. He illustrates issues of children's magazines, like *Boys' Life*.

_____

4. Norman paints scenes from everyday small-town life.

_____

5. Norman calls himself a storyteller.

_____

6. A fire destroys many of Norman's paintings.

_____

7. Norman Rockwell receives the Presidential Medal of Freedom in 1976.

_____

## Try It

1. Write a sentence in the present tense that describes a piece of art you have seen or made.

_____

2. Now, rewrite the same sentence in the past tense.

_____

# Lesson 3.5 Irregular Past-Tense Verbs: *Ate, Said, Grew, Made, Rode*

Some verbs do not follow the pattern of regular verbs. The past tenses of these verbs are different. To form the past tense, do not add **ed** or **d** to these verbs. Instead, you must change the entire word.

| **Present tense** | **Past tense** |
|---|---|
| She *eats* a snack every day. | She *ate* a snack every day. |
| Mario *says* it will rain tonight. | Mario *said* it will rain tonight. |
| The tiny pine tree *grows* quickly. | The tiny pine tree *grew* quickly. |
| Catalina *makes* bracelets. | Catalina *made* bracelets. |
| I *ride* the bus downtown. | I *rode* the bus downtown. |

**Proof It**

Some of the verbs below are in the wrong tense. Cross out the verbs in bold type. Use this symbol (^), and write the correct word above it.

When my mom was a little girl, her family owned a bakery. Mom **says** that she loved the sweet smell of bread and pastries baking in the ovens. Every morning, Mom **eats** a cinnamon roll for breakfast. She **rides** her bike to school when the weather was nice. In her bag, she carried fresh muffins for her teachers and her friends.

In the afternoon, she and her dad **make** crusty rolls and chewy bagels. Grandpa put all the ingredients in a big bowl. He and Mom took turns kneading the dough. Then, he covered it with a clean towel. The dough **grows** and **grows**. Mom **says** she loved to punch it down. Finally, she and Grandpa shaped the dough and popped it into the ovens. Mom's family **eats** fresh bread with dinner every night!

## Lesson 3.5 Irregular Past-Tense Verbs: *Ate, Said, Grew, Made, Rode*

**Solve It**

Read each sentence below. On the line, write the past tense of the underlined verb.

1. Grandma always <u>eats</u> a blueberry bagel with cream cheese for breakfast. _____

2. The Larsons <u>say</u> that Hot Cross Buns was the best bakery in town.

   _____

3. Mom's cousin, Eddie, <u>rides</u> his bike around town and delivered bread.

   _____

4. Mom <u>grows</u> up helping her parents at the bakery. _____

5. Every Saturday, Mom and Grandpa <u>make</u> 12 loaves of wheat bread, 15 loaves of French bread, and 100 dinner rolls. _____

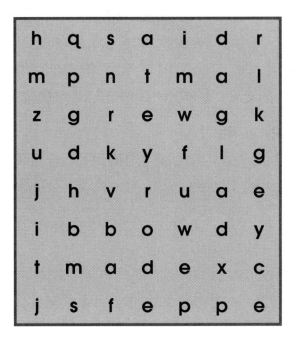

Now, find each past-tense verb in the word search puzzle. Circle the words you find. Words are written across and down.

**Try It**

1. What did you eat for dinner last night? Use a complete sentence to answer the question.

   _____

2. Write a sentence that uses the past tense of one of these words: *say, grow, make,* or *ride.*

   _____

## Lesson 3.6 Irregular Past-Tense Verbs: *Gave, Flew, Brought, Thought, Wrote*

The past tenses of some verbs do not follow the patterns of regular verbs. To form the past tense, do not add **ed** or **d**. Instead, you must change the entire word.

| **Present tense** | **Past tense** |
| --- | --- |
| Franklin *gives* her an orange. | Franklin *gave* her an orange. |
| The goose *flies* over the pond. | The goose *flew* over the pond. |
| Marisa *brings* some games. | Marisa *brought* some games. |
| Beth *thinks* she got an A. | Beth *thought* she got an A. |
| I *write* a letter to my grandma. | I *wrote* a letter to my grandma. |

**Rewrite It**

The sentences below are all in the present tense. Rewrite them in the past tense.

1. Ms. Lucetta gives the class an assignment.

_____

2. Nicholas and Liv write a play about a giant who lives in the forest.

_____

3. They think the giant should be kind, not scary.

_____

4. A small bluebird flies many miles to save the kind giant.

_____

5. The bluebird brings him an important message.

_____

6. The giant gives the bluebird shelter in his cave.

_____

# Lesson 3.6 Irregular Past-Tense Verbs: *Gave, Flew, Brought, Thought, Wrote*

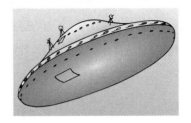

## Proof It

Some of the verbs below are in the wrong tense. Cross out the underlined verbs. Use this symbol (^), and write the correct past-tense verbs above them.

Pradeep and Kent <u>write</u> a play for Ms. Lucetta's class. Their play was about a brother and sister who <u>think</u> that an alien spaceship landed near their house. They named the brother and sister Harry and Carrie. In the play, something very large <u>flies</u> over Harry and Carrie's house one night. It made a loud whirring noise. Its lights flashed on and off.

Carrie ran to the window. She <u>thinks</u> it was a helicopter until she saw how big it was. Harry ran into the backyard. He <u>brings</u> his camera with him. Harry took as many photos as he could. Then, the ship grew silent and quickly <u>flies</u> away.

Pradeep and Kent <u>think</u> the play they <u>write</u> was fun and exciting. They were not sure how to end it though. Did aliens actually visit Harry and Carrie's house? Was it all a dream? They knew they would have to decide before they <u>give</u> their play to Ms. Lucetta.

## Try It

In the selection above, why did the spaceship fly away? Use the past tense of the verb *fly* in your answer.

_____

_____

# Lesson 3.7 Forming the Future Tense

To write or speak about something that is happening right now, use the **present tense**. When something has already happened, use the **past tense**. When something has not happened yet, use the **future tense**.

> **Past:** I *used* all the shampoo.
> **Present:** I *use* all the shampoo.
> **Future:** I *will use* all the shampoo.

The future tense is formed by using the word *will* with a verb. The word *will* means that something has not taken place yet, but it will happen in the future.

> Seamus *will come* home in three days.
> The plumber *will fix* the leaky pipe.
> The water *will boil* in a minute or two.
> Ms. Webster *will make* lasagna for dinner.

## Complete It

Complete each sentence with the future tense of the verb in parentheses ( ).

1. Charlotte _____ a doctor when she grows up. (be)

2. Fernando _____ to speak eight languages. (learn)

3. Maddy _____ for the Olympics. (train)

4. Travis _____ a cure for a serious disease. (find)

5. Akio _____ wild animals. (photograph)

6. Elena _____ all around the world. (travel)

# Lesson 3.7 Forming the Future Tense

**Rewrite It**

On the line, write **PA** if a sentence takes place in the past. Write **PR** if it takes place in the present. Then, rewrite each sentence in the future tense.

Example: __PA__ The movie ended at 8:00.

  __The movie will end at 8:00.__ _____

1. _____ The sheepdog barked at the mail carrier.

   _____

2. _____ The gardener picks flowers from her wildflower garden.

   _____

3. _____ The robin pulls a fat earthworm from the soil.

   _____

4. _____ A ladybug landed on Layla's shoulder.

   _____

**Try It**

1. Write a sentence about someplace you have been in the past. Underline the verb.

   _____

2. Write a sentence about where you are right now. Underline the verb.

   _____

3. Write a sentence about somewhere you will go or something you will do in the future. Underline the verb.

   _____

# Lesson 3.8 Contractions with *Not, Will,* and *Have*

A **contraction** is a short way of saying something by combining two words into one. An apostrophe (') takes the place of the missing letters.

Many contractions are formed when a verb and the word *not* are combined. The apostrophe takes the place of the letter **o** in *not*.

| | | |
|---|---|---|
| is not = isn't | are not = aren't | was not = wasn't |
| were not = weren't | does not = doesn't | did not = didn't |
| do not = don't | can not = can't | |

Some contractions can be formed with pronouns and the verb *will*. An apostrophe takes the place of the letters **wi** in *will*.

| | | |
|---|---|---|
| I will = I'll | it will = it'll | you will = you'll |
| we will = we'll | she will = she'll | they will = they'll |
| he will = he'll | | |

Contractions can also be made with the verb *have*. An apostrophe takes the place of the letters **ha** in *have*.

| | |
|---|---|
| I have = I've | we have = we've |
| you have = you've | they have = they've |

## Proof It

Cross out the five incorrect contractions below. Use this proofreading mark (^), and write the correct contraction above it.

My neighborhood is having a giant yard sale on Saturday. Wel'l post signs all around town. This week, I'ill go through the boxes under my bed and in the attic. There are many things I know we do'nt need. At first, my little brother did'nt want to help. Then, I told him all the money would go to the animal shelter where we got our dog Maisy. I think he'ill be happy to help now.

# Lesson 3.8 Contractions with *Not, Will,* and *Have*

## Rewrite It

Circle the two words in each sentence that could be combined to make a contraction. Then, rewrite the sentences using contractions.

1. We were not even open for business yet when the first customers arrived.

   _____

2. "I will give you 15 dollars for the tricycle," said Mrs. Smythe.

   _____

3. "You will find many great bargains," Justin told our customers.

   _____

4. Our free lemonade did not last long.

   _____

5. We have raised hundreds of dollars for the animal shelter!

   _____

6. Maisy and I can not wait to give the check to the shelter's director.

   _____

## Try It

1. Write a sentence about something you do not like doing. Use a contraction with *not* in your sentence. Circle the contraction.

   _____

2. Write a sentence about something you will do in the future. Use a contraction with *will* in your sentence. Circle the contraction.

   _____

# Lesson 3.9 Contractions with *Am, Is, Are,* and *Would*

**Contractions** can be made with different forms of the verb *to be*. The apostrophe takes the place of the first vowel in *am, is,* and *are*.

| | |
|---|---|
| I am = I'm | it is = it's |
| you are = you're | we are = we're |
| he is = he's | they are = they're |
| she is = she's | |

Contractions formed with the word *would* are a little different. The apostrophe takes the place of the entire word, except for the **d**.

| | |
|---|---|
| I would = I'd | it would = it'd |
| you would = you'd | we would = we'd |
| he would = he'd | they would = they'd |
| she would = she'd | |

## Match It

Match each pair of underlined words with its contraction. Write the letter of the contraction in the space.

1. _____ I am going to take gymnastics lessons with my friend, Elise.

2. _____ She is a year older than I am.

3. _____ Elise said she would show me some warm-up stretches.

4. _____ Our class meets on Wednesdays. It is in an old building on Fourth Street.

5. _____ We are going to carpool to class.

6. _____ Elise's dad teaches gymnastics. He is also the high school coach.

7. _____ I would like to be on his team when I am in high school.

**a.** We're

**b.** she'd

**c.** He's

**d.** I'm

**e.** I'd

**f.** It's

**g.** She's

# Lesson 3.9 Contractions with *Am, Is, Are,* and *Would*

## Complete It

Fill in each blank below with a contraction from the box.

| I'm | It's | He's | It'd |
|-----|------|------|------|
| We're | she'd | I'd | She's |

1. _____ like to meet Olympic gold-medal gymnast Carly Patterson one day.

2. _____ from my hometown of Baton Rouge, Louisiana.

3. In an interview, Carly said _____ like to try a career in singing.

4. Elise's favorite gymnast is Blaine Wilson. _____ a three-time Olympic gymnast.

5. _____ each going to write a letter to Carly and Blaine.

6. _____ sure they will write back to us when they hear what big fans we are.

7. _____ be an amazing experience to see the Olympic Games live.

8. _____ my dream to travel to the Olympics.

## Try It

1. Write a sentence about a famous person you would like to meet. Use a contraction in your sentence. Underline the contraction.

_____

2. Write a sentence that includes a contraction with the word *am, is,* or *are.* Underline the contraction.

_____

# Lesson 3.10 Negative Words and Double Negatives

**Negative words** are words like *no, none, never, nothing, nobody, nowhere,* and *no one.* The word *not* and contractions that use *not* are also negative words. A sentence needs only one negative word. It is incorrect to use a **double negative**, or more than one negative word, in a sentence.

**Correct:** There were *not* any oranges in the refrigerator.
There were *no* oranges in the refrigerator.
**Incorrect:** There were *not no* oranges in the refrigerator.

**Correct:** Kevin *never* saw anyone he knew at the store.
Kevin saw *no one* he knew at the store.
**Incorrect:** Kevin *never* saw *no one* he knew at the store.

**Correct:** *None* of the students were born in another country.
**Incorrect:** *None* of the students *weren't* born in another country.

## Proof It

Read the paragraphs below. There are five double negatives. Cross out one negative word or phrase in the incorrect sentences to correct them.

If you haven't never heard of Jellyfish Lake, you should learn more about it. This amazing saltwater lake is in Palau, an island in the Philippines. You do not never want to get too close to a jellyfish in the ocean. Ocean jellyfish sting their prey. The jellyfish of Jellyfish Lake do not have no stingers. Instead, they use algae and sunlight to get the nutrients they need.

These jellyfish have only one predator—the sea anemone. This is why there are so many of them. No one can never swim in the lake without seeing millions of these jellyfish. It is a special experience for humans. Not nowhere else in the world can people swim surrounded by more than 25 million harmless jellyfish.

# Lesson 3.10 Negative Words and Double Negatives

**Complete It**

Read each sentence below. Circle the word or words from the pair in parentheses ( ) that correctly complete each sentence.

1. The jellyfish don't (never, ever) stop moving.

2. They don't do (anything, nothing) but follow the sun across the lake all day long.

3. My aunt said there (is, is not) nowhere on Earth she would rather go snorkeling.

4. People who swim with the jellyfish shouldn't (ever, never) lift or throw the delicate animals.

5. There aren't (no, any) jellyfish without stingers in the oceans of the world.

6. Because the jellyfish don't have to hunt for their food, there (was, was not) no need for stingers.

7. The beautiful jellyfish don't (never, ever) seem to be too bothered by human visitors.

8. El Niño brought high temperatures to Palau in the late 1990s. Suddenly, there weren't (any, no) jellyfish in the lake.

**Try It**

1. Write a sentence using one of these negative words: *no, none, never, nothing, nobody, nowhere, no one,* or *not.*

_____

2. On another piece of paper, write a sentence using a double negative. Trade papers with a classmate. On the line below, write your classmate's sentence correctly.

_____

# Lesson 3.11 Forming Plurals with **s** and **es**

The word **plural** means *more than one*. To make many nouns plural, add **s**.

one egg → two egg**s**        one dog → six dog**s**

one pencil → many pencil**s**        one photo → nine photo**s**

If a noun ends in **sh**, **ch**, **s**, or **x**, form the plural by adding **es**.

one bu**sh** → three bush**es**        one pea**ch** → five peach**es**

one fo**x** → two fox**es**        one bu**s** → several bus**es**

If a noun ends with a consonant and a **y**, drop the **y** and add **ies** to form the plural.

one bab**y** → all the bab**ies**        one cit**y** → many cit**ies**

## Complete It

Read each sentence below. Complete it with the plural form of the word in parentheses ( ).

1. Ethan made two _____ as he blew out his birthday candles. (wish)

2. All the _____ in the yard came down during the huge thunderstorm last week. (branch)

3. Jacob takes care of the _____ next door when our neighbors go out of town. (cat)

4. We need about six ripe _____ to make apple pie. (apple)

5. Hallie left her _____ at a friend's house. (glass)

6. Claudia and Crista picked sour _____ from the tree in the yard. (cherry)

7. Please recycle the _____ in the garage. (box)

8. Four _____ have volunteered to organize the book sale. (family)

# Lesson 3.11 Forming Plurals with **s** and **es**

**Solve It**

Read the clues below. Find the word in the box that matches each clue. Then, make the word plural, and write it in the numbered space in the crossword puzzle.

| airplane | dress |
|----------|-------|
| bed | beach |
| giraffe | fox |
| dish | baby |

## Across

**2** very young people

**4** machines that let people fly in the sky

**5** sandy places near lakes or oceans

**6** red animals with pointy ears and fluffy tails

**7** pieces of clothing worn by girls

## Down

**1** tall animals with long, skinny necks

**3** cups, plates, and bowls

**5** soft pieces of furniture that you sleep in

**Try It**

1. Write a sentence using the plural form of one of these words: *peach, watch, wish, bush, dress, class,* or *box.*

_____

2. Write a sentence using the plural form of any word. Circle the plural word.

_____

# Lesson 3.12 Irregular Plurals

Some plural words do not follow the rules. Instead of adding an ending to these words, you need to remember their plural forms.

one *man*, seven *men*                one *foot*, two *feet*

one *woman*, five *women*          one *goose*, ten *geese*

one *ox*, six *oxen*                      one *child*, a lot of *children*

one *mouse*, many *mice*            one *die*, two *dice*

Some words do not change at all. The singular and plural forms are the same.

one *deer*, six *deer*                  one *fish*, forty *fish*

one *moose*, two *moose*          one *sheep*, a dozen *sheep*

one *trout*, five *trout*               one *series*, three *series*

one *species*, nine *species*

## Match It

Match each phrase below to the correct plural form. Write the letter on the line.

1. _____ one woman          **a.** fifty womans          **b.** fifty women

2. _____ one die              **a.** six dice                **b.** six dies

3. _____ a moose             **a.** many moose           **b.** many mooses

4. _____ the trout            **a.** hundreds of trout     **b.** hundreds of trouts

5. _____ one species        **a.** eight species          **b.** eight specieses

6. _____ the goose           **a.** four gooses            **b.** four geese

7. _____ one ox               **a.** a herd of oxes         **b.** a herd of oxen

8. _____ a child              **a.** most childs            **b.** most children

# Lesson 3.12 Irregular Plurals

## Solve It

On the lines below, write the plural form of each word in the box.

| | | |
|---|---|---|
| foot _____ | ox _____ | deer _____ |
| man _____ | mouse _____ | sheep _____ |

Use the words in the box to complete the rhymes below.

1. The room was filled with 25 _____, and every single man's name was Ken.

2. "Hurry, hurry, hurry!" said all of the _____. "Walking's too slow, let's take the jeep!"

3. I am only one tiny gray _____, and yet there are dozens of cats in this house.

4. Please do me a favor and move your _____. I do not want footprints all over my seat!

5. In the garden I see dozens of _____, and they've eaten all of my lettuce, I fear.

6. The man scratched his head and looked at the _____. "Was it you who ate my bagel and lox?"

7. If I've told you once, I've told you twice. There's no room in this house for any more _____!

## Try It

On the lines below, make up two of your own rhymes using one of the plurals from the exercise above.

1. _____

2. _____

# Lesson 3.13 Singular Possessives

When something belongs to a person or thing, they *possess* it. An apostrophe (') and the letter **s** at the end of a word show that the person or thing is the owner in a **possessive**.

Julianne**'s** violin

Ichiro**'s** basketball

the park**'s** gates

the school**'s** gym

the tiger**'s** stripes

Trent**'s** sister

**Proof It**

The possessives below are missing apostrophes. To add an apostrophe, use this symbol (v̌).

1. The White Houses address is 1600 Pennsylvania Avenue.

2. Two fires almost destroyed the home of the nations president.

3. The Presidents House, the Presidents Palace, and the Executive Mansion were early names for the White House.

4. The Oval Offices shape was chosen by President Taft.

5. Some of the worlds best artists have work displayed in the White House.

6. President Bushs dogs, Barney and Miss Beazley, were Scottish terriers.

## **Lesson 3.13** Singular Possessives

**Rewrite It**

Rewrite the sentences below. Replace the underlined words in each sentence with a possessive.

Example: <u>The capital of Hawaii</u> is Honolulu.

**Hawaii's capital is Honolulu.**

1. <u>The hometown of Ronald Reagan</u> was Tampico, Illinois.

   _____

2. <u>The nickname of Benjamin Harrison</u> was "Little Ben."

   _____

3. Theodore Roosevelt was <u>the youngest president of the nation</u>.

   _____

4. Michelle Obama, <u>the wife of the President Obama</u>, is an advocate for healthy eating.

   _____

5. <u>The 39th president of America</u> was Jimmy Carter.

   _____

6. Before he became president, one of <u>the jobs of Harry Truman</u> was farming.

   _____

**Try It**

Write a sentence about a well-known figure from history. Use a possessive in your sentence.

   _____

   _____

# Lesson 3.14 Plural Possessives

To form the **possessive of a plural** word that ends in **s**, add an apostrophe after the **s**.

| | |
|---|---|
| the girls' room | the monkeys' food |
| the berries' juice | the teachers' decision |

For plural words that do not end in **s**, add an apostrophe and an **s** to form the possessive.

| | |
|---|---|
| the people**'s** goals | the men**'s** clothes |

**Complete It**

Read each sentence below. Replace the words in parentheses ( ) with a possessive. Write the possessive in the space.

1. (The thick white fur of polar bears) _____ keeps them warm during Arctic winters.

2. (The mother of the bear cubs) _____ protects her babies from wolves and other predators.

3. (The coats of caribous) _____ change colors, depending on the seasons.

4. (The flippers of seals) _____ make them strong, speedy swimmers.

5. When the young girl listened quietly, she could hear (the songs of walruses) _____.

| Tip | Apostrophes are the key to telling the difference between a plural and a possessive. | |
|---|---|---|
| | **Plural** | **Possessive** |
| | thousands of bugs | a bug's wings |
| | several boys | the boys' clubhouse |
| | four watermelons | the watermelon's seeds |

# Lesson 3.14 Plural Possessives

**Identify It**

Read each phrase below. If it is plural, write **PL** on the line. If it is plural possessive, write **PP**.

1. _____ the playful baby seals

2. _____ the igloos' walls

3. _____ the floating icebergs

4. _____ the Arctic rivers

5. _____ hundreds of salmon

6. _____ the puffins' brightly-colored beaks

7. _____ the explorers' route

8. _____ the people's warm clothing

**Try It**

Write two sentences that include plural words.

1. _____

2. _____

Now, write two sentences that use the possessive form of the plural words from above.

3. _____

4. _____

# Lesson 3.15 Subject and Object Pronouns

**Pronouns** are words that take the places of nouns and proper nouns.
**Subject pronouns** take the place of subjects in sentences. Some subject pronouns are *I, you, he, she, it, we,* and *they.*

| | |
|---|---|
| *Eduardo* likes to rollerblade. | *He* likes to rollerblade. |
| *The mall* was crowded. | *It* was crowded. |
| *Serena and Libby* were in the newspaper. | *They* were in the newspaper. |

**Object pronouns** often follow action words or words like *to, at, from, with,* and *of.* Some object pronouns are *me, you, him, her, it, us,* and *them.*

| | |
|---|---|
| The horse **jumped** the fence. | The horse **jumped** it. |
| Joey went **with** Mr. Simms. | Joey went **with** him. |

I put the letter on top **of** *the dresser.*
I put the letter on top **of** *it.*

## Identify It

Read the sentences below. Underline each pronoun. Write **SP** above it if it is a subject pronoun. Write **OP** above it if it is an object pronoun.

1. The librarian gave him the book.

2. Heather and Chase took the puppy with them.

3. It will be sunny and 65 degrees today.

4. The children sang the song to her.

5. I will ask the owner tomorrow.

6. Ngozi received all the information from you.

| Tip | When you are talking about yourself and another person, always put the other person before you. |
|---|---|
| | Jaya and I    Lee and me    He and I |

# Lesson 3.15 Subject and Object Pronouns

**Proof It**

Read the sentences below. Cross out the incorrect pronouns. Then, use this symbol (^), and write the correct pronouns above them.

1. The students in Ms. Curry's class are going on a field trip. Them are going to the museum.

2. Ms. Curry told we that the museum is her favorite field trip.

3. The bus will leave at 8:30 in the morning. She will be parked in the school's west lot.

4. Casey and Allison will sit together. Them are best friends.

5. Ibrahim or Peter might sit with I.

6. The Goose Creek museum is not far away. It did not take we long to drive to him.

7. Michael forgot to bring his lunch. Ms. Curry gave he half of her sandwich and an apple.

8. Me loved seeing all the fossils.

**Try It**

1. Write a sentence using a subject pronoun. Circle the pronoun.

_____

2. Write a sentence using an object pronoun. Circle the pronoun.

_____

# Lesson 3.16 Comparative Adjectives

**Adjectives** can be used to compare people or things that are similar. Add **er** to an adjective to compare two things.

> "The medium chair is hard**er** than the small chair," said Little Red Riding Hood.

Add **est** to compare three or more things.

> Papa Bear's bed is soft. Mama Bear's bed is soft**er**. Baby Bear's bed is soft**est**.

For adjectives that end in **e**, just add **r** or **st**.

> nic**e**, nic**er**, nic**est**   clos**e**, clos**er**, clos**est**   gentl**e**, gentl**er**, gentl**est**

For adjectives that end in a consonant and a **y**, drop the **y** and add **ier** or **iest**.

> tin**y**, tin**ier**, tin**iest**   spic**y**, spic**ier**, spic**iest**   bus**y**, bus**ier**, bus**iest**

**Identify It**

Read the sentences below. Choose the correct adjective from the pair in parentheses, and circle it.

## 4th Annual Fitness Challenge a Success!

Here are the results from last week's Fitness Challenge.

- Brad Dexter and Ariela Vega were the (faster, fastest) sprinters.
- The (youngest, young) student to participate was six-year-old Emily Yu.
- Most students said the obstacle course this year was (hardest, harder) than the one last year.
- Everyone agreed that the (easyest, easiest) event was the beanbag toss.
- The weather was both (sunnyer, sunnier) and (coldest, colder) than last year.
- The (stranger, strangest) thing that happened all week was when the clown made a homerun at the kickball game. No one knows who was wearing the clown costume!
- The cafeteria was (busiest, busier) after the challenges than it usually is at lunchtime.
- Morgan Bonaventure won the award for (Greatest, Greater) Overall Performance.

# Lesson 3.16 Comparative Adjectives

## Complete It

Read each sentence below. Complete it with the correct comparative form of the adjective in parentheses ( ).

1. I wish it had been _____ during the Kite Race. (windy)

2. The _____ cheers came at the end of the day when Principal Sneed did jumping jacks wearing a suit. (loud)

3. Micah is _____ than Jack, but Jack can sink more basketballs. (tall)

4. The _____ race was between Nadia and Kyle. (close)

5. It is much _____ to ride a bike wearing a helmet than to ride a bike without one. (safe)

6. This year's awards were even _____ than they have been in other years. (nice)

## Try It

1. Write a sentence using a comparative adjective to compare two types of animals.

   _____

   _____

2. Write a sentence using a comparative adjective to compare two things that you can see from where you are sitting.

   _____

   _____

## Lesson 3.17 Comparative Adverbs

**Adverbs** can be used to make comparisons. Some adverbs follow the same rules that adjectives do. For most one-syllable adverbs, add **er** or **est** to make a comparison.

> The boy in the blue shorts ran *faster* than I did.
> Over the summer, Katherine grew *taller* than Jane.

To make a comparison using adverbs that end in **ly**, use the words *more* or *most*.

> Aunt Peg read the book *more slowly* than Uncle Calvin.
> My sister sang *most beautifully* of all the girls in her class.

### Complete It

Fill in the spaces in the chart with the correct adverbs. Remember that some comparative adverbs need to be used with the words *more* or *most*.

| | | |
|---|---|---|
| slowly | _____ | most slowly |
| fast | faster | _____ |
| skillfully | _____ | _____ |
| happily | more happily | _____ |
| _____ | more patiently | most patiently |
| _____ | _____ | latest |
| safely | _____ | most safely |
| playfully | _____ | _____ |

# Lesson 3.17 Comparative Adverbs

## Proof It

Read the diary entry below. There are seven comparative adverb mistakes. Cross out each mistake. To add a word, use this symbol (^) and write the correct word above it.

Saturday, September 24

Dear Diary,

Today was the first day of Flannery's obedience class. We got there soonest than most of the other dogs and owners. Flannery sniffed and greeted the dogs as they arrived. She wagged her tail most cheerfully than any other dog.

The class leader helped everyone teach their dogs some basic commands. He laughed more harder than anyone when Flannery stole a treat out of his pocket. I'm sure he will hide them carefullier next time. The little dachshund standing next to us fetched more eagerly of all the dogs. She had short little legs, but she could run more fast than many of the bigger dogs. At the end of the class, Mom and I clapped most loudest of all the owners! Flannery will get her diploma in no time!

## Try It

1. Write a sentence comparing two or more people or things. Use some form of the adverb *playfully*.

_____

## Lesson 3.18 Synonyms and Antonyms

**Synonyms** are words that have the same, or almost the same, meanings. Using synonyms in your writing can help you avoid using the same words over and over. They can make your writing more interesting.

| | | |
|---|---|---|
| quick, fast | present, gift | sad, unhappy |
| close, near | jump, hop | tired, sleepy |

**Antonyms** are words that have opposite meanings.

| | | |
|---|---|---|
| old, young | wide, narrow | true, false |
| never, always | funny, serious | smile, frown |

### Complete It

Read each sentence below. If the sentence is followed by the word *synonym*, write a synonym for the underlined word on the line. If it is followed by the word *antonym*, write an antonym for the underlined word.

1. The rocks in the walls of the Grand Canyon are millions of years <u>old</u>. (antonym) _____

2. Limestone is the <u>top</u> layer in the nine layers of rocks. (antonym) _____

3. The waters of the Colorado River formed the <u>enormous</u> canyon. (synonym) _____

4. Francisco Vásquez de Coronado led the <u>first</u> Europeans to see the canyon. (antonym) _____

5. Native Americans lived in the canyon <u>before</u> Europeans arrived. (antonym) _____

6. If you <u>yell</u> into the canyon, you will hear echoes of your voice. (synonym) _____

7. People <u>like</u> taking burro rides through the canyon. (synonym) _____

## Lesson 3.18 Synonyms and Antonyms

**Solve It**

Write a synonym from the box beside each word in numbers 1–5. Write an antonym from the box beside each word in numbers 6–10.

| difficult | wrong | destroy | sleepy | giggle |
|-----------|-------|---------|--------|--------|
| close | cheap | speak | loose | same |

1. laugh _____

2. wreck _____

3. talk _____

4. shut _____

5. tired _____

6. right _____

7. expensive _____

8. tight _____

9. easy _____

10. different _____

| r | t | j | d | e | g | h | o | s | q | d |
|---|---|---|---|---|---|---|---|---|---|---|
| f | d | i | f | f | i | c | u | l | t | g |
| j | e | i | b | w | g | h | m | e | y | y |
| o | s | a | m | e | g | e | d | e | u | r |
| a | t | w | b | k | l | a | e | p | z | n |
| w | r | o | n | g | e | p | n | y | u | o |
| l | o | o | s | e | k | c | l | o | s | e |
| g | y | c | l | n | s | p | e | a | k | d |

Now, find the words from the box in the word search puzzle. Circle each word you find. Words are written across and down.

**Try It**

1. Write a sentence using a synonym for *terrific*.

_____

2. Write a sentence using an antonym for *boring*.

_____

## Lesson 3.19 Homophones

**Homophones** are words that sound alike but have different spellings and meanings. Here are some examples of homophones.

Did you *hear* that noise?                    The party is *here*.
Connor *knew* it would rain today.           I like your *new* haircut.
There is only *one* pancake left.            I *won* the raffle!
*Our* family is very large.                   Pick Sam up in an *hour*.
*Your* mom speaks Spanish.                    *You're* my best friend.

### Identify It

Read each sentence below. If the word in **bold** type is used correctly, make a check mark (✓) on the line. If it is not used correctly, write its homophone on the line.

1. _____ Mei **new** the best way to get from Seattle, Washington, to Portland, Oregon.

2. _____ We are meeting for lunch an **hour** before we go up in the Space Needle.

3. _____ **You're** sister said that it rains a lot in Seattle.

4. _____ The Seattle Mariners **won** the game on Friday night!

5. _____ **Hour** class is going on a field trip to Pike Place Market.

6. _____ Is **your** boat docked in Puget Sound?

7. _____ The 1962 World's Fair was held **hear** in Seattle.

8. _____ The **knew** Seattle Central Library is a beautiful glass and steel building located downtown.

# Lesson 3.19 Homophones

**Complete It**

Read the following sentences. Complete each sentence with a word from the pair of homophones in parentheses. Write the word on the line.

1. Jada _____ they would take the Washington State Ferry to Bainbridge Island. (knew, new)

2. _____ family moved to Seattle because Mom works with computers. (Hour, Our)

3. I can see the Cascade Mountains from _____! (hear, here)

4. I am excited that _____ going hiking at Mount Rainier this weekend. (your, you're)

5. _____ of Seattle's most famous residents is computer giant Bill Gates. (Won, One)

6. Brendan did not _____ the guide say that Smith Tower was Seattle's first skyscraper. (hear, here)

7. The Seattle Seahawks moved into their _____ football stadium in 2002. (new, knew)

8. Does _____ uncle still work at the Seattle Children's Museum? (you're, your)

**Try It**

On the lines below, write two sentences. Use the word *won* in the first sentence. Use the word *one* in the second sentence.

1. _____

2. _____

## Lesson 3.20 Multiple-Meaning Words

**Multiple-meaning words** are words that are spelled the same but have different meanings. Look at how the word is used in the sentence to figure out which meaning it has.

In the first sentence below, the word *trunk* means *an elephant's snout*. In the second sentence, it means *a sturdy box used for storage*.

> The elephant used its *trunk* to pick up the stick.
>
> Grandpa's old photos are stored in a *trunk* in the attic.

In the first sentence below, the word *fair* means *a carnival*. In the second sentence, it means *equal* or *just*.

> Jonah rode on a Ferris wheel at the county *fair*.
>
> It is not *fair* that I have to go to bed an hour earlier than Amanda.

### Find It

The dictionary entry below shows two different meanings for the same word. Each meaning is a different part of speech. Use the dictionary entry to answer the questions below.

> **watch** *noun*: a small device that is worn on the wrist and used to keep time
>
> *verb*: to look at or follow with one's eyes

1. Mikayla's grandparents gave her a watch for her birthday.
   Which definition of *watch* is used in this sentence? _____
   **a.** the first definition               **b.** the second definition

2. Did you watch the movie you rented?
   Which definition of *watch* is used in this sentence? _____
   **a.** the first definition               **b.** the second definition

3. What part of speech is *watch* when it is used to mean *a device used to keep time*? _____
   **a.** a noun                             **b.** a verb

# Lesson 3.20 Multiple-Meaning Words

## Match It

Read each sentence below. Choose the definition that matches the way the word in **bold** type is used in the sentence. Write the letter of the definition on the line.

1. _____ If you don't hurry, you'll miss the **train**!
   **a.** to teach something by repeating it
   **b.** a line of cars that move together along a track

2. _____ Mark scored a **goal** in the second half of the game.
   **a.** something that people work hard to achieve
   **b.** a score in a game when a puck or ball is shot into a certain area

3. _____ Eloise is the **second** child in a family of four girls.
   **a.** number two; the one that comes after the first
   **b.** a moment in time; a small part of a minute

4. _____ We dropped pennies in the **well** and made a wish for each one.
   **a.** healthy; good
   **b.** a deep hole in the ground, used to get water or oil

5. _____ Gabrielle's piano teacher is **patient** when she makes mistakes.
   **a.** not easily irritated or annoyed
   **b.** someone who is getting medical treatment

## Try It

1. Write a sentence using one of the multiple-meaning words from the exercise above (*train, goal, second, well, patient*).

   _____

2. Now, write a sentence using the other meaning of the word you chose.

   _____

Before you start writing, you need to make a plan. **Brainstorming** is one way to come up with ideas. You may not use all of your ideas. Still, you will find the one or two great ideas you were looking for.

Sit down with a pen and a piece of paper. Make a list of things you know a lot about or would like to learn more about.

| | |
|---|---|
| life in the Sahara desert | Eiffel Tower |
| basketball | space shuttles |
| islands | being an artist |

Which topic is most interesting? Once you choose your topic, you can start learning more about it. You may need to go to the library. You may need to use the Internet. You may even need to interview someone.

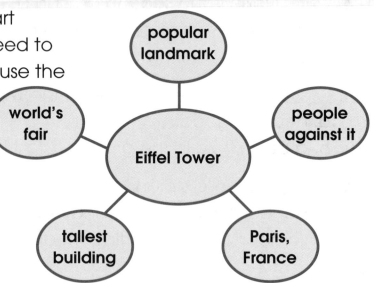

Once you have all your information, make an **idea web**. It can help you put your ideas in order before you start writing.

**Try It**

On a separate piece of paper, brainstorm your own list of ideas. Let your imagination go, and have fun! Choose the most interesting topic. If you need to, look for more information. Then, create an idea web.

# Lesson 4.2 Writer's Guide: Writing

When you first begin writing, do not worry about mistakes. You are just writing a **rough draft**. Look at the idea web you made when you were planning. Turn your ideas into sentences and paragraphs.

Do not worry about editing right now. After you have written your first draft, you can make changes and corrections. For now, just write. Here are some things to keep in mind as you write:

- Stay on topic.
- Include all the important details.
- Use complete sentences.

Here is an example of a rough draft. Can you see how the writer used the idea web to help write this paragraph?

The Eiffel Tower is an intresting place to visit. It was built in Paris France. It was made for a world's fair The Louvre is a famous museum in Paris. The tower is very tall. It was the tallest building in the world many people did not think it should be built. it looks like they were wrong, though. Millions of people visit it every year! It is one of the most famus landmarks.

**Try It**

Use the idea web you made to write a rough draft on another piece of paper. Remember, this stage is all about writing, so write! You'll be able to edit your work later.

# Lesson 4.3 Writer's Guide: Revising

Now that you have finished writing, it is time to **revise**. Read what you have written. Sometimes it helps to read your work out loud. Ask yourself these questions:

- Do all of my sentences tell about the main idea?
- Can I add any details that make my writing more interesting?
- Are there any words or sentences that do not belong?

*in 1889*

The Eiffel tower is an intresting place to visit. It was built ^in

Paris France. It was made for a world's fair. ~~The Louvre is a famous~~

~~museum in Paris.~~ The tower is ^*986 feet* ~~very~~ tall. It was the tallest building in

*for 41 years*                               *They thought it would be ugly.*

the world ^many people did not think it should be built. ^it looks like

*About 6*                         *the Eiffel tower*

they were wrong, though. ^Million~~s~~ people visit ~~it~~ ^every year! It is

*in the world*

one of the most famus landmarks. ^

In the paragraph above, the writer added some details. For example, explaining that the Eiffel Tower is very tall does not tell the reader much. It is more helpful to know that the Eiffel Tower is 986 feet tall.

The writer also took out a sentence that was not needed. The Louvre is in Paris, but it does not have anything to do with the Eiffel Tower. The writer decided that the sentence about the Louvre was not on topic.

**Try It**

Look at all the changes the writer made. Can you see why each change was needed? Now, revise your rough draft. Doesn't it sound better already?

# Lesson 4.4 Writer's Guide: Proofreading

**Proofreading** makes your writing stronger and clearer. Here are some things to ask yourself when you are proofreading:

- Do sentences and proper nouns start with a capital letter?
- Does each sentence end with a punctuation mark?
- Are any words misspelled? Use a dictionary if you are not sure.
- Are commas used in the right places?

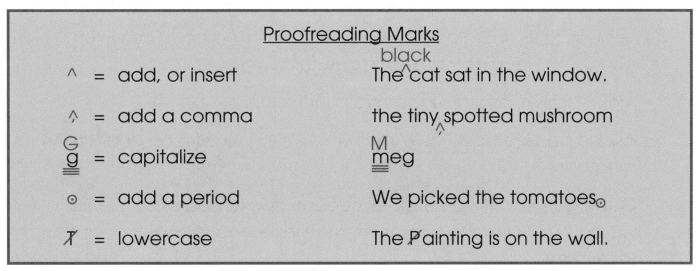

The Eiffel Tower is an intresting place to visit. It was built in 1889 in Paris France. It was made for a world's fair. The tower is 986 feet tall. It was the tallest building in the world for 41 years many people did not think it should be built. They thought it would be ugly. it looks like they were wrong, though. About six Million people visit the Eiffel tower every year! It is one of the most famus landmarks in the world.

**Try It**

Use proofreading marks to edit your writing. Trade papers with a friend. It can be easier to spot mistakes in someone else's work.

# Lesson 4.5 Writer's Guide: Publishing

After all your changes have been made, write or type a final copy of your work. Your paper should look neat and clean. Now, you are ready to publish. **Publishing** is a way of sharing your writing with others. Here are some ways to publish your work:

- Read your writing to your family, your friends, or your classmates.

- Make a copy of your writing. Send it to someone who lives far away.

- Read your writing aloud. Have a teacher or parent record you. You can use a video camera or a tape recorder.

- Make copies, and give them to your friends.

- Ask an adult to help you e-mail your writing to a friend or a family member.

- Get together with some other students. Make copies of everyone's writing. Combine the copies into a booklet that each student can take home.

---

**From:** Tucker Boone

**Date:** May 20, 2014

**To:** auntlouisa@smileyhorse.net; grandpajoe@21stcentury.com

**Subject:** Eiffel Tower report

    The Eiffel Tower is an interesting place to visit. It was built in 1889 in Paris, France. It was made for a world's fair. The tower is 986 feet tall. It was the tallest building in the world for 41 years. Many people did not think it should be built. They thought it would be ugly. It looks like they were wrong, though. About six million people visit the Eiffel Tower every year! It is one of the most famous landmarks in the world.

---

## Try It

Choose one of the ways listed above to share your work. What kinds of comments do your friends and family have? Can you think of any other ways to share your writing?

# Lesson 4.6 Writer's Guide: Writing a Paragraph

A **paragraph** is a group of sentences. Each paragraph is about one main idea. All the sentences tell more about the main idea. When you are ready to write about a new idea, start a new paragraph. When the paragraphs are put together, they make a letter, a story, or a report.

LA TOUR EIFFEL

A new paragraph does not start at the left edge of a piece of paper. It starts about five spaces from the edge. Leave an **indent**, or a space, about the size of the word **write**. This space tells the reader a new paragraph is starting.

The first sentence in a paragraph is the **topic sentence**. It tells what the paragraph will be mostly about. The next few sentences give more details about the topic. The last sentence is a **closing sentence**. It sums up the paragraph.

In the paragraph below, each important part is labeled.

**indent**        **topic sentence**

⟶ <u>The Eiffel Tower is an interesting place to visit.</u> It was built in 1889 in Paris, France. It was made for a world's fair. The tower is 986 feet tall. It was the tallest building in the world for 41 years. Many people did not think it should be built. They thought it would be ugly. It looks like they were wrong, though. About six million people visit the Eiffel Tower every year! <u>It is one of the most famous landmarks in the world.</u>

**details**

**closing sentence**

# Lesson 4.7 Writer's Guide: Writing a Friendly Letter

Writing a letter can be fun. It is exciting to open the mailbox and see a letter waiting. Writing letters can also be a good way to keep in touch with people who live far away.

Here are some things to keep in mind when you write a letter:

- **Write the date in the top right corner.** Remember to start the name of the month with a capital letter. Use a comma between the day and the year.
- **Begin your letter with a greeting.** Follow it with the person's name and a comma. Most letters begin with the word **Dear**.
- **Share some news in your letter.** What is new in your life? Have you done anything fun? Have you been someplace exciting?
- **Ask questions.** It is polite to ask how others are doing.
- **End your letter with a closing.** Some popular closings are **Sincerely**, **Yours truly**, **Love**, and **Your friend**. Use a capital letter to begin your closing. Use a comma after it.
- **Sign your name below the closing.**

May 20, 2014

Dear Grandma,

How are you? I am doing fine. Last week, I wrote a report about the Eiffel Tower. Mom helped me do some research on the Internet. I learned many interesting facts. For example, did you know that the Eiffel Tower has 1,665 steps? Mr. Strasser said my report was excellent. I told him that I plan to see the Eiffel Tower in person someday.

Please write back to me, and tell me what's new in Park City. I miss you a lot and hope you can visit soon.

Love,
Tucker

# Lesson 4.8 Writer's Guide: Writing to Convince

Have you ever tried to convince someone of something? To **convince** means **to get people to see things your way**. Maybe you have tried to convince your teacher that recess should be longer. Maybe you have tried to convince your parents to give you a later bedtime.

Words can be very powerful. You can change people's ideas with your words. Here are some tips for writing to convince:

- Think of all the reasons you feel a certain way. Make a list of your ideas.

- Now, think about why people might not agree with you. What could you say to change their minds? Add these ideas to your list.

- You are ready to begin writing. First, write a topic sentence about what you want or believe. Next, list your reasons. Finally, write a sentence that sums up your ideas.

| | |
|---|---|
| **Eiffel Tower should be free** | it's a public place |
| | more people might visit if free |
| | people could donate money |
| | money used to care for tower |

     People should not have to pay to visit the Eiffel Tower. The tower is like a park or a library. It belongs to everyone. People should be able to enjoy it at any time. Instead of paying to see it, people could donate money if they wanted to. This money could be used to take care of the tower. More people might visit the Eiffel Tower if they did not have to pay. It should be free for everyone to enjoy.

# SPECTRUM®

# Reading

# Two Boys, Big Plans

*Read to see what Sam and Kent are planning.*

1  "Okay, I'm going to ask my parents right now. Are you?" Sam waited for Kent's reply over the phone.

2  "I think so," said Kent after a moment. "My dad just got home a little while ago. Are you bringing crackers?"

3  Sam laughed. Kent was always hungry. "Yes, I'll bring the crackers," he said. "And be sure to tell them that we'll turn the lights out by 9:30. Okay?"

4  "Nine-thirty. Right," Kent agreed. "Okay, I'm going to go ask. I'll talk to you in a little bit."

5  "Okay," answered Sam, and he hung up. *Now, if only we can talk our parents into letting us do this,* he thought to himself. He put on a big smile and entered the family room.

6  "Dad?" said Sam quietly so he wouldn't make his father jump. "I cleaned up those grass clippings for you."

7  "Oh, good," nodded Mr. Hume. "Thanks, Sam."

8  "Mom? Dad?" started Sam again. Both his parents looked over their newspapers. The words rushed out of Sam. "Kent and I were wondering if we could sleep out in the tent tonight. We'd be warm enough in our sleeping bags, and we won't eat too much, and it'll be lights out at 9:30, we promise."

9  Mr. and Mrs. Hume blinked, then looked at each other. *How do they talk to each other without saying anything?* wondered Sam.

10  "Did Kent's parents say it was okay?" asked Mrs. Hume.

11  "He's asking right now." Sam shifted from one foot to the other. Another look passed between his parents.

12  Mr. Hume nodded. "If Kent's parents say it's okay, it's okay with us."

13  "Thanks, Dad! Thanks, Mom!" called Sam as he dashed for the phone. He dialed and held his breath. Then, he heard Kent's voice.

14  "Okay?" asked Sam.

15  "Okay!" said Kent.

**1.** This story is mostly about

_____ a sleepover.

_____ Sam's parents.

_____ two boys' plans.

**2.** At the beginning, when Sam and Kent are talking on the phone, what did you think they might be talking about?

_____

_____

**3.** In the story, when did you find out what the boys are planning?

_____

**4.** Why do you think Sam told his dad about the grass clippings?

_____

_____

**5.** Why does Sam mention being warm enough and when the lights will be turned out?

_____

_____

**6.** Now that the boys have permission, what do you think they will do next?

_____

_____

**7.** In paragraph 5, why are the words *Now, if we can only talk our parents into letting us do this* in italics?

_____

**8.** What is the author's purpose in writing this selection?

_____

**9.** Have you ever been worried about asking your parents to do something? What was it, and how did you ask them?

_____

_____

# One Tent, Lots of Stuff

*What do the boys need for their night in the tent?*

1 "Lantern?"

2 "Got it."

3 "Sleeping bags?"

4 "Got it—both of them."

5 "Pillows?"

6 "Two fat ones."

7 "Crackers?"

8 "Three kinds."

9 "Three kinds? Great!"

10 Sam and Kent had made a list of all the things they needed for sleeping out in the tent. Now, they were sitting cross-legged in the tent, checking things off the list.

11 "Are you going to bring a bathrobe and slippers?" Kent asked Sam.

12 "Oh, no! We're camping. Those are just for in the house," answered Sam, looking as if he knew all about camping.

13 "Oh, right," said Kent, who had never been camping before. He didn't think Sam had been camping before either. Still, it was Sam's dad's tent, so he must know.

14 "Oh, I almost forgot. Can you bring your baseball glove?" Sam looked very serious.

15 Kent couldn't figure this one out. "My baseball glove? What do we need that for?"

16 "Well, we just might. You never know," said Sam with mystery and authority.

17 "Okay," shrugged Kent, "I'll bring it when I come after supper. What time do you think you'll be able to come out?"

18 Sam thought for a moment. "We usually eat at 5:45. Then, I have to clear the table. I should be done by 6:30. What about you?"

19 "My dad doesn't get home until six o'clock," said Kent, regretfully. "Maybe if I offer to help Mom with supper, things will go quickly."

20 Sam shrugged. "It's worth a try. Come out as soon as you can." Sam looked around the tent. "Okay, I think everything's ready. I'll see you later."

21 "See you later," said Kent, and the boys both ran home.

**1.** One of the boys usually has the ideas. The other one seems to go along with those ideas. Which boy is the "leader"?

_____

**2.** What details from the story helped you answer question 1?

_____

_____

**3.** Kent says he might help his mom with supper. What does that tell you about Kent?

_____

**4.** Based on what you know about camping, how do you feel about all the stuff the boys have in their tent? List what you think they need and what they don't need.

**What They Need**

_____

**What They Don't Need**

_____

**5.** In some stories, the author tells you what is happening. In this story, the author uses mostly dialogue, what the characters say, to let you know what is going on. Choose one line of dialogue and write what it helps you know about the character.

Dialogue: _____

_____

_____

**6.** Why does Kent think that Sam knows more about camping?

_____

_____

**7.** How do you think the boys feel about camping out together? Explain your answer.

_____

_____

# How to Pitch a Tent

*Follow these instructions to learn how to pitch a tent.*

These general instructions should allow anyone to pitch any size or style of tent. Keep in mind that pitching a tent alone, even if you have experience, is difficult.

1. Choose a flat area on which to pitch your tent. Remove any stones or rocks that might poke through the tent's floor.

2. Take the tent and all equipment out of the storage bag. Lay everything on the ground neatly.

3. Spread a groundcloth over the chosen spot. Then, lay the tent floor over the groundcloth. Fold the edges of the groundcloth under, so they do not stick out from the edges of the tent.

4. Make sure the tent door is zipped shut. Then, pound a stake through each loop, pulling snugly as you go so the floor gets stretched to its full size.

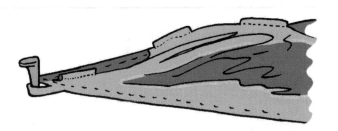

5. Put together the tent poles, if necessary. Thread each one through its loops or channels. Do not step or walk on the tent to do this. If necessary, crawl or lie down on your stomach to reach the center of the tent.

6. Raise the poles. If you have a partner, work on opposite sides of the tent.

7. Pull the guy lines straight out from the sides of the tent. Peg each one.

1. What do you know about pitching a tent? Do you have anything to add to these instructions?

   _____

   _____

2. Number the sentences to show the order of steps to pitch a tent.
   _____ Spread out groundcloth.
   _____ Tighten and peg guy lines.
   _____ Choose and clear an area.
   _____ Put together tent poles.
   _____ Lay out equipment.
   _____ Pound stakes through loops.
   _____ Raise the poles.

3. If you don't know or understand what a guy line is, which illustration helps you figure it out? Tell how.

   _____

   _____

4. Choose one illustration. Explain what it shows.

   _____

   _____

   _____

5. In the first paragraph, the author says that pitching a tent alone is difficult. Why do you think this is?

   _____

   _____

6. What is the purpose of a groundcloth?

   _____

7. Which two steps explain what to do with the poles?
   _____ and _____

8. After reading these instructions, do you think you could pitch a tent? Why or why not?

   _____

   _____

# One Tent...What Next?

*What do the boys expect to happen?*

1   "Then, there was the time my brother and I nearly got blown away with the tent! Did I tell you about that one?" Sam shook his head and tried not to look impatient. His dad had been telling camping stories for almost an hour. *How can I get him to stop without saying anything?* thought Sam to himself. He really wanted to get out to the tent.

2   Finally, his dad stopped for a bite of dessert, and Sam asked to be excused. When his mom nodded her head okay, it took only four trips to clear the table. Then, he was off and across the backyard.

3   "Caught you!" yelled Sam as he flipped back the tent flap. Kent jumped and turned red. "Ha! I knew it! In the crackers already." Then, he laughed. "Have you been waiting long?"

4   Kent shook his head because his mouth was full. Finally, he said, "Not long. My dad got home late."

5   Sam shrugged. "Oh, well. We're here now. Let's get ready."

6   "Ready for what?" asked Kent.

7   "For whatever's going to happen," answered Sam. *Well, he must know,* thought Kent. He helped Sam straighten the sleeping bags and stash stuff in the corners. They played catch across the tent for a little while. *Ah, the baseball glove,* thought Kent. They played badminton with crackers, but then Sam discovered crumbs in his sleeping bag, so they stopped.

8   They turned on the lantern and read. After a while, Sam retold some of his dad's camping stories. Then, Kent turned out the light, and they listened for noises in the dark. They didn't hear any for a very long time.

9   Finally, Kent heard something at the tent flap. He half crawled and half flew across the tent to warn Sam. Sam yelled when Kent landed on top of him.

10   "Hey, are you guys all right?" It was Sam's mom. "Breakfast is ready."

11   Sam and Kent looked at each other in disbelief. They had slept through the whole night, and nothing had happened.

**1.** Which sentence best describes this story?

_____ Nothing exciting happens to the boys in the tent.

_____ The boys have a crazy night in the tent.

_____ In the morning, Kent plays a trick on Sam and scares him.

**2.** Why did the boys stop playing badminton?

_____

_____

**3.** Read the sentences below. Write **F** next to sentences that are facts and **O** next to sentences that are opinions.

_____ Kent eats too many crackers.

_____ Sam's dad had been telling camping stories for almost an hour.

_____ Breakfast is ready.

_____ Sam's dad tells the best camping stories.

**4.** What do you think the boys were hoping would happen?

_____

_____

_____

**5.** In paragraph 3, why does Kent turn red?

_____

_____

**6.** Write **C** next to the sentence below that is the cause. Write **E** next to the sentence that is the effect.

_____ Kent landed on top of Sam.

_____ Sam's mom startled the boys.

**7.** This story has two settings. What are they?

_____ and _____

# Night Lights

*What is keeping Mikki awake?*

1   There were lights flashing outside. No matter what I did, I could see those lights. I couldn't figure out what they were, so I started worrying.

2   I turned away from the window and closed my eyes. But then I had to open them, just a crack, to see if the lights were still there. *Flash-flash, off, flash!*

3   I rolled toward the window and watched. Maybe I could figure it out. I started listing things. Car lights? Not bright enough. Police car flashers? Not blue and red enough. Spaceships? Not likely. All right, this is really bugging me. I have to go ask Mom, I finally concluded.

4   I padded downstairs where my mom was reading a magazine. She was a little surprised to see me.

5   "The lights are flashing upstairs," I said.

6   "They are?" She said it with that "this is a great excuse for being out of bed" look on her face.

7   "I can't figure out what it is," I continued, hoping for some comfort. To my relief, she put down her magazine and steered me back upstairs.

8   We laid across my bed on our stomachs and watched out the window. Mom knew right away.

9   "Mikki, do you remember driving up to visit Uncle Walt last month?" she asked. I nodded. "Do you remember how long it took?" I nodded again. "Well, Uncle Walt is having a thunderstorm way up north where his house is. The lightning is sort of shining off the clouds, so we can see the flashing down here, even though the storm is far away from us."

10   "Oh," I said. I thought to myself, *Well, that makes sense.* After all, what else causes lights to flash in the sky? Aliens? Not likely.

**1.** What is causing Mikki to worry?

_____

**2.** What does Mikki do to try to get to sleep?

First, she _____

_____

Then, she _____

_____

**3.** What is causing the flashing lights?

_____

_____

**4.** Have you ever been kept awake at night by something that bothered or puzzled you? Write about it.

_____

_____

_____

**5.** From whose point of view is this story told?

_____ Mom's    _____ Mikki's    _____ Uncle Walt's

**6.** Which word best describes Mom in the story?

_____ impatient    _____ confused    _____ kind

**7.** Is this story realistic? Why or why not?

_____

_____

**8.** Name three things that Mikki thinks the lights could be.

_____  _____  _____

# Thunder and Lightning

*What causes thunder and lightning?*

1   The story of thunder and lightning is a lesson on electricity. Lightning is really just a giant electrical spark. Thunder is a direct result of the activity of that spark.

## Lightning First

2   Imagine a single water droplet high above Earth. It is in a cloud among millions of other water droplets. As this water droplet falls toward Earth, it gets bigger by collecting more moisture. When the droplet gets to just about the size of a pea, it splits. This splitting action causes an electrical charge to build up on the two new droplets.

3   If the droplets fall straight to Earth, the electrical charge is very small and will have no effect. If the droplets get swept upward by air currents, however, the whole process begins again. The droplets fall, grow, split, and become more strongly charged with electricity each time.

4   In time, the electrical charge in the droplets becomes so strong that it has to discharge itself. The result is a huge spark. It may leap from a cloud to the ground in less than one-tenth of a second. We know it as lightning.

## Thunder Second

5   When lightning flashes, the air is suddenly heated, and then it quickly cools. These rapid changes in the air cause the cracking sound of thunder. During a storm, we see lightning first, and then wait to hear the thunder. That's because light travels faster than sound. We see the lightning as it happens, but the sound of the thunder may take any number of seconds to reach us, depending on how far away the lightning was. The rumbling sound of thunder is actually an echo from the sound waves bouncing off Earth or off the clouds.

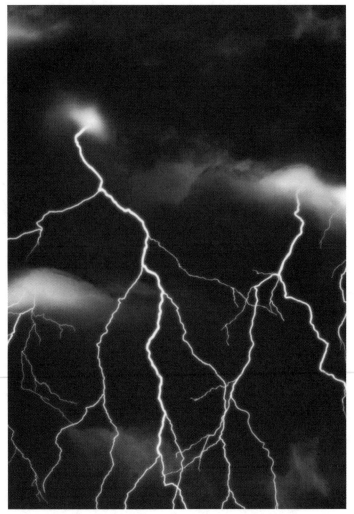

**I.** The author wrote this article to

_____ entertain.

_____ give information.

_____ persuade.

**2.** Which comes first, thunder or lightning?

_____

**3.** What causes lightning? Give a brief answer.

_____

_____

_____

**4.** How does lightning cause thunder?

_____

_____

_____

**5.** If you read only the two headings in this article, what would you learn?

_____

_____

_____

**6.** Write **T** for true or **F** for false next to each statement below.

_____ Thunder always takes the same amount of time to reach Earth.

_____ Light travels faster than sound.

_____ Thunder and lightning are not related to each other.

**7.** What is the main idea of paragraph 4?

_____

_____

_____

**8.** Which of the following is the purpose of paragraph 1?

_____ introduction _____ author's purpose _____ conclusion

# Smokey the Bear

*Read to find out how Smokey the Bear became famous.*

1 Smokey the Bear's story doesn't start with a bear. It starts with a problem, a solution, and then a drawing.

2 In the 1940s, during World War II, the leaders of the United States had a problem. They were worried about having enough wood to build ships and other equipment for the war. The solution: To protect America's forests (and the wood that might be needed for ships), the U.S. Forest Service started a campaign to prevent forest fires.

3 The Forest Service created posters reminding people about fire safety. The posters featured a deer named Bambi from a popular movie. Before long, however, the poster images were switched to a popular toy animal—a bear. An illustrator, Albert Staehle, drew that first bear with a park ranger's hat in 1944 and named him *Smokey.*

4 Six years later, while fighting a forest fire in New Mexico, firefighters found a black bear cub clinging to a tree. They rescued the cub and called it Hotfoot. Soon, however, the cub was renamed Smokey after the drawings on the posters.

5 Once he recovered from his injuries, Smokey was taken to the National Zoo in Washington, D.C. Thousands of people visited him there until he died in 1976. Smokey was 26 years old. His message is still with us, however, as we see him reminding us to prevent forest fires all across the nation.

Put a check next to the sentences that are true.

**1.** _____ The idea for Smokey the Bear started in the 1940s.

**2.** _____ Smokey the Bear lives in New Mexico.

**3.** _____ The Forest Service made posters in honor of a bear cub that died in a fire.

**4.** _____ Smokey the Bear was a drawing first, and then a real bear.

Write **M** next to the sentences that tell about make-believe things.

**5.** _____ Smokey the Bear lived in a zoo for many years.

**6.** _____ Smokey the Bear speaks to campers about the danger of forest fires.

**7.** _____ Smokey the Bear used to help firefighters put out fires.

**8.** Why was Smokey the Bear created? Write the phrase or sentence from the article that tells you.

_____

_____

_____

**9.** In paragraph 2, what problem did U.S. leaders have?

_____

**10.** What was the solution?

_____

**11.** What organization created the fire safety posters?

_____

**12.** In the posters, did Smokey the Bear look realistic? Explain.

_____

_____

# Planting Dreams

*What does Rosa dream about?*

1   She was walking home from work one evening when she got the idea. Rosa didn't like her job at the factory, but it was better than no job at all. So, while she was trying not to think about work, she saw the pots stacked up in an alley. They were cheap plastic pots, but there were dozens of them piled up behind the flower shop. *Such a waste*, she thought. When the pots were still there three days later, Rosa went in and asked if she could take some. The flower shop lady said she didn't mind, so Rosa carried home a tower of pots, pretending she was a circus performer on the way.

2   At home, Rosa set the pots on the fire escape outside her tiny apartment. And there they sat. Once, a gust of wind sent them clattering to the street three floors below, and she had to go and chase them before the gathering storm.

3   Every day, Rosa went to work and thought about her pots. She was waiting for something, but she had patience.

4   At last, the newspaper brought good news. A hardware store had a sale on potting soil. Rosa carefully counted her money, and then she walked the six blocks to the store. She bought six bags and carried them home. She bought seeds, too. Rosa slept well that night and dreamed of masses of flowers and fat, glowing fruits.

5   Sundays were always good days. Rosa didn't have to work on Sundays. But Rosa couldn't remember when she had had *such* a good Sunday. She got up early and ate her breakfast on the fire escape with her pots. Then, she began to scoop dirt into the pots. She hummed a little song until all six of her bags of soil were empty. Then, she laid her precious seed packets out and planned her garden. Tomatoes for the biggest pots, and peppers for the next-biggest ones. Flowers in all the rest.

6   At the end of the day, Rosa sat in her garden and watched the sunset. *Soon*, she thought, *there will be masses of flowers and fat, glowing fruits.*

A **fact** is something that can be proven true. An **opinion** is what someone thinks or feels. Check the sentences that are facts.

1. _____ Vegetables can be grown in pots.

2. _____ Creating a garden on a fire escape is difficult.

3. _____ Any garden is beautiful.

4. _____ Plants need soil and water.

5. Number the sentences to show the order in which things happened.
   _____ Rosa bought potting soil.
   _____ Rosa took the pots home.
   _____ Rosa planted her seeds.
   _____ Rosa saw the pots.

6. Check the words or phrases that best describe Rosa.
   _____ selfish
   _____ tends to waste time
   _____ likes the outdoors
   _____ appreciates beauty

7. Why do you think Rosa slept well the night after she bought seeds and soil?

   _____

   _____

   _____

8. The author repeats a line from paragraph 4 in the last paragraph. What line is it? Why do you think the author repeats it?

   _____

   _____

   _____

9. Have you ever planted something and watched it grow? Tell about how it made you feel.

   _____

   _____

   _____

   _____

# Dreaming of the Harvest

*Read to see how Rosa's garden is doing.*

1    Rosa hurried home from work. She knew it had been quite warm that day, and it hadn't rained since last week. She was worried that her tiny seedlings might have gotten too much sun. When she got to her building, she raced up the stairs, two at a time, up to the third floor.

2    Rosa was still panting when she stepped out onto the fire escape. *Oh, you poor things!* was all she could think. Even her strongest, tallest tomato plant looked as if it had just given up. It was pale and dry looking, not green and smooth like it had been this morning. Rosa got her watering can and went right to work. She watered each pot until it began to drip out the holes in the bottom. She made sure each plant got just the right amount. Then, she went in to fix something to eat.

3    In the kitchen, Rosa bit into an apple and imagined that it was a big, juicy tomato. She chopped a carrot and imagined that it was a shiny, green pepper getting ready to join some tomatoes in a pot of rich, spicy sauce.

4    She carried her dinner out to the fire escape. The apartment building across the street cast its shadow on her garden, letting it rest from the day's hot sun. Rosa leaned against the wall and closed her eyes. She let her hard day of work at the factory fade away as she imagined taking her flowers to her friends at work. Just think how surprised they would be. They would think she had robbed the flower shop!

5    Rosa watched her garden grow until after dark. Then, she went inside and dreamed of running her own shop filled with trays of fresh vegetables and baskets of flowers fresh from her own garden.

1. Why is Rosa worried about her plants on this day?

_____

_____

Write **T** if the sentence is true. Write **F** if the sentence is false.

2. _____ This story is mostly about Rosa worrying about her garden.

3. _____ Rosa is careless about her garden.

4. _____ Rosa plans to share her flowers with others.

5. _____ Too much sun causes Rosa's plants to dry up.

Compare how things really are with how they used to be, or with what Rosa imagines.

6. The strongest, tallest tomato plant is _____.

   It had been _____.

7. Rosa bites into an _____.

   She imagines that it is a _____.

8. She chops a _____.

   She imagines that it is a _____.

9. For now, Rosa works at a _____.

   She dreams of _____.

10. Why do you think Rosa spends so much time daydreaming?

_____

_____

11. What details from the story helped you answer question 10?

_____

_____

12. Which of these is mostly likely to be true?
   _____ Rosa lives in the country.
   _____ Rosa lives in a city.

# Peppers

*Which kind of pepper do you like best?*

1   What comes in many colors and is high in vitamins A and C? Some people like them hot; some prefer them mild. They are a common sight in backyard gardens throughout the United States. Have you guessed yet? They are peppers.

2   Whether green, yellow, or red, peppers add flavor to many types of foods. People eat them raw, pickled, or cooked. They go in salads, in sauces, on sandwiches, and, of course, on pizza.

## Bell Peppers

3   The mildest variety of pepper is the bell pepper. They are sometimes called *sweet peppers*, but they are not sweet like sugar. They are simply less spicy, or hot, than other types of peppers. The round, apple-sized fruits of bell pepper plants are green, yellow, or red. Some people eat them before they get fully ripe. Bell peppers are by far the most common pepper found in gardens and on grocery store shelves.

## Chili Peppers

4   "Chili pepper" is a general name for a number of quite spicy peppers that come in many sizes and appear red, yellow, or green. These hotter peppers tend to be long and skinny. Chili peppers don't actually burn your mouth, but they can cause pain. A certain chemical in the fruit causes this feeling. Chili peppers, whether fresh or dried, add an almost fiery zing to foods. Dishes from Mexico, India, and Africa are noted for including the hottest types of peppers. Eating these foods may take some getting used to. In addition to the discomfort in your mouth, hot peppers may cause your eyes to water, your nose to run, and your ears to feel warm.

5   Whatever their color or flavor, peppers add variety and spice to fancy or even everyday foods. When was the last time you had a pepper?

**I.** What do you know about peppers, or what experiences have you had growing or eating peppers?

_____

_____

**2.** Do you like peppers? Write why or why not.

_____

**3.** How are bell peppers and chili peppers the same? How are they different? Write what the article tells you about each kind.

**Bell Peppers**

Size _____

Shape _____

Color _____

Flavor _____

**Chili Peppers**

Size _____

Shape _____

Color _____

Flavor _____

**4.** What two headings does the author divide the article into? How is this helpful?

_____

_____

**5.** Write **T** for true or **F** for false next to each statement below.

_____ Hot peppers can make your eyes water.

_____ Bell peppers are very spicy.

_____ Peppers can be prepared in many ways.

_____ Bell peppers are red, and chili peppers are green.

**6.** What makes chili peppers burn your mouth?

_____

**7.** What two vitamins are peppers high in?

_____ and _____

# Soccer Blues

*Why is Perry so unhappy about soccer practice?*

1 "Okay, everybody, come over here and listen up!" Coach's voice carried across the soccer field. Kids of all sizes and shapes stopped what they were doing and walked or trotted toward the coach. When the several dozen boys and girls were in a ring around him, the coach continued. "I want all of you to practice dribbling on your own for at least half an hour a day outside of practice. Okay?"

2 "Okay, Coach!" yelled the circle. Everyone smiled. Coach always liked answers to his questions.

3 Satisfied with the response, Coach went on. "Most of the passing we do in games is when we're only 10, maybe 20, yards apart. We need to be able to deliver the ball within that range *every time we pass,*" Coach explained. "Now, we're going to do a one-on-one passing exercise. One partner over here, the other over there," he said, pointing to one touch line and another invisible line about half-way across the field. "What I want you to do is...."

4 Around the circle, heads nodded as eager players listened to Coach. One head, though, wasn't nodding; it was bobbing. Perry was so tired and hungry that his knees felt shaky. He was sure he had dribbled his soccer ball a hundred miles already this afternoon. He felt as if one more passing exercise would pretty much finish him off. Somehow, he stumbled through. He was pretty sure he did not impress Coach, though, when one of his passes went wildly across the field.

5 At the end of practice, Perry flopped into the back seat of the car and buckled his seatbelt. He didn't even wait for his mom's usual question.

6 "Practice was awful," said Perry without even opening his eyes. "I don't ever want to go back."

**1.** In most stories, a character has a problem. What is Perry's problem?

_____

**2.** What information in the story helped you answer question 1?

_____

_____

**3. Dialogue** is what the characters in a story say. What did you learn about Perry from his dialogue?

_____

_____

**4.** Find a line of the coach's dialogue. What does it tell you about the coach?

Dialogue: _____

_____

What it tells: _____

_____

**5.** Coach thinks that a passing exercise is important because

_____

_____.

**6.** What is the setting for this story?

_____

**7. Practice was awful.** Is this a fact or an opinion?

_____

**8.** The last line of paragraph 5 says that Perry didn't even wait for his mom's usual question. What do you think her question is?

_____

**9.** Which word or phrase best describes Perry in this story?
_____ confident    _____ full of energy    _____ exhausted

**10.** Have you ever wished you could quit an activity? Tell about it.

_____

_____

# Mom to the Rescue

*Have you ever solved a mystery?*

1     Mrs. Rothman was speechless. The only thing Perry had talked about all winter was soccer. Now, Perry wanted to quit soccer. Not knowing whether to laugh or cry, she drove home and fixed dinner.

2     After dinner, Mrs. Rothman tried to get to the bottom of the problem.

3     "Do you think Coach is too tough?"

4     "No."

5     "Are you having trouble with one of the other kids?"

6     "No."

7     "Did you get hurt?"

8     "No."

9     "Do you feel as if you're not good enough? If that's the case, you should talk to Coach...."

10     "Well, that's sort of it. I just felt so weak during practice. My knees were shaky. I could hardly lift my feet." Perry shook his head. "I just don't have what it takes. A soccer player has to run and run and not even get winded."

11     *Hmm*, thought Mrs. Rothman. *Weak? Shaky knees?* She softened her questioning a little. "Did you have a good lunch today?"

12     Perry thought for a second. "Um, yes, I guess so. Oh, except that there was a fire drill, and I didn't get to finish."

13     *Aha, that's it! A boy can't make it through school and soccer practice without the proper fuel.*

14     "I'll tell you what, Perry," said Mrs. Rothman, patting his knee. "Why don't you try it for one more day. I'll meet you after school with a power snack, and we'll see if that helps." Perry agreed, but he wondered what a power snack was and how it could possibly help.

I. Mrs. Rothman is speechless because

_____.

2. Check two words that tell how Perry probably felt.
_____ disappointed
_____ proud
_____ eager
_____ frightened

3. Perry says he wants to quit soccer because

_____.

4. Have you ever tried to do something that was hard, or that you had to work at? What was it?

_____

_____

Did you get discouraged? Did you quit?

_____

_____

5. Do you think Perry's decision is reasonable, or do you think he is giving up too easily? Explain.

_____

_____

6. Mrs. Rothman probably feels
_____ surprised      _____ angry      _____ entertained

7. What problem does Mrs. Rothman think Perry is having?

_____

8. How does she plan to help Perry?

_____

_____

9. What do you think would be a good example of a power snack? Explain your choice.

_____

_____

# Power Snack

*Have you ever had a power snack?*

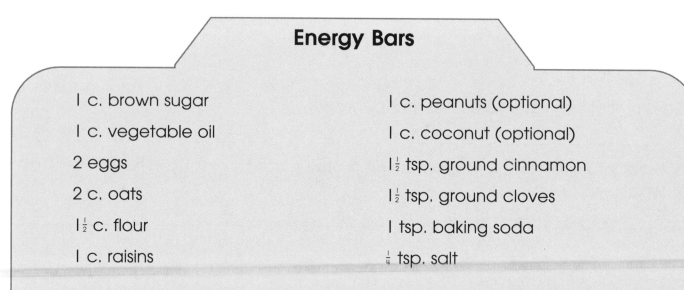

## Energy Bars

1 c. brown sugar

1 c. vegetable oil

2 eggs

2 c. oats

$1\frac{1}{2}$ c. flour

1 c. raisins

1 c. peanuts (optional)

1 c. coconut (optional)

$1\frac{1}{2}$ tsp. ground cinnamon

$1\frac{1}{2}$ tsp. ground cloves

1 tsp. baking soda

$\frac{1}{4}$ tsp. salt

Heat oven to 350° F. Grease 11" x 17" pan. Mix brown sugar, oil, and eggs until smooth. Stir in remaining ingredients. Spread mixture into pan, pressing with fingers until even. Bake until center is set, but not firm, 16–22 minutes. Remove from oven and cool for 15 minutes. Drizzle honey glaze* over bars. Let cool completely. Cut into squares. Store covered for two weeks. Or, wrap tightly and freeze for up to six months.

*Directions for honey glaze: Place $\frac{1}{4}$ c. honey and 2 T. butter or margarine in a sauce pan. Heat and stir until well blended and heated through. Drizzle over bars.

(Note: Always ask a grown-up for help in the kitchen.)

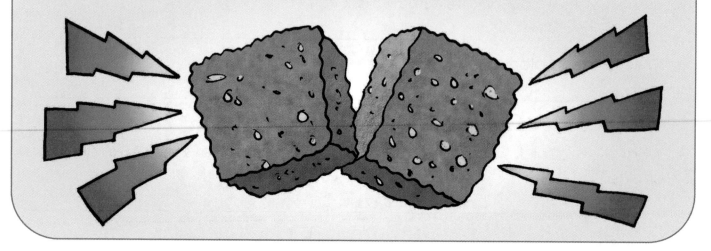

Write these steps in the correct order. (Not all of the recipe's steps are here.)
- spread mixture into pan
- drizzle glaze
- grease the pan
- mix sugar, oil, and eggs
- remove from oven and cool

1. _____

2. _____

3. _____

4. _____

5. _____

6. How long do the directions say to bake the bars?

_____

7. The directions say to "drizzle honey glaze over bars." How did you know what honey glaze was?

_____

Recipes often use short forms of words called **abbreviations**. Match the common recipe words in the box with their abbreviations.

| cup | teaspoon |
|---|---|
| Fahrenheit | tablespoon |

8. T. _____    10. F _____

9. c. _____    11. tsp. _____

12. The directions say, "Bake until center is set but not firm." What does this mean?

_____

13. How long do the energy bars need to cool?

_____

14. What is the longest you could keep these bars? What would you need to do to them?

_____

_____

# And It's Out of the Park!

*What happens at the soccer game?*

1   "Okay, everybody listen up!" Coach said. It took only a moment for the team to gather. It was the first game of the season. Perry could tell that everyone was nervous and excited, just like he was.

2   "This is where all those drills pay off. You guys have dribbled to the moon and back since we started practice. You've done a good job. Now, let's remember everything we learned and play a good game. Okay?"

3   "Okay!" the team yelled, and Coach smiled. He liked their spirit.

4   "All right! Let's go, Bobcats!" Perry and his teammates roared onto the field and took their positions.

5   It seemed as if Coach's hopes were coming true. The midfielders stayed in position. The center backs defended the goal well. Coach even heard some of the other team's parents admiring how his team handled the ball.

6   Neither team scored in the first half. During the second half, there was a great play that almost put a goal on the scoreboard in the final seconds.

7   There was a terrific jumble around the ball. Perry and another player were down, leaving two other players battling it out. Perry rolled out of the way and scrambled to his feet. Just then, the ball somehow broke free and came his way. Without hesitating for a moment, he reeled back and kicked.

8   *Now that was a solid kick*, Perry thought to himself. Time seemed to stop as everyone on the field watched the arc of the ball's flight. It was beautiful. When the ball disappeared from sight, someone in the crowd yelled, "It's a home run!" The crowd and the players exploded in laughter. In the midst of all the end-of-game confusion, Perry's only thought was, *Wow, those power snacks really work.*

1. When you read the story's title, did you guess about how the story ended? Was your guess close to being correct? Explain.

   _____

   _____

   _____

2. Circle the word that best describes the coach's words before the game.

   angry        encouraging

3. Have you ever been in a sporting event or a performance that didn't turn out the way you expected? Did something funny or weird happen? Write about it.

   _____

   _____

   _____

4. At the end of paragraph 2, Coach says that the players have "dribbled to the moon and back." This is a figure of speech. What does it mean?

   _____

   _____

5. Give one example of dialogue in the story.

   _____

   _____

   Now, give one example of a character's thought that is not spoken out loud.

   _____

   _____

6. How are the two examples in question 5 written differently from each other?

   _____

   _____

7. Why is it funny that someone in the crowd says, "It's a home run!"?

   _____

   _____

# History of Soccer

*Read to see how soccer had its start.*

### Earliest Record

1 The earliest written evidence of a soccer-like game comes from China. During the second and third centuries B.C., Chinese soldiers took part in an activity that involved kicking a ball into a small net. Historians think the game was a skill-building exercise for the soldiers.

### Years of Development

2 In ancient Greece and Rome, teams of up to 27 players played a soccer-type game. In Britain hundreds of years later, during the thirteenth century A.D., whole villages played against each other. With hundreds of people playing, these games were both long and rough. Kicking, punching, and biting were common and allowed.

3 In 1331, English King Edward III passed a law in an attempt to put a stop to the popular but violent game. The king of Scotland spoke against the game a hundred years later. Queen Elizabeth I, during the late 1500s, passed a law that called for a week of jail for anyone caught playing "football," or soccer, as we call it. But the game could not be stopped.

### The Modern Game Emerges

4 Two hundred and fifty years later, people in Britain were still playing a game we would recognize as soccer. A well-known English college, Eton, developed a set of rules in 1815. A number of other colleges soon agreed to use the same rules, and those schools played against each other. Finally, 50 years later, a formal association formed to oversee the playing of the game and its rules. In 1869, a rule against handling the ball with the hands transformed the game into the sport of soccer that is wildly popular all around the world.

**1.** This article is mostly about
_____ how soccer was named.
_____ the rules of soccer.
_____ soccer's history.

**2.** Historians think that soccer might have started out as a

_____.

**3.** Why did King Edward III pass a law against soccer?

_____

_____

**4.** What punishment did Queen Elizabeth have for soccer players?

_____

**5.** What important rule change made the game into what we know as soccer? When did it happen?

_____

_____

**6.** If you wanted to find out about the beginnings of soccer, under which heading should you look?

_____

**7.** Under which heading would you find information about soccer during the last century or so?

_____

**8.** Write **T** for **true** or **F** for **false** next to each statement below.
_____ Today, you are allowed to touch the ball with your hands in soccer.
_____ Kicking and biting were common in soccer games long ago.
_____ In Britain, soccer is called "football."

**9.** At the end of paragraph 3, it says, "the game could not be stopped." Why do you think this was true?

_____

_____

**10.** What was the author's purpose for writing this article?

_____

# Why Soccer?

*Why do you think soccer is so popular?*

1   On what topic do more than 13 million American kids agree? Soccer! The Soccer Industry Council of America reported in 1999 that all those kids were playing organized soccer. Add adults into the mix, and you come up with more than 18 million Americans playing soccer. What makes soccer so popular?

2   First, I think there's the international appeal. Americans see that people in many other countries in the world are wildly excited about soccer. The excitement must be catching.

3   Second, soccer takes less equipment than some other sports, especially football. For that reason, it's not very costly for a kid to join a soccer team.

4   Third, parents view soccer as a safer sport than some other sports. Though accidents may occur, body contact isn't supposed to be part of the game. Therefore, fewer injuries occur.

5   Fourth, soccer appeals to both boys and girls. Though soccer was at first only a male sport (just like all other sports), soccer has caught on with girls. This is good for the sport, I think. Interest in the sport extends to whole families, so there are more players, more fans, more coaches, and so on.

6   Finally, I think there is the running factor. Running up and down a field chasing a ball is such a healthy, all-American thing to do. Kids love it, and few parents can object to it.

**1.** The person who wrote this article is the **author**. The author probably wrote this article to

_____ make you laugh.

_____ give information.

_____ persuade you to do something.

The author states some facts in the article. She also gives her opinion. Write **F** next to each sentence that is a fact. Write **O** next to each sentence that gives an opinion.

**2.** _____ Add adults into the mix, and you come up with more than 18 million Americans playing soccer.

**3.** _____ First, I think there's the international appeal.

**4.** _____ Though accidents may occur, body contact isn't supposed to be part of the game.

**5.** _____ And finally, I think there is the running factor.

**6.** Look back at the sentences you marked as opinions. What do you notice about them?

_____

_____

**7.** What is the main idea of paragraph 5?

_____ Soccer is only for boys, just like other sports.

_____ Soccer is a good sport for both boys and girls.

_____ Soccer has caught on with girls.

**8.** Why is soccer less expensive than some other sports?

_____

_____

**9.** Look at the focus question under the title. What do you think its purpose is?

_____

_____

**10.** Have you ever played soccer? If so, tell about your experience. If not, explain why you would or would not like to try it.

_____

_____

# A Teacher's Journal

*Do you think the girls will be able to work together?*

April 14

1     When my students work together on projects, everything usually works out. I had my doubts today, though, when I put Sharla, Tess, and Lee together to make a volcano. At one point, I knew something was going to blow up, and it wasn't the volcano!

2     I knew the girls weren't good friends, but I encourage my students to learn to work with all of their classmates. I could tell they felt a little shy when they sat down for their first planning meeting. Students in other groups had questions, so I didn't notice the girls for quite a few minutes. When I looked back in their direction, one looked mad, one looked sad, and one was nearly in tears. Good grief!

3     As I approached, they all started talking at once. Tess didn't want to have to touch "that icky paste" to build the volcano. Sharla had some design ideas that she couldn't get across to the other two. Lee thought they should just stop talking and get to work.

4     I calmed the girls down and suggested that they make a list of things on which they agreed. They agreed they were making a volcano out of flour, salt, and water, and that's all. They couldn't agree on the size, on a base for the volcano, or on who should get to mix the paste. Each girl had her own ideas and would not budge for the sake of working together or moving ahead.

5     By this time, the work session was over and it was time for lunch. The girls had made very little progress, and I was wondering if I had made a big mistake. Maybe this was one group of students who just couldn't work together.

1. Do you think Sharla, Tess, and Lee will be able to work together? Write why or why not.

   _____

   _____

2. Think of times when you worked with classmates on projects. Was it hard or easy? Explain.

   _____

   _____

   _____

3. Would you say that you are more like Sharla—full of ideas—or more like Lee— eager to stop talking and get to work? Write why.

   _____

   _____

4. Does the teacher who is writing the journal seem thoughtful or worn out? Write why you think so.

   _____

   _____

5. At the end of the first paragraph, the teacher says, "I knew something was going to blow up, and it wasn't the volcano." What does she mean?

   _____

   _____

6. From whose point of view is this selection told?

   _____ Sharla    _____ Lee    _____ the teacher

7. What do you predict will happen next in the story?

   _____

   _____

8. If you wrote a journal entry, what would you write about?

   _____

   _____

# A Student's Journal

*Read to see how the girls are moving ahead with their volcano.*

April 16

1  Tess and Lee and I have to make a volcano together. Mrs. Holt put us in a group on Tuesday, and we had such a big argument! Tess was fussing about the paste, and Lee didn't want to plan anything. She just wanted to jump in and start working. It was awful. We didn't get anything done. Yesterday, Mrs. Holt made us stay in during recess so we could finish planning our volcano. Missing recess was so unfair!

2  Anyway, we finally said we would make the volcano about a foot high, and we'd add a little village around the base. That way, Tess can make the little village since she refuses to touch the volcano paste. (I think Mrs. Holt should make her.)

3  Today, Lee and I mixed up the paste. It was really goopy but kind of fun. We set up a plastic water bottle and some wadded-up aluminum foil as a base for the volcano. Then, we started plopping paste on. Tess just watched (no fair).

4  I was making my side all nice and smooth. I told Lee she should smooth out her side, too. She said, "No, Sharla, it should look lumpy, like a real mountain," just as if she were the boss. I said it would just look messy and that we should make it smooth. Well, the whole thing went downhill from there. Our paste started to dry out, and we didn't have time to finish. I suppose that means we'll have to miss recess again tomorrow, and it's all Lee's fault.

This story is written in the form of a journal entry. The person who is writing uses *I* to refer to herself. She is the **narrator**, or the person telling the story.

1. Find a sentence that tells you that the narrator actually took part in the action of the story. Write the sentence here.

   _____

   _____

2. The narrator, Sharla, disagreed with Lee about

   _____.

3. Sharla was upset because

   _____

   _____

4. Did you expect this journal to be written by Mrs. Holt, the teacher? Why or why not?

   _____

   _____

5. Why did the girls decide to make a village around the base?

   _____

6. Which of these words best describes Sharla's attitude toward the other two girls?
   _____ impatient      _____ understanding      _____ comforting

7. Explain how the picture adds to your understanding of the story.

   _____

   _____

8. Write **C** next to the sentence below that is the cause. Write **E** next to the sentence that is the effect.
   _____ The girls didn't make much progress on their volcano.
   _____ Mrs. Holt made the girls stay in at recess.

# The Great Volcano Debate

*What is the great volcano debate all about?*

1   "Sharla? Lee? Tess? Can you come here for a minute, please?" Mrs. Holt called the girls to her desk. It was Friday morning.

2   "Now, you know today is the last work session on our projects, right?" she asked.

3   The girls all nodded.

4   "Are you ready to finish up?"

5   No one answered.

6   "Is there a problem?" Mrs. Holt asked, knowing perfectly well that there was a problem. She wanted the girls to put it in their own words, though.

7   Sharla glanced at the other two, and then began. "Well, I think the volcano should be smooth so it looks nice."

8   "And," jumped in Lee, "I think it should look rough and rocky, like a real mountain."

9   "I see," said Mrs. Holt, stalling for time. "What do you think, Tess?"

10   "Well, I've been making buildings for the village," she said quickly, to make sure Mrs. Holt knew she had been helping. "I think it would be neat if we could show lava flowing down toward the village, sort of like Pompeii...."

11   "Hey!" cut in Sharla, "that's a great idea. The flowing lava would be smooth. Right, Mrs. Holt?"

12   "Yes, I guess so." Mrs. Holt had never actually seen flowing lava, but it seemed reasonable.

13   Sharla continued. "The other side of the mountain, where there's no lava, would look rocky and bumpy. Right?"

14   Tess caught on. "So one side can be smooth, and the other side can be rough. Come on, you guys, let's go finish!"

15   Mrs. Holt wasn't sure, but she thought the girls might have solved their own problem.

**1.** In most stories, the characters have a problem. What problem do the characters in this story have?

_____

**2.** What caused Mrs. Holt to call the girls up to her desk?

_____

**3.** What is Tess's idea?
_____ to show flowing lava
_____ to make both sides smooth
_____ to make the village larger

**4.** What is the result of Tess's idea?

_____

_____

**5.** Where in the story do we learn that the teacher, Mrs. Holt, knows the girls are not getting along?

_____

_____

**6.** What is the main difference in the way this story is written, compared to the other two about the same characters?
_____ This story is told from Lee's point of view.
_____ Sharla is not a character in this story.
_____ It is not written as a journal entry.

**7.** How do you think Mrs. Holt feels about the girls solving their own problem? Explain.

_____

_____

**8.** What is the setting for this story?

_____

**9.** The girls learned how to build a volcano by doing this project. What else do you think they learned?

_____

_____

# The End of a Volcano Tale

*What did the girls learn from their project?*

1   Sharla, Tess, and Lee stood proudly behind their model volcano. Tess straightened a tiny building in the village at the base of the mountain.

2   Mrs. Holt quieted the class. "Girls, you may begin."

3   Lee felt something wiggly in her stomach. She was supposed to go first.

4   "This is our volcano," she said. *Oh, that was stupid*, thought Lee, trying not to roll her eyes. *They can probably figure that out.* "We made it this shape because that's how a lot of volcanoes are shaped."

5   Next, Sharla told about what happens when a volcano erupts. After that, Tess told about a famous volcano and the town nearby that got covered up with ash and mud.

6   When it looked as if they were done, Mrs. Holt had a question. "Can you tell about the steps you went through to complete your project, girls?"

7   The girls looked at each other. They hadn't expected this. Sharla felt her face turn red, but she spoke up.

8   "Well, at first we didn't agree about what we wanted and how we wanted to do it." Sharla shrugged. "It took us a while to make a plan and get it done."

9   Tess went on. "We figured out that everybody had a job to do."

10   "And everybody has good ideas, even if they're not what you expect," added Lee.

11   Mrs. Holt looked pleased. *It only took one volcano and two explosions to figure out how to work together*, she thought. *Not bad.*

**1.** This story is mostly about
_____ becoming best friends after working together.
_____ what the girls learned from their project.
_____ how a teacher helped the girls get along.

**2.** How do the girls feel about their volcano project?

_____

_____

**3.** When it is Lee's turn to speak, she feels
_____ nervous.
_____ happy.
_____ cross.

**4.** Why did Sharla's face turn red when Mrs. Holt asked about how they completed their project?

_____

_____

**5.** What experiences have you had working with other people? Were there times when you didn't agree or get along? Write about it.

_____

_____

_____

**6.** When it is Tess's turn to speak, what does she tell about?

_____

_____

**7.** Make a check mark next to the thing that happened first.
_____ Mrs. Holt had a question.
_____ Lee said, "This is our volcano."
_____ Mrs. Holt looked pleased.

**8.** If the girls had to work together again, how do you think they would do? Explain.

_____

_____

# Volcanoes

*Read to find out why volcanoes erupt.*

[1] The surface of Earth is not a solid place. There are many holes, some of which allow magma to reach Earth's surface from deep inside.

[2] Magma comes from deep inside Earth where it's hot. It's so hot that rocks melt. Magma is **molten**, or melted, rock. Because of the heat, there is also pressure. When things such as air, gases, or molten rock get hot, they **expand**, or get bigger. That means they need space. Weak parts of Earth's crust get pushed aside, or opened up. The magma follows the easiest path, usually along **fissures**, or cracks, toward the surface.

[3] When it does reach the surface, magma is called *lava*. If there is a great deal of pressure behind the magma, it explodes through the crust's surface, sending dust, ash, lava, and rocks high into the air. When there is only a little pressure, the magma may simply bubble up and form a lava flow that spreads across the land.

[4] A volcano may be **active**, or experience eruptions, on a fairly regular basis. Or it may lie **dormant**, or inactive, for hundreds of years. Scientists, called *volcanologists*, are always ready to learn more because each volcano is unique and may teach them something new about the inner workings of Earth.

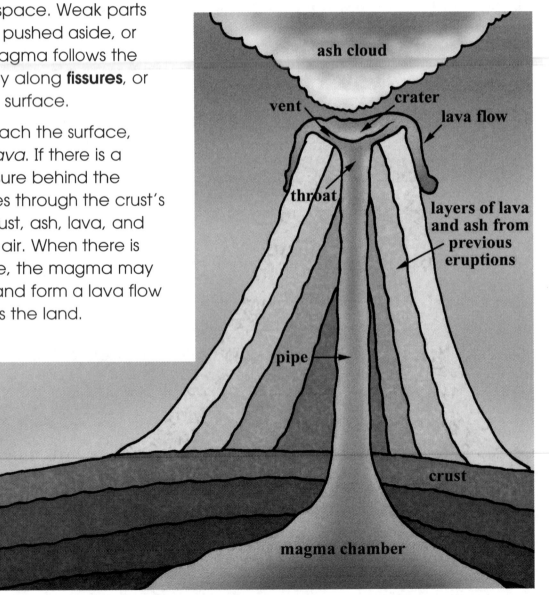

In nonfiction writing, the author sometimes calls attention to words that the reader may not know. Those words appear in **bold** type. The author usually gives the meaning of the bold word in the same sentence.

Below are the bold words from the article. Write the meaning of each word.

1. molten _____

2. expand _____

3. fissures _____

4. active _____

5. dormant _____

Write **F** next to each sentence that is a fact. Write **O** next to each sentence that is an opinion.

6. _____ Volcanic eruptions are one of the most striking natural events.

7. _____ A volcanic eruption is more frightening than a hurricane.

8. _____ Volcanoes are located in many places in the world.

9. What does the illustration show?

_____

_____

10. Trace with your finger the path that magma would take from under Earth's crust to the surface. Describe the path in your own words.

_____

_____

11. Write **C** next to the sentence below that is the cause. Write **E** next to the sentence that is the effect.

_____ Parts of Earth's crust open up.

_____ The molten rock gets very hot and expands.

12. What are scientists who study volcanoes called?

_____

# Forest Mammals

*Do you know what a mammal is?*

## Common Characteristics

1   What does a moose have in common with a porcupine? How about a bear with a mouse? How can more than 4,000 different kinds of mammals have much of anything in common? In fact, mammals have four distinct characteristics:

1. Mammals have warm blood, which means they can maintain a steady body temperature.

2. Mammals have backbones.

3. Female mammals produce milk to feed their babies.

4. Mammals have fur or hair, though the amount of it varies widely.

## North American Forest Dwellers

2   Forest mammals are alike in that they live in the same natural conditions, or **habitat**. Trees and the leafy undergrowth provide shelter and food for the many types of mammals that live in a North American forest.

3   **Insect eaters:** Moles and shrews are just two types of **insectivores** that live on or under the forest floor. They find insects in the dirt or in rotting tree trunks or leaf matter.

4   **Gnawing animals:** This large family of mammals, called **rodents**, includes beavers, squirrels, mice, and porcupines. Whether on the ground or in trees, these animals gnaw on nuts, seeds, and branches with their strong front teeth.

5   **Hare-like animals:** Rabbits and hares make up this group. Leafy sprouts and sometimes the bark of young trees are the main diet of these animals.

6   **Meat eaters:** In North America, the largest meat eaters, or **carnivores**, are bears and mountain lions. Wolves and coyotes are also members of this group. They eat smaller mammals such as rabbits, mice, and moles.

7   **Hoofed animals:** In North America, moose and deer are the most common forest-dwelling hoofed animals. The forest provides both shelter and food for them.

**1.** What four common characteristics do mammals have?

_____

_____

In the article, the author showed some words in bold type. The meanings of those words are given as well. Find the meanings of the words, and write them here.

**2.** habitat _____

_____

**3.** insectivores _____

_____

**4.** rodents _____

_____

**5.** carnivores _____

_____

**6.** Hoofed animals are named for the kind of _____ they have.

**7.** Give one example of each kind of forest dweller.

insect eaters: _____          gnawing animals: _____

hare-like animals: _____          meat eaters: _____

hoofed animals: _____

**8.** Why do you think a forest is a good habitat for many different kinds of mammals?

_____

_____

**9.** Think about what you know about mammals. Name two kinds of mammals that are not mentioned in the article.

_____ and _____

**10. Meat eaters eat smaller mammals, such as rabbits, mice, and moles.** Is this sentence a fact or an opinion?

_____

# Snakes: Love Them or Leave Them?

*Why do you think snakes are not popular?*

1  I think it is safe to say that most people really don't like snakes. It would be hard to find a person who is neutral, or simply doesn't care one way or the other. What I can't figure out is why something that doesn't even have any legs causes such alarm.

2  Snakes are reptiles, of course, not mammals. Do you think there is some ancient hatred between mammals and reptiles? Maybe their cold-bloodedness is what makes us dislike snakes. Or perhaps age-old stories about frightening creatures with scales cause us to turn away from our neighbors, the snakes.

3  Snakes are quite useful, but that doesn't seem to matter. Snakes help control the rodent population. Without snakes, perhaps we would be overrun with mice. Most of us, however, would rather see a mouse than a snake.

4  The poison argument is a strong one. Some snakes are poisonous, and people all over the world do die from snake bites each year. However, the poisonous varieties are only a small percentage of the world's snakes. We can't say the whole batch is bad just because of a few rotten ones.

5  And what do we do with the people who really like snakes? They like snakes even more strongly than we dislike them. These people learn about them, seek them out, and observe them. Why? The only reason I can think of is that these people are truly generous and open-minded. They are able to put aside differences and welcome the snake as a fellow living being.

6  Whatever the reason for our like or dislike, snakes are a vital part of the circle of life. They would prefer to be left alone, and that is what we should do. If you're lucky, you might not run across more than a few of them in an entire lifetime. That would be fine with most of us.

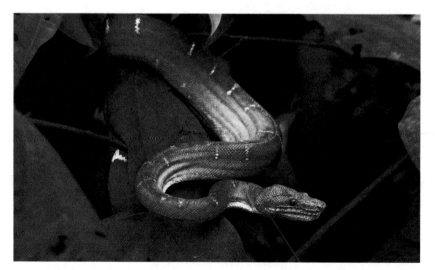

The author of this article chose to share her own point of view. Find a sentence in which the author uses the word *I*. What idea is the author sharing in that sentence?

1. The sentence begins with

_____.

The author is saying _____

_____.

2. Do you think the author likes snakes, dislikes snakes, or is neutral? Write a sentence from the article that supports your answer.

_____

_____

Write **F** next to each sentence that is a fact. Write **O** next to each sentence that is an opinion.

3. _____ People dislike snakes because they have no legs.

4. _____ Snakes control the rodent population.

5. _____ Not meeting many snakes is a good thing.

6. Name one difference between mammals and reptiles.

_____

_____

7. What is one way in which snakes are useful?

_____

8. What is the main idea of paragraph 4?

_____ If you get bitten by a poisonous snake, seek medical help.

_____ Some snakes are poisonous, but that's not a good reason to dislike all snakes.

_____ Poisonous snakes are very vicious.

9. Tell how you feel about snakes and why.

_____

_____

_____

# Redwood Giants

*Read to learn about America's biggest trees.*

1 From a seed that is smaller than a pea grows the tallest of trees. The coast redwood is the unchallenged giant of North America's trees.

## What's special about redwoods?

2 Redwoods are special for a couple of reasons. The first is their size. Imagine standing next to a tree that is the height of a 20- or 30-story building. The second is their age. Redwoods commonly make it to 600 years or so. Some have been found that are more than 2,000 years old.

## Where do redwoods grow?

3 To find a coast redwood, you'll have to go to Oregon or California. A strip of coastline about 450 miles long and up to 35 miles wide is home to the redwoods. Coast redwoods do not grow anywhere else in the world.

## Why do redwoods grow there?

4 The coast of the Pacific Ocean provides a special environment for the redwoods. Cool, moist air comes off the ocean and keeps the trees moist all year. That is important because almost all of the area's rain falls between October and May. During the dry summer months, the trees depend on moisture from the thick fog that often hangs over the coast.

## How do redwoods survive?

5 Redwoods have a couple of built-in protection systems. Most of a redwood's branches and leaves are high up on the tree. This keeps them safe from forest fires. Also, the bark of a mature redwood tree is as much as 12 inches thick. The thick covering protects the lower part of the tree from fire damage. Redwoods are safe from insect damage because the wood contains a bitter-tasting chemical called *tannin*.

## What should I do?

6 If you ever get a chance, visit a redwood forest. Look among the tree trunks and imagine who might have camped there a thousand years ago. Look upward and just imagine how high the trees might grow if we preserve and protect them.

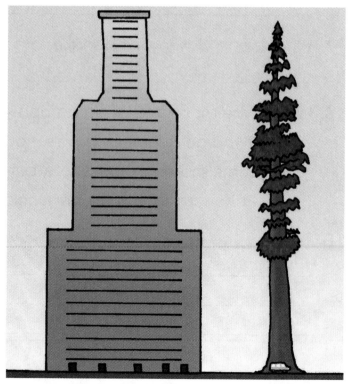

**1.** To see a redwood tree, you have to go to _____.

**2.** Why do redwoods grow there?

_____

_____

**3.** What might happen if someone tried to grow a redwood tree in Kansas or Missouri, for example?

_____

_____

**4.** What do you think is most special about redwood trees? Write why.

_____

_____

**5.** Why do you think the author chose to use questions for the headings?

_____

_____

**6.** If you want to find out what conditions redwoods need to grow, under which heading would you look?

_____

**7.** If you wonder what the big deal is about redwoods, under which heading should you look?

_____

**8.** What three objects are shown in the diagram?

_____

**9.** What is the author's purpose for writing this selection?

_____ to entertain

_____ persuade

_____ to inform

**10.** About how long can a redwood live?

_____

# Problem Solved

*What will Miss Eller decide the class should study?*

1   So far, Miss Eller's idea had worked out. Her students had done some research on whatever they wanted to know about the natural world. They had all really enjoyed uncovering facts about snails or redwood trees or grasshoppers. And Enzo's plastic snakes had been a big hit.

2   Now, it all fell back to Miss Eller, though. She had to decide whose ideas to accept and whose to reject. She thought back on the students' reports and tried to sort them into groups. Furry things in this group, and crawling things in that group? No, that didn't really work.

3   Suddenly, her gaze shifted and she realized that the answer was right in front of her. A poster on the wall showed a lush woodland scene that included many different kinds of trees, forest creatures, birds, and, yes, even some snakes and crawly things. Miss Eller smiled. *A picture is worth a thousand words—or a thousand ideas,* she thought. She had the solution.

4   After lunch, the students gathered on the meeting rug. "What if I told you that we are going to have one topic, but that you are all going to be able to study what you want?"

5   "How can that be?" questioned Tara. "We all had different ideas."

6   Miss Eller shrugged. "It all depends on how you group things together. What if our topic is 'Redwood Forests'? What do you suppose lives in a redwood forest?"

7   Hands shot up left and right. Everything the students could think of fit into Miss Eller's topic: redwood trees, of course, cute and fuzzy mammals, snails, snakes—you name it.

8   Within a few weeks, the classroom had been transformed. A sign appeared outside the classroom door.

> ## Welcome to our
> # redwood forest.
> If something lives, grows, eats, breathes, or crawls in a redwood forest, we know all about it.
> ## Come on in.

Complete each sentence with the correct word.

| author | dialogue | narrator |
|--------|----------|----------|

1. When characters speak, their words make up the story's

   _____.

2. The person who wrote the story is the _____.

3. Within the story, the person or character who tells the story is the

   _____.

4. In most stories, the main character has a problem. Miss Eller's problem is that

   _____

5. Look at the illustration. What did Miss Eller's students do during their study of redwood forests?

   _____

   _____

   _____

6. Where did Miss Eller get the idea of how to solve the problem?

   _____

7. How do you think Miss Eller's class feels about the project?

   _____ excited

   _____ worried

   _____ upset

8. The last paragraph says that the classroom had been transformed. What does this mean?

   _____

9. Write **C** next to the sentence below that is the cause. Write **E** next to the sentence that is the effect.

   _____ Students raise their hands to answer the question.

   _____ Miss Eller asks what lives in a redwood forest.

# Magic with Flowers

*What are Josh and Gary trying to do?*

1   *"Ala-ka-ZAM!"* said Gary, trying to make his voice sound big. He waved his arms in and out in what he hoped was a fancy pattern, and then tapped the box sitting on the table with a magic wand. He held his breath. The box jiggled a little. Then, the table jiggled a little.

2   *"Ahhhhh!"* The exclamation erupted from under the table.

3   "What's the matter?" called Gary. "Did it work?"

4   Gary's friend Josh came out from under the table. His hair was wet. His shirt was wet. He was holding a vase of fake flowers. "Well, it worked if you don't count spilling water all over," Josh grumbled. The boys had put water in the vase because they thought it would make it all seem more real.

5   "Maybe we should use real flowers," suggested Gary.

6   "They'd just wilt," Josh shook his head.

7   Gary shrugged. "Yeah, I guess so. Aside from spilling, how did it go under there?"

8   Josh told what had happened. When Gary tapped the box, Josh was supposed to open the secret door on the bottom of the box and pull the vase of flowers down, and then close up the box again. But the bottom had gotten stuck and the vase had tipped. The boys sat down to rethink their plan.

9   The boys had thought the old broken table was almost too good to be true. Its worn-out wicker top had a hole that was just the right size for covering with the box as well as for making stuff disappear by pulling it through.

10   "This whole magic thing just isn't as easy as I thought it would be," noted Gary.

11   "Yeah, I know," Josh agreed. "How do you suppose the real magicians did it? They made stuff disappear all the time."

12   An idea popped into Gary's head and his face brightened. "Maybe it is the fake flowers. The real ones used real stuff, like rabbits. We need a rabbit. Go get Wiggles!"

**1.** This story is mostly about

_____ two boys trying to do a magic trick.

_____ a boy teaching another boy a magic trick.

_____ how to do a magic trick.

**2.** Josh got wet because _____

_____ .

**3.** Why was Josh under the table?

_____

_____

**4.** Write **C** next to the sentence below that is the cause. Write **E** next to the sentence that is the effect.

_____ The vase tipped and got Josh wet.

_____ The bottom of the box got stuck.

**5.** Why were the boys so excited about the old table they found?

_____

_____

**6.** Doing magic is (easier, harder) than the boys had expected.

**7.** Gary thinks that he and Josh need real things, so he tells Josh to go get a real

_____ .

**8.** Read the sentences below. Write **F** next to sentences that are facts and **O** next to sentences that are opinions.

_____ Gary held his breath.

_____ The boys should use real flowers.

_____ Being a magician is hard work.

_____ Josh's hair was wet.

**9.** What do you think will happen next?

_____

_____

_____

# Magic with Wiggles

*Read to see whether Josh and Gary's new trick works.*

1   *Well, okay*, thought Josh. Every magician they had ever read about had used rabbits. Josh couldn't believe they hadn't thought of Wiggles earlier. He had a good feeling about this.

2   Gary put a lettuce leaf in the box, and then Josh put Wiggles in the box and closed one of the top flaps. Josh got into position under the table so he could pull Wiggles through the hole in the bottom of the box and make him disappear.

3   Gary cleared his throat and raised his arms slowly. *"Ala-ka-...."*

4   "Hey, wait," called Josh from underneath the table. He crawled part way out. "Maybe we should try a new word. A rabbit-y word."

5   "A rabbit-y word?" Gary looked doubtful. "Like what?"

6   "Well, I don't know." Josh thought for a moment. "How about *rabbit-o-zam*?

7   *"Rabbit-o-ZAM!"* Gary tried it out. Both boys shook their heads.

8   Josh tried again. *"Shish-rabbit-ka-zam!"* Nope.

9   *"Abra-ca-DAB-rabbit!"* tried Gary.

10   *"Abra-ca-DAB-rabbit?"* Josh was laughing so hard he could barely get the word out.

11   After a good laughing spell, the boys got back down to business. They agreed to go back to good old *abracadabra*.

12   Josh took his position, and Gary did his part, complete with arms waving and stick tapping. The box jiggled a tiny bit. The table jiggled.

13   *"Ahhhhh!"* The cry from under the table was truly alarming.

14   "Now what's wrong?" cried Gary.

15   *"It worked!"* screamed Josh, scrambling out from under the table. *"It worked! Wiggles is gone!"*

16   "It worked?" cried Gary, and he dived under the table in disbelief. When he came out, the boys did a little dance, and then they bowed to the imaginary crowd, quite certain that they heard wild clapping.

17   Wiggles had, indeed, disappeared.

1. How was the magic trick supposed to work?

   _____

2. What actually happened?

   _____

   _____

Write the best word to complete each sentence below.

3. They should have thought of Wiggles _____. (brighter, sooner, calmer)

4. The magic words made the boys _____ so hard. (laugh, lame, learn)

5. It made Gary feel like a real magician when he _____ his arms. (waved, cried, tapped)

6. The boys couldn't _____ Wiggles was gone. (agree, scramble, believe)

7. Write **R** next to the sentences that tell about something real. Write **M** next to the sentences that are about made-up things.

   _____ Rabbits eat lettuce.

   _____ Rabbits disappear and reappear.

   _____ Magicians say magic words.

8. In the story, who is the magician, and who is the assistant?

   _____

   _____

9. Do you think the boys were surprised that Wiggles was actually gone? Why or why not?

   _____

   _____

10. Which words best describe the boys?

    _____ good-natured

    _____ sneaky

    _____ irritated

11. What do you think will happen next in the story?

    _____

    _____

# Houdini

*What made Harry Houdini so great?*

1   Do you believe in magic? The greatest magician of all time didn't. Harry Houdini was known as "The King of Cards" and "The Great Escape Artist." But he was the first to say that his magic tricks were tricks, not magic.

2   Houdini's early interest in magic tricks led him to read about famous magicians. He studied and then practiced and practiced. His first magic shows, begun when he was 17, included mostly card tricks. He added new tricks, such as escaping from an ordinary box, once he had perfected them.

3   From those simple beginnings, Houdini's magic tricks became more showy and more daring. He escaped from handcuffs. Then, he allowed audience members to bring their own handcuffs to prove he could escape from *any* pair of handcuffs. Then, he escaped from a straitjacket, hanging upside down by his ankles.

4   How can a performer top his own top performance? Think of a trick that seems truly impossible. Houdini had himself locked into a crate and thrown into a river. He also had himself sealed into a lead coffin, which was placed into a hotel swimming pool. An hour later, Houdini waved to the waiting fans and newspaper reporters.

5   Houdini strongly supported the work of magicians but just as strongly spoke against "fake" magicians who claimed that they had special powers or communicated with "spirits." Houdini would expose these false magicians by visiting their shows and then writing magazine or newspaper articles to reveal how they fooled their audiences.

6   To set himself apart from the "spiritual" magicians, Houdini practiced his tricks, perfected them, and then practiced again. Though Harry Houdini died more than 75 years ago, the man and his tricks have never been matched.

1. The author wrote this article to

_____ persuade.

_____ make you laugh.

_____ give you information.

Write **F** next to each sentence that is a fact. Write **O** next to each sentence that is an opinion.

2. _____ Harry Houdini died more than 75 years ago.

3. _____ Houdini could escape from handcuffs.

4. _____ Harry Houdini was the only "real" magician.

5. _____ Houdini's magic tricks were wonderful.

6. The article gives details about Houdini and his life. Number the details in the order in which the author tells about them.

_____ He escaped from a straitjacket, hanging upside down.

_____ Houdini had his first magic shows when he was 17.

_____ Houdini exposed "fake" magicians.

_____ Houdini's magic tricks became more showy and daring.

7. Which of these old sayings would Houdini have agreed with?

_____ Practice makes perfect.

_____ You are what you eat.

_____ A watched pot never boils.

8. **Houdini believed he had special powers and could talk to spirits.** Is this statement true or false?

_____

# David Copperfield

*What kind of a magician is David Copperfield?*

[1]    An illusion is something that fools the senses or the mind. An illusion may make you think something exists when it really does not. It may be something that appears to be one thing, but is really something else. David Copperfield calls himself an *illusionist*. He is someone who makes or creates illusions.

[2]    Many people are interested in magic, but most of them are not performing and getting paid for it by age 12. Nor are they teaching college-level classes in magic at age 16. Copperfield was the youngest person ever to be allowed to join the Society of American Magicians. When he got to college himself, Copperfield got the leading part in a play called *The Magic Man*. In addition to acting and singing, he created all the magic in the show.

The show ran for longer than any other musical in Chicago's history.

[3]    Copperfield is a huge success as a showy illusionist, but he has other projects as well. He says that his best work is Project Magic. Copperfield developed a number of tricks done with the hands. These tricks help hospital patients who need to improve their hand strength or coordination to move and control their fingers. Learning to do the tricks also builds confidence. Patients in the program can boast that they can do tricks that able-bodied people can't do.

[4]    Like many magicians, Copperfield has an interest in the history of magic. He has created a museum and library in which books, articles, and old magic props, or equipment, are stored and displayed. By keeping track of history, Copperfield hopes to save magic for future generations.

**1.** David Copperfield is an _____.

**2.** What did he start doing at age 12?

_____

**3.** What was he doing by age 16?

_____

Check all answers that are correct.

**4.** Which of these words do you think best describe Copperfield?
_____ thoughtless
_____ lazy
_____ hard-working
_____ talented

**5.** What do you think a magician could learn from Copperfield's collection of old magic books and equipment?

_____

_____

**6.** If you were a magician or an illusionist, what kinds of tricks would you like to do?

_____

_____

**7.** The headings below belong in this article. To which paragraph does each heading belong?
Copperfield's Beginnings _____
What Is an Illusion? _____
Saving Magic for the Future _____
Project Magic _____

**8.** In your own words, explain what an illusion is.

_____

_____

**9.** The youngest person ever to be allowed to join the Society of American Magicians was _____.

**10.** Why do you think Copperfield believes that his best work is Project Magic?

_____

_____

# Wiggles Reappears

*How do the boys get Wiggles back?*

1  "Which word do you think did it?" asked Josh.

2  "What do you mean?" asked Gary, still feeling great because their magic trick had worked. They had finally gotten something to disappear.

3  "Was it *shish-rabbit-ka-zam* or *abra-ca-dab-rabbit*?" Josh asked, working hard to repeat the magic words they had thought up.

4  Gary laughed again, remembering the words. "Oh, I think it was definitely *abra-ca-dab-rabbit*, don't you?"

5  "I don't know," shrugged Josh. "I guess we'll have to try each of them backward to get him back."

6  All of a sudden, it was very quiet. Gary looked at Josh. How in the world were they going to get Wiggles back?

7  "I think I remember all the words," Gary said, trying to encourage Josh. Wiggles was Josh's pet, after all.

8  The boys sat down on the back steps of Josh's house to figure out how to say the words backward so the magic would work the other way.

9  "Okay," said Gary, thinking hard. "We have *zam-ka-rabbit-shish* and *rabbit-dab-ca-abra*."

10  Josh continued, "And *zam-o-rabbit* and just plain old *dabra-ca-abra*."

11  Gary nodded, "I think that's it."

12  "*Ahhhhh!*" The cry came from around the corner of the house. It was Josh's mom.

13  "Mom? What's the matter?" called Josh, as both boys went running.

14  "Now, how many times have I told you not to chew on my..." Josh heard his mom's voice. Just around the corner, both boys stopped short.

15  "Wiggles! He reappeared!" Josh cried.

16  Mom looked at the boys. "Wiggles? Reappeared? Who's going to make my flowers reappear?"

17  The boys looked at each other, smiled, and nodded. They waved their arms and said, in their best magician voices, "*Zam-ka-flowers-SHISH!*"

1. Number the sentences to show the order in which events happened in the story.

_____ Gary laughed about their magic words.

_____ The boys heard Josh's mom.

_____ The boys discovered Mom and Wiggles.

_____ The boys figured out how to say the words backward.

_____ Gary felt great because their trick worked.

_____ The boys tried to make Mom's flowers reappear.

2. What problem do the boys have in this story?

_____

_____

3. What problem does Mom have?

_____

_____

4. How do the boys try to help Mom? Do you think it will work?

_____

_____

_____

5. Who does Wiggles belong to?

_____

6. Do you think Wiggles has escaped before? What details in the story helped you answer this question?

_____

_____

_____

7. Do you think the boys will continue working on their magic tricks? Why or why not?

_____

_____

_____

# Caught in Traffic

*What happens on the way back from the field trip?*

1 Jason was winning. He and his friends had been trying to see who could list the most cool things that they had seen on the field trip. Jason had 27 so far. Steven was starting to catch up, though.

2 As Luisa thought up more ideas, she gazed out the bus window and realized that the bus wasn't moving. She saw long lines of cars beside them and stretching around a curve in front of them.

3 "Hey, I wonder what's happening," she said, pointing out the window. "Everyone is stopped."

4 The bus driver heard Luisa and nodded his head. "This often happens on the outer edges of the city, especially on Friday afternoons. Everyone has to be somewhere, and right now they're all right here," he said, turning to frown, but in a friendly way, at Luisa.

5 Jason was a little worried. "What if we don't get back to school on time?"

6 "Oh, we have plenty of time," Mrs. Mason quickly assured him. "And if it does get late, the bus driver can radio the school and let them know what's happening. It'll be all right."

7 "Just look at them all," said Luisa, still gazing out the window. "How many do you think there are?"

8 "Let's see!" suggested Steven. "One, two, three, four, five, six, seven, eight...."

9 "Okay, okay," cut in Luisa, waving a hand at Steven, "that's annoying." She grinned at Steven, and Steven grinned right back.

10 Jason had a different thought. "I wonder where they're all going and where they came from." The three friends all looked out the window at the cars disappearing into the distance. Each of them wondered about all the different kinds of people and all of their different reasons for being here right now, clogging up the highway.

Write the best word to complete each sentence below.

1. Up ahead, the line of cars went around a _____.
   (curve, ledge, movement)

2. Jason was worried about the bus being _____. (hard, late, extra)

3. Steven wanted to _____ the cars. (spin, read, count)

4. Have you ever been stuck in traffic? Write about how it felt.

   _____

   _____

   _____

   _____

5. What might cause a traffic jam? List as many reasons as you can.

   _____

   _____

   _____

6. How do you think the bus driver feels about the traffic jam?
   _____ amused
   _____ joyful
   _____ frustrated

7. If the bus is late, what will the bus driver do?

   _____

   _____

8. Write **C** next to the sentence below that is the cause. Write **E** next to the
   sentence that is the effect.

   _____ Lots of cars are on the highway at the same time.

   _____ The cars are causing a traffic jam.

# How Many Are There?

*Read to see why we count things.*

[1] Look in any newspaper and you are likely to see numbers. We like to know how many inches of rain we've had, or how many students are in our schools. We want to know how much the city government is spending, or how many people have voted. We like to see numbers.

[2] Fortunately, many people like to count or keep track of things. They count traffic accidents and help us decide where to put stop signs and traffic lights. They count people to help us decide when we need more houses or more schools. They count how many people catch the flu and tell us when to get shots.

[3] Some numbers help us see that we need to change something. Other numbers show how things are changing. The numbers in the graph on this page show how the population and the number of cars in the United States have changed. How has the growth in population affected or changed the United States? How has the increase in the number of cars affected the country? Think about how this growth has affected you and your community.

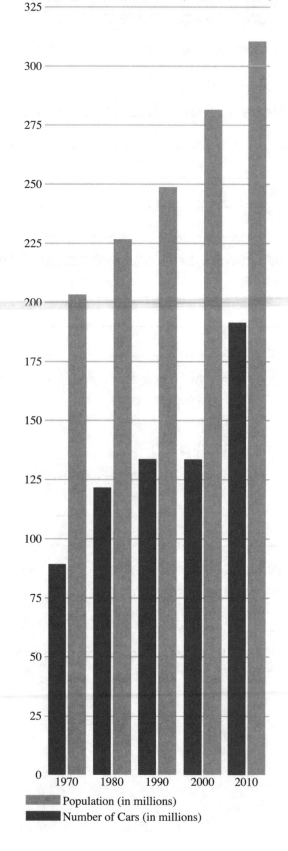

**Population and Number of Cars in the United States (1970–2010)**

Population (in millions)
Number of Cars (in millions)

1. What kinds of things do we count? List two examples from the article.

   _____

2. What do we learn from counting things?

   _____

   _____

3. How do you think the information shown in this graph affects you and your community?

   _____

   _____

4. What can the number of traffic accidents tell us?

   _____

   _____

5. How many years does this chart cover?

   _____

6. Why is the title of the chart important?

   _____

Use the bar graph to answer these questions.

7. For each year, which is greater, the population or the number of cars?

   _____

8. If you want population data for 1950, would this graph help you? How can you tell?

   _____

   _____

9. What was the population of the United States in 1970?

   _____

10. How many cars were there in 1990?

   _____

# Sidewalk Art

*How do a sister and brother fill a long, hot afternoon?*

1   I feel like a cactus. No, that's too dry. I feel like the glass greenhouse at the city park, all steamy and cloudy inside because the plants like it warm and moist. I feel like…

2   Oh, it's no use. I don't feel like anything. I'm just hot. It's hot outside. It's hot inside. There is nothing to do. I sit on the front steps of our building, trying to stay in a small triangle of shade. At the same time, I try to touch as little of the step as possible because everything feels hot and sticky, including my own skin.

3   I squint toward the sun to make bright, fuzzy patterns with my eyelashes. I watch a tree across the street. I can count on the fingers of one hand the number of leaves moving in the breeze. That's how weak the breeze is.

4   I try to think of something to do. I give myself a deadline. When the shade of my building gets to that crack in the sidewalk, I will do something. It happens slowly, just like everything else in the heat. When it gets close, I go down to the crack and watch. Yes, it's time. What should I do?

5   My brother Fujio's box of chalk is sitting forgotten at the bottom of the steps. I take out a piece of yellow chalk and make a blazing sun on the sidewalk. I surround it with white, then with every color in the chalk box.

6   Fujio appears at my side. "What's that, Tatsu?" he asks.

7   I don't say anything, but I write "Heat" at the bottom of my drawing. He just shrugs. Then, he gets the black chalk (his favorite color) and starts coloring. He fills a whole square of the sidewalk.

8   "What's that?" I ask.

9   "Shade," he says.

10   "Fujio, that's not…," I begin to say, but then I stop. It doesn't really matter. It's something to do, and that's a bonus on a hot day.

**1.** Tatsu is sitting in the shade on the front steps because

_____.

**2.** Tatsu titles her drawing "Heat" because

_____

_____.

**3.** Write **R** next to the sentences that tell about something real. Write **M** next to the sentences that are about made-up things.

_____ A person can make shade by drawing a picture of it.

_____ A person can draw a picture of heat.

_____ A person can draw a picture of the sun.

The **narrator** is the person who tells a story. Answer these questions.

**4.** Because the narrator is also a character, she uses the words *I* and *me* to tell her story. Find a place in the story where one of these words is used. Write the sentence here.

_____

_____

**5.** Where in the story do you discover what the narrator's name is?

_____

**6.** Do you think Tatsu and Fujio live in the city, in the country, or in a small town? Why?

_____

_____

**7.** From whose point of view is the story told?

_____ Tatsu's      _____ Fujio's      _____ Not enough information is given.

**8.** The author uses lots of descriptions to tell how hot it is. List three details from the story that help you imagine the heat.

_____

_____

_____

**9.** What do you like to do on a super hot summer day?

_____

# Wishes on the Sidewalk

*How do the children try to cool themselves off?*

1   It's late afternoon now, and it's getting a little better. The heat, I mean. The shade came around to the front of the building, so at least the sidewalk doesn't burn you anymore.

2   I tease Fujio about drawing a picture of shade. He's pretty cool about it. He just says, "It helped me think about not being hot."

3   I look at my own picture of the hot, hot sun. Maybe I should have tried it Fujio's way. Maybe my sun picture just makes it hotter here.

4   I see our neighbors Mario and Katie coming down the sidewalk. They stop and look at our pictures. Mario points at Fujio's black square and raises his eyebrows.

5   "Shade," sighs Fujio, as if he is tired of being an artist who is not understood. Mario wrinkles his brow for a moment, and then bends down and picks up the blue chalk. He begins at a corner, just like Fujio did, and covers a square with blue.

6   It's too hot to talk, so we just wait. We figure he'll explain. When Mario is done, he stands up and gives a little bow. "Cool water," he says. Fujio and I smile. Then, Katie jumps up and grabs the white chalk.

7   "Watch this, Tatsu," she says to me. Mario steps aside as Katie begins in the middle of a square. The square fills with white as the chalk gets smaller and smaller.

8   Finally, she stands. "A snow bank," she announces.

9   Fujio, Mario, and I cheer and clap. "Bravo! Bravo!"

10   Katie sits back down on the steps and leans back. I can tell she and the boys are thinking cool thoughts. I get up and make a big black "X" across my hot sun picture. Then, I go and sit right in the middle of Katie's snow bank. It's so cool it doesn't even melt.

**1.** Why do Mario and Katie choose to draw pictures of cool water and a snow bank?

_____

_____

**2.** Why does Tatsu cross out her own picture of the sun?

_____

_____

**3.** Which word best describes the group of friends?

_____ energetic

_____ creative

_____ anxious

**4.** Mario doesn't use words to ask Fujio what he drew. How does he ask instead?

_____

**5.** What is the author's purpose in writing this story?

_____ to teach      _____ to persuade      _____ to entertain

**6.** Why is the story titled "Wishes on the Sidewalk"?

_____

_____

_____

**7.** Do you think that thinking about cool things can help a person cool down? Write why or why not.

_____

_____

_____

**8.** Can you remember a hot day? How did it feel? Describe it so that someone else can imagine it easily.

_____

_____

_____

# Drawings on the Wall

*What might you have been doing if you lived 17,000 years ago?*

1   The year, if anyone were counting, would be around 15,000 B.C. You were probably looking for food, maybe using an animal skin to carry water, and possibly tending a fire to keep warm. Oh, and there's one other thing. You might have been drawing pictures on the walls of your cave.

2   We don't know why you drew the pictures. You had to go deep into the cave to do it, so you must have had a plan. You probably took a lamp made out of animal fat with you. Some of us think you drew pictures to bring good luck when you hunted. Others think the spears in some of the pictures mean that you were teaching other people to hunt.

3   For paint, you mixed animal fat with various things, such as dirt or berries. You used the ragged end of a stick to brush or dab the paint onto the wall. Sometimes, you didn't feel like using any color and you used the end of a stick that had been burned in the fire. It made broad black marks, much like modern artists make with chalk.

4   You drew what you saw around you—animals such as buffalo, deer, horses, and sometimes birds and fish. You drew people, but not very often. Sometimes, you made handprints or basic shape patterns on the wall.

5   You'll be happy to know that we think your pictures are really quite good. The buffalo look strong and powerful. And many of the horses and deer look graceful. You drew their shapes well.

6   We have found your drawings in more than 130 caves, mostly in France and England. We wonder if there are more that we haven't found yet. We wonder so many things, but we'll just have to satisfy ourselves with admiring your drawings. We're glad you made them.

**1.** This article is mostly about

_____ animals that lived thousands of years ago.

_____ early cave art.

_____ how early people survived.

**2.** What did early cave artists use for paint?

_____

**3.** Where did early artists make their drawings?

_____

**4.** Early cave art has been found in more than _____ caves.

**5.** How do you like the cave art shown on this page? How is it the same or different from other drawings you have seen of mammoths?

_____

_____

_____

**6.** Who is the author addressing, or talking to, in this article?

_____ the reader

_____ the people who made the cave paintings

_____ artists of today

**7.** Why is this an unusual way to write the article?

_____

_____

_____

**8.** Most of the cave drawings have been found in _____ and

_____.

**9.** What is the main idea of paragraph 4?

_____

_____

**10.** About how many years ago were the cave paintings made?

_____

# Phone Troubles

*What happens when Kyle doesn't pay attention to a telephone message?*

1 Somebody called for Mom. It was somebody from school. I didn't really catch the name. I said my mom was mowing the lawn, and so the lady asked if I could take a message. I said, "Sure."

2 Then, she started talking about cakes and Thursday after school and I said sure, cakes were great. I was trying to get my math homework done because Raj was waiting for me next door. Then, the lady said something about the principal and I said, "Sure, I know," because everyone knows the principal. Finally, she stopped talking and said, "Okay?"

3 I said, "Okay." Then, I remembered to say, "Thank you for calling," just like Mom taught me. Then, I hung up, finished my math, and headed for Raj's house.

4 I didn't remember the call until the next morning at breakfast. "Oh, you had a call yesterday while you were out mowing the lawn, Mom."

5 "Oh? Who was it, Kyle?" she said, between toast bites.

6 *Uhhh. Think, think.* "It was about Thursday after school," I said, announcing the only detail I could remember.

7 "What about it?" Mom was getting a little prickly. I knew I had to handle this well.

8 "There's a bake sale. The principal was asking for stuff." I felt good about remembering the principal.

9 Well, to make a long story short, it was the president of the PTO who called. Mom said she's very important. She was asking if Mom could bake a cake for the principal because they were going to surprise him for his birthday.

10 Mom showed up on Thursday after school with a little plate of cookies, thinking there was a bake sale. Mrs. Essman looked at her like she was from Mars and asked where the cake was. Of course, Mom didn't know anything about a cake or a birthday or anything. Now, I'm in the doghouse, and my brother and I have to learn telephone manners from Mom.

1. Number the sentences to show the order in which things happened.

   _____ Kyle gives Mom the phone message.

   _____ Mom goes to school on Thursday.

   _____ Mom goes out to mow the lawn.

   _____ Kyle takes a phone call for Mom.

   _____ Mrs. Essman asks Mom where the cake is.

2. Why does Mom take cookies to school on Thursday?

   _____

   _____

3. While he is talking on the phone, Kyle is also _____

   _____.

4. What is the setting for this story?

   _____

   _____

5. What type of story is this?

   _____ realistic fiction     _____ science fiction     _____ a tall tale

6. In paragraph 7, the author says that Mom is getting a little prickly. What does this mean?

   _____

   _____

7. What do you think Kyle will do the next time he answers the phone? Why?

   _____

   _____

8. Do you think it was fair for Kyle's mom to be frustrated with him? Explain.

   _____

   _____

   _____

# Phone Manners

*What telephone manners does Mom teach her sons?*

1 "Now, repeat after me. When we answer the phone, we say: 'Hello. Reese residence. This is so-and-so speaking.'"

2 My brother and I repeated after Mom in slow, droning tones, "Hello. Reese residence. This is Kyle-thony speaking." We each said our names in the "so-and-so" spot, so Kyle and Anthony came out *Kyle-thony*. I thought about giggling, but the look on Mom's face told me not to.

3 "That's very good." Mom was talking to us as if we were four-year-olds. "Now," she continued, "if the person on the other end of the phone says, 'May I speak to your mother?', what do you say? Kyle?" I knew this one.

4 I recited just like Mom had taught us. "Yes, you may. May I ask who is calling, please?"

5 "That's very good," said Mom in her sing-songy teacher voice. "Okay, you seem to have the basics. Let's talk about taking phone messages." She shot me a look. I had goofed up on one little phone message the other day. That's why my brother and I were in the Phone Manners from Mom class. "What are the three basic parts of a phone message?"

6 Anthony and I recited: "Name. Number. Write it down."

7 "Very good," sang Mom. "Oh, and there's actually a fourth part. Can anyone figure out what it is?" She looked right at me. I couldn't think.

8 "Deliver the message," Mom answered her own question, "on the same day the call comes in." I smiled weakly. That was a small detail that I had overlooked the other day, along with name, number, and writing it down.

9 "Any questions?" Mom asked brightly. Anthony raised his hand. "Yes?"

10 "Will there be a test?"

11 "Every time the phone rings," said Mom, quite seriously. "Class dismissed."

1. What important parts of a phone message did Kyle forget the other day?

   _____

   _____

2. Look at the illustration. What do you think Mom is saying? Write the dialogue.

   _____

   _____

3. Why is Mom talking to the boys as though they are four years old?

   _____

   _____

4. Look at the picture of Kyle and Anthony. What do you learn about the boys from the picture that isn't in the story?

   _____

   _____

5. How will the boys be tested?

   _____

   _____

6. Do you think Mom's phone class will be a success? Why or why not?

   _____

   _____

You have just attended the Phone Manners from Mom class. How should you respond to these telephone situations?

7. The phone rings. You answer it by saying, "_____

   _____."

8. Your dad is reading a book on the porch. The phone rings and the person says, "May I speak to your father?" What do you say?

   _____

9. Your mom is washing her hair and can't come to the phone, so you must take a message. What are the four important parts of a phone message?

   _____

# Hold the Phone!

*What do the boys notice about Uncle Dale?*

1 Kyle hung up the phone and tore the top sheet off the message pad. He posted it in the middle of the refrigerator door with his favorite magnet. Ever since Mom's Phone Manners class, he had followed the rules: Get the name. Get the number. Write it down. Deliver it.

2 As Kyle positioned the polar bear magnet, his uncle Dale walked into the kitchen. "Hey, Uncle Dale. What's up?"

3 "Oh, not much," shrugged Uncle Dale. "Your mom invited me over for supper." Uncle Dale often dropped by just in time for a meal.

4 "Oh, cool," said Kyle, on his way out the door with Anthony. Just then, the phone rang. Uncle Dale answered it.

5 "Yeah?" he said. Kyle and Anthony froze. Their mom had taught them not to say "yeah" on the phone. She said it was bad manners. They wondered how Uncle Dale had missed that lesson. "Yeah." Uncle Dale said again and nodded. "Yeah, okay." Silence. "Sure." He hung up.

6 After a moment, Anthony was too curious not to ask. "Who was that?"

7 "It was for your mom," said Uncle Dale, paging through a magazine. Kyle and Anthony looked at each other.

8 "Um, there's a message pad here," offered Kyle, "if you want to write a message down."

9 Uncle Dale looked up for a moment. "Oh, it's okay. I'll remember. It was someone from school about a meeting."

10 "What meeting?" asked Mom, peeling off her garden gloves at the kitchen door. Uncle Dale looked up.

11 "Oh, hi, Sis. Ahh, there's a meeting … on Saturday morning." Uncle Dale's face suddenly looked a little pained.

12 "Where? What about?" asked Mom. Kyle and Anthony grilled their teeth.

13 "Oh, you know, one of those school meetings," said Uncle Dale slowly. "It starts at 9:30…I think."

14 Mom made a face. She looked at her sons. All three of them turned to Uncle Dale and recited: "Get the name! Get the number! Write it down! Deliver it!"

1. What surprised Kyle and Anthony about Uncle Dale's phone conversation?

_____ the fact that he had even answered the phone

_____ the way he spoke

_____ the length of the conversation

2. Number the sentences to show the order in which events happened.

_____ Uncle Dale gets a lesson on how to take phone messages.

_____ Uncle Dale arrives.

_____ Uncle Dale answers the phone.

_____ Kyle takes a phone message.

_____ Mom enters the kitchen.

_____ Kyle greets Uncle Dale.

3. Why does Uncle Dale's face look a little pained in paragraph 11?

_____

_____

4. Why are Kyle and Anthony not supposed to say "yeah" on the phone?

_____

_____

5. How are Uncle Dale and Mom related to each other?

_____

_____

6. Do you think that Uncle Dale will use better phone manners in the future? Explain.

_____

_____

# Telephones: How Do They Work?

*Read to find out how telephones work.*

1  We're going to take a little trip. We're going to travel with your voice as it leaves your mouth, goes through a telephone, moves through the telephone network, and arrives at your friend's telephone.

2  Let's say you already dialed the telephone. A computer instantly connected you to your friend's telephone, based on the numbers you pressed. The sound waves made by your voice enter the microphone in your telephone. The sound waves then travel by wire. With the help of an electric power supply, an electric current runs along the wire. Your sound waves disrupt that flow of electricity. When the current is flowing smoothly, your friend hears no sound. When your sound waves have affected the flow, the varying electrical current reaches the speaker in the earpiece of your friend's telephone. A device there changes the electrical currents back into sound waves. The sound waves enter your friend's ear, and your conversation has begun.

3  As technology goes, telephones are thought to be quite simple. People knew almost 400 years ago that sound waves could travel along a wire. Then, in 1875, Alexander Graham Bell invented a telephone that could be put to practical use. Imagine what he would think if he could see his fellow Americans on the telephone today.

1. The article says it's not your voice, but _____ made by your voice, that enter the telephone's microphone.

2. When the current in a telephone wire is flowing smoothly, what does the person on the other end hear?

   _____

3. When sound waves interrupt the flow of current, what does the person on the other end hear?

   _____

4. How long ago did people know that sound could travel along a wire?

   _____

5. How long ago did Alexander Graham Bell invent the telephone?

   _____

Write **F** next to each sentence that is a fact. Write **O** next to each sentence that is an opinion.

6. _____ Sound waves travel along a wire with the help of an electrical current.

7. _____ The telephone is the most important invention of the last 200 years.

8. _____ Without the telephone, modern businesses would fail.

9. How does the computer know to connect you to the person you are trying to call?

   _____

10. **Telephones have been around for less than a hundred years.** Is this statement true or false?

   _____

11. How do you and other members of your family use the telephone today?

   _____

   _____

12. What would it be like if you had to get along without telephones? How else would you communicate?

   _____

   _____

# Math Grade 3 Answers

## Chapter 1

### Lesson 1.1, page 6

|    | a  | b  | c  | d  | e  | f  |
|----|----|----|----|----|----|----|
| 1. | 5  | 16 | 7  | 8  | 3  | 14 |
| 2. | 9  | 6  | 9  | 11 | 7  | 13 |
| 3. | 7  | 11 | 14 | 11 | 14 | 6  |
| 4. | 0  | 11 | 14 | 7  | 8  | 12 |
| 5. | 7  | 4  | 6  | 10 | 16 | 9  |
| 6. | 20 | 15 | 20 | 15 | 18 | 12 |

### Lesson 1.2, page 7

|    | a  | b  | c  | d  | e  | f  |
|----|----|----|----|----|----|----|
| 1. | 5  | 6  | 1  | 5  | 7  | 5  |
| 2. | 3  | 3  | 3  | 8  | 9  | 2  |
| 3. | 5  | 3  | 6  | 3  | 7  | 7  |
| 4. | 11 | 1  | 16 | 8  | 5  | 13 |
| 5. | 7  | 2  | 1  | 9  | 4  | 6  |
| 6. | 2  | 17 | 8  | 4  | 1  | 6  |

### Lesson 1.3, page 8

|    | a  | b  | c  | d  | e  | f  |
|----|----|----|----|----|----|----|
| 1. | 39 | 33 | 30 | 28 | 88 | 76 |
| 2. | 27 | 48 | 27 | 83 | 92 | 55 |
| 3. | 26 | 47 | 59 | 80 | 77 | 44 |
| 4. | 59 | 55 | 56 | 48 | 69 | 69 |
| 5. | 27 | 58 | 65 | 93 | 97 | 58 |
| 6. | 53 | 93 | 99 | 65 | 68 | 77 |

### Lesson 1.4, page 9

|    | a  | b  | c  | d  | e  | f  |
|----|----|----|----|----|----|----|
| 1. | 11 | 64 | 22 | 20 | 81 | 32 |
| 2. | 52 | 70 | 21 | 42 | 12 | 56 |
| 3. | 41 | 22 | 27 | 13 | 44 | 30 |
| 4. | 41 | 21 | 12 | 22 | 21 | 12 |
| 5. | 30 | 21 | 11 | 54 | 21 | 16 |
| 6. | 10 | 16 | 23 | 31 | 61 | 41 |

### Lesson 1.5, page 10

|    | a  | b  | c  | d  | e  | f  |
|----|----|----|----|----|----|----|
| 1. | 41 | 91 | 90 | 52 | 81 | 48 |
| 2. | 63 | 91 | 64 | 80 | 83 | 72 |
| 3. | 81 | 81 | 45 | 32 | 56 | 70 |
| 4. | 81 | 45 | 81 | 31 | 90 | 54 |
| 5. | 80 | 45 | 41 | 52 | 54 | 91 |
| 6. | 46 | 61 | 70 | 51 | 60 | 91 |

### Lesson 1.6, page 11

|    | a  | b  | c  | d  | e  | f  |
|----|----|----|----|----|----|----|
| 1. | 8  | 3  | 25 | 14 | 36 | 59 |
| 2. | 17 | 6  | 34 | 19 | 17 | 19 |
| 3. | 35 | 15 | 46 | 29 | 25 | 24 |
| 4. | 7  | 40 | 59 | 67 | 35 | 19 |
| 5. | 48 | 27 | 23 | 57 | 36 | 19 |
| 6. | 36 | 47 | 68 | 55 | 18 | 39 |

### Lesson 1.7, page 12

|    | a  | b  | c  | d  | e  | f  |
|----|----|----|----|----|----|----|
| 1. | 84 | 92 | 64 | 68 | 48 | 90 |
| 2. | 98 | 72 | 60 | 53 | 71 | 84 |
| 3. | 83 | 52 | 19 | 91 | 74 | 85 |
| 4. | 96 | 92 | 93 | 66 | 91 | 89 |
| 5. | 95 | 68 | 91 | 55 | 58 | 75 |

## Chapter 2

### Lesson 2.1, page 13

|    | a   | b   | c   | d   | e   | f   |
|----|-----|-----|-----|-----|-----|-----|
| 1. | 118 | 103 | 140 | 118 | 110 | 162 |
| 2. | 94  | 119 | 105 | 113 | 158 | 114 |
| 3. | 102 | 119 | 161 | 115 | 127 | 121 |
| 4. | 114 | 104 | 119 | 102 | 105 | 170 |
| 5. | 100 | 107 | 120 | 111 | 139 | 86  |
| 6. | 139 | 187 | 150 | 118 | 126 | 139 |

### Lesson 2.2, page 14

|    | a   | b   | c   | d   | e   | f   |
|----|-----|-----|-----|-----|-----|-----|

| | a | b | c | d | e | f |
|---|---|---|---|---|---|---|
| 1. | 140 | 61 | 151 | 111 | 94 | 92 |
| 2. | 81 | 110 | 104 | 111 | 121 | 145 |
| 3. | 141 | 44 | 120 | 93 | 91 | 111 |
| 4. | 81 | 134 | 121 | 94 | 62 | 80 |
| 5. | 43 | 101 | 80 | 141 | 127 | 92 |
| 6. | 114 | 122 | 120 | 94 | 88 | 77 |
| 7. | 93 | 124 | 92 | 70 | 122 | 71 |

**Lesson 2.2, page 15**

| | a | b | c | d | e | f |
|---|---|---|---|---|---|---|
| 1. | 89 | 78 | 88 | 86 | 77 | 39 |
| 2. | 79 | 79 | 67 | 66 | 68 | 86 |
| 3. | 26 | 8 | 48 | 89 | 69 | 88 |
| 4. | 78 | 58 | 69 | 86 | 59 | 76 |
| 5. | 28 | 58 | 29 | 58 | 74 | 87 |
| 6. | 85 | 69 | 79 | 75 | 87 | 58 |
| 7. | 79 | 89 | 57 | 88 | 78 | 87 |

**Lesson 2.3, page 16**

| | a | b | c | d | e | f |
|---|---|---|---|---|---|---|
| 1. | 685 | 1,153 | 933 | 1,123 | 444 | 1,656 |
| 2. | 1,175 | 1,030 | 1,570 | 1,042 | 1,280 | 868 |
| 3. | 1,282 | 1,001 | 681 | 973 | 1,356 | 1,194 |
| 4. | 982 | 944 | 367 | 404 | 414 | 1,234 |
| 5. | 1,424 | 850 | 1,378 | 1,350 | 446 | 812 |
| 6. | 1,334 | 1,070 | 880 | 1,251 | 1,125 | 839 |
| 7. | 465 | 922 | 1,334 | 521 | 967 | 874 |

**Lesson 2.4, page 17**

| | a | b | c | d | e | f |
|---|---|---|---|---|---|---|
| 1. | 212 | 593 | 489 | 120 | 480 | 148 |
| 2. | 408 | 206 | 279 | 106 | 377 | 190 |
| 3. | 331 | 399 | 519 | 189 | 577 | 321 |
| 4. | 114 | 208 | 529 | 171 | 448 | 220 |
| 5. | 86 | 627 | 25 | 350 | 86 | 838 |
| 6. | 281 | 349 | 225 | 336 | 129 | 485 |

**Lesson 2.5, page 18**

| | a | b | c | d | e | f |
|---|---|---|---|---|---|---|
| 1. | 369 | 901 | 417 | 732 | 521 | 290 |
| 2. | 1,108 | 606 | 1,075 | 1,005 | 397 | 476 |
| 3. | 847 | 711 | 931 | 550 | 531 | 506 |
| 4. | 1,055 | 589 | 812 | 902 | 382 | 695 |

**Lesson 2.6, page 19**

| | a | b | c | d | e | f |
|---|---|---|---|---|---|---|
| 1. | 570 | 238 | 33 | 326 | 165 | 222 |
| 2. | 121 | 15 | 226 | 112 | 129 | 296 |
| 3. | 399 | 220 | 106 | 263 | 264 | 405 |
| 4. | 187 | 462 | 437 | 303 | 215 | 198 |

**Chapter 3**

**Lesson 3.1, page 20**

| | a | b | c | d | e | f |
|---|---|---|---|---|---|---|
| 1. | 18 | 20 | 31 | 44 | 97 | 16 |
| 2. | 133 | 153 | 123 | 83 | 142 | 150 |
| 3. | 251 | 120 | 120 | 223 | 157 | 55 |
| 4. | 163 | 183 | 188 | 39 | 120 | 212 |
| 5. | 224 | 202 | 215 | 73 | 181 | 202 |

**Lesson 3.2, page 21**

| | a | b | c | d | e | f |
|---|---|---|---|---|---|---|
| 1. | 1,040 | 1,594 | 650 | 1,794 | 1,616 | 914 |
| 2. | 1,612 | 973 | 2,417 | 445 | 1,100 | 723 |
| 3. | 2,027 | 2,158 | 1,489 | 1,673 | 1,239 | 1,867 |
| 4. | 660 | 1,612 | 1,285 | 1,279 | 1,802 | 1,353 |
| 5. | 2,533 | 1,487 | 1,980 | 525 | 1,774 | 2,280 |

**Lesson 3.2, page 22**

1. 135; 213; 159; 507
2. 186; 175; 182; 543 **3.** 2,325 **4.** 442

**Lesson 3.3, page 23**

| | a | b | c | d | e | f |
|---|---|---|---|---|---|---|
| 1. | 9,057 | 9,873 | 7,389 | 7,464 | 9,469 | 9,803 |
| 2. | 3,764 | 9,990 | 9,311 | 7,296 | 9,793 | 8,052 |
| 3. | 7,757 | 9,281 | 8,405 | 4,065 | 9,173 | 8,485 |
| 4. | 8,420 | 9,465 | 3,578 | 8,874 | 9,717 | 9,512 |

# Math Grade 3 Answers

**5.** 7,413 9,232 5,532 9,044 9,768 6,708
**6.** 7,437 7,309 6,858 9,914 9,292 9,905

## Lesson 3.3, page 24
**1.** 1,523; 1,695; 3,218
**2.** 1,200; 1,320; 2,520 **3.** 2,122 **4.** 2,600

## Lesson 3.4, page 25

|    | a | b | c | d | e |
|----|------|------|------|------|------|
| **1.** | 7483 | 6736 | 4661 | 1742 | 894 |
| **2.** | 1882 | 8080 | 6982 | 7882 | 3872 |
| **3.** | 4092 | 595 | 1582 | 5291 | 7481 |
| **4.** | 6891 | 2795 | 7492 | 3493 | 2791 |
| **5.** | 8891 | 2893 | 1781 | 2892 | 7641 |
| **6.** | 4672 | 3480 | 6891 | 3294 | 4573 |

## Lesson 3.4, page 26
**1.** 2,532; 1,341; 1,191
**2.** 1,250; 495; 755
**3.** 1,986; 103; 1,883 **4.** 54 **5.** 191

## Lesson 3.5, page 27

|    | a | b | c | d |
|----|-------|-------|-------|-------|
| **1.** | 960 | 150 | 190 | 4,030 |
| **2.** | 130 | 3,450 | 8,660 | 7,990 |
| **3.** | 8,800 | 1,000 | 3,300 | 7,900 |
| **4.** | 500 | 1,300 | 800 | 4,400 |
| **5.** | 8,600 | 1,900 | 360 | 1,540 |
| **6.** | 1,900 | 770 | 900 | 90 |
| **7.** | 450 | 8,710 | 500 | 5,330 |
| **8.** | 3,700 | 120 | 490 | 2,400 |

## Lesson 3.5, page 28

|    | a | b | c | d |
|----|-------|-------|-------|-------|
| **1.** | 540 | 800 | 480 | 960 |
| **2.** | 5,700 | 9,650 | 7,400 | 1,610 |
| **3.** | 600 | 90 | 5,400 | 980 |
| **4.** | 4,930 | 9,700 | 600 | 700 |
| **5.** | 1,100 | 7,090 | 7,450 | 1,140 |

**6.** 4,600 3,900 5,100 700
**7.** 90 960 7,700 540
**8.** 300 720 150 800

## Lesson 3.6, page 29

|    | a | b | c | d |
|----|------|------|-------|------|
| **1.** | 70 | 30 | 110 | 130 |
| **2.** | 140 | 170 | 260 | 250 |
| **3.** | 500 | 500 | 1100 | 800 |
| **4.** | 1500 | 1600 | 6200 | 5300 |
| **5.** | 5000 | 1300 | 12000 | 5000 |

## Lesson 3.6, page 30
**1.** 900 **2.** 30 **3.** 800 **4.** 130 **5.** 500

## Lesson 3.7, page 31

|    | a | b | c | d |
|----|------|------|------|------|
| **1.** | 20 | 40 | 10 | 30 |
| **2.** | 380 | 930 | 730 | 480 |
| **3.** | 200 | 400 | 300 | 500 |
| **4.** | 800 | 2400 | 4100 | 7000 |
| **5.** | 5000 | 6000 | 1000 | 8000 |

## Lesson 3.7, page 32
**1.** 20 **2.** 100 **3.** 200 **4.** 110 **5.** 110

# Chapter 4

## Lesson 4.1, page 33

|    | a | b | c | d | e |
|----|----|----|----|----|----|
| **1.** | 6 | 14 | 12 | 18 | 16 |
| **2.** | 4 | 2 | 15 | 18 | 9 |
| **3.** | 6 | 3 | 12 | 21 | 8 |
| **4.** | 16 | 4 | 20 | 36 | 32 |
| **5.** | 12 | 8 | 10 | 24 | 27 |
| **6.** | 24 | 28 | 6 | 21 | 18 |

## Lesson 4.2, page 34

|    | a | b | c | d | e | f |
|----|----|----|----|----|----|----|
| **1.** | 10 | 15 | 3 | 4 | 12 | 10 |
| **2.** | 0 | 1 | 15 | 4 | 0 | 12 |

# Math Grade 3 Answers

| | | | | | | |
|---|---|---|---|---|---|---|
| **3.** | 16 | 10 | 20 | 6 | 25 | 0 |
| **4.** | 8 | 0 | 9 | 16 | 6 | 2 |
| **5.** | 0 | 9 | 8 | 0 | 6 | 20 |
| **6.** | 5 | 0 | 3 | 25 | 0 | 8 |

## Lesson 4.3, page 35

**1.** 4; 5; 20 **2.** 3; 2; 6 **3.** 4; 2; 8

**4.** Answers may vary—solution is 5

**5.** Answers may vary—solution is 12

## Lesson 4.4, page 36

| | a | b | c | d | e | f |
|---|---|---|---|---|---|---|
| **1.** | 0 | 27 | 30 | 4 | 5 | 18 |
| **2.** | 18 | 40 | 40 | 0 | 18 | 12 |
| **3.** | 24 | 21 | 6 | 14 | 15 | 4 |
| **4.** | 12 | 25 | 9 | 8 | 21 | 0 |
| **5.** | 0 | 18 | 35 | 30 | 6 | 8 |
| **6.** | 28 | 9 | 9 | 14 | 0 | 3 |

## Lesson 4.5, page 37

| | a | b | c | d | e | f |
|---|---|---|---|---|---|---|
| **1.** | 27 | 42 | 20 | 63 | 48 | 0 |
| **2.** | 12 | 40 | 36 | 0 | 35 | 18 |
| **3.** | 5 | 24 | 16 | 48 | 0 | 0 |
| **4.** | 3 | 24 | 18 | 12 | 18 | 30 |
| **5.** | 24 | 18 | 42 | 81 | 32 | 15 |
| **6.** | 12 | 64 | 27 | 28 | 0 | 49 |

## Lesson 4.6, page 38

**1.** 6; 5; 30 **2.** 7; 9; 63

**3.** 4; 8; 32

**4.** Answers may vary—solution is 35

**5.** Answers may vary—solution is 36

## Lesson 4.7, page 39

| | a | b | c | d | e | f |
|---|---|---|---|---|---|---|
| **1.** | 90 | 20 | 90 | 240 | 160 | 490 |
| **2.** | 200 | 400 | 540 | 80 | 400 | 480 |
| **3.** | 180 | 50 | 140 | 150 | 210 | 150 |
| **4.** | 80 | 30 | 360 | 630 | 120 | 250 |

## Lesson 4.7, page 40

| | a | b | c | d | e | f |
|---|---|---|---|---|---|---|
| **1.** | 100 | 150 | 30 | 40 | 120 | 100 |
| **2.** | 150 | 40 | 180 | 40 | 210 | 120 |
| **3.** | 160 | 160 | 240 | 140 | 300 | 250 |
| **4.** | 320 | 0 | 350 | 360 | 60 | 80 |
| **5.** | 140 | 240 | 180 | 300 | 480 | 320 |
| **6.** | 450 | 630 | 30 | 450 | 0 | 160 |
| **7.** | 180 | 560 | 540 | 490 | 640 | 240 |
| **8.** | 350 | 810 | 270 | 360 | 560 | 210 |

## Lesson 4.8, page 41

**1.** 60; 3; 180 **2.** 20; 4; 80

**3.** 30; 4; 120 **4.** 20 **5.** 60

## Lesson 4.9, page 42

**1.** 84 **2.** 70 **3.** 25 **4.** 98

## Chapter 5

## Lesson 5.1, page 43

**1.** 12; 2 **2.** 24; 3 **3.** 36; 9 **4.** 4; 8; 2

**5.** 7; 35; 5 **6.** 20; 4 **7.** 27; 3 **8.** 6; 3

**9.** 3; 15; 5 **10.** 2 ; 14 ; 7

## Lesson 5.1, page 44

**1a.** 4; 4; 4 × 3 = 12

**1b.** 3; 3; 3 × 4 = 12

**2a.** 4; 5; 5; 5 × 4 = 20

**2b.** 5; 4; 4; 4 × 5 = 20

**3a.** 12; 2; 6; 6; 6 × 2 = 12

**3b.** 12; 6; 2; 2; 2 × 6 = 12

## Lesson 5.2, page 45

**1a.** 2; 3 × 2 = 6 **1b.** 7; 2 × 7 = 14

**1c.** 5; 1 × 5 = 5 **1d.** 2; 2 × 2 = 4

**1e.** 4; 1 × 4 = 4 **2a.** 9; 3 × 9 = 27

**2b.** 3; 1 × 3 = 3 **2c.** 9; 2 × 9 = 18

**2d.** 7; 1 × 7 = 7 **2e.** 7; 3 × 7 = 21

**3a.** 4; 3 × 4 = 12 **3b.** 8; 2 × 8 = 16

# Math Grade 3 Answers

**3c.** 5; 1 × 5 = 5 **3d.** 6; 3 × 6 = 18
**3e.** 5; 2 × 5 = 10 **4a.** 6; 1 × 6 = 6
**4b.** 8; 1 × 8 = 8 **4c.** 4; 2 × 4 = 8
**4d.** 2; 1 × 2 = 2 **4e.** 1; 1 × 1 = 1
**5a.** 8; 3 × 8 = 24 **5b.** 3; 3 × 3 = 9
**5c.** 9; 1 × 9 = 9 **5d.** 3; 2 × 3 = 6
**5e.** 1; 2 × 1 = 2

## Lesson 5.3, page 46

**1a.** 9 ; 6 × 9 = 54 **1b.** 9 ; 3 × 9 = 27
**1c.** 8 ; 6 × 8 = 48 **1d.** 5 ; 5 × 5 = 25
**1e.** 9 ; 4 × 9 = 36 **2a.** 6 ; 5 × 6 = 30
**2b.** 6 ; 4 × 6 = 24 **2c.** 8 ; 4 × 8 = 32
**2d.** 4 ; 4 × 4 = 16 **2e.** 5 ; 4 × 5 = 20

|       | a | b | c | d | e |
|-------|---|---|---|---|---|
| **3.** | 6 | 7 | 7 | 4 | 7 |
| **4.** | 9 | 2 | 8 | 8 | 3 |
| **5.** | 4 | 8 | 3 | 9 | 3 |
| **6.** | 3 | 7 | 6 | 1 | 9 |

## Lesson 5.3, page 47

**1.** 24; 6; 4 **2.** 30; 6; 5 **3.** 42; 6; 7
**4.** 3 **5.** 8

## Lesson 5.4, page 48

**1a.** 1; 7 × 1 = 7 **1b.** 4; 6 × 4 = 24
**1c.** 7; 8 × 7 = 56 **1d.** 5; 6 × 5 = 30
**1e.** 8; 8 × 8 = 64 **2a.** 2; 6 × 2 = 12
**2b.** 5; 7 × 5 = 35 **2c.** 3; 8 × 3 = 24
**2d.** 4; 7 × 4 = 28 **2e.** 6; 6 × 6 = 36

|       | a | b | c | d | e |
|-------|---|---|---|---|---|
| **3.** | 7 | 9 | 8 | 7 | 3 |
| **4.** | 2 | 2 | 3 | 6 | 5 |
| **5.** | 7 | 2 | 3 | 1 | 6 |
| **6.** | 3 | 6 | 1 | 9 | 5 |

## Lesson 5.4, page 49

**1.** 72; 9; 8 **2.** 40; 8; 5 **3.** 16; 8; 2 **4.** 9

## Lesson 5.5, page 50

|        | a | b | c | d | e |
|--------|---|---|---|---|---|
| **1.** | 5 | 4 | 3 | 9 | 3 |
| **2.** | 9 | 9 | 8 | 7 | 1 |
| **3.** | 8 | 7 | 4 | 7 | 9 |
| **4.** | 2 | 2 | 5 | 3 | 3 |
| **5.** | 6 | 5 | 1 | 9 | 3 |
| **6.** | 4 | 9 | 4 | 6 | 9 |
| **7.** | 1 | 8 | 6 | 9 | 8 |
| **8.** | 6 | 5 | 7 | 6 | 5 |
| **9.** | 3 | 4 | 9 | 2 | 1 |
| **10.** | 7 | 7 | 9 | 2 | 7 |

## Lesson 5.6, page 51

|        | a | b | c | d | e | f |
|--------|---|---|---|---|---|---|
| **1.** | 2 | 2 | 9 | 9 | 9 | 2 |
| **2.** | 5 | 6 | 3 | 3 | 8 | 4 |
| **3.** | 8 | 3 | 4 | 7 | 1 | 6 |
| **4.** | 6 | 2 | 9 | 1 | 4 | 5 |
| **5.** | 100 | 60 | 320 | 20 | 50 | 270 |
| **6.** | 42 | 300 | 400 | 90 | 280 | 80 |
| **7.** | 60 | 70 | 350 | 480 | 180 | 18 |
| **8.** | 400 | 280 | 140 | 160 | 200 | 270 |

## Lesson 5.7, page 52

**1.** 6 **2.** 40 **3.** 11 **4.** 7

## Chapter 6

## Lesson 6.1, page 53

|        | a | b | c |
|--------|---|---|---|
| **1.** | $\frac{1}{3}$ | $\frac{3}{4}$ | $\frac{4}{5}$ |
| **2.** | $\frac{1}{10}$ | $\frac{3}{8}$ | $\frac{1}{2}$ |
| **3.** | $\frac{2}{3}$ | $\frac{4}{8}$ | $\frac{2}{5}$ |
| **4.** | $\frac{2}{4}$ | $\frac{3}{5}$ | $\frac{4}{10}$ |

## Lesson 6.2, page 54

|        | a | b | c |
|--------|---|---|---|
| **3.** | $\frac{4}{5}$ | $\frac{1}{4}$ | $\frac{4}{8}$ |

# Math Grade 3 Answers

**3.** $\frac{1}{10}$     $\frac{2}{3}$     $\frac{3}{8}$

**3.** $\frac{1}{2}$     $\frac{2}{5}$     $\frac{9}{10}$

| | a | b | c | d |
|---|---|---|---|---|

**4.**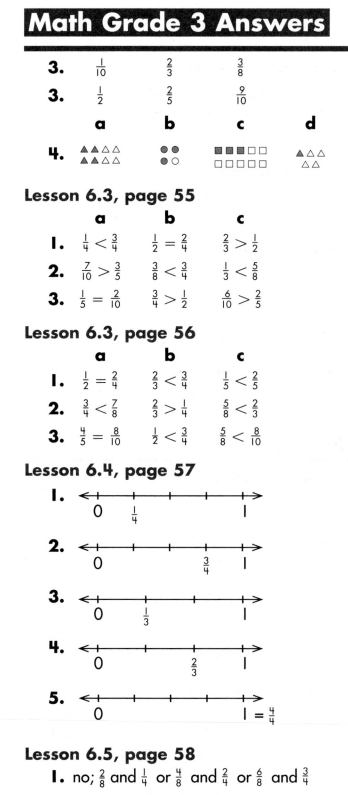

## Lesson 6.3, page 55

| | a | b | c |
|---|---|---|---|
| **1.** | $\frac{1}{4} < \frac{3}{4}$ | $\frac{1}{2} = \frac{2}{4}$ | $\frac{2}{3} > \frac{1}{2}$ |
| **2.** | $\frac{7}{10} > \frac{3}{5}$ | $\frac{3}{8} < \frac{3}{4}$ | $\frac{1}{3} < \frac{5}{8}$ |
| **3.** | $\frac{1}{5} = \frac{2}{10}$ | $\frac{3}{4} > \frac{1}{2}$ | $\frac{6}{10} > \frac{2}{5}$ |

## Lesson 6.3, page 56

| | a | b | c |
|---|---|---|---|
| **1.** | $\frac{1}{2} = \frac{2}{4}$ | $\frac{2}{3} < \frac{3}{4}$ | $\frac{1}{5} < \frac{2}{5}$ |
| **2.** | $\frac{3}{4} < \frac{7}{8}$ | $\frac{2}{3} > \frac{1}{4}$ | $\frac{5}{8} < \frac{2}{3}$ |
| **3.** | $\frac{4}{5} = \frac{8}{10}$ | $\frac{1}{2} < \frac{3}{4}$ | $\frac{5}{8} < \frac{8}{10}$ |

## Lesson 6.4, page 57

**1.** number line: 0, $\frac{1}{4}$, 1

**2.** number line: 0, $\frac{3}{4}$, 1

**3.** number line: 0, $\frac{1}{3}$, 1

**4.** number line: 0, $\frac{2}{3}$, 1

**5.** number line: 0, $1 = \frac{4}{4}$

## Lesson 6.5, page 58

**1.** no; $\frac{2}{8}$ and $\frac{1}{4}$ or $\frac{4}{8}$ and $\frac{2}{4}$ or $\frac{6}{8}$ and $\frac{3}{4}$

**2.** no; $\frac{1}{3}$ and $\frac{2}{6}$ or $\frac{2}{3}$ and $\frac{4}{6}$

## Lesson 6.6, page 59

**1.** $\frac{4}{4}$ **2.** $\frac{3}{3}$ **3.** $\frac{2}{2}$ **4.** $\frac{5}{5}$ **5.** $\frac{10}{10}$ **6.** $\frac{8}{8}$

---

# Chapter 7

## Lesson 7.1, page 60

**1.** 90 kilograms **2.** 500 liters
**3.** 5,000 grams **4.** 1 gram **5.** 46
**6.** 2 **7.** 7 **8.** 10

## Lesson 7.1, page 61

**1.** 1,000 liters **2.** 1 gram **3.** 2 liters
**4.** 700 grams **5.** 36 **6.** 100 **7.** 24 **8.** 5

## Lesson 7.2, page 62

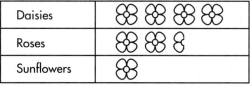

**Flowers In My Garden**

| Daisies | |
|---|---|
| Roses | |
| Sunflowers | |

Key: = 2 flowers

15 total flowers

## Lesson 7.3, page 63

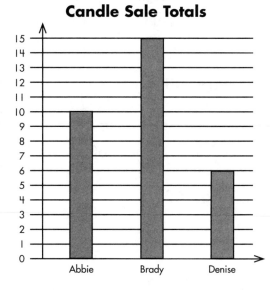

**Candle Sale Totals**

9 more candles

# Math Grade 3 Answers

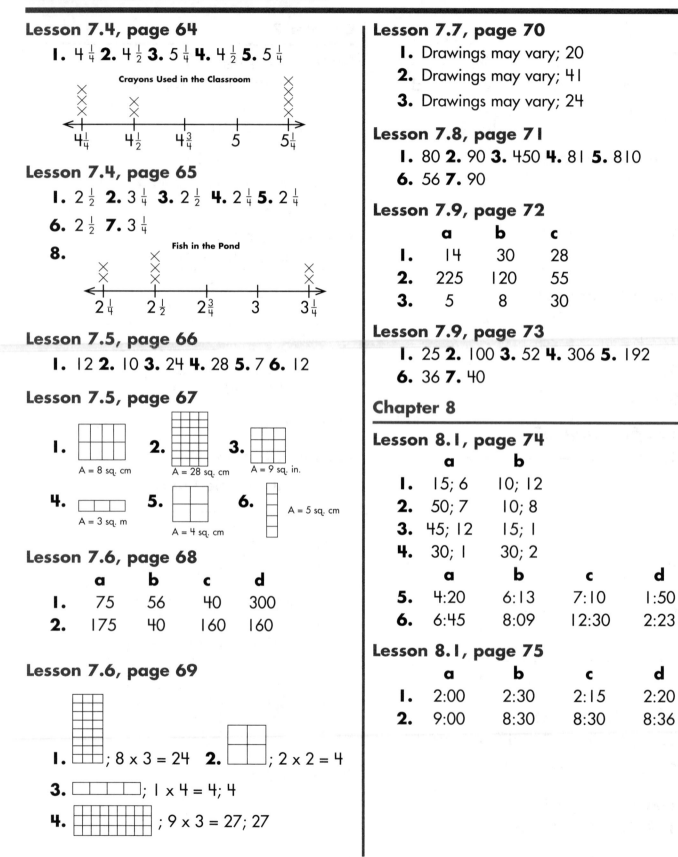

**Lesson 7.4, page 64**

1. $4\frac{1}{4}$ 2. $4\frac{1}{2}$ 3. $5\frac{1}{4}$ 4. $4\frac{1}{2}$ 5. $5\frac{1}{4}$

**Crayons Used in the Classroom**

$4\frac{1}{4}$  $4\frac{1}{2}$  $4\frac{3}{4}$  5  $5\frac{1}{4}$

**Lesson 7.4, page 65**

1. $2\frac{1}{2}$ 2. $3\frac{1}{4}$ 3. $2\frac{1}{2}$ 4. $2\frac{1}{4}$ 5. $2\frac{1}{4}$

6. $2\frac{1}{2}$ 7. $3\frac{1}{4}$

8.

**Fish in the Pond**

$2\frac{1}{4}$  $2\frac{1}{2}$  $2\frac{3}{4}$  3  $3\frac{1}{4}$

**Lesson 7.5, page 66**

1. 12 2. 10 3. 24 4. 28 5. 7 6. 12

**Lesson 7.5, page 67**

1.  A = 8 sq. cm  2.  A = 28 sq. cm  3.  A = 9 sq. in.

4.  A = 3 sq. m  5.  A = 4 sq. cm  6.  A = 5 sq. cm

**Lesson 7.6, page 68**

|    | a | b | c | d |
|----|-----|-----|-----|-----|
| 1. | 75 | 56 | 40 | 300 |
| 2. | 175 | 40 | 160 | 160 |

**Lesson 7.6, page 69**

1. ; 8 x 3 = 24  2. ; 2 x 2 = 4

3. ; 1 x 4 = 4; 4

4. ; 9 x 3 = 27; 27

**Lesson 7.7, page 70**

1. Drawings may vary; 20
2. Drawings may vary; 41
3. Drawings may vary; 24

**Lesson 7.8, page 71**

1. 80 2. 90 3. 450 4. 81 5. 810
6. 56 7. 90

**Lesson 7.9, page 72**

|    | a | b | c |
|----|-----|-----|-----|
| 1. | 14 | 30 | 28 |
| 2. | 225 | 120 | 55 |
| 3. | 5 | 8 | 30 |

**Lesson 7.9, page 73**

1. 25 2. 100 3. 52 4. 306 5. 192
6. 36 7. 40

## Chapter 8

**Lesson 8.1, page 74**

|    | a | b |
|----|-------|-------|
| 1. | 15; 6 | 10; 12 |
| 2. | 50; 7 | 10; 8 |
| 3. | 45; 12 | 15; 1 |
| 4. | 30; 1 | 30; 2 |

|    | a | b | c | d |
|----|------|------|-------|------|
| 5. | 4:20 | 6:13 | 7:10 | 1:50 |
| 6. | 6:45 | 8:09 | 12:30 | 2:23 |

**Lesson 8.1, page 75**

|    | a | b | c | d |
|----|------|------|------|------|
| 1. | 2:00 | 2:30 | 2:15 | 2:20 |
| 2. | 9:00 | 8:30 | 8:30 | 8:36 |

# Math Grade 3 Answers

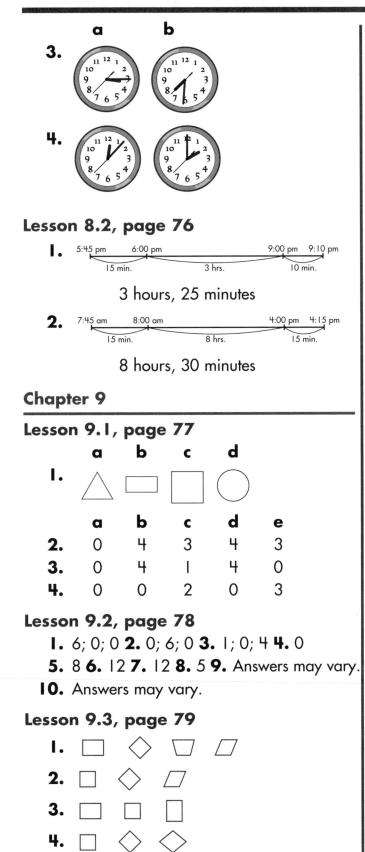

**a**        **b**

**3.**

**4.**

## Lesson 8.2, page 76

**1.**

| 5:45 pm | 6:00 pm | | 9:00 pm | 9:10 pm |
|---|---|---|---|---|
| 15 min. | 3 hrs. | | 10 min. | |

### 3 hours, 25 minutes

**2.**

| 7:45 am | 8:00 am | | 4:00 pm | 4:15 pm |
|---|---|---|---|---|
| 15 min. | 8 hrs. | | 15 min. | |

### 8 hours, 30 minutes

## Chapter 9

### Lesson 9.1, page 77

|     | **a** | **b** | **c** | **d** | |
|-----|---|---|---|---|---|
| **1.** | △ | ▭ | ☐ | ○ | |

|     | **a** | **b** | **c** | **d** | **e** |
|-----|---|---|---|---|---|
| **2.** | 0 | 4 | 3 | 4 | 3 |
| **3.** | 0 | 4 | 1 | 4 | 0 |
| **4.** | 0 | 0 | 2 | 0 | 3 |

### Lesson 9.2, page 78

**1.** 6; 0; 0 **2.** 0; 6; 0 **3.** 1; 0; 4 **4.** 0

**5.** 8 **6.** 12 **7.** 12 **8.** 5 **9.** Answers may vary.

**10.** Answers may vary.

### Lesson 9.3, page 79

**1.** ☐ ◇ ▱ ▱

**2.** ☐ ◇ ▱

**3.** ☐ ☐ ☐

**4.** ☐ ◇ ◇

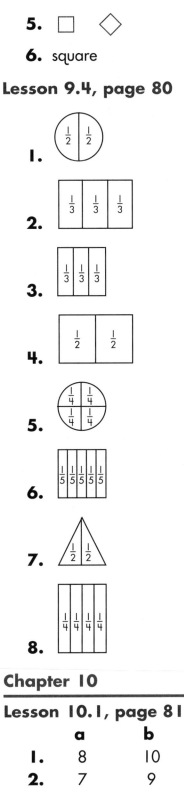

**5.** ☐ ◇

**6.** square

## Lesson 9.4, page 80

**1.**

**2.**

**3.**

**4.**

**5.**

**6.**

**7.**

**8.**

## Chapter 10

### Lesson 10.1, page 81

|     | **a** | **b** | **c** |
|-----|---|---|---|
| **1.** | 8 | 10 | 12 |
| **2.** | 7 | 9 | 11 |
| **3.** | 14 | 12 | 10 |

# Math Grade 3 Answers

| | | | |
|---|---|---|---|
| **4.** | 6 | 3 | 1 |
| **5.** | 10 | 9 | 8 |
| **6.** | 20 | 25 | 30 |
| **7.** | 12 | 15 | 18 |
| **8.** | 70 | 110 | 160 |
| **9.** | 7 | 4 | 1 |
| **10.** | 7 | 6 | 5 |

## Lesson 10.2, page 82

| | a | b | c | d |
|---|---|---|---|---|
| **1.** | 4 | 6 | 0 | 0 |
| **2.** | 2 | 5 | 1 | 1 |
| **3.** | 2 | 4 | 1 | 4 |
| **4.** | 5 | 3 | 5 | 4 |
| **5.** | 4 | 6 | 2 | 5 |
| **6.** | 5 | 5 | 2 | 6 |
| **7.** | 3 | 6 | 2 | 3 |

## Lesson 10.2, page 83

**1a.** 8 x 3 = 24; 24 x 2 = 48; d = 48

**1b.** 2 x 9 = 18; 18 x 2 = 36; h = 36

**2a.** 4 x 6 = 24; 24 x 2 = 48; e = 48

**2b.** 7 x 4 = 28; 28 x 2 = 56; g = 56

**3a.** 6; 24 + 24; 48

**3b.** 6; 24 + 18; 42

**4a.** 10; 18 + 20; 38

**4b.** 9; 35 + 45; 80

# Language Arts Grade 3 Answers

## Lesson 1.1 Common and Proper Nouns

A **common noun** can be a person, place, or thing.

*teacher* (person)          *museum* (place)
*notebook* (thing)

A **proper noun** is a noun that names a specific person, place, or thing. Proper nouns are capitalized to show that they are important.

Here are some examples of common and proper nouns:

| Common nouns | Proper nouns |
|---|---|
| school | Hickory Hills Elementary School |
| zoo | Memphis Zoo |
| brother | Alexander |
| city | Tallahassee |
| day | Sunday |
| cat | Sasha |

### Complete It

Complete the sentences below with a noun from the box. If there is a **P** after the space, use a proper noun. If there is a **C** after the space, use a common noun.

| Walnut High School | Saturday | town |
|---|---|---|
| dog | Jordan Lake | brother |

1. Uncle Dale is taking me fishing at ___Jordan Lake___ (P).

2. We will leave early on ___Saturday___ (P) morning.

3. My ___brother___ (C), Kris, is coming with us.

4. Uncle Dale lives an hour away in a ___town___ (C) called Rockvale.

5. He is a math teacher at ___Walnut High School___ (P).

6. Uncle Dale's ___dog___ (C), Patches, always comes fishing with us.

86

## Lesson 1.1 Common and Proper Nouns

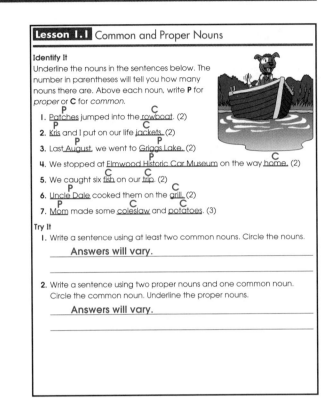

### Identify It

Underline the nouns in the sentences below. The number in parentheses will tell you how many nouns there are. Above each noun, write **P** for *proper* or **C** for *common*.

1. <u>Patches</u>(P) jumped into the <u>rowboat</u>(C). (2)
2. <u>Kris</u>(P) and I put on our life <u>jackets</u>(C). (2)
3. Last <u>August</u>(P), we went to <u>Griggs Lake</u>(P). (2)
4. We stopped at <u>Elmwood Historic Car Museum</u>(P) on the way <u>home</u>(C). (2)
5. We caught six <u>fish</u>(C) on our <u>trip</u>(C). (2)
6. <u>Uncle Dale</u>(P) cooked them on the <u>grill</u>(C). (2)
7. <u>Mom</u>(P) made some <u>coleslaw</u>(C) and <u>potatoes</u>(C). (3)

### Try It

1. Write a sentence using at least two common nouns. Circle the nouns.

   **Answers will vary.**

2. Write a sentence using two proper nouns and one common noun. Circle the common noun. Underline the proper nouns.

   **Answers will vary.**

87

## Lesson 1.2 Abstract Nouns

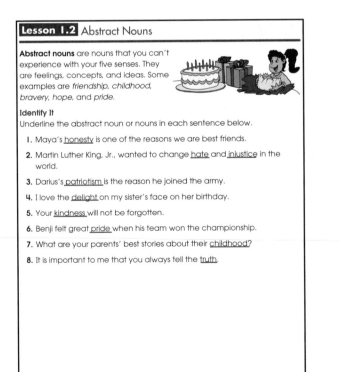

**Abstract nouns** are nouns that you can't experience with your five senses. They are feelings, concepts, and ideas. Some examples are *friendship, childhood, bravery, hope,* and *pride*.

### Identify It

Underline the abstract noun or nouns in each sentence below.

1. Maya's <u>honesty</u> is one of the reasons we are best friends.
2. Martin Luther King, Jr., wanted to change <u>hate</u> and <u>injustice</u> in the world.
3. Darius's <u>patriotism</u> is the reason he joined the army.
4. I love the <u>delight</u> on my sister's face on her birthday.
5. Your <u>kindness</u> will not be forgotten.
6. Benji felt great <u>pride</u> when his team won the championship.
7. What are your parents' best stories about their <u>childhood</u>?
8. It is important to me that you always tell the <u>truth</u>.

88

## Lesson 1.2 Abstract Nouns

### Complete It

Fill in each blank below with an abstract noun from the box.

| wisdom | liberty | freedom | knowledge |
|---|---|---|---|
| courage | joy | kindness | |

1. Our country was founded on the ideas of ___liberty___ and ___freedom___ for all.
2. It took great ___courage___ to rebuild after the hurricane.
3. Uncle Zane's ___knowledge___ of birds amazes me.
4. The room was filled with ___joy___ when Will found his lost puppy.
5. Neighbors showed us much ___kindness___ when my baby sister was born.
6. Grandpa has the ___wisdom___ that comes with a long life.

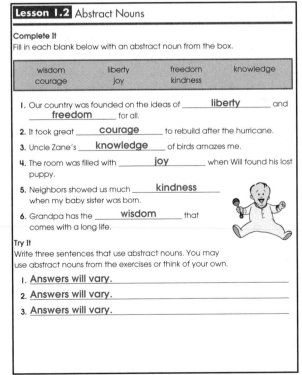

### Try It

Write three sentences that use abstract nouns. You may use abstract nouns from the exercises or think of your own.

1. **Answers will vary.**
2. **Answers will vary.**
3. **Answers will vary.**

89

# Language Arts Grade 3 Answers

## Lesson 1.3 Pronouns

A **pronoun** is a word that takes the place of a noun. Pronouns keep you from using the same noun or nouns over and over again.

Some pronouns take the place of a single person or thing: *I, me, you, he, she, him, her,* and *it*. Other pronouns take the place of plural nouns: *we, us, they,* and *them*.

In the examples below, pronouns take the place of the underlined nouns.

> The <u>grizzly bears</u> waded into the stream.
> *They* waded into the stream.
> <u>Molly</u> finished her report at noon.
> *She* finished her report at noon.
> Put <u>the bowl</u> on the table.
> Put *it* on the table.

### Identify It

Read the paragraphs below. Circle each pronoun. You should find 15 pronouns.

Sonja Henie was an amazing figure skater. (She) was born in Oslo, Norway, in 1912. When Sonja was only five years old, (she) won (her) first skating contest. (It) was the start of a great career. (She) was a world champion for ten years. People around the world became interested in skating. (They) followed the career of the talented young girl.

Sonja also wanted to be a movie star. (She) moved to Hollywood and began acting. (She) also performed in a traveling ice show. (It) was very popular. Huge crowds came to watch Sonja perform. (They) could not get enough of (her). Sonja enjoyed (her) fame and the money (it) brought (her). But (her) first and greatest love was always skating.

**90**

## Lesson 1.3 Pronouns

### Rewrite It

Read the sentences below. Rewrite each sentence using a pronoun in place of the underlined noun or nouns.

Example: <u>David</u> kicked the ball toward the goal.
*He* kicked the ball toward the goal.

1. <u>Bryan and Anna</u> had their first skating lesson on Tuesday.
   **They had their first skating lesson on Tuesday.**

2. <u>Bryan</u> had never skated before.
   **He had never skated before.**

3. <u>The ice</u> was slick and shiny.
   **It was slick and shiny.**

4. The teacher helped <u>Anna</u> tighten the skates.
   **The teacher helped her tighten the skates.**

5. The teacher told <u>Bryan and Anna</u> that they did a great job.
   **The teacher told them that they did a great job.**

### Try It

1. Think about the first time you tried something new. Write a sentence about your experience. Circle the pronoun.
   **Answers will vary.**

2. Write a sentence using the pronoun *he, she,* or *it*.
   **Answers will vary.**

**91**

## Lesson 1.4 Verbs

**Verbs** are often action words. They tell what happens in a sentence. Every sentence has a verb.

Ramon *put* on his running shoes. He *grabbed* his headphones. He *opened* the door and *took* a deep breath. Ramon *stretched* for a few minutes. Then, he *ran* down the street toward the park.

### Complete It

A verb is missing from each sentence below. Complete the sentences with verbs from the box.

| breathed | moved | attached | invented |
|----------|-------|----------|----------|
| gave | kept | carried | helped |

1. In 1819, August Siebe ____**invented**____ the first diving suit.
2. The large helmet ____**attached**____ to a leather and canvas suit.
3. Weights ____**helped**____ divers stay underwater.
4. The divers underwater ____**breathed**____ air through hoses.
5. Later on, rubber suits ____**kept**____ divers dry.
6. The invention of scuba gear ____**gave**____ divers more freedom.
7. Divers ____**moved**____ from place to place on their own.
8. They ____**carried**____ their air with them.

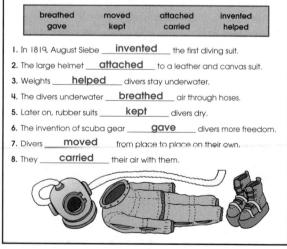

**92**

## Lesson 1.4 Verbs

### Identify It

Circle the 10 action verbs in the paragraphs below.

Jacques Cousteau (explored) many of Earth's oceans. In 1950, he (bought) a ship called *Calypso*. On the *Calypso*, Jacques (traveled) to bodies of water around the world. He (wrote) many books and (made) many movies about his travels. He (won) prizes for some of his work. Jacques also (invented) things, like an underwater camera and the first scuba equipment.

Jacques Cousteau (believed) it was important to protect ocean life. He (created) a group called the *Cousteau Society*. More than 300,000 people (belong) to the Cousteau Society today.

### Try It

1. Write a sentence about a place you would like to visit one day. Circle the verb.
   **Answers will vary.**

2. Write a sentence about your favorite thing to do during the weekend. Circle the verb.
   **Answers will vary.**

**93**

# Language Arts Grade 3 Answers

## Lesson 1.5 Linking Verbs

A **linking verb** links the subject to the rest of the sentence. Linking verbs are not action words.

The verb *to be* is a linking verb. Some different forms of the verb *to be* are *is, am, are, was,* and *were.* Some other linking verbs are *become, feel,* and *seem.*

**Identify It**
Read the sentences below. Underline the linking verbs. Circle the action verbs. Some sentences may have more than one verb.

1. My grandmother <u>is</u> a marine biologist.
2. She (studies) undersea life.
3. She <u>was</u> always a good student.
4. She (loved) the ocean and animals as a child.
5. It <u>was</u> hard for her to become a scientist.
6. When she <u>was</u> young, some people <u>felt</u> women could not <u>be</u> good at science.
7. My grandma (proved) she <u>was</u> smart and hardworking.
8. One day, I might <u>become</u> a marine biologist myself.

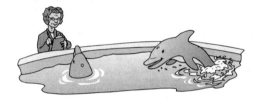

**94**

## Lesson 1.5 Linking Verbs

**Solve It**
Use the linking verbs from the box to complete each sentence. Some may work for more than one sentence. Then, look for the linking verbs in the word search puzzle. Circle each word you find.

1. Today, my grandfather _____is_____ a stage actor.
2. He first _____became_____ a movie star at the age of 22.
3. He _____feels_____ lucky to have had such an amazing career.
4. I _____am_____ going to see him in a Broadway play next week.
5. When my dad _____was_____ little, he was in one of Grandpa's movies.

| feels | am | became |
|-------|-----|--------|
| was | is | |

```
a  d  r  j  k (f  p
b  e  c  a  m  e) i
d (w  a  s) b  e  y
a  f  v  c  u  l  p
m  u  f  q (i  s) g
```

**Try It**
1. Write a sentence using a linking verb.
   **Answers will vary.**

2. Write a sentence using a linking verb and an action verb.
   **Answers will vary.**

**95**

## Lesson 1.6 Adjectives and Articles

**Adjectives** are words that describe. They give more information about nouns. Adjectives answer the questions *What kind?* and *How many?* They often come before the nouns they describe.
  Fat raindrops bounced off the umbrella. (what kind of raindrops?)

Adjectives can also appear other places in the sentence. If you are not sure a word is an adjective, look for the noun you think it describes.
  The robot was *helpful.*      The package is *huge!*

An **article** is a word that comes before a noun. *A, an,* and *the* are articles.

Use *the* to talk about a specific person, place, or thing.
  *the* computer    *the* jacket    *the* bicycle    *the* starfish

Use *a* or *an* to talk about any person, place, or thing. If the noun begins with a consonant sound, use *a*. If it begins with a vowel sound, use *an*.
  *a* wig    *a* bed    *an* apple    *an* envelope

**Complete It**
Complete each item below with an adjective from the box.

| shy | electric | prickly | warty | smelly |
|-----|----------|---------|-------|--------|
| seven | skinny | tiny | howling | wrinkled |

1. the _____prickly_____ porcupine
2. the _____warty_____ toad
3. the _____electric_____ eel
4. the gray, _____wrinkled_____ elephant
5. the _____tiny_____ hummingbird
6. the tall, _____skinny_____ giraffe
7. the _____smelly_____ skunk
8. the _____shy_____ deer
9. the _____howling_____ wolf
10. _____seven_____ flamingos

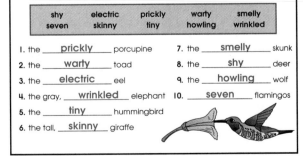

**96**

## Lesson 1.6 Adjectives and Articles

**Rewrite It**
The senten[ Answers will vary. Possible answers: ]. Rewrite the sentences.

1. The dog barked at the squirrel as it ran up the tree.
   **The small, fierce dog barked at the gray squirrel as it ran up the old, gnarled tree.**

2. The dolphin dove into the waves and swam toward the sunset.
   **The friendly dolphin dove into the gentle waves and swam toward the colorful sunset.**

**Proof It**
Read the paragraph below. Circle the 20 articles you find. Six of the articles are incorrect. Cross them out, and write the correct articles above them.

(A) time capsule is (a) ~~an~~ interesting way to communicate with people in (a) ~~the~~ future. (A) time capsule is (a) group of items from (the) present time. (An) ~~The~~ items tell something about (a) person, (a) place, or (a) moment in time. They are sealed in (a) container. (A) glass jar or (the) plastic box with (a) tight lid works well. Then, (the) capsule is buried or put in (an) ~~a~~ safe place. (An) attached note should say when (the) capsule will be opened. Some capsules are opened in (the) ~~a~~ year or in ten years. Others will stay buried or hidden for (a) thousand or even five thousand years!

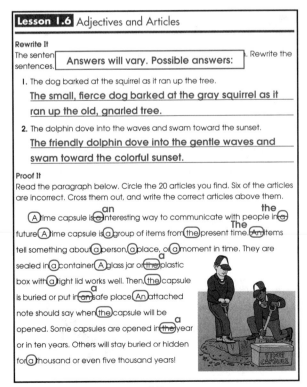

**97**

# Language Arts Grade 3 Answers

## Lesson 1.7 Adverbs

**Adverbs** are words that describe verbs. Adverbs often answer the questions *When? Where?* or *How?*

She *joyfully* cheered for them.     *Joyfully* tells *how* she cheered.

*Yesterday*, I had a picnic.     *Yesterday* tells *when* I had a picnic.

Brady put the box *downstairs*.     *Downstairs* tells *where* Brady put the box.

Adverbs can also describe adjectives. They usually answer the question *How?*

Sierra was **too** late.     The sunset was **really** beautiful.

Adverbs can describe other adverbs, too.

Luke spoke **extremely** quietly.     Shawn **very** sadly said good-bye.

### Complete It

An adverb is missing from each sentence below. Choose the adverb from the box that best completes each sentence. Write it on the line. Then, circle the word the adverb describes.

| | | |
|---|---|---|
| loudly | brightly | often |
| beside | suddenly | completely |

1. Dylan (sat) **beside** Amina at the school play.
2. The two friends **often** (went) to plays together.
3. The room was **completely** (dark)
4. **Suddenly**, the curtain (opened.)
5. The scenery onstage was **brightly** (painted.)
6. The children (said) their lines **loudly** so that everyone could hear them.

98

## Lesson 1.7 Adverbs

### Solve It

Read the sentences below. Find the adverb in each sentence. Write it on the lines after the sentence.

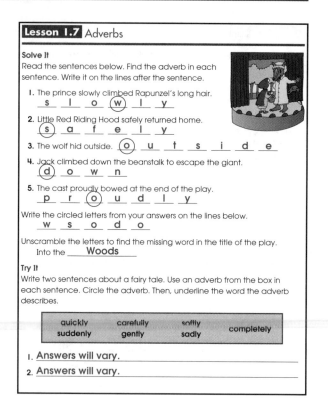

1. The prince slowly climbed Rapunzel's long hair.
   s   l   o  (w)  l   y
2. Little Red Riding Hood safely returned home.
   (s)  a   f   e   l   y
3. The wolf hid outside. (o)  u   t   s   i   d   e
4. Jack climbed down the beanstalk to escape the giant.
   (d)  o   w   n
5. The cast proudly bowed at the end of the play.
   p   r  (o)  u   d   l   y

Write the circled letters from your answers on the lines below.

w   s   o   d   o

Unscramble the letters to find the missing word in the title of the play.

Into the **Woods**

### Try It

Write two sentences about a fairy tale. Use an adverb from the box in each sentence. Circle the adverb. Then, underline the word the adverb describes.

| | | | |
|---|---|---|---|
| quickly | carefully | softly | |
| suddenly | gently | sadly | completely |

1. **Answers will vary.**
2. **Answers will vary.**

99

## Lesson 1.8 Conjunctions

A **conjunction** joins together words, phrases, and parts of sentences. The most common conjunctions are *and, or,* and *but*. Other conjunctions are *since, because, although, if, while, unless,* and *however*.

Chloe loves Brussels sprouts, *but* Haley won't eat them.

*Since* you play soccer, can you give me some tips?

### Complete It

Choose a conjunction to complete each sentence. Write it on the line.

1. Do you want to play the violin **or** the piano? (or, but)
2. Mr. Randall canceled Lucy's lesson **because** he had a cold. (unless, because)
3. Let's play a duet at the recital **if** we can learn it in time. (while, if)
4. Owen plays the drums, **and** Marcus plays the trombone. (and, or)
5. Mrs. Klein likes to knit **while** Ezra practices singing. (however, while)
6. Liam always practices his scales, **but** Alla never does. (but, if)
7. Jade can buy a drum set, **however** her parents want her to help pay for it. (however, or)
8. **Although** Vikram's lesson is at 11:00, he often arrives at 10:30. (While, Although)

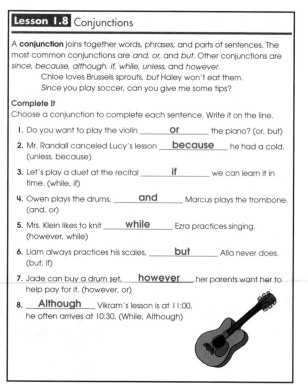

100

## Lesson 1.8 Conjunctions

### Rewrite It

Combine each pair [ **Possible answers:** ] . There may be more than one correct ans

1. Jack wants to take violin lessons. His sister has been taking them for years.

   **Jack wants to take violin lessons since his sister has been taking them for years.**

2. Nora plays piano by ear. She can't read notes at all.

   **Nora plays piano by ear, but she can't read notes at all.**

3. Dion enjoys listening to music. He doesn't play any instruments yet.

   **Although Dion enjoys listening to music, he doesn't play any instruments yet.**

4. Mr. Santiago hums. He practices every afternoon.

   **Mr. Santiago hums while he practices every afternoon.**

### Try It

Write a short paragraph about music. Use at least four conjunctions, and circle them.

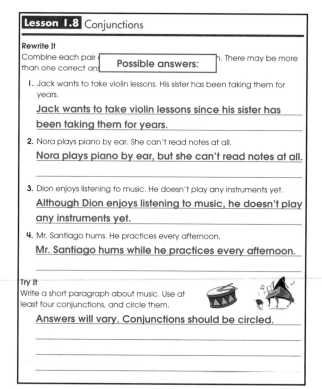

**Answers will vary. Conjunctions should be circled.**

101

# Language Arts Grade 3 Answers

## Lesson 1.9 Statements and Commands

A **statement** is a sentence that begins with a capital letter and ends with a period. A statement gives information.

    **D**iego will be 13 in April.    **S**udan is a country in Africa.

**Commands** are sentences that tell you to do something. Commands also begin with a capital letter and end with a period.

    **U**se the bright blue marker.    **C**hop the onions.

| Tip | Statements usually begin with a noun or a pronoun. Commands often begin with a verb. |
|---|---|

**Complete It**

The statements below are missing periods. Add periods where they are needed. Circle each period you add so that it is easy to see.

Monday, July 16

Dear Diary,

    On Saturday, Shi-Ann and I set up a lemonade stand⊙We made colorful signs to hang around the neighborhood⊙Dad helped us make cookies and chocolate pretzels⊙We wanted to make sure our customers would be thirsty⊙

    At the store, we bought a tablecloth, cups, and napkins⊙Dad let us borrow some money to use in our change box⊙Once we opened for business, we had tons of customers⊙Shi-Ann and I had to keep making fresh lemonade all day⊙

    We each made ten dollars from our lemonade stand⊙I had fun, but now I know that owning a business is a lot of work⊙

**102**

## Lesson 1.9 Statements and Commands

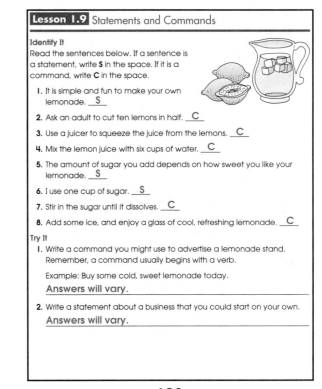

**Identify It**

Read the sentences below. If a sentence is a statement, write **S** in the space. If it is a command, write **C** in the space.

1. It is simple and fun to make your own lemonade. __S__

2. Ask an adult to cut ten lemons in half. __C__

3. Use a juicer to squeeze the juice from the lemons. __C__

4. Mix the lemon juice with six cups of water. __C__

5. The amount of sugar you add depends on how sweet you like your lemonade. __S__

6. I use one cup of sugar. __S__

7. Stir in the sugar until it dissolves. __C__

8. Add some ice, and enjoy a glass of cool, refreshing lemonade. __C__

**Try It**

1. Write a command you might use to advertise a lemonade stand. Remember, a command usually begins with a verb.

    Example: Buy some cold, sweet lemonade today.

    **Answers will vary.**

2. Write a statement about a business that you could start on your own.

    **Answers will vary.**

**103**

## Lesson 1.10 Questions

**Questions** are sentences that ask something. When a person asks a question, he or she is looking for information. A question begins with a capital letter and ends with a question mark.

    **W**ill you go to the party with me**?**
    **W**hat is the weather like in Phoenix**?**

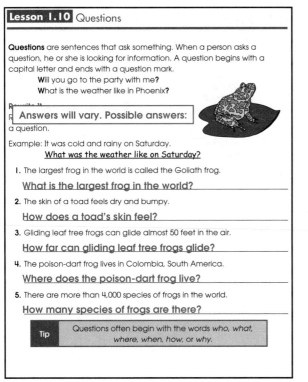

**Rewrite It**

R | **Answers will vary. Possible answers:**
a question.

Example: It was cold and rainy on Saturday.
    __What was the weather like on Saturday?__

1. The largest frog in the world is called the Goliath frog.
    __What is the largest frog in the world?__

2. The skin of a toad feels dry and bumpy.
    __How does a toad's skin feel?__

3. Gliding leaf tree frogs can glide almost 50 feet in the air.
    __How far can gliding leaf tree frogs glide?__

4. The poison-dart frog lives in Colombia, South America.
    __Where does the poison-dart frog live?__

5. There are more than 4,000 species of frogs in the world.
    __How many species of frogs are there?__

| Tip | Questions often begin with the words *who, what, where, when, how,* or *why*. |
|---|---|

**104**

## Lesson 1.10 Questions

**Proof It**

Read the following paragraphs. There are seven incorrect end marks. Cross out the mistakes. Then, write the correct end marks above them.

    Have you ever heard someone say it was "raining frogs"**?** You might have thought that it was just a figure of speech. But in rare cases, it has actually rained frogs**⊙** How could this happen**?** It sounds impossible. During a tornado or a powerful thunderstorm, water from a pond or lake can be sucked into the air. This includes anything that is in the water.

    The storm continues to move**⊙** As it travels, it releases the water into the air. Does this mean that frogs and fish come raining down from the sky**?** Yes, this is exactly what happens.

    Cases of strange things falling from the sky have been reported for many years**⊙** People have seen small frogs, fish, grasshoppers, and snails drop from the sky in places like France, India, Louisiana, and Kansas. Are animals the only things that get swept up by storms**?** No. In fact, in 1995, it rained soda cans in the Midwest.

**Try It**

1. Write a question you would like to ask a frog expert.
    __Answers will vary.__

2. Write a question you would like to ask a weather expert.
    __Answers will vary.__

**105**

# Language Arts Grade 3 Answers

## Lesson 1.11 Exclamations

**Exclamations** are sentences that show excitement or surprise. Exclamations begin with a capital letter and end with an exclamation point.

The Gold Nuggets won the championship!
We missed the bus!

Sometimes an exclamation can be a single word. Sometimes it can contain a command.

Oops!   Uh-oh!   Watch out!   Come back!

### Complete It
Read the advertisement below. Some of the end marks are missing. Write the correct end marks on the lines.

**106**

## Lesson 1.11 Exclamations

### Proof It
Read the sentences below. If the end mark is correct, make a check mark (✓) on the line. If the end mark is not correct, cross it out and write the correct end mark in the space.

1. Watch out✗ _!_
2. Did you take the dog for a walk✗ _?_
3. Luis is going to learn how to play the trumpet✗ _._
4. We won the game✗ _!_
5. I lost my wallet✗ _!_
6. How old is Ella✗ _?_
7. My grandma had 16 brothers and sisters! _✓_
8. Harry wore a new suit to the wedding. _✓_

### Try It
Imagine that you were going on a jungle animal safari. Think of two exclamations you might make. Write them on the lines below.
Examples: Watch out for that big snake!
That leopard runs really fast!

__Answers will vary.__

**107**

## Lesson 1.12 Parts of a Sentence: Subject

The **subject** of a sentence is what a sentence is about. In a statement, the subject is usually found at the beginning of the sentence before the verb. A subject can be a single word or it can be several words.

*The entire team* cheered when the winning goal was scored.
*Irina* loves to eat oatmeal for breakfast.
*Brian Adams and Brian Rowley* are in the same class.
*Four raccoons, three chipmunks, and an opossum* live in my backyard.

### Identify It
Underline the subject in each sentence below.

1. <u>The Golden Gate Bridge</u> is located in San Francisco, California.
2. <u>The bridge</u> was built in 1937.
3. <u>It</u> was the longest suspension bridge in the world until 1964.
4. <u>A suspension bridge</u> is a bridge that hangs from cables.
5. <u>Joseph Strauss</u> was the engineer who designed the amazing bridge.
6. <u>The Verrazano Narrows Bridge and the Mackinac Bridge</u> are two other famous bridges.
7. <u>The bridge's orange color</u> was chosen so that it would be easy to see on foggy days.
8. <u>Many movies and TV shows</u> have included views of the bridge.
9. <u>You</u> can walk or bike across the Golden Gate Bridge during the day.

**108**

## Lesson 1.12 Parts of a Sentence: Subject

### Complete It
Each sentence below is missing a subject. Find the subject in the box that best fits each sentence. Write the subject on the line.

| The Golden Gate Bridge | A statue of Joseph B. Strauss |
| People and cars | Maria |
| The cost to build the bridge | About nine million people |

1. _____Maria_____ learned all about different kinds of bridges from her teacher.
2. __The Golden Gate Bridge__ is 1.7 miles long.
3. __A statue of Joseph B. Strauss__ celebrates the famous engineer.
4. __About nine million people__ visit the bridge every year.
5. _____People and cars_____ that travel north on the bridge do not have to pay a toll.
6. __The cost to build the bridge__ was 27 million dollars.

### Try It
1. Write a sentence in which the subject is a person's name. Underline the subject.
   __Answers will vary.__
2. Write a sentence in which the subject is more than one word. Underline the subject.
   __Answers will vary.__

**109**

# Language Arts Grade 3 Answers

## Lesson 1.13 Parts of a Sentence: Predicate

A **predicate** tells what happens in a sentence. It tells what the subject is or does. The predicate always includes the verb. Finding the verb in a sentence can help you identify the predicate.

In the sentences below, the verbs are in bold type. The predicates are in italics.

> Evelina **recycles** *all her cans and bottles.*
> The seagull **soared** *above the stormy waters.*
> Jermaine **took** *a picture of the dog with his camera.*

**Identify It**
Read the paragraph below. Underline the predicate in each sentence.

In the United States, April 22 <u>is Earth Day</u>. On Earth Day, people <u>celebrate the planet Earth</u>. They <u>take the time to remember that the environment is fragile</u>. The first Earth Day <u>was held in 1970</u>. About 20 million Americans <u>celebrated that year</u>. Today, more than 500 million people around the world <u>take part in Earth Day activities.</u>

On Earth Day, people <u>learn about different types of pollution.</u> They also <u>learn what they can do to help save the planet.</u> Many people <u>recycle things.</u> Paper, glass, and aluminum <u>can be reused in new ways.</u> Some groups <u>plant trees to help keep the air clean.</u> Others <u>pick up litter in their parks and neighborhoods.</u> For some caring people, every day <u>is Earth Day!</u>

110

## Lesson 1.13 Parts of a Sentence: Predicate

**Rewrite It**
One box below is filled with subjects. One box is filled with predicates. Draw a line to match each subject to a predicate. Then, write the complete sentences on the lines below. (There is more than one correct way to match the subjects and predicates.)

| Subjects | Predicates |
| --- | --- |
| Roma and Patrick | held an Earth Day 5K Run. |
| Alexis | clean ... McCoy Park. |
| Ms. Piazza | ... many ways to reuse newspapers. |
| My sister and I | donated ten dollars to a fund for endangered animals. |
| The students at Waxhill Elementary | planted eight small trees on Earth Day. |

Answers will vary.

1. _____
2. _____
3. _____
4. _____
5. _____

Answers will vary.

**Try It**
Write two sentences about something you can do every day to protect the planet. Underline the predicate in each sentence.

Answers will vary.

111

## Lesson 1.14 Sentence Fragments and Run-On Sentences

A sentence is a group of words that contains a complete thought or idea. All sentences have a subject and a predicate. Part of a sentence, or an incomplete sentence, is called a **sentence fragment**. Sentence fragments cannot stand alone.

Examples: *Drove to the store.* (no subject)
*Because the sun.* (group of words)
*The girls on the porch.* (no predicate)

**Run-on sentences** are sentences that are too long. They are hard to follow, so they need to be split into two separate sentences. If the two sentences are about the same idea, they can be joined with a comma and a conjunction like *and* or *but.*

> Clare likes cheese her brother Miles does not. (run-on)
> Clare likes cheese. *Her* brother Miles does not. (split into two sentences)
> Clare likes cheese, *but* her brother Miles does not. (combined with a comma and conjunction)

**Identify It**
Read each item below. If it is a complete sentence, write **C** on the line. If it is a sentence fragment, write **F** on the line.

1. **F** Threw the ball.
2. **F** After Madeline made a basket.
3. **C** James scored a goal.
4. **F** Cheered, clapped, and yelled.
5. **C** The volleyball bounced off the net.

112

## Lesson 1.14 Sentence Fragments and Run-On Sentences

**Proof It**
Read the paragraphs below. There are four run-on sentences. Make a slash (/) where you would break the run-on sentences into two sentences.

Example: The clown wore enormous shoes / he had a large, red nose.

There are many different breeds of dogs/each one has a special personality. Basset hounds are often thought of as hunting dogs. They have long, floppy ears and wrinkly skin/they can be loyal, friendly, and stubborn. Some people think their droopy eyes are sweet/others think these hounds always look sad.

Cocker spaniels are good dogs for families. They are friendly and good with children/they have beautiful, long silky ears. Cocker spaniels are usually tan or black in color.

**Try It**
On a separate piece of paper, write two sentence fragments. Trade papers with a classmate. On the lines below, turn your classmate's fragments into complete sentences.

1. Answers will vary.
2. Answers will vary.

113

# Language Arts Grade 3 Answers

## Lesson 1.15 Combining Sentences: Subjects and Objects

Sometimes sentences that tell about the same thing can be combined. Then, the writer does not have to repeat words. Instead, the writer can combine two sentences into one by using the word *and*.

Terrence likes popcorn.          Peter likes popcorn.
Terrence *and* Peter like popcorn.

Because the subject (Terrence and Peter) is plural, the verb form has to change from *likes* to *like*.

In the example below, both sentences tell about what Jill read, so they can be combined.

Jill read a new book.          Jill read a magazine.
Jill read a new book *and* a magazine.

**Identify It**
Read each pair of sentences below. If the sentences tell about the same thing and can be combined with the word *and*, make a check mark (✓) on the line. If they tell about different things and cannot be combined, make an **X** on the line.

1. ___✓___ Snakes are reptiles. Lizards are reptiles.
2. ___X___ Cheetahs are mammals. Toads are amphibians.
3. ___✓___ The robin ate some berries. The robin ate a worm.
4. ___✓___ Tarantulas are spiders. Black widows are spiders.
5. ___X___ The dolphin swam beside its baby. The whale headed for deeper waters.

**114**

## Lesson 1.15 Combining Sentences: Subjects and Objects

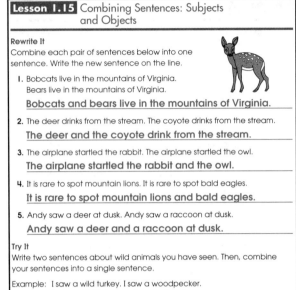

**Rewrite It**
Combine each pair of sentences below into one sentence. Write the new sentence on the line.

1. Bobcats live in the mountains of Virginia. Bears live in the mountains of Virginia.
   **Bobcats and bears live in the mountains of Virginia.**

2. The deer drinks from the stream. The coyote drinks from the stream.
   **The deer and the coyote drink from the stream.**

3. The airplane startled the rabbit. The airplane startled the owl.
   **The airplane startled the rabbit and the owl.**

4. It is rare to spot mountain lions. It is rare to spot bald eagles.
   **It is rare to spot mountain lions and bald eagles.**

5. Andy saw a deer at dusk. Andy saw a raccoon at dusk.
   **Andy saw a deer and a raccoon at dusk.**

**Try It**
Write two sentences about wild animals you have seen. Then, combine your sentences into a single sentence.

Example:  I saw a wild turkey. I saw a woodpecker.
          I saw a wild turkey and a woodpecker.

**Answers will vary.**

**115**

## Lesson 1.16 Combining Sentences: Verbs

When two sentences tell about the same thing, they can sometimes be combined using the word *and*. The first two sentences below are about what Veronica did at breakfast, so they can be combined.

Veronica ate some cereal. Veronica drank a glass of orange juice.
Veronica ate some cereal *and* drank a glass of orange juice.

Some sentences can be combined using the word *or*. Use *or* if there are several choices about what might happen. In the example below, we do not know which choice Habib will make, so the word *or* is used.

Habib might walk home. Habib might ride his bike home. Habib might run home.
Habib might walk, ride his bike, *or* run home.

If you list several things in a row, place a comma after each one except the last.

**Complete It**
Read the sentences below. Fill in each blank with the missing word.

1. Grandpa spread out the tent. Grandpa hammered the stakes.
   Grandpa spread out the tent __and__ hammered the stakes.

2. Will might look for sticks. Will might cook dinner.
   Will might look for sticks __or__ cook dinner.

3. Will put the pillows in the tent. Will unrolled the sleeping bags.
   Will put the pillows in the tent __and__ unrolled the sleeping bags.

4. Grandpa and Will might make sandwiches. Grandpa and Will might grill hamburgers.
   Grandpa and Will might make sandwiches __or__ grill hamburgers.

**116**

## Lesson 1.16 Combining Sentences: Verbs

**Rewrite It**
Combine each set of sentences below into one sentence. Write the new sentence on the line.

1. Grandpa stacked the wood. Grandpa found the matches. Grandpa lit the fire.
   **Grandpa stacked the wood, found the matches, and lit the fire.**

2. Grandpa toasted a marshmallow. Grandpa placed it between two graham crackers.
   **Grandpa toasted a marshmallow and placed it between two graham crackers.**

3. Will read in the tent with a flashlight. Will finished his book.
   **Will read in the tent with a flashlight and finished his book.**

4. Grandpa and Will looked at the night sky. Grandpa and Will found the Big Dipper.
   **Grandpa and Will looked at the night sky and found the Big Dipper.**

5. Next summer, they might sail down the coast. Next summer, they might go fishing.
   **Next summer, they might sail down the coast or go fishing.**

**Try It**
1. Write two sentences that tell about things you do in the morning. Use a different verb in each sentence.
   **Answers will vary.**

2. Now, combine the two sentences you wrote using the word *and*.
   **Answers will vary.**

**117**

# Language Arts Grade 3 Answers

---

### Lesson 1.17 Combining Sentences: Adjectives

Sometimes, sentences can be combined.

> The leaves are green. They are shiny. They are large.

The adjectives *green*, *shiny*, and *large* all describe *leaves*. The sentences can be combined into one by using the word *and*. Remember to use a comma after each adjective except the last.

> The leaves are green, shiny, *and* large.

In the example below, only a comma is needed to combine the two sentences. Both sentences describe the jacket.

> The red jacket is Amelia's favorite. The jacket is warm.
> The warm, red jacket is Amelia's favorite.

**Identify It**

Read each set of sentences below. If the adjectives describe the same thing, the sentences can be combined. Make a check mark (✓) on the line. If they describe different things, the sentences cannot be combined. Make an **X** on the line.

1. __✓__ The strawberries are red. They are juicy.

2. __X__ The lemons are tart. The lemonade is sweet.

3. __✓__ I like wild blueberries. I like fresh blueberries.

4. __✓__ The grapes are ripe. They are dark purple. They are plump.

5. __✓__ The fuzzy kiwi is on the table. It is round.

6. __X__ Oranges are tropical. Apples can be red, green, or yellow.

118

---

### Lesson 1.17 Combining Sentences: Adjectives

**Rewrite It**

Combine each set of sentences below into one sentence. Write the new sentence on the line.

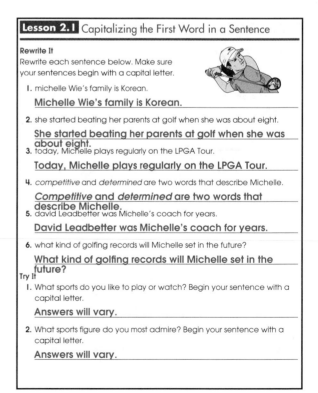

1. Cucumbers are long. They are thin. They are green.

   **Cucumbers are long, thin, and green.**

2. Sam grew some huge tomatoes in his garden. They were juicy.

   **Sam grew some huge, juicy tomatoes in his garden.**

3. The rabbits seem to love Mom's lettuce. It is leafy.

   **The rabbits seem to love Mom's leafy lettuce.**

4. The seedlings are tiny. They are pale green.

   **The seedlings are tiny and pale green.**

5. Rohan's peppers were small. They were spicy.

   **Rohan's peppers were small and spicy.**

**Try It**

1. Write two sentences that describe a piece of clothing you are wearing. Use a different adjective in each sentence.

   Example: I am wearing a new shirt. My shirt is striped.

   **Answers will vary.**

2. Now, write a sentence that combines the two sentences you wrote.

   Example: I am wearing a new, striped shirt.

   **Answers will vary.**

119

---

### Lesson 2.1 Capitalizing the First Word in a Sentence

The first word of a sentence always begins with a **capital letter**. A capital letter is a sign to the reader that a new sentence is starting.

> *I* live on the third floor of the apartment building.
> *Do* you like green beans?
> *Here* comes the parade!
> *Maya* grinned at Jeff.

**Proof It**

Read the paragraphs below. The first word of every sentence should be capitalized. To capitalize a letter, underline it three times (≡). Then, write the capital letter above it.

Example: <u>M</u>y sister taught me a new computer game.

<u>H</u>ave you ever played golf? <u>I</u>f you have, you know that it can be harder than it looks. <u>G</u>olfer Michelle Wie makes it look pretty easy. <u>T</u>hat's because she can hit a golf ball more than 300 yards! <u>A</u>t the age of 13, Michelle became the youngest winner ever of the Women's Amateur Public Links. <u>S</u>he has even played on the famous men's golf tour, the PGA Tour. <u>S</u>ome people think that this amazing six-foot-tall golfer will be the next Tiger Woods.

120

---

### Lesson 2.1 Capitalizing the First Word in a Sentence

**Rewrite It**

Rewrite each sentence below. Make sure your sentences begin with a capital letter.

1. michelle Wie's family is Korean.

   **Michelle Wie's family is Korean.**

2. she started beating her parents at golf when she was about eight.

   **She started beating her parents at golf when she was about eight.**

3. today, Michelle plays regularly on the LPGA Tour.

   **Today, Michelle plays regularly on the LPGA Tour.**

4. *competitive* and *determined* are two words that describe Michelle.

   ***Competitive* and *determined* are two words that describe Michelle.**

5. david Leadbetter was Michelle's coach for years.

   **David Leadbetter was Michelle's coach for years.**

6. what kind of golfing records will Michelle set in the future?

   **What kind of golfing records will Michelle set in the future?**

**Try It**

1. What sports do you like to play or watch? Begin your sentence with a capital letter.

   **Answers will vary.**

2. What sports figure do you most admire? Begin your sentence with a capital letter.

   **Answers will vary.**

121

---

# Language Arts Grade 3 Answers

---

**Lesson 2.2** Capitalizing Names and Titles

Capitalize the **specific names of people and pets**.

> My cousin *Umeko* moved here from Japan.
> We named the puppy *George*.

A **title** is a word that comes before a person's name. A title gives more information about who a person is. Titles that come before a name are capitalized.

> *Grandpa* Bruce          *Aunt* Juliet
> *Captain* Albrecht       *President* Abraham Lincoln
> *Senator* Barbara Boxer  *Judge* Naser

**Titles of respect** are also capitalized.

> *Mr.* Watterson    *Miss* Newton    *Mrs.* Cohen
> *Dr.* Gupta        *Ms.* Liang

> **Tip**
> If a title is not used with a name, it is not capitalized.
> My *aunt* is funny. The *judge* was here.
> But, if a title is used as a name, it is capitalized.
> Tell *Mom* I am going to the park.
> *Grandpa* will fix the computer.

**Complete It**

Complete each sentence below with the words in parentheses ( ). Some of the words will need to be capitalized. Others will not.

1. Kelly took her dog, _____**Abby**_____, for a walk to the park. (abby)

2. My school has a new _____**principal**_____. (principal)

3. On Tuesday, _____**Grandma**_____ is coming to visit. (grandma)

4. The best teacher I ever had was _____**Mr. Butler**_____. (mr. butler)

5. The baby dolphin at the zoo is named _____**Michi**_____. (michi)

122

---

**Lesson 2.2** Capitalizing Names and Titles

**Proof It**

Read the letter below. There are ten mistakes. To capitalize a letter, underline it three times, and write the capital letter above it. To lowercase a letter (or change it from a capital letter to a small letter), make a slash through it. Then, write the small letter above it.

Example: Olivia and m̲a̲t̲t̲ asked their G̶randma if she knew m̲r̲. Buckman.

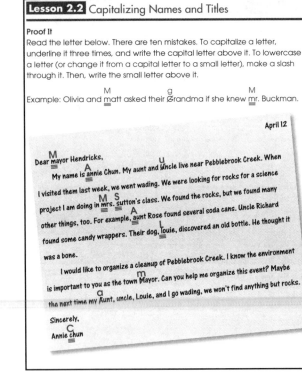

April 12

Dear M̲ayor Hendricks,

My name is A̲nnie Chun. My aunt and U̲ncle live near Pebblebrook Creek. When I visited them last week, we went wading. We were looking for rocks for a science project I am doing in M̲r̲s̲. S̲utton's class. We found the rocks, but we found many other things, too. For example, A̲unt Rose found several soda cans. Uncle Richard found some candy wrappers. Their dog, L̲ouie, discovered an old bottle. He thought it was a bone.

I would like to organize a cleanup of Pebblebrook Creek. I know the environment is important to you as the town M̶ayor. Can you help me organize this event? Maybe the next time my A̶unt, uncle, Louie, and I go wading, we won't find anything but rocks.

Sincerely,
Annie C̲hun

123

---

**Lesson 2.3** Capitalizing Place Names

The **names of specific places** always begin with a capital letter.

> *Madison, Wisconsin*              *Rocky Mountains*
> *Italy*                          *Liberty Avenue*
> *Science Museum of Minnesota*    *Jupiter*
> *Jones Middle School*           *Los Angeles Public Library*

**Complete It**

Complete each sentence below with the word or words in parentheses ( ). Remember to capitalize the names of specific places.

1. There are many _____**towns**_____ (towns) across _____**America**_____ (america) that have interesting names.

2. Have you ever heard of Okay, _____**Arkansas**_____ (arkansas)?

3. Some towns are named after foods, like Avocado, California, and _____**Two Egg**_____ (two egg), Florida.

4. Some names, like Chickasawhatchee and _____**Goochland**_____ (goochland) are fun to say.

5. A person from _____**Russia**_____ (russia) might be surprised to find a town named Moscow in Vermont.

6. If you're on your way to visit _____**Mount Rushmore**_____ (mount rushmore), look for Igloo, South Dakota.

7. Would you like to go to _____**Boring Elementary School**_____ (boring elementary school) in Boring, Oregon?

> **Tip**
> In the names of specific places, some words are not capitalized. All the important words begin with a capital letter. Small words, like *of, the, and,* and *a,* do not begin with a capital letter unless they are at the beginning of a sentence.

124

---

**Lesson 2.3** Capitalizing Place Names

**Proof It**

Read the directions below. Capitalize the names of specific places. To capitalize a letter, underline it three times (=), and write the capital letter above it.

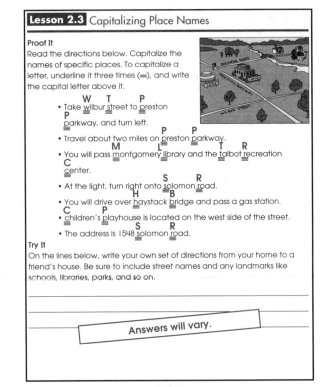

- Take w̲ilbur s̲treet to p̲reston p̲arkway, and turn left.
- Travel about two miles on p̲reston p̲arkway.
- You will pass m̲ontgomery l̲ibrary and the t̲albot r̲ecreation c̲enter.
- At the light, turn right onto s̲olomon r̲oad.
- You will drive over h̲aystack b̲ridge and pass a gas station.
- c̲hildren's p̲layhouse is located on the west side of the street.
- The address is 1548 s̲olomon r̲oad.

**Try It**

On the lines below, write your own set of directions from your home to a friend's house. Be sure to include street names and any landmarks like schools, libraries, parks, and so on.

Answers will vary.

125

---

# Language Arts Grade 3 Answers

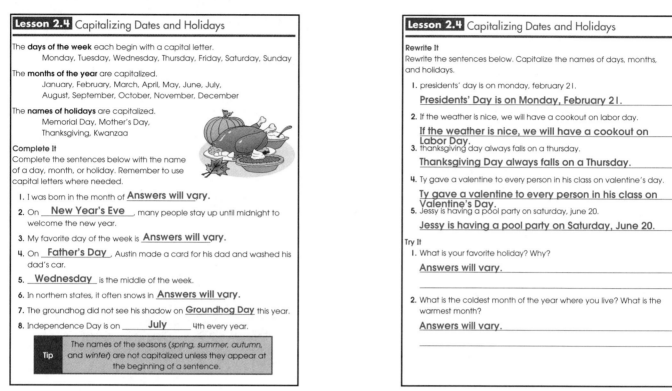

**Lesson 2.4** Capitalizing Dates and Holidays

The **days of the week** each begin with a capital letter.
  Monday, Tuesday, Wednesday, Thursday, Friday, Saturday, Sunday

The **months of the year** are capitalized.
  January, February, March, April, May, June, July,
  August, September, October, November, December

The **names of holidays** are capitalized.
  Memorial Day, Mother's Day,
  Thanksgiving, Kwanzaa

**Complete It**
Complete the sentences below with the name of a day, month, or holiday. Remember to use capital letters where needed.

1. I was born in the month of **Answers will vary.**
2. On **New Year's Eve**, many people stay up until midnight to welcome the new year.
3. My favorite day of the week is **Answers will vary.**
4. On **Father's Day**, Austin made a card for his dad and washed his dad's car.
5. **Wednesday** is the middle of the week.
6. In northern states, it often snows in **Answers will vary.**
7. The groundhog did not see his shadow on **Groundhog Day** this year.
8. Independence Day is on **July** 4th every year.

**Tip** The names of the seasons (*spring, summer, autumn,* and *winter*) are not capitalized unless they appear at the beginning of a sentence.

126

---

**Lesson 2.4** Capitalizing Dates and Holidays

**Rewrite It**
Rewrite the sentences below. Capitalize the names of days, months, and holidays.

1. presidents' day is on monday, february 21.

   **Presidents' Day is on Monday, February 21.**

2. If the weather is nice, we will have a cookout on labor day.

   **If the weather is nice, we will have a cookout on Labor Day.**

3. thanksgiving day always falls on a thursday.

   **Thanksgiving Day always falls on a Thursday.**

4. Ty gave a valentine to every person in his class on valentine's day.

   **Ty gave a valentine to every person in his class on Valentine's Day.**

5. Jessy is having a pool party on saturday, june 20.

   **Jessy is having a pool party on Saturday, June 20.**

**Try It**

1. What is your favorite holiday? Why?

   **Answers will vary.**

2. What is the coldest month of the year where you live? What is the warmest month?

   **Answers will vary.**

127

---

**Lesson 2.5** Capitalizing Book, Movie, and Song Titles

The titles of books, movies, and songs are capitalized. Small words, like *of, the, and, in, to, a, an,* and *from,* do not begin with a capital letter unless they are the first or last word of a title.

| Books | Movies | Songs |
|---|---|---|
| Stuart Little | Epic | "Down by the Bay" |
| Ramona the Brave | The Secret Garden | "Pop Goes the Weasel" |
| A Light in the Attic | Jumanji | "When You Wish Upon a Star" |

**Rewrite It**
Rewrite the sentences below. Capitalize the names of books, movies, and song titles.

1. It took Shakhil only two days to read the book how to eat fried worms.

   **It took Shakhil only two days to read the book How to Eat Fried Worms.**

2. Sara is sleeping over tonight, and we are going to watch toy story 2.

   **Sara is sleeping over tonight, and we are going to watch Toy Story 2.**

3. The song "let it go" is from the movie frozen.

   **The song "Let It Go" is from the movie Frozen.**

4. I love the poems in Bruce Lansky's book no more homework, no more tests.

   **I love the poems in Bruce Lansky's book No More Homework, No More Tests.**

5. Devon listened to the song "yellow submarine" on his mom's Beatles CD.

   **Devon listened to the song "Yellow Submarine" on his mom's Beatles CD.**

128

---

**Lesson 2.5** Capitalizing Book, Movie, and Song Titles

**Proof It**
Read the sentences below. There are 24 words that should begin with a capital letter but do not. To capitalize a letter, underline it three times. Then, write the capital letter above it.

1. I love to sing "<u>h</u>akuna <u>m</u>atata" from <u>t</u>he Lion King because the words are fun to say.
   *(H, M, T)*

2. Have you seen the old version or the new version of The <u>p</u>arent <u>t</u>rap?
   *(P, T)*

3. Felipe borrowed <u>t</u>he <u>w</u>ay <u>t</u>hings <u>w</u>ork by David Macaulay from the library.
   *(T, W, T, W)*

4. If you watch Schoolhouse Rock, you can learn the song "<u>c</u>onjunction junction."
   *(C)*

5. Last week, Lottie read Freckle <u>j</u>uice and Chocolate <u>f</u>ever.
   *(J, F)*

6. <u>m</u>adeline is the name of a book and a movie.
   *(M)*

7. Reading <u>t</u>he <u>g</u>reat <u>k</u>apok <u>t</u>ree by Lynne Cherry is a good way to learn about rain forests.
   *(T, G, K, T)*

8. My little sister sings "<u>s</u>hake <u>y</u>our <u>s</u>illies <u>o</u>ut" every morning.
   *(S, Y, S, O)*

9. Paul and Tyler saw <u>w</u>alking <u>w</u>ith <u>d</u>inosaurs three times in the movie theater!
   *(W, W, D)*

**Try It**

1. Imagine that you were shipwrecked on a desert island. If you could bring only one book with you, what would it be?

   **Answers will vary.**

2. What is the funniest movie you have seen in the last year?

   **Answers will vary.**

129

# Language Arts Grade 3 Answers

## Lesson 2.6 Periods

A **period** is an end mark that follows a statement or a command.

    Put your bike in the garage.      Natalie has four brothers.

Periods are also used after initials. An **initial** is a letter that stands for a name.

    Darren *B.* Johnson    *P. L.* Travers    *J. P.* O'Bryan

The **days of the week** are often written as abbreviations, or in a shorter form. A period follows the abbreviation.

    Mon.  Tues.  Wed.  Thurs.  Fri.  Sat.  Sun.

The **months of the year** can also be abbreviated. May, June, and July are not abbreviated because their names are short.

    Jan.  Feb.  Mar.  Apr.  Aug.  Sept.  Oct.  Nov.  Dec.

**People's titles** are usually abbreviated when they come before a name.

    *Mrs.* = mistress    *Mr.* = mister    *Dr.* = doctor

**Types of streets** are written as abbreviations in addresses.

    *St.* = street    *Ave.* = avenue    *Dr.* = drive    *Ln.* = lane
    *Rd.* = road    *Blvd.* = boulevard    *Ct.* = court    *Cir.* = circle

### Match It

Write the letter of the correct abbreviation on the line.

1. **a**   October 2      **a.** Oct. 2      **b.** Octob. 2
2. **b**   John Fitzgerald Kennedy    **a.** John F Kennedy    **b.** John F. Kennedy
3. **b**   Tuesday      **a.** Tu.      **b.** Tues.
4. **b**   Chester Avenue      **a.** Chester Avn.      **b.** Chester Ave.
5. **a**   December 19      **a.** Dec. 19      **b.** Dcmbr. 19
6. **b**   Madison Anne Hall      **a.** Madison A Hall      **b.** Madison A. Hall

**130**

## Lesson 2.6 Periods

### Proof It

Read the schedule below. Cross out words that can be written as abbreviations. Write the correct abbreviations above them.

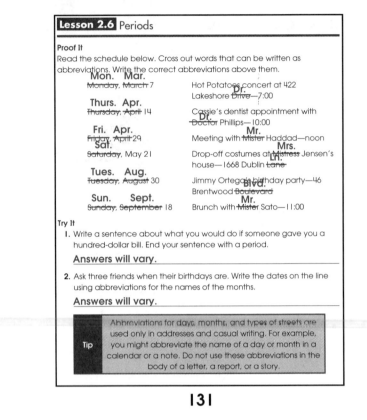

**Mon. Mar.**
~~Monday, March~~ 7      Hot Potatoes concert at 422 Lakeshore ~~Drive~~ **Dr.**—7:00

**Thurs. Apr.**
~~Thursday, April~~ 14      Cassie's dentist appointment with ~~Doctor~~ **Dr.** Phillips— 10:00

**Fri. Apr.**
~~Friday, April~~ 29      Meeting with ~~Mister~~ **Mr.** Haddad—noon

**Sat.**
~~Saturday,~~ May 21      Drop-off costumes at ~~Mistress~~ **Mrs.** Jensen's house—1668 Dublin ~~Lane~~ **Ln.**

**Tues. Aug.**
~~Tuesday, August~~ 30      Jimmy Ortega's birthday party—46 Brentwood ~~Boulevard~~ **Blvd.**

**Sun. Sept.**
~~Sunday, September~~ 18      Brunch with ~~Mister~~ **Mr.** Sato—11:00

### Try It

1. Write a sentence about what you would do if someone gave you a hundred-dollar bill. End your sentence with a period.

    **Answers will vary.**

2. Ask three friends when their birthdays are. Write the dates on the line using abbreviations for the names of the months.

    **Answers will vary.**

> **Tip**   Abbreviations for days, months, and types of streets are used only in addresses and casual writing. For example, you might abbreviate the name of a day or month in a calendar or a note. Do not use these abbreviations in the body of a letter, a report, or a story.

**131**

## Lesson 2.7 Question Marks

Use a **question mark** to end a sentence that asks a question.

    Would you like some fruit punch**?**    How many books did you read**?**
    Where is Connor going**?**    Can all birds fly**?**

### Complete It

Read each an [**Answers will vary. Possible answers:**] the answer.

Example: **Q:** How tall is Mr. Stein?

    **A:** Mr. Stein is six feet tall.

1. **Q:** **How many moons does Jupiter have?**

    **A:** Jupiter has at least 63 known moons.

2. **Q:** **What is the largest body in the solar system?**

    **A:** The sun is the largest body in the solar system.

3. **Q:** **Is Mars or Saturn closer to the sun?**

    **A:** Mars is closer to the sun than Saturn.

4. **Q:** **When did Galileo make his first telescope?**

    **A:** Galileo made his first telescope in 1608.

5. **Q:** **How long has Shannon Lucid spent in space?**

    **A:** Astronaut Shannon Lucid has spent more than 200 days in space.

6. **Q:** **What is the smallest planet?**

    **A:** Mercury is the smallest planet.

**132**

## Lesson 2.7 Question Marks

### Proof It

Read the paragraphs below. Cross out the six incorrect end marks. Add the correct end marks, and circle them.

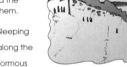

Have you ever visited the Sleeping Bear Dunes**(?)** They are located along the shore of Lake Michigan. The enormous dunes, or sand hills, are more than 400 feet tall in places. Many people travel to Michigan every year to climb the dunes**(?)** Most visitors come in the summer, but some people come in the winter, instead. Why would they visit the icy shores of the lake in the winter**(?)** Sledding down the steep slopes can be a lot of fun!

Do you know where the dunes got their name**(?)** A Native American legend says that a mother bear lay on the beach to watch for her cubs after a fire. Over time, sand covered the bear**(?)** Some people still think they can see the shape of a bear sleeping on the beach. This is how the dunes came to be called the Sleeping Bear Dunes**(?)**

### Try It

On the lines below, write a question you could ask a park ranger at Sleeping Bear Dunes National Lakeshore.

**Answers will vary.**

**133**

# Language Arts Grade 3 Answers

## Lesson 2.8 Exclamation Points

An **exclamation point** is used to end a sentence that is exciting or expresses strong feeling. Sometimes exclamation points are used to show surprise or fear.

That pan is hot!          Lindsay won first prize!
I can't believe you broke the chair!          There's a snake!

**Proof It**
Read the diary entry below. Five of the periods should be exclamation points. Find the five incorrect periods, and cross them out. Then, add exclamation points where they are needed.

Saturday, May 6

Dear Diary,

Something interesting happened today. I am going to be in a movie! The movie The Time Travelers is being filmed in my town. My mom works at the library. The director was learning about the history of the town at the library. My mom helped the director find what she needed. The director saw my picture on my mom's desk. She asked my mom if I would be interested in a small part in the movie. Would I ever!

I will have only two lines to say. Mom said she will help me memorize them. My scene will last about five minutes. Do you know what the best part is? I get to work with my favorite actor! I can't wait to start filming! Who knows? Maybe I'll be famous one day!

134

## Lesson 2.8 Exclamation Points

**Complete It**
The sentences below are missing end marks. Add the correct end mark in the space following each sentence. You should add four periods, two question marks, and three exclamation points.

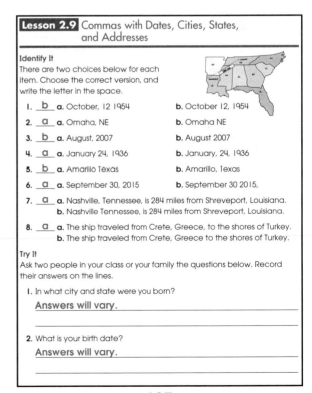

1. Evan and Tanner have been jumping on the trampoline all morning .
2. Have you read the book <u>A Cricket in Times Square</u> ?
3. Kazuki's swimming lesson was cancelled .
4. Watch out !
5. Please clean your room before bedtime .
6. The Bradview Tigers won the championship !
7. Would you like cheese on your sandwich ?
8. There's a huge spider in my bed !
9. Tereza traded stickers with her little brother .

**Try It**
1. Write a sentence that shows excitement. Your sentence should end with an exclamation point.
   **Answers will vary.**

2. Write a sentence that shows fear. Your sentence should end with an exclamation point.
   **Answers will vary.**

135

## Lesson 2.9 Commas with Dates, Cities, States, and Addresses

Commas are used in dates. They are used in between the day and the year.
March 4, 2006    September 22, 1750    June 1, 1991

Commas are also used in between the names of cities and states or cities and countries.
Portland, Oregon    Paris, France    Minneapolis, Minnesota

When the names of cities and states (or countries) are in the middle of a sentence, a comma goes after the state or country, too.
Bethany stopped in Burlington, Vermont, on her way home.

In an address, a comma is used between the city name and state abbreviation.
Richmond, VA    Juneau, AK

**Proof It**
Read the sentences below. Add commas by using this symbol (∧).

Example: The Rock and Roll Hall of Fame is in Cleveland∧Ohio.

1. Basketball star LeBron James was born on December 30∧1984.
2. Sarah Hughes skated in the Winter Olympics in Salt Lake City∧Utah.
3. In 2004, Lance Armstrong traveled to Liege∧Belgium∧to ride in the Tour de France.
4. Olympic swimmer Michael Phelps was born in Baltimore∧Maryland∧ in 1985.

| Tip | When only a month and year are given, do not separate them with a comma. August 1999    February 2014    December 1941 |

136

## Lesson 2.9 Commas with Dates, Cities, States, and Addresses

**Identify It**
There are two choices below for each item. Choose the correct version, and write the letter in the space.

1. **b** a. October, 12 1954          b. October 12, 1954
2. **a** a. Omaha, NE          b. Omaha NE
3. **b** a. August, 2007          b. August 2007
4. **a** a. January 24, 1936          b. January, 24, 1936
5. **b** a. Amarillo Texas          b. Amarillo, Texas
6. **a** a. September 30, 2015          b. September 30 2015,
7. **a** a. Nashville, Tennessee, is 284 miles from Shreveport, Louisiana.
   b. Nashville Tennessee, is 284 miles from Shreveport, Louisiana.
8. **a** a. The ship traveled from Crete, Greece, to the shores of Turkey.
   b. The ship traveled from Crete, Greece to the shores of Turkey.

**Try It**
Ask two people in your class or your family the questions below. Record their answers on the lines.

1. In what city and state were you born?
   **Answers will vary.**

2. What is your birth date?
   **Answers will vary.**

137

# Language Arts Grade 3 Answers

## Lesson 2.10 Commas in a Series

A **series** is a list of words. Use a comma after each word in a series except the last word.

Ms. Pinckney asked Alonzo, Erica, and Charley to work on the project together.

Dakota put a sandwich, an apple, and a granola bar in her lunchbox.

Our neighbors have two dogs, three cats, seven chickens, and a goat.

### Proof It

Read the note below. Twelve commas are missing. Add commas where they are needed by using this symbol (∧).

Dear Dillon,

Please go to the store for me when you get home from school. Tonight we are going to make muffins for Grandad's birthday breakfast. We will need blueberries∧eggs∧sugar∧ and lemon juice. I left some money on the kitchen table.

Ellie is going swimming with Rob∧Aliya∧Eve∧and Hunter. She will be home around 4:00. Please remind her to let the dog out∧hang up her swimsuit∧and start her homework.

I made a list of the things you said you will need for your science project. I put glue∧ sand∧newspaper∧vinegar∧and baking soda on the list. Is anything missing? We can go shopping tomorrow afternoon.

See you in a couple of hours!

Love,

Mom

138

---

## Lesson 2.10 Commas in a Series

### Rewrite It

The numbered sentences are missing commas. Rewrite each numbered sentence in the recipe, using commas where needed.

**Lemony Blueberry Muffins**

| | |
|---|---|
| 1½ cups flour | ½ cup milk |
| ⅓ cup yellow cornmeal | ½ cup plain yogurt |
| ⅓ cup sugar | 3 tablespoons oil |
| 1½ teaspoons baking powder | 1 tablespoon lemon juice |
| ½ teaspoon baking soda | 1 egg |
| ¼ teaspoon salt | 1 cup blueberries |

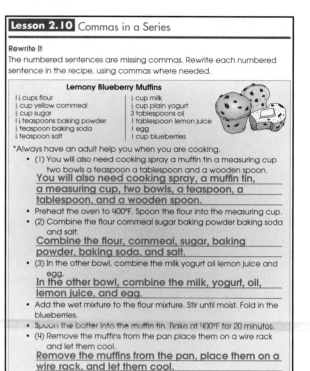

*Always have an adult help you when you are cooking.

- (1) You will also need cooking spray a muffin tin a measuring cup two bowls a teaspoon a tablespoon and a wooden spoon.
  **You will also need cooking spray, a muffin tin, a measuring cup, two bowls, a teaspoon, a tablespoon, and a wooden spoon.**
- Preheat the oven to 400°F. Spoon the flour into the measuring cup.
- (2) Combine the flour cornmeal sugar baking powder baking soda and salt.
  **Combine the flour, cornmeal, sugar, baking powder, baking soda, and salt.**
- (3) In the other bowl, combine the milk yogurt oil lemon juice and egg.
  **In the other bowl, combine the milk, yogurt, oil, lemon juice, and egg.**
- Add the wet mixture to the flour mixture. Stir until moist. Fold in the blueberries.
- Spoon the batter into the muffin tin. Bake at 400°F for 20 minutes.
- (4) Remove the muffins from the pan place them on a wire rack and let them cool.
  **Remove the muffins from the pan, place them on a wire rack, and let them cool.**

139

---

## Lesson 2.11 Commas in Compound Sentences

A **simple sentence** tells about one complete thought. A **compound sentence** is made of two or more simple sentences. To form a compound sentence, use a comma and the conjunction *and, or,* or *but* to join the simple sentences.

In the examples below, the underlined parts of each compound sentence can stand alone as simple sentences. Notice that a comma follows the first simple sentence.

Sadie likes orange juice, *but* her brother prefers apple juice.
Do you want to go to the zoo, *or* would you rather go to the art museum?
Alejandro collects baseball cards, *and* Adam collects coins.

### Identify It

Read each sentence below. If it is a simple sentence, write **S** on the line. If it is a compound sentence, write **C** on the line. Then, underline each simple sentence in the compound sentence.

1. __S__ Have you noticed birds in your yard or your neighborhood?
2. __C__ Feeding birds can be fun, and it can be educational.
3. __C__ Some birds like birdseed, but others like suet, a type of fat.
4. __S__ In the winter, many birds prefer fatty foods, like peanut butter.
5. __C__ Bird food placed on the ground will attract birds, but it will also attract other animals.
6. __S__ Squirrels are known for eating bird food and scaring birds away.
7. __S__ Once birds notice that you are feeding them, they will come to visit often.
8. __C__ Finches love thistle seed, and orioles love oranges.

140

---

## Lesson 2.11 Commas in Compound Sentences

### Proof It

Read the paragraph below. Three commas are missing from compound sentences. Add each comma by using this symbol (∧).

If you have a plastic soda bottle, you can make your own bird feeder. With an adult's help, make two holes on opposite sides of the bottle∧ and push a twig through each hole. Small birds can perch on the twig. Then, make several other holes in the bottle. The birds will be able to eat seeds from these holes. Tie some string around the neck of the bottle∧and hang it from a sturdy tree branch. Enjoy watching the birds from a window∧ but don't forget to feed them.

### Try It

1. Write a simple sentence about birds you have seen at a park or in your neighborhood.
   **Answers will vary.**

2. Write a compound sentence about other city wildlife you have seen.
   **Answers will vary.**

141

# Language Arts Grade 3 Answers

---

## Lesson 2.12 Punctuating Dialogue

The exact words a person says are called **dialogue**. One set of quotation marks is used before the first word of dialogue. A second set of quotation marks is used after the last word of dialogue.

"I love to sail."          "Is the fruit ripe?"

If the dialogue does not end the sentence, put a comma (not a period) inside the quotation marks. The period belongs at the very end of the sentence.

"I love to sail," Chloe said.          "The fruit isn't ripe," said Geoff.

If the dialogue is a question and does not end the sentence, keep the question mark inside the quotation marks.

"Do you love sailing?" Chloe asked.

"Are the bananas ripe?" asked Geoff.

If part of the sentence comes before the dialogue, put a comma after that part of the sentence. The period at the end of the sentence belongs inside the quotation marks.

Chloe said, "I love to sail."          Geoff asked, "Is the fruit ripe?"

**Proof It**

Read each sentence below. If the sentence is correct, make a check mark on the line (✓). If it is not correct, make an **X** on the line. Then, use the proofreading marks in the box to show the changes.

| | |
|---|---|
| ∧ | = insert comma |
| ⊙ | = insert period |
| ⌄ | = insert quotation marks |

Example: __X__ Our suitcases are in the attic," said Dad⊙

1. __X__ "This summer, I am going to take Spanish lessons," said Mackenzie.

2. __✓__ "My family is driving all the way across the country in an RV," Ryan said.

3. __X__ Nicolae said, "I plan to go swimming at the lake every day⊙"

142

---

## Lesson 2.12 Punctuating Dialogue

**Rewrite It**

The sentences below are missing commas, periods, and quotation marks. Rewrite each sentence. Add punctuation marks where needed.

1. I have never been to a farm before replied Audrey

   **"I have never been to a farm before," replied Audrey.**

2. Neither have I agreed Nicolae

   **"Neither have I," agreed Nicolae.**

3. My grandparents have cows, horses, goats, and barn cats said Van

   **"My grandparents have cows, horses, goats, and barn cats," said Van.**

4. He added I stay with them every summer, and there is always something to do

   **He added, "I stay with them every summer, and there is always something to do."**

5. I would love to learn how to ride a horse or milk a cow said Audrey

   **"I would love to learn how to ride a horse or milk a cow," said Audrey.**

6. Van grinned at Audrey and said My grandparents can always use an extra hand

   **Van grinned at Audrey and said, "My grandparents can always use an extra hand."**

**Try It**

Ask two of your classmates what they plan to do next summer. Record their answers on the lines below. Remember to use quotation marks to show the exact words your classmates use.

1. **Answers will vary but quotation marks should be used correctly.**

2. **Answers will vary but quotation marks should be used correctly.**

143

---

## Lesson 2.13 Punctuating Titles

**Titles of books, movies, and plays** are underlined.

Lucas did a book report on Two Heads Are Better Than One.

The movie Two Brothers is an adventure about twin tiger cubs.

For Dionne's birthday, her family went to see the play Peter Pan.

**Titles of songs, poems, and stories** are set in quotation marks.

Judith Viorst wrote the poem "If I Were in Charge of the World."

The story "The Emperor's Clothes" is in my book of fairy tales.

My favorite song is "Bright Eyes" by Remy Zero.

**Complete It**

Read each sentence below. Underline the titles of books, movies, and plays. Put quotation marks around the titles of songs, stories, and poems.

1. Before the first softball game of the season, we always sing "Take Me Out to the Ballgame."

2. Scotty Smalls is the main character in the movie The Sandlot.

3. My favorite poem is "Eletelephony" by Laura E. Richards.

4. In the play Annie, Bridget McCabe had the lead role.

5. Laura Ingalls Wilder wrote Little House in the Big Woods.

6. The movie The Incredibles won an award for Best Animated Film.

7. When it was time for bed, Dad told me a story called "Gregory and Grandpa's Wild Balloon Ride."

8. I memorized Edward Lear's poem "The Owl and the Pussycat."

9. Singing the song "Purple People Eater" makes my sister laugh.

| Tip | Remember to place periods inside quotation marks if a title comes at the end of a sentence. |
|---|---|

144

---

## Lesson 2.13 Punctuating Titles

**Proof It**

Read the diary entry below. Find the titles, and underline them or place them in quotation marks. To add quotation marks, use this symbol (⌄).

POETRY WEEK

Thursday, October 8

Dear Diary,

    I had a very busy week. On Monday, I went to the library after school. I worked on the story I am writing. It is called "The Mystery of the Golden Toothbrush." I borrowed the books Summer of the Sea Serpent, Stone Fox, and Pink and Say. I am going to write a book report on one of them, but I haven't decided which one.

    On Wednesday, I recited two poems for Poetry Week. I chose "The Shadow" by Robert Louis Stevenson and "Jellyfish Stew" by Jack Prelutsky. After school, I tried out for the play The Princess and the Pea. I hope I land the role of the princess.

    On Friday night, Ankit and Kendra came over to watch some movies. We rented Antz and My Neighbor Totoro. Antz is Kendra's favorite movie. My parents made subs and popcorn for us. We had a lot of fun, but I'm glad this crazy week is over!

**Try It**

1. What is your favorite song? Write the title on the line.

   **Answers will vary, but the song title should be set in quotation marks.**

2. Think of an idea for a story you could write. Then, write two possible titles for your story on the lines below.

   **Answers will vary, but both titles should be set in quotation marks.**

145

---

# Language Arts Grade 3 Answers

## Lesson 3.1 Subject-Verb Agreement: Adding **s** and **es**

The **subject** of a sentence tells who or what the sentence is about. When the subject is **singular**, it is only one person, place, or thing. When there is a singular subject, the verb ends with **s** or **es**.

Add **s** to most regular verbs that have a single subject.

*The boat* sail**s** close to shore.       *The woman* water**s** the flower.

Add **es** to regular verbs that have a single subject and end in **sh, ch, s, x,** and **z**.

*Gran* kiss**es** us good-bye.       *Jake* crunch**es** his cereal loudly.

When the subject is **plural**, it is more than one person, place, or thing. When the subject is plural, the verb does not end with **s** or **es**.

*The kittens* sleep on the sofa.       *Zared and Nina* latch the gate.

**Proof It**

Read the paragraph below. Underline the subjects. Find the verbs that do not agree with their subjects. Add or delete **s** or **es** from the verbs so that they agree with their subjects. Use this symbol (^) to add a letter or letters. Cross out letters that don't belong.

<u>Mr. Ruskin</u> wash^**es** his historic car on Saturdays. <u>Aaron and Ali</u> help~~s~~ him. <u>Mr. Ruskin</u> sprays the old car with warm water. <u>He</u> scrub^**s** every inch of the car with a big sponge. <u>The children</u> polish^**es** the windshield and <u>the mirrors</u>. <u>They</u> use clean, soft rags. <u>Aaron</u> wax^**es** the beautiful red car. <u>It</u> shine^**s** in the sunlight. <u>He wishes</u> to have a car just like his dad's one day. <u>Mr. Ruskin</u> take^**s** Aaron and Ali for a drive in the shiny car every Saturday afternoon. <u>They</u> buy ice-cream cones. Then, <u>they</u> walk~~s~~ in the park.

**146**

## Lesson 3.1 Subject-Verb Agreement: Adding **s** and **es**

**Complete It**

Read each sentence below. Then, read the pair of verbs in parentheses ( ). Choose the correct verb form. Write it on the line.

1. Emily and Mateo ____**toss**____ a ball in the backyard. (toss, tosses)
2. The Jorgensons ____**harvest**____ their pumpkins every autumn. (harvest, harvests)
3. My little brother ____**brushes**____ his teeth with an electric toothbrush. (brush, brushes)
4. Britta ____**bikes**____ ten miles a day when she is in training for the race. (bike, bikes)
5. The blender ____**mixes**____ the ingredients. (mix, mixes)
6. The Guzmans ____**camp**____ near a crystal-clear mountain lake every summer. (camp, camps)
7. The shaggy Irish setter ____**catches**____ the ball each time I throw it. (catch, catches)
8. Aunt Celeste ____**lives**____ about two hours away. (live, lives)

**Try It**

1. Write a sentence using one of the following verbs: *climb, skate, twirl, travel, race, point,* or *bake.* Underline the subject in your sentence, and circle the verb. Make sure that the subject and the verb agree.

   **Answers will vary.**

2. Write a sentence using one of the following verbs: *push, crash, finish, pitch, watch, miss,* or *fix.* Underline the subject in your sentence, and circle the verb. Make sure that the subject and the verb agree.

   **Answers will vary.**

**147**

## Lesson 3.2 Irregular Verbs: *Am, Is, Are*

*Am, is,* and *are* are all different forms of the verb *to be.*

*Am* is used only with the subject *I.*

   *I* **am** sleepy.   *I* **am** hungry.   *I* **am** under the bed.

*Is* is used when the subject is singular.

   *Mickey* **is** sixteen.   *Annabelle* **is** tall.   *The beach* **is** rocky.

*Are* is used with the subject *you.*

   *You* **are** very funny.   *You* **are** correct.   *You* **are** first in line.

*Are* is also used when the subject is plural.

   *Haley Joel Osment and Dakota Fanning* **are** actors.
   *The boys* **are** at home.

**Rewrite It**

Rewrite each sentence below. If it has a plural subject, rewrite it with a single subject. If it has a single subject, rewrite it with a plural subject. Remember that the form of the verb must agree with the subject and verb.

Example: The salad dressing and the salad are on the table.
   The salad dressing is on the table.

1. Nissa and Toby are eight.

   **Nissa is eight. OR Toby is eight.**

2. The photograph is in an album.

   **The photographs are in an album.**

3. The CDs on the shelf are from the library.

   **The CD on the shelf is from the library.**

4. We are excited about traveling to Mexico.

   **Answers will vary.**

**148**

## Lesson 3.2 Irregular Verbs: *Am, Is, Are*

**Proof It**

Read the paragraphs below. There are 11 mistakes with the verbs *am, is,* and *are.* Cross out each mistake. Then, write the correct form of the verb above it.

A topiary (*toe pee air ee*) ~~are~~ **is** a kind of sculpture made from plants. Topiaries ~~is~~ **are** cut to look like many different things. Some ~~am~~ **are** shaped like animals. For example, a topiary can look like an elephant, a bear, a horse, or even a dinosaur. Other topiaries ~~is~~ **are** trimmed to look like castles, cones, or mazes.

A topiary gardener ~~are~~ **is** an artist. He or she can turn simple shrubs into beautiful sculptures. Boxwood, holly, bay laurel, and yew ~~am~~ **are** some of the best plants to use for topiary. They ~~is~~ **are** easy to train and to trim.

In May, I ~~are~~ **am** going to visit the Green Animals Topiary Garden in Rhode Island. It ~~am~~ **is** one of the oldest topiary gardens in the country. There ~~am~~ **are** 80 pieces of topiary there! It ~~are~~ **is** fun to imagine all the green animals coming to life and roaming the gardens.

**Try It**

Write three sentences on the lines below. Use the verbs *am, is,* or *are* in each sentence.

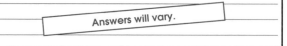

**Answers will vary.**

**149**

# Language Arts Grade 3 Answers

## Lesson 3.3 Irregular Verbs: *Has, Have*

*Has* and *have* are different forms of the verb *to have.*

*Have* is used when the subject is *I* or *you.*
    *I **have** a cold.*             *You **have** two brothers.*

*Have* is also used with plural subjects.
    *We **have** a book about dinosaurs.*
    *Roberto and Chiara **have** a baby sister.*
    *They **have** a yellow house.*    *Both cars **have** flat tires.*

*Has* is used when there is a single subject like *he, she,* or *it.*
    *She **has** blonde hair.*    *The librarian **has** a cheerful smile.*
    *A male deer **has** antlers.*

**Complete It**
Complete each sentence below with the word *has* or *have.* Write the correct word in the space.

1. Gus and Emily **have** a shell collection.

2. A horse conch **has** a cone shape and can grow to be almost two feet long.

3. Shells **have** value when they are beautiful or rare.

4. The shapes of some shells **have** interesting names, like helmet, basket, lamp, frog, and trumpet.

5. Oysters and clams **have** shells that are hinged at the back.

6. Emily **has** a necklace made from polished pieces of shell.

7. Cowrie shells **have** been used as money on Indian and Pacific islands.

8. If Gus **has** more than one of a certain shell, he will trade it with other collectors.

**150**

## Lesson 3.3 Irregular Verbs: *Has, Have*

**Proof It**
Read the letter below. There are eight mistakes with the verbs *have* and *has.* Cross out each incorrect verb. Then, write the correct form of the verb above it.

August 6, 2015

Dear Kyra,

    How is life at home in Massachusetts? We are having a great time in Florida. Gus and I ~~has~~ **have** 40 new shells to add to our collection! We ~~has~~ **have** been busy searching the beaches here. Gus and I already ~~has~~ **have** labels for our new shells. We don't want to forget their names by the time we get home.

    Some shells still ~~has~~ **have** animals living in them. We never collect those shells. Our parents ~~has~~ **have** helped us look in rock crevices and tide pools. That is how we found a true tulip shell. It ~~have~~ **has** a pretty peachy color and an interesting pattern.

    I ~~has~~ **have** a surprise to bring home for you. You ~~has~~ **have** never seen a shell like this. I can't wait to see you. Wish you were here!

Your friend,

Emily

**151**

## Lesson 3.4 Forming the Past Tense by Adding **ed**

Verbs in the **present tense** tell about things that are happening right now. Verbs in the **past tense** tell about things that have already happened.

Add **ed** to a regular verb to change it to the past tense. If the verb already ends in **e**, just add **d**.
    The concert end**ed** at 9:00.    It snow**ed** 16 inches yesterday!
    Uncle Donny tasted the pudding.    The waitress smile**d** at the girl.

If a verb ends in **y**, change the **y** to **i** and add **ed**.
    We hurry to catch the bus.    We hurr**ied** to catch the bus.
    I dry the laundry outside.    I dr**ied** the laundry outside.

**Complete It**
Read the sentences below. Complete each sentence with the past tense of the verb in parentheses ( ).

1. Leonardo da Vinci **painted** the mysterious *Mona Lisa.* (paint)

2. Women and children often **posed** for artist Mary Cassatt. (pose)

3. The Impressionists **showed** the world that not all paintings had to look realistic. (show)

4. Grandma Moses **loved** to paint cheerful pictures of life in the country. (love)

5. Jackson Pollack, who made colorful paint-splattered paintings, **studied** with Thomas Hart Benton. (study)

6. Vincent van Gogh **created** more than 800 oil paintings during his lifetime! (create)

7. Chinese artist Wang Yani **started** painting when she was only two. (start)

**152**

## Lesson 3.4 Forming the Past Tense by Adding **ed**

**Rewrite It**
Read the sentences below. They are all in the present tense. Underline the verb in each sentence. Then, rewrite the sentences in the past tense.

1. Norman Rockwell <u>lives</u> from 1894 until 1978.
   **Norman Rockwell lived from 1894 until 1978.**

2. Norman <u>studies</u> at the National Academy of Design in New York.
   **Norman studied at the National Academy of Design in New York.**

3. He <u>illustrates</u> issues of children's magazines, like *Boys' Life.*
   **He illustrated issues of children's magazines, like *Boys' Life.***

4. Norman <u>paints</u> scenes from everyday small-town life.
   **Norman painted scenes from everyday small-town life.**

5. Norman <u>calls</u> himself a storyteller.
   **Norman called himself a storyteller.**

6. A fire <u>destroys</u> many of Norman's paintings.
   **A fire destroyed many of Norman's paintings.**

7. Norman Rockwell <u>receives</u> the Presidential Medal of Freedom in 1976.
   **Norman Rockwell received the Presidential Medal of Freedom in 1976.**

**Try It**
1. Write a sentence in the present tense that describes a piece of art you have seen or made.
   **Answers will vary.**

2. Now, rewrite the same sentence in the past tense.
   **Answers will vary.**

**153**

# Language Arts Grade 3 Answers

---

**Lesson 3.5** Irregular Past-Tense Verbs: *Ate, Said, Grew, Made, Rode*

Some verbs do not follow the pattern of regular verbs. The past tenses of these verbs are different. To form the past tense, do not add **ed** or **d** to these verbs. Instead, you must change the entire word.

| **Present tense** | **Past tense** |
|---|---|
| She *eats* a snack every day. | She *ate* a snack every day. |
| Mario *says* it will rain tonight. | Mario *said* it will rain tonight. |
| The tiny pine tree *grows* quickly. | The tiny pine tree *grew* quickly. |
| Catalina *makes* bracelets. | Catalina *made* bracelets. |
| I *ride* the bus downtown. | I *rode* the bus downtown. |

**Proof It**

Some of the verbs below are in the wrong tense. Cross out the verbs in bold type. Use this symbol (^), and write the correct word above it.

When my mom was a little girl, her family owned a bakery. Mom ~~says~~ *said*^
that she loved the sweet smell of bread and pastries baking in the ovens.
Every morning, Mom ~~eats~~ *ate*^ a cinnamon roll for breakfast. She ~~rides~~ *rode*^ her bike
to school when the weather was nice. In her bag, she carried fresh muffins
for her teachers and her friends.

In the afternoon, she and her dad ~~make~~ *made*^ crusty rolls and chewy
bagels. Grandpa put all the ingredients in a big bowl. He and Mom took
turns kneading the dough. Then, he covered it with a clean towel. The
dough ~~grows~~ *grew*^ and ~~grows~~ *grew*^. Mom ~~says~~ *said*^ she loved to punch it down. Finally, she
and Grandpa shaped the dough and popped it into the ovens.
Mom's family ~~eats~~ *ate*^ fresh bread with dinner every night!

**154**

---

**Lesson 3.5** Irregular Past-Tense Verbs: *Ate, Said, Grew, Made, Rode*

**Solve It**

Read each sentence below. On the line, write the past tense of the underlined verb.

1. Grandma always <u>eats</u> a blueberry bagel with cream cheese for breakfast. _____**ate**_____

2. The Larsons <u>say</u> that Hot Cross Buns was the best bakery in town. _____**said**_____

3. Mom's cousin, Eddie, <u>rides</u> his bike around town and delivered bread. _____**rode**_____

4. Mom <u>grows</u> up helping her parents at the bakery. _____**grew**_____

5. Every Saturday, Mom and Grandpa <u>make</u> 12 loaves of wheat bread, 15 loaves of French bread, and 100 dinner rolls. _____**made**_____

Now, find each past-tense verb in the word search puzzle. Circle the words you find. Words are written across and down.

**Try It**

1. What did you eat for dinner last night? Use a complete sentence to answer the question.

   **Answers will vary.**

2. Write a sentence that uses the past tense of one of these words: *say, grow, make,* or *ride.*

   **Answers will vary.**

**155**

---

**Lesson 3.6** Irregular Past-Tense Verbs: *Gave, Flew, Brought, Thought, Wrote*

The past tenses of some verbs do not follow the patterns of regular verbs. To form the past tense, do not add **ed** or **d**. Instead, you must change the entire word.

| **Present tense** | **Past tense** |
|---|---|
| Franklin *gives* her an orange. | Franklin *gave* her an orange. |
| The goose *flies* over the pond. | The goose *flew* over the pond. |
| Marisa *brings* some games. | Marisa *brought* some games. |
| Beth *thinks* she got an A. | Beth *thought* she got an A. |
| I *write* a letter to my grandma. | I *wrote* a letter to my grandma. |

**Rewrite It**

The sentences below are all in the present tense. Rewrite them in the past tense.

1. Ms. Lucetta gives the class an assignment.

   **Ms. Lucetta gave the class an assignment.**

2. Nicholas and Liv write a play about a giant who lives in the forest.

   **Nicholas and Liv wrote a play about a giant who lives in the forest.**

3. They think the giant should be kind, not scary.

   **They thought the giant should be kind, not scary.**

4. A small bluebird flies many miles to save the kind giant.

   **A small bluebird flew many miles to save the kind giant.**

5. The bluebird brings him an important message.

   **The bluebird brought him an important message.**

6. The giant gives the bluebird shelter in his cave.

   **The giant gave the bluebird shelter in his cave.**

**156**

---

**Lesson 3.6** Irregular Past-Tense Verbs: *Gave, Flew, Brought, Thought, Wrote*

**Proof It**

Some of the verbs below are in the wrong tense. Cross out the underlined verbs. Use this symbol (^), and write the correct past-tense verbs above them.

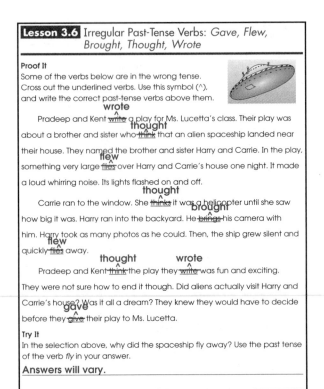

Pradeep and Kent ~~write~~ *wrote*^ a play for Ms. Lucetta's class. Their play was
about a brother and sister who ~~think~~ *thought*^ that an alien spaceship landed near
their house. They named the brother and sister Harry and Carrie. In the play,
something very large ~~flies~~ *flew*^ over Harry and Carrie's house one night. It made
a loud whirring noise. Its lights flashed on and off.

Carrie ran to the window. She ~~thinks~~ *thought*^ it was a helicopter until she saw
how big it was. Harry ran into the backyard. He ~~brings~~ *brought*^ his camera with
him. Harry took as many photos as he could. Then, the ship grew silent and
quickly ~~flies~~ *flew*^ away.

Pradeep and Kent ~~think~~ *thought*^ the play they ~~write~~ *wrote*^ was fun and exciting.
They were not sure how to end it though. Did aliens actually visit Harry and
Carrie's house? Was it all a dream? They knew they would have to decide
before they ~~give~~ *gave*^ their play to Ms. Lucetta.

**Try It**

In the selection above, why did the spaceship fly away? Use the past tense of the verb *fly* in your answer.

**Answers will vary.**

**157**

---

# Language Arts Grade 3 Answers

## Lesson 3.7 Forming the Future Tense

To write or speak about something that is happening right now, use the **present tense**. When something has already happened, use the **past tense**. When something has not happened yet, use the **future tense**.

**Past:** I *used* all the shampoo.
**Present:** I *use* all the shampoo.
**Future:** I *will use* all the shampoo.

The future tense is formed by using the word *will* with a verb. The word *will* means that something has not taken place yet, but it will happen in the future.

Seamus *will come* home in three days.
The plumber *will fix* the leaky pipe.
The water *will boil* in a minute or two.
Ms. Webster *will make* lasagna for dinner.

### Complete It
Complete each sentence with the future tense of the verb in parentheses ( ).

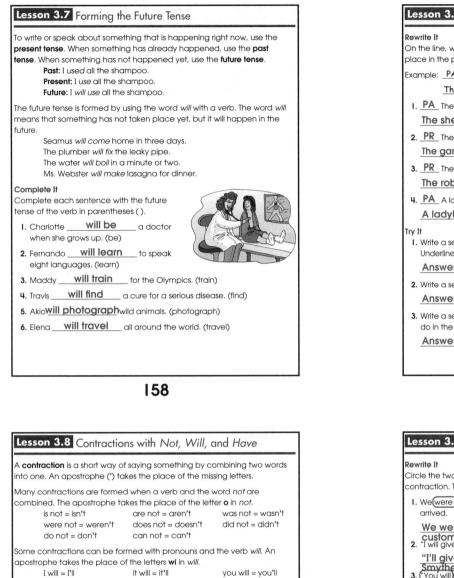

1. Charlotte _____ **will be** _____ a doctor when she grows up. (be)

2. Fernando _____ **will learn** _____ to speak eight languages. (learn)

3. Maddy _____ **will train** _____ for the Olympics. (train)

4. Travis _____ **will find** _____ a cure for a serious disease. (find)

5. Akio **will photograph** wild animals. (photograph)

6. Elena _____ **will travel** _____ all around the world. (travel)

158

## Lesson 3.7 Forming the Future Tense

### Rewrite It
On the line, write **PA** if a sentence takes place in the past. Write **PR** if it takes place in the present. Then, rewrite each sentence in the future tense.

Example: _PA_ The movie ended at 8:00.

The movie will end at 8:00.

1. _PA_ The sheepdog barked at the mail carrier.

**The sheepdog will bark at the mail carrier.**

2. _PR_ The gardener picks flowers from her wildflower garden.

**The gardener will pick flowers from her wildflower garden.**

3. _PR_ The robin pulls a fat earthworm from the soil.

**The robin will pull a fat earthworm from the soil.**

4. _PA_ A ladybug landed on Layla's shoulder.

**A ladybug will land on Layla's shoulder.**

### Try It
1. Write a sentence about someplace you have been in the past. Underline the verb.

**Answers will vary.**

2. Write a sentence about where you are right now. Underline the verb.

**Answers will vary.**

3. Write a sentence about somewhere you will go or something you will do in the future. Underline the verb.

**Answers will vary.**

159

## Lesson 3.8 Contractions with *Not, Will,* and *Have*

A **contraction** is a short way of saying something by combining two words into one. An apostrophe (') takes the place of the missing letters.

Many contractions are formed when a verb and the word *not* are combined. The apostrophe takes the place of the letter **o** in *not*.

| | | |
|---|---|---|
| is not = isn't | are not = aren't | was not = wasn't |
| were not = weren't | does not = doesn't | did not = didn't |
| do not = don't | can not = can't | |

Some contractions can be formed with pronouns and the verb *will*. An apostrophe takes the place of the letters **wi** in *will*.

| | | |
|---|---|---|
| I will = I'll | it will = it'll | you will = you'll |
| we will = we'll | she will = she'll | they will = they'll |
| he will = he'll | | |

Contractions can also be made with the verb *have*. An apostrophe takes the place of the letters **ha** in *have*.

| | |
|---|---|
| I have = I've | we have = we've |
| you have = you've | they have = they've |

### Proof It
Cross out the five incorrect contractions below. Use this proofreading mark (^), and write the correct contraction above it.

My neighborhood is having a giant yard sale on Saturday. ~~We'll~~ **We'll** post signs all around town. This week, ~~I'll~~ **I'll** go through the boxes under my bed and in the attic. There are many things I know we ~~do'nt~~ **don't** need. At first, my little brother ~~did'nt~~ **didn't** want to help. Then, I told him all the money would go to the animal shelter where we got our dog Maisy. I think ~~he'll~~ **he'll** be happy to help now.

160

## Lesson 3.8 Contractions with *Not, Will,* and *Have*

### Rewrite It
Circle the two words in each sentence that could be combined to make a contraction. Then, rewrite the sentences using contractions.

1. We (were not) even open for business yet when the first customers arrived.

**We weren't even open for business yet when the first customers arrived.**

2. "I will give you 15 dollars for the tricycle," said Mrs. Smythe.

**"I'll give you 15 dollars for the tricycle," said Mrs. Smythe.**

3. "(You will) find many great bargains," Justin told our customers.

**"You'll find many great bargains," Justin told our customers.**

4. Our free lemonade (did not) last long.

**Our free lemonade didn't last long.**

5. (We have) raised hundreds of dollars for the animal shelter!

**We've raised hundreds of dollars for the animal shelter!**

6. Maisy and I (can not) wait to give the check to the shelter's director.

**Maisy and I can't wait to give the check to the shelter's director.**

### Try It
1. Write a sentence about something you do not like doing. Use a contraction with *not* in your sentence. Circle the contraction.

**Answers will vary.**

2. Write a sentence about something you will do in the future. Use a contraction with *will* in your sentence. Circle the contraction.

**Answers will vary.**

161

# Language Arts Grade 3 Answers

## Lesson 3.9 Contractions with *Am, Is, Are,* and *Would*

**Contractions** can be made with different forms of the verb *to be*. The apostrophe takes the place of the first vowel in *am, is,* and *are*.

| | |
|---|---|
| I am = I'm | it is = it's |
| you are = you're | we are = we're |
| he is = he's | they are = they're |
| she is = she's | |

Contractions formed with the word *would* are a little different. The apostrophe takes the place of the entire word, except for the **d**.

| | |
|---|---|
| I would = I'd | it would = it'd |
| you would = you'd | we would = we'd |
| he would = he'd | they would = they'd |
| she would = she'd | |

### Match It

Match each pair of underlined words with its contraction. Write the letter of the contraction in the space.

1. __d__ <u>I am</u> going to take gymnastics lessons with my friend, Elise.
2. __g__ <u>She is</u> a year older than I am.
3. __b__ Elise said <u>she would</u> show me some warm-up stretches.
4. __f__ Our class meets on Wednesdays. <u>It is</u> in an old building on Fourth Street.
5. __a__ <u>We are</u> going to carpool to class.
6. __c__ Elise's dad teaches gymnastics. <u>He is</u> also the high school coach.
7. __e__ <u>I would</u> like to be on his team when I am in high school.

a. We're
b. she'd
c. He's
d. I'm
e. I'd
f. It's
g. She's

162

## Lesson 3.9 Contractions with *Am, Is, Are,* and *Would*

### Complete It

Fill in each blank below with a contraction from the box.

| I'm | It's | He's | It'd |
|---|---|---|---|
| We're | she'd | I'd | She's |

1. __I'd__ like to meet Olympic gold-medal gymnast Carly Patterson one day.
2. __She's__ from my hometown of Baton Rouge, Louisiana.
3. In an interview, Carly said __she'd__ like to try a career in singing.
4. Elise's favorite gymnast is Blaine Wilson. __He's__ a three-time Olympic gymnast.
5. __We're__ each going to write a letter to Carly and Blaine.
6. __I'm__ sure they will write back to us when they hear what big fans we are.
7. __It'd__ be an amazing experience to see the Olympic Games live.
8. __It's__ my dream to travel to the Olympics.

### Try It

1. Write a sentence about a famous person you would like to meet. Use a contraction in your sentence. Underline the contraction.
   Answers will vary.

2. Write a sentence that includes a contraction with the word *am, is,* or *are*. Underline the contraction.
   Answers will vary.

163

## Lesson 3.10 Negative Words and Double Negatives

**Negative words** are words like *no, none, never, nothing, nobody, nowhere,* and *no one*. The word *not* and contractions that use *not* are also negative words. A sentence needs only one negative word. It is incorrect to use a **double negative**, or more than one negative word, in a sentence.

**Correct:** There were *not* any oranges in the refrigerator.
There were *no* oranges in the refrigerator.
**Incorrect:** There were *not no* oranges in the refrigerator.

**Correct:** Kevin *never* saw anyone he knew at the store.
Kevin saw *no one* he knew at the store.
**Incorrect:** Kevin *never* saw *no one* he knew at the store.

**Correct:** *None* of the students were born in another country.
**Incorrect:** *None* of the students *weren't* born in another country.

### Proof It

Read the paragraphs below. There are five double negatives. Cross out one negative word or phrase in the incorrect sentences to correct them.

If you haven't ~~never~~ heard of Jellyfish Lake, you should learn more about it. This amazing saltwater lake is in Palau, an island in the Philippines. You do not ~~never~~ want to get too close to a jellyfish in the ocean. Ocean jellyfish sting their prey. The jellyfish of Jellyfish Lake do not have ~~no~~ stingers. Instead, they use algae and sunlight to get the nutrients they need.

These jellyfish have only one predator—the sea anemone. This is why there are so many of them. No one can ~~never~~ swim in the lake without seeing millions of these jellyfish. It is a special experience for humans. ~~Not~~ Nowhere else in the world can people swim surrounded by more than 25 million harmless jellyfish.

164

## Lesson 3.10 Negative Words and Double Negatives

### Complete It

Read each sentence below. Circle the word or words from the pair in parentheses ( ) that correctly complete each sentence.

1. The jellyfish don't (never, (ever)) stop moving.
2. They don't do ((anything), nothing) but follow the sun across the lake all day long.
3. My aunt said there ((is), is not) nowhere on Earth she would rather go snorkeling.
4. People who swim with the jellyfish shouldn't ((ever), never) lift or throw the delicate animals.
5. There aren't (no, (any)) jellyfish without stingers in the oceans of the world.
6. Because the jellyfish don't have to hunt for their food, there ((was), was not) no need for stingers.
7. The beautiful jellyfish don't (never, (ever)) seem to be too bothered by human visitors.
8. El Niño brought high temperatures to Palau in the late 1990s. Suddenly, there weren't ((any), no) jellyfish in the lake.

### Try It

1. Write a sentence using one of these negative words: *no, none, never, nothing, nobody, nowhere, no one,* or *not*.
   Answers will vary.

2. On another piece of paper, write a sentence using a double negative. Trade papers with a classmate. On the line below, write your classmate's sentence correctly.
   Answers will vary.

165

# Language Arts Grade 3 Answers

## Lesson 3.11 Forming Plurals with **s** and **es**

The word **plural** means *more than one*. To make many nouns plural, add **s**.

one egg → two egg**s**        one dog → six dog**s**
one pencil → many pencil**s**        one photo → nine photo**s**

If a noun ends in **sh**, **ch**, **s**, or **x**, form the plural by adding **es**.

one bush → three bush**es**        one peach → five peach**es**
one fox → two fox**es**        one bus → several bus**es**

If a noun ends with a consonant and a **y**, drop the **y** and add **ies** to form the plural.

one baby → all the bab**ies**        one cit**y** → many cit**ies**

**Complete It**
Read each sentence below. Complete it with the plural form of the word in parentheses ( ).

1. Ethan made two _____wishes_____ as he blew out his birthday candles. (wish)

2. All the _____branches_____ in the yard came down during the huge thunderstorm last week. (branch)

3. Jacob takes care of the _____cats_____ next door when our neighbors go out of town. (cat)

4. We need about six ripe _____apples_____ to make apple pie. (apple)

5. Hallie left her _____glasses_____ at a friend's house. (glass)

6. Claudia and Crista picked sour _____cherries_____ from the tree in the yard. (cherry)

7. Please recycle the _____boxes_____ in the garage. (box)

8. Four _____families_____ have volunteered to organize the book sale. (family)

166

## Lesson 3.11 Forming Plurals with **s** and **es**

**Solve It**
Read the clues below. Find the word in the box that matches each clue. Then, make the word plural, and write it in the numbered space in the crossword puzzle.

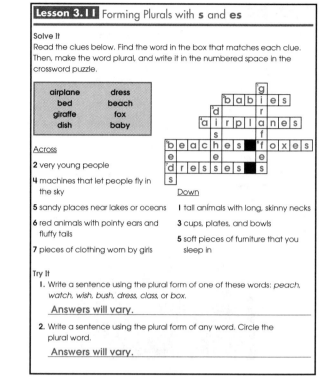

| airplane | dress |
| bed | beach |
| giraffe | fox |
| dish | baby |

Across

**2** very young people

**4** machines that let people fly in the sky

**5** sandy places near lakes or oceans

**6** red animals with pointy ears and fluffy tails

**7** pieces of clothing worn by girls

Down

**1** tall animals with long, skinny necks

**3** cups, plates, and bowls

**5** soft pieces of furniture that you sleep in

**Try It**

1. Write a sentence using the plural form of one of these words: *peach, watch, wish, bush, dress, class,* or *box.*

   _Answers will vary._

2. Write a sentence using the plural form of any word. Circle the plural word.

   _Answers will vary._

167

## Lesson 3.12 Irregular Plurals

Some plural words do not follow the rules. Instead of adding an ending to these words, you need to remember their plural forms.

one *man*, seven *men*        one *foot*, two *feet*
one *woman*, five *women*        one *goose*, ten *geese*
one *ox*, six *oxen*        one *child*, a lot of *children*
one *mouse*, many *mice*        one *die*, two *dice*

Some words do not change at all. The singular and plural forms are the same.

one *deer*, six *deer*        one *fish*, forty *fish*
one *moose*, two *moose*        one *sheep*, a dozen *sheep*
one *trout*, five *trout*        one *series*, three *series*
one *species*, nine *species*

**Match It**
Match each phrase below to the correct plural form. Write the letter on the line.

1. **b** one woman     a. fifty womans     **b.** fifty women

2. **a** one die     **a.** six dice     b. six dies

3. **a** a moose     **a.** many moose     b. many mooses

4. **a** the trout     **a.** hundreds of trout     b. hundreds of trouts

5. **a** one species     **a.** eight species     b. eight specieses

6. **b** the goose     a. four gooses     **b.** four geese

7. **b** one ox     a. a herd of oxes     **b.** a herd of oxen

8. **b** a child     a. most childs     **b.** most children

168

## Lesson 3.12 Irregular Plurals

**Solve It**
On the lines below, write the plural form of each word in the box.

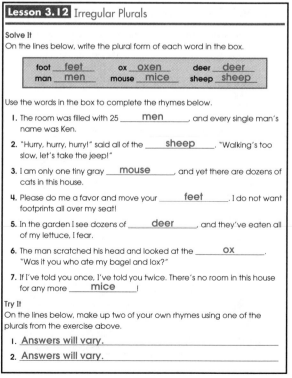

| foot _feet_ | ox _oxen_ | deer _deer_ |
| man _men_ | mouse _mice_ | sheep _sheep_ |

Use the words in the box to complete the rhymes below.

1. The room was filled with 25 _____men_____, and every single man's name was Ken.

2. "Hurry, hurry, hurry!" said all of the _____sheep_____. "Walking's too slow, let's take the jeep!"

3. I am only one tiny gray _____mouse_____, and yet there are dozens of cats in this house.

4. Please do me a favor and move your _____feet_____. I do not want footprints all over my seat!

5. In the garden I see dozens of _____deer_____, and they've eaten all of my lettuce, I fear.

6. The man scratched his head and looked at the _____ox_____. "Was it you who ate my bagel and lox?"

7. If I've told you once, I've told you twice. There's no room in this house for any more _____mice_____!

**Try It**
On the lines below, make up two of your own rhymes using one of the plurals from the exercise above.

1. _Answers will vary._

2. _Answers will vary._

169

# Language Arts Grade 3 Answers

## Lesson 3.13 Singular Possessives

When something belongs to a person or thing, they *possess* it. An apostrophe (') and the letter **s** at the end of a word show that the person or thing is the owner in a **possessive**.

| | |
|---|---|
| Julianne**'s** violin | the school**'s** gym |
| Ichiro**'s** basketball | the tiger**'s** stripes |
| the park**'s** gates | Trent**'s** sister |

### Proof It
The possessives below are missing apostrophes. To add an apostrophe, use this symbol (ⱽ).

1. The White Houses address is 1600 Pennsylvania Avenue.
2. Two fires almost destroyed the home of the nations president.
3. The Presidents House, the Presidents Palace, and the Executive Mansion were early names for the White House.
4. The Oval Offices shape was chosen by President Taft.
5. Some of the worlds best artists have work displayed in the White House.
6. President Bushs dogs, Barney and Miss Beazley, were Scottish terriers.

**170**

## Lesson 3.13 Singular Possessives

### Rewrite It
Rewrite the sentences below. Replace the underlined words in each sentence with a possessive.

Example: The capital of Hawaii is Honolulu.
<u>Hawaii's capital is Honolulu.</u>

1. The hometown of Ronald Reagan was Tampico, Illinois.
   **Ronald Reagan's hometown was Tampico, Illinois.**

2. The nickname of Benjamin Harrison was "Little Ben."
   **Benjamin Harrison's nickname was "Little Ben."**

3. Theodore Roosevelt was the youngest president of the nation.
   **Theodore Roosevelt was the nation's youngest president.**

4. Michelle Obama, the wife of the President Obama, is an advocate for healthy eating.
   **Michelle Obama, President Obama's wife, is an advocate for healthy eating.**

5. The 39th president of America was Jimmy Carter.
   **America's 39th president was Jimmy Carter.**

6. Before he became president, one of the jobs of Harry Truman was farming.
   **Before he became president, one of Harry Truman's jobs was farming.**

### Try It
Write a sentence about a well-known figure from history. Use a possessive in your sentence.

**Answers will vary.**

**171**

## Lesson 3.14 Plural Possessives

To form the **possessive of a plural** word that ends in **s**, add an apostrophe after the **s**.

| | |
|---|---|
| the girls' room | the monkeys' food |
| the berries' juice | the teachers' decision |

For plural words that do not end in **s**, add an apostrophe and an **s** to form the possessive.

| | |
|---|---|
| the people**'s** goals | the men**'s** clothes |

### Complete It
Read each sentence below. Replace the words in parentheses ( ) with a possessive. Write the possessive in the space.

1. (The thick white fur of polar bears) **The polar bears' thick white fur** keeps them warm during Arctic winters.
2. (The mother of the bear cubs) **The bear cubs' mother** protects her babies from wolves and other predators.
3. (The coats of caribou) **The caribous' coats** change colors, depending on the seasons.
4. (The flippers of seals) **The seals' flippers** make them strong, speedy swimmers.
5. When the young girl listened quietly, she could hear (the songs of walruses) **the walruses' songs**.

| Tip | Apostrophes are the key to telling the difference between a plural and a possessive. | |
|---|---|---|
| | **Plural** | **Possessive** |
| | thousands of bugs | a bug's wings |
| | several boys | the boys' clubhouse |
| | four watermelons | the watermelon's seeds |

**172**

## Lesson 3.14 Plural Possessives

### Identify It
Read each phrase below. If it is plural, write **PL** on the line. If it is plural possessive, write **PP**.

1. **PL** the playful baby seals
2. **PP** the igloos' walls
3. **PL** the floating icebergs
4. **PL** the Arctic rivers
5. **PL** hundreds of salmon
6. **PP** the puffins' brightly-colored beaks
7. **PP** the explorers' route
8. **PP** the people's warm clothing

### Try It
Write two sentences that include plural words.

1. **Answers will vary.**
2. **Answers will vary.**

Now, write two sentences that use the possessive form of the plural words from above.

3. **Answers will vary.**
4. **Answers will vary.**

**173**

# Language Arts Grade 3 Answers

## Lesson 3.15 Subject and Object Pronouns

**Pronouns** are words that take the places of nouns and proper nouns.
**Subject pronouns** take the place of subjects in sentences. Some subject pronouns are *I, you, he, she, it, we,* and *they.*

| | |
|---|---|
| *Eduardo* likes to rollerblade. | *He* likes to rollerblade. |
| *The mall* was crowded. | *It* was crowded. |
| *Serena and Libby* were in the newspaper. | *They* were in the newspaper. |

**Object pronouns** often follow action words or words like *to, at, from, with,* and *of.* Some object pronouns are *me, you, him, her, it, us,* and *them.*

| | |
|---|---|
| The horse **jumped** the fence. | The horse **jumped** it. |
| Joey went **with** Mr. Simms. | Joey went **with** him. |
| I put the letter on top **of** the dresser. | |
| I put the letter on top **of** it. | |

### Identify It
Read the sentences below. Underline each pronoun. Write **SP** above it if it is a subject pronoun. Write **OP** above it if it is an object pronoun.

1. The librarian gave <u>him</u> [OP] the book.
2. Heather and Chase took the puppy with <u>them.</u> [OP]
3. <u>It</u> [SP] will be sunny and 65 degrees today.
4. The children sang the song to <u>her.</u> [OP]
5. <u>I</u> [SP] will ask the owner tomorrow.
6. Ngozi received all the information from <u>you.</u> [OP]

| Tip | When you are talking about yourself and another person, always put the other person before you. Jaya and I    Lee and me    He and I |
|---|---|

174

## Lesson 3.15 Subject and Object Pronouns

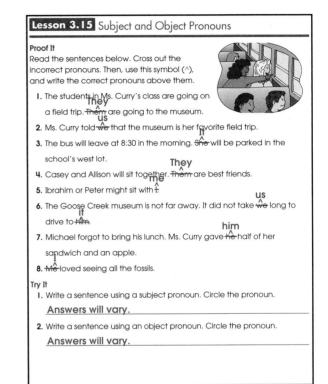

### Proof It
Read the sentences below. Cross out the incorrect pronouns. Then, use this symbol (^), and write the correct pronouns above them.

1. The students in Ms. Curry's class are going on a field trip. ~~Them~~ [They] are going to the museum.
2. Ms. Curry told ~~we~~ [us] that the museum is her favorite field trip.
3. The bus will leave at 8:30 in the morning. ~~She~~ [It] will be parked in the school's west lot.
4. Casey and Allison will sit together. ~~Them~~ [They] are best friends.
5. Ibrahim or Peter might sit with ~~I~~ [me].
6. The Goose Creek museum is not far away. It did not take ~~we~~ [us] long to drive to ~~him~~ [it].
7. Michael forgot to bring his lunch. Ms. Curry gave ~~he~~ [him] half of her sandwich and an apple.
8. ~~Me~~ [I] loved seeing all the fossils.

### Try It
1. Write a sentence using a subject pronoun. Circle the pronoun.

   <u>Answers will vary.</u>

2. Write a sentence using an object pronoun. Circle the pronoun.

   <u>Answers will vary.</u>

175

## Lesson 3.16 Comparative Adjectives

**Adjectives** can be used to compare people or things that are similar. Add **er** to an adjective to compare two things.

> "The medium chair is hard**er** than the small chair," said Little Red Riding Hood.

Add **est** to compare three or more things.

> Papa Bear's bed is soft. Mama Bear's bed is soft**er**. Baby Bear's bed is soft**est**.

For adjectives that end in **e**, just add **r** or **st**.

> nice, nicer, nicest    close, closer, closest    gentle, gentler, gentlest

For adjectives that end in a consonant and a **y**, drop the **y** and add **ier** or **iest**.

> tiny, tinier, tiniest    spicy, spicier, spiciest    busy, busier, busiest

### Identify It
Read the sentences below. Choose the correct adjective from the pair in parentheses, and circle it.

> #### 4th Annual Fitness Challenge a Success!
> Here are the results from last week's Fitness Challenge.
> - Brad Dexter and Ariela Vega were the (faster, (fastest)) sprinters.
> - The ((youngest), young) student to participate was six-year-old Emily Yu.
> - Most students said the obstacle course this year was (hardest, (harder)) than the one last year.
> - Everyone agreed that the (easyest, (easiest)) event was the beanbag toss.
> - The weather was both (sunnyer, (sunnier)) and (coldest, (colder)) than last year.
> - The (stranger, (strangest)) thing that happened all week was when the clown made a homerun at the kickball game. No one knows who was wearing the clown costume!
> - The cafeteria was (busiest, (busier)) after the challenges than it usually is at lunchtime.
> - Morgan Bonaventure won the award for ((Greatest), Greater) Overall Performance.

176

## Lesson 3.16 Comparative Adjectives

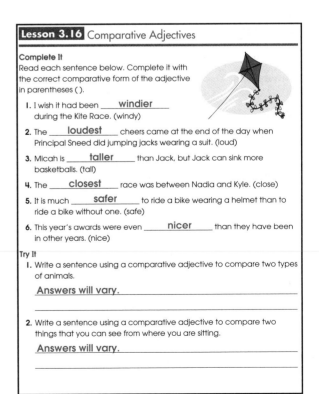

### Complete It
Read each sentence below. Complete it with the correct comparative form of the adjective in parentheses ( ).

1. I wish it had been _____windier_____ during the Kite Race. (windy)
2. The _____loudest_____ cheers came at the end of the day when Principal Sneed did jumping jacks wearing a suit. (loud)
3. Micah is _____taller_____ than Jack, but Jack can sink more basketballs. (tall)
4. The _____closest_____ race was between Nadia and Kyle. (close)
5. It is much _____safer_____ to ride a bike wearing a helmet than to ride a bike without one. (safe)
6. This year's awards were even _____nicer_____ than they have been in other years. (nice)

### Try It
1. Write a sentence using a comparative adjective to compare two types of animals.

   <u>Answers will vary.</u>

2. Write a sentence using a comparative adjective to compare two things that you can see from where you are sitting.

   <u>Answers will vary.</u>

177

# Language Arts Grade 3 Answers

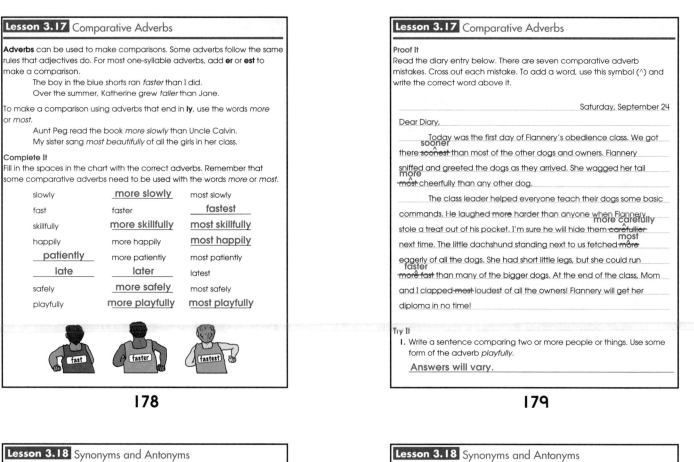

## Lesson 3.17 Comparative Adverbs

**Adverbs** can be used to make comparisons. Some adverbs follow the same rules that adjectives do. For most one-syllable adverbs, add **er** or **est** to make a comparison.

> The boy in the blue shorts ran *faster* than I did.
> Over the summer, Katherine grew *taller* than Jane.

To make a comparison using adverbs that end in **ly**, use the words *more* or *most*.

> Aunt Peg read the book *more slowly* than Uncle Calvin.
> My sister sang *most beautifully* of all the girls in her class.

**Complete It**
Fill in the spaces in the chart with the correct adverbs. Remember that some comparative adverbs need to be used with the words *more* or *most*.

| slowly | more slowly | most slowly |
| fast | faster | fastest |
| skillfully | more skillfully | most skillfully |
| happily | more happily | most happily |
| patiently | more patiently | most patiently |
| late | later | latest |
| safely | more safely | most safely |
| playfully | more playfully | most playfully |

fast | faster | fastest

**178**

## Lesson 3.17 Comparative Adverbs

**Proof It**
Read the diary entry below. There are seven comparative adverb mistakes. Cross out each mistake. To add a word, use this symbol (^) and write the correct word above it.

Saturday, September 24

Dear Diary,

    Today was the first day of Flannery's obedience class. We got there ~~soonest~~ sooner than most of the other dogs and owners. Flannery sniffed and greeted the dogs as they arrived. She wagged her tail ~~most~~ more cheerfully than any other dog.

    The class leader helped everyone teach their dogs some basic commands. He laughed ~~more~~ harder than anyone when Flannery stole a treat out of his pocket. I'm sure he will hide them ~~carefuller~~ more carefully next time. The little dachshund standing next to us fetched more^most eagerly of all the dogs. She had short little legs, but she could run ~~more fast~~ faster than many of the bigger dogs. At the end of the class, Mom and I clapped ~~most~~ loudest of all the owners! Flannery will get her diploma in no time!

**Try It**
1. Write a sentence comparing two or more people or things. Use some form of the adverb *playfully*.

    <u>Answers will vary.</u>

**179**

## Lesson 3.18 Synonyms and Antonyms

**Synonyms** are words that have the same, or almost the same, meanings. Using synonyms in your writing can help you avoid using the same words over and over. They can make your writing more interesting.

| quick, fast | present, gift | sad, unhappy |
| close, near | jump, hop | tired, sleepy |

**Antonyms** are words that have opposite meanings.

| old, young | wide, narrow | true, false |
| never, always | funny, serious | smile, frown |

**Complete It**
Read each sentence below. If the sentence is followed by the word *synonym*, write a synonym for the underlined word on the line. If it is followed by the word *antonym*, write an antonym for the underlined word.

1. The rocks in the walls of the Grand Canyon are millions of years <u>old</u>. (antonym) <u>young</u>

2. Limestone is the <u>top</u> layer in the nine layers of rocks. (antonym) <u>bottom</u>

3. The waters of the Colorado River formed the <u>enormous</u> canyon. (synonym) <u>Possible answers: huge, giant</u>

4. Francisco Vásquez de Coronado led the <u>first</u> Europeans to see the canyon. (antonym) <u>last</u>

5. Native Americans lived in the canyon <u>before</u> Europeans arrived. (antonym) <u>after</u>

6. If you <u>yell</u> into the canyon, you will hear echoes of your voice. (synonym) <u>Possible answers: scream, shout, holler</u>

7. People <u>like</u> taking burro rides through the canyon. (synonym) <u>enjoy</u>

**180**

## Lesson 3.18 Synonyms and Antonyms

**Solve It**
Write a synonym from the box beside each word in numbers 1–5. Write an antonym from the box beside each word in numbers 6–10.

| difficult | wrong | destroy | sleepy | giggle |
| close | cheap | speak | loose | same |

1. laugh <u>giggle</u>
2. wreck <u>destroy</u>
3. talk <u>speak</u>
4. shut <u>close</u>
5. tired <u>sleepy</u>
6. right <u>wrong</u>
7. expensive <u>cheap</u>
8. tight <u>loose</u>
9. easy <u>difficult</u>
10. different <u>same</u>

```
r  t  j  d  e (g  h  o  s) q  d
f (d  i  f  f  i  c  u  l  t) g
j  e  i  b  w  g  h  m  e  y  y
o (s  a  m  e) g  e  d  e  u  r
a  t  w  b  k  l  a  e  p  z  n
(w  r  o  n  g) e (p  n  y  u  o
(l  o  o  s  e) k (c  l  o  s  e)
g  y  c  l  n (s  p  e  a  k) d
```

Now, find the words from the box in the word search puzzle. Circle each word you find. Words are written across and down.

**Try It**
1. Write a sentence using a synonym for *terrific*.

    <u>Answers will vary.</u>

2. Write a sentence using an antonym for *boring*.

    <u>Answers will vary.</u>

**181**

# Language Arts Grade 3 Answers

## Lesson 3.19 Homophones

**Homophones** are words that sound alike but have different spellings and meanings. Here are some examples of homophones.

Did you *hear* that noise?     The party is *here*.
Connor *knew* it would rain today.     I like your *new* haircut.
There is only *one* pancake left.     I *won* the raffle!
*Our* family is very large.     Pick Sam up in an *hour*.
*Your* mom speaks Spanish.     *You're* my best friend.

### Identify It

Read each sentence below. If the word in **bold** type is used correctly, make a check mark (✓) on the line. If it is not used correctly, write its homophone on the line.

1. __knew__ Mei **new** the best way to get from Seattle, Washington, to Portland, Oregon.
2. __✓__ We are meeting for lunch an **hour** before we go up in the Space Needle.
3. __Your__ **You're** sister said that it rains a lot in Seattle.
4. __✓__ The Seattle Mariners **won** the game on Friday night!
5. __Our__ **Hour** class is going on a field trip to Pike Place Market.
6. __✓__ Is **your** boat docked in Puget Sound?
7. __here__ The 1962 World's Fair was held **hear** in Seattle.
8. __new__ The **knew** Seattle Central Library is a beautiful glass and steel building located downtown.

**182**

## Lesson 3.19 Homophones

### Complete It

Read the following sentences. Complete each sentence with a word from the pair of homophones in parentheses. Write the word on the line.

1. Jada __knew__ they would take the Washington State Ferry to Bainbridge Island. (knew, new)
2. __Our__ family moved to Seattle because Mom works with computers. (Hour, Our)
3. I can see the Cascade Mountains from __here__! (hear, here)
4. I am excited that __you're__ going hiking at Mount Rainier this weekend. (your, you're)
5. __One__ of Seattle's most famous residents is computer giant Bill Gates. (Won, One)
6. Brendan did not __hear__ the guide say that Smith Tower was Seattle's first skyscraper. (hear, here)
7. The Seattle Seahawks moved into their __new__ football stadium in 2002. (new, knew)
8. Does __your__ uncle still work at the Seattle Children's Museum? (you're, your)

### Try It

On the lines below, write two sentences. Use the word *won* in the first sentence. Use the word *one* in the second sentence.

1. __Answers will vary.__
2. __Answers will vary.__

**183**

## Lesson 3.20 Multiple-Meaning Words

**Multiple-meaning words** are words that are spelled the same but have different meanings. Look at how the word is used in the sentence to figure out which meaning it has.

In the first sentence below, the word *trunk* means *an elephant's snout*. In the second sentence, it means *a sturdy box used for storage*.

    The elephant used its *trunk* to pick up the stick.
    Grandpa's old photos are stored in a *trunk* in the attic.

In the first sentence below, the word *fair* means *a carnival*. In the second sentence, it means *equal* or *just*.

    Jonah rode on a Ferris wheel at the county *fair*.
    It is not *fair* that I have to go to bed an hour earlier than Amanda.

### Find It

The dictionary entry below shows two different meanings for the same word. Each meaning is a different part of speech. Use the dictionary entry to answer the questions below.

    **watch** *noun*: a small device that is worn on the wrist and used to keep time
       *verb*: to look at or follow with one's eyes

1. Mikayla's grandparents gave her a watch for her birthday.
Which definition of *watch* is used in this sentence? __a__
   **a.** the first definition       **b.** the second definition

2. Did you watch the movie you rented?
Which definition of *watch* is used in this sentence? __b__
   **a.** the first definition       **b.** the second definition

3. What part of speech is *watch* when it is used to mean *a device used to keep time*? __a__
   **a.** a noun       **b.** a verb

**184**

## Lesson 3.20 Multiple-Meaning Words

### Match It

Read each sentence below. Choose the definition that matches the way the word in **bold** type is used in the sentence. Write the letter of the definition on the line.

1. __b__ If you don't hurry, you'll miss the **train**!
   **a.** to teach something by repeating it
   **b.** a line of cars that move together along a track

2. __b__ Mark scored a **goal** in the second half of the game.
   **a.** something that people work hard to achieve
   **b.** a score in a game when a puck or ball is shot into a certain area

3. __a__ Eloise is the **second** child in a family of four girls.
   **a.** number two; the one that comes after the first
   **b.** a moment in time; a small part of a minute

4. __b__ We dropped pennies in the **well** and made a wish for each one.
   **a.** healthy; good
   **b.** a deep hole in the ground, used to get water or oil

5. __a__ Gabrielle's piano teacher is **patient** when she makes mistakes.
   **a.** not easily irritated or annoyed
   **b.** someone who is getting medical treatment

### Try It

1. Write a sentence using one of the multiple-meaning words from the exercise above (*train, goal, second, well, patient*).
   __Answers will vary.__

2. Now, write a sentence using the other meaning of the word you chose.
   __Answers will vary.__

**185**

# Reading Grade 3 Answers

---

1. This story is mostly about
   _____ a sleepover.
   _____ Sam's parents.
   __X__ two boys' plans.

2. At the beginning, when Sam and Kent are talking on the phone, what did you think they might be talking about?
   **Answers will vary.**

3. In the story, when did you find out what the boys are planning?
   **when Sam asks his parents for permission**

4. Why do you think Sam told his dad about the grass clippings?
   **Answers will vary.**

5. Why does Sam mention being warm enough and when the lights will be turned out?
   **Answers will vary.**

6. Now that the boys have permission, what do you think they will do next?
   **Answers will vary.**

7. In paragraph 5, why are the words *Now, if we can only talk our parents into letting us do this* in italics?
   **Sam is not speaking out loud. He is thinking those words.**

8. What is the author's purpose in writing this selection?
   **to entertain**

9. Have you ever been worried about asking your parents to do something? What was it, and how did you ask them?
   **Answers will vary.**

197

---

1. One of the boys usually has the ideas. The other one seems to go along with those ideas. Which boy is the "leader"?
   **Sam**

2. What details from the story helped you answer question 1?
   **Answers will vary.**

3. Kent says he might help his mom with supper. What does that tell you about Kent?
   **Answers will vary.**

4. Based on what you know about camping, how do you feel about all the stuff the boys have in their tent? List what you think they need and what they don't need.
   **What They Need**
   **Answers will vary.**

   **What They Don't Need**
   **Answers will vary.**

5. In some stories, the author tells you what is happening. In this story, the author uses mostly dialogue, what the characters say, to let you know what is going on. Choose one line of dialogue and write what it helps you know about the character.
   Dialogue: **Ex.: "Oh, no! We're camping. Those are just for in the house..."**
   **Answers will vary.**

6. Why does Kent think that Sam knows more about camping?
   **Possible answer: The tent belongs to Sam's dad, so Kent figures Sam knows something about camping.**

7. How do you think the boys feel about camping out together? Explain your answer.
   **Answers will vary.**

199

---

1. What do you know about pitching a tent? Do you have anything to add to these instructions?
   **Answers will vary.**

2. Number the sentences to show the order of steps to pitch a tent.
   __3__ Spread out groundcloth.
   __7__ Tighten and peg guy lines.
   __1__ Choose and clear an area.
   __5__ Put together tent poles.
   __2__ Lay out equipment.
   __4__ Pound stakes through loops.
   __6__ Raise the poles.

3. If you don't know or understand what a guy line is, which illustration helps you figure it out? Tell how.
   **The illustration that goes with Step 7; the guy lines are stretched out, just as the text describes.**

4. Choose one illustration. Explain what it shows.
   **Answers will vary.**

5. In the first paragraph, the author says that pitching a tent alone is difficult. Why do you think this is?
   **Possible answer: It is hard to put in the poles and raise the tent alone.**

6. What is the purpose of a groundcloth?
   **Possible answer: to protect the bottom of the tent**

7. Which two steps explain what to do with the poles?
   **5** and **6**

8. After reading these instructions, do you think you could pitch a tent? Why or why not?
   **Answers will vary.**

201

---

1. Which sentence best describes this story?
   __X__ Nothing exciting happens to the boys in the tent.
   _____ The boys have a crazy night in the tent.
   _____ In the morning, Kent plays a trick on Sam and scares him.

2. Why did the boys stop playing badminton?
   **Sam finds crumbs in his sleeping bag.**

3. Read the sentences below. Write F next to sentences that are facts and O next to sentences that are opinions.
   __O__ Kent eats too many crackers.
   __F__ Sam's dad had been telling camping stories for almost an hour.
   __F__ Breakfast is ready.
   __O__ Sam's dad tells the best camping stories.

4. What do you think the boys were hoping would happen?
   **Answers will vary.**

5. In paragraph 3, why does Kent turn red?
   **Answers will vary.**

6. Write C next to the sentence below that is the cause. Write E next to the sentence that is the effect.
   __E__ Kent landed on top of Sam.
   __C__ Sam's mom startled the boys.

7. This story has two settings. What are they?
   **Sam's kitchen** and **the tent**

203

---

# Reading Grade 3 Answers

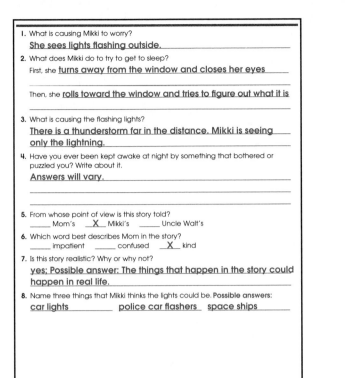

**205**

1. What is causing Mikki to worry?
   She sees lights flashing outside.

2. What does Mikki do to try to get to sleep?
   First, she turns away from the window and closes her eyes

   Then, she rolls toward the window and tries to figure out what it is

3. What is causing the flashing lights?
   There is a thunderstorm far in the distance. Mikki is seeing only the lightning.

4. Have you ever been kept awake at night by something that bothered or puzzled you? Write about it.
   Answers will vary.

5. From whose point of view is this story told?
   _____ Mom's   _X_ Mikki's   _____ Uncle Walt's

6. Which word best describes Mom in the story?
   _____ impatient   _____ confused   _X_ kind

7. Is this story realistic? Why or why not?
   yes; Possible answer: The things that happen in the story could happen in real life.

8. Name three things that Mikki thinks the lights could be. Possible answers:
   car lights       police car flashers   space ships

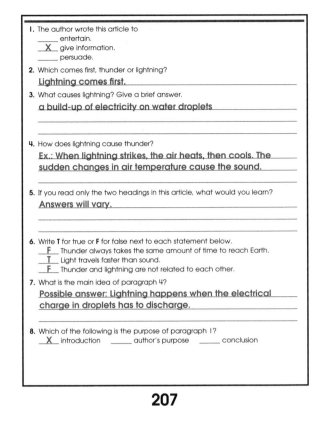

**207**

1. The author wrote this article to
   _____ entertain.
   _X_ give information.
   _____ persuade.

2. Which comes first, thunder or lightning?
   Lightning comes first.

3. What causes lightning? Give a brief answer.
   a build-up of electricity on water droplets

4. How does lightning cause thunder?
   Ex.: When lightning strikes, the air heats, then cools. The sudden changes in air temperature cause the sound.

5. If you read only the two headings in this article, what would you learn?
   Answers will vary.

6. Write **T** for true or **F** for false next to each statement below.
   _F_ Thunder always takes the same amount of time to reach Earth.
   _T_ Light travels faster than sound.
   _F_ Thunder and lightning are not related to each other.

7. What is the main idea of paragraph 4?
   Possible answer: Lightning happens when the electrical charge in droplets has to discharge.

8. Which of the following is the purpose of paragraph 1?
   _X_ introduction   _____ author's purpose   _____ conclusion

**209**

Put a check next to the sentences that are true.

1. _✓_ The idea for Smokey the Bear started in the 1940s.

2. _____ Smokey the Bear lives in New Mexico.

3. _____ The Forest Service made posters in honor of a bear cub that died in a fire.

4. _✓_ Smokey the Bear was a drawing first, and then a real bear.

Write **M** next to the sentences that tell about make-believe things.

5. _____ Smokey the Bear lived in a zoo for many years.

6. _M_ Smokey the Bear speaks to campers about the danger of forest fires.

7. _M_ Smokey the Bear used to help firefighters put out fires.

8. Why was Smokey the Bear created? Write the phrase or sentence from the article that tells you.
   to protect America's forests

9. In paragraph 2, what problem did U.S. leaders have?
   They were worried about having enough wood for the war.

10. What was the solution?
    to start a campaign to prevent forest fires

11. What organization created the fire safety posters?
    the Forest Service

12. In the posters, did Smokey the Bear look realistic? Explain.
    Possible answer: No, he was wearing a park ranger's hat.

**211**

A **fact** is something that can be proven true. An **opinion** is what someone thinks or feels. Check the sentences that are facts.

1. _✓_ Vegetables can be grown in pots.

2. _____ Creating a garden on a fire escape is difficult.

3. _____ Any garden is beautiful.

4. _✓_ Plants need soil and water.

5. Number the sentences to show the order in which things happened.
   _3_ Rosa bought potting soil.
   _2_ Rosa took the pots home.
   _4_ Rosa planted her seeds.
   _1_ Rosa saw the pots.

6. Check the words or phrases that best describe Rosa.
   _____ selfish
   _____ tends to waste time
   _✓_ likes the outdoors
   _✓_ appreciates beauty

7. Why do you think Rosa slept well the night after she bought seeds and soil?
   Possible answer: She felt happy and content.

8. The author repeats a line from paragraph 4 in the last paragraph. What line is it? Why do you think the author repeats it?
   masses of flowers and fat, glowing fruits; Possible answer: It's something Rosa likes to repeat to herself to remind her of what her garden will be like.

9. Have you ever planted something and watched it grow? Tell about how it made you feel.
   Answers will vary.

# Reading Grade 3 Answers

---

**213**

1. Why is Rosa worried about her plants on this day?
   **She is afraid the heat and lack of rain will hurt her plants.**

Write **T** if the sentence is true. Write **F** if the sentence is false.

2. **F** This story is mostly about Rosa worrying about her garden.
3. **F** Rosa is careless about her garden.
4. **T** Rosa plans to share her flowers with others.
5. **T** Too much sun causes Rosa's plants to dry up.

Compare how things really are with how they used to be, or with what Rosa imagines.

6. The strongest, tallest tomato plant is **pale and dry looking**.
   It had been **green and smooth**.
7. Rosa bites into an **apple**.
   She imagines that it is a **big, juicy tomato**.
8. She chops a **carrot**.
   She imagines that it is a **shiny green pepper**.
9. For now, Rosa works at a **factory**.
   She dreams of **running her own flower shop**.
10. Why do you think Rosa spends so much time daydreaming?
    **Possible answer: She doesn't like her job, and her life is not very colorful or interesting.**
11. What details from the story helped you answer question 10?
    **Answers will vary.**

12. Which of these is mostly likely to be true?
    _____ Rosa lives in the country.
    __✓__ Rosa lives in a city.

---

**215**

1. What do you know about peppers, or what experiences have you had growing or eating peppers?
   **Answers will vary.**

2. Do you like peppers? Write why or why not.
   **Answers will vary.**

3. How are bell peppers and chili peppers the same? How are they different? Write what the article tells you about each kind.
   **Bell Peppers**
   Size **apple-sized**
   Shape **round**
   Color **red, yellow, or green**
   Flavor **less spicy**
   **Chili Peppers**
   Size **many sizes**
   Shape **long and skinny**
   Color **red, yellow, or green**
   Flavor **hot or spicy**

4. What two headings does the author divide the article into? How is this helpful?
   **bell peppers and chili peppers; Possible answer: The sections help you know where to look for information in the article.**

5. Write **T** for true or **F** for false next to each statement below.
   **T** Hot peppers can make your eyes water.
   **F** Bell peppers are very spicy.
   **T** Peppers can be prepared in many ways.
   **F** Bell peppers are red, and chili peppers are green.

6. What makes chili peppers burn your mouth?
   **a chemical in them**

7. What two vitamins are peppers high in?
   **A** _____ and **C** _____

---

**217**

1. In most stories, a character has a problem. What is Perry's problem?
   **He feels awful during soccer practice.**

2. What information in the story helped you answer question 1?
   **Answers will vary.**

3. **Dialogue** is what the characters in a story say. What did you learn about Perry from his dialogue?
   **He doesn't ever want to go back to soccer practice.**

4. Find a line of the coach's dialogue. What does it tell you about the coach?
   Dialogue: **Answers will vary.**

   What it tells: **Answers will vary.**

5. Coach thinks that a passing exercise is important because
   **the players need to be able to pass the ball well during a game**

6. What is the setting for this story?
   **the soccer field**

7. **Practice was awful.** Is this a fact or an opinion?
   **an opinion**

8. The last line of paragraph 5 says that Perry didn't even wait for his mom's usual question. What do you think her question is?
   **Possible answer: How was practice?**

9. Which word or phrase best describes Perry in this story?
   _____ confident  _____ full of energy  __✓__ exhausted

10. Have you ever wished you could quit an activity? Tell about it.
    **Answers will vary.**

---

**219**

1. Mrs. Rothman is speechless because
   **Perry has just said he wants to quit soccer.**

2. Check two words that tell how Perry probably felt.
   __✓__ disappointed
   _____ proud
   _____ eager
   __✓__ frightened

3. Perry says he wants to quit soccer because
   **he is weak; doesn't have what it takes**

4. Have you ever tried to do something that was hard, or that you had to work at? What was it?
   **Answers will vary.**

   Did you get discouraged? Did you quit?
   **Answers will vary.**

5. Do you think Perry's decision is reasonable, or do you think he is giving up too easily? Explain.
   **Answers will vary.**

6. Mrs. Rothman probably feels
   __✓__ surprised  _____ angry  _____ entertained

7. What problem does Mrs. Rothman think Perry is having?
   **He didn't have a good lunch, so he was low on energy.**

8. How does she plan to help Perry?
   **She's going to make him a power snack to eat right before the next practice.**

9. What do you think would be a good example of a power snack? Explain your choice.
   **Answers will vary.**

---

# Reading Grade 3 Answers

Write these steps in the correct order. (Not all of the recipe's steps are here.)
- spread mixture into pan
- drizzle glaze
- grease the pan
- mix sugar, oil, and eggs
- remove from oven and cool

1. grease the pan

2. mix sugar, oil, and eggs

3. spread mixture into pan

4. remove from oven and cool

5. drizzle glaze

6. How long do the directions say to bake the bars?
16 to 22 minutes

7. The directions say to "drizzle honey glaze over bars." How did you know what honey glaze was?
Answers will vary.

Recipes often use short forms of words called **abbreviations**. Match the common recipe words in the box with their abbreviations.

| cup | teaspoon |
|---|---|
| Fahrenheit | tablespoon |

8. T. tablespoon

9. c. cup

10. F Fahrenheit

11. tsp. teaspoon

12. The directions say, "Bake until center is set but not firm." What does this mean?
Possible answer: The middle should not be gooey, but it should not be overbaked either.

13. How long do the energy bars need to cool?
They need to cool completely.

14. What is the longest you could keep these bars? What would you need to do to them?
six months; freeze them

**221**

---

1. When you read the story's title, did you guess about how the story ended? Was your guess close to being correct? Explain.
Answers will vary.

2. Circle the word that best describes the coach's words before the game.
angry    (encouraging)

3. Have you ever been in a sporting event or a performance that didn't turn out the way you expected? Did something funny or weird happen? Write about it.
Answers will vary.

4. At the end of paragraph 2, Coach says that the players have "dribbled to the moon and back." This is a figure of speech. What does it mean?
Possible answer: They have dribbled a great distance.

5. Give one example of dialogue in the story.
Possible answer: "Okay, everybody listen up!"

Now, give one example of a character's thought that is not spoken out loud.
Possible answer: Now that was a solid kick.

6. How are the two examples in question 5 written differently from each other?
The first one is in quotation marks, and the second one is in italics.

7. Why is it funny that someone in the crowd says, "It's a home run!"?
Possible answer: There are no home runs in soccer. The person was confusing soccer with baseball.

**223**

---

1. This article is mostly about
____ how soccer was named.
____ the rules of soccer.
✓ soccer's history.

2. Historians think that soccer might have started out as a
skill-building exercise for soldiers.

3. Why did King Edward III pass a law against soccer?
the game was rough or violent

4. What punishment did Queen Elizabeth have for soccer players?
a week of jail

5. What important rule change made the game into what we know as soccer? When did it happen?
In 1869 a rule against handling the ball with the hands was made.

6. If you wanted to find out about the beginnings of soccer, under which heading should you look?
Earliest Record

7. Under which heading would you find information about soccer during the last century or so?
The Modern Game Emerges

8. Write T for **true** or F for **false** next to each statement below.
F Today, you are allowed to touch the ball with your hands in soccer.
T Kicking and biting were common in soccer games long ago.
T In Britain, soccer is called "football."

9. At the end of paragraph 3, it says, "the game could not be stopped." Why do you think this was true?
Possible answer: It was popular, and people loved it too much to stop playing.

10. What was the author's purpose for writing this article?
to tell about the history of soccer

**225**

---

1. The person who wrote this article is the **author**. The author probably wrote this article to
____ make you laugh.
X give information.
____ persuade you to do something.

The author states some facts in the article. She also gives her opinion. Write **F** next to each sentence that is a fact. Write **O** next to each sentence that gives an opinion.

2. F Add adults into the mix, and you come up with more than 18 million Americans playing soccer.

3. O First, I think there's the international appeal.

4. F Though accidents may occur, body contact isn't supposed to be part of the game.

5. O And finally, I think there is the running factor.

6. Look back at the sentences you marked as opinions. What do you notice about them?
Answers will vary.

7. What is the main idea of paragraph 5?
____ Soccer is only for boys, just like other sports.
✓ Soccer is a good sport for both boys and girls.
____ Soccer has caught on with girls.

8. Why is soccer less expensive than some other sports?
You don't need a lot of equipment.

9. Look at the focus question under the title. What do you think its purpose is?
Possible answer: It tells you something to look for or think about as you read.

10. Have you ever played soccer? If so, tell about your experience. If not, explain why you would or would not like to try it.
Answers will vary.

**227**

# Reading Grade 3 Answers

---

**I.** Do you think Sharla, Tess, and Lee will be able to work together? Write why or why not.

   **Answers will vary.**

**2.** Think of times when you worked with classmates on projects. Was it hard or easy? Explain.

   **Answers will vary.**

**3.** Would you say that you are more like Sharla—full of ideas—or more like Lee—eager to stop talking and get to work? Write why.

   **Answers will vary.**

**4.** Does the teacher who is writing the journal seem thoughtful or worn out? Write why you think so.

   **Answers will vary.**

**5.** At the end of the first paragraph, the teacher says, "I knew something was going to blow up, and it wasn't the volcano." What does she mean?

   **Possible answer: She knows that the girls may end up having a fight.**

**6.** From whose point of view is this selection told?

   _____ Sharla   _____ Lee   _✓_ the teacher

**7.** What do you predict will happen next in the story?

   **Answers will vary.**

**8.** If you wrote a journal entry, what would you write about?

   **Answers will vary.**

**229**

---

This story is written in the form of a journal entry. The person who is writing uses *I* to refer to herself. She is the **narrator**, or the person telling the story.

**I.** Find a sentence that tells you that the narrator actually took part in the action of the story. Write the sentence here.

   **Answers will vary.**

**2.** The narrator, Sharla, disagreed with Lee about

   **whether to make the sides of the volcano smooth or rough**.

**3.** Sharla was upset because

   **she thought it was unfair to have to stay inside at recess.**

**4.** Did you expect this journal to be written by Mrs. Holt, the teacher? Why or why not?

   **Answers will vary.**

**5.** Why did the girls decide to make a village around the base?

   **Tess could do something without touching the volcano paste.**

**6.** Which of these words best describes Sharla's attitude toward the other two girls?

   _✓_ impatient   _____ understanding   _____ comforting

**7.** Explain how the picture adds to your understanding of the story.

   **Possible answer: I can get an idea of what the volcano will look like. I can see that Tess is not really helping.**

**8.** Write **C** next to the sentence below that is the cause. Write **E** next to the sentence that is the effect.

   _C_ The girls didn't make much progress on their volcano.

   _E_ Mrs. Holt made the girls stay in at recess.

**231**

---

**I.** In most stories, the characters have a problem. What problem do the characters in this story have?

   **They had disagreed about how to finish their project.**

**2.** What caused Mrs. Holt to call the girls up to her desk?

   **They weren't done with their project.**

**3.** What is Tess's idea?

   _X_ to show flowing lava

   _____ to make both sides smooth

   _____ to make the village larger

**4.** What is the result of Tess's idea?

   **The girls agree to make one side smooth and one side rough. Sharla and Lee can both get what they want.**

**5.** Where in the story do we learn that the teacher, Mrs. Holt, knows the girls are not getting along?

   **Where it says, "knowing perfectly well that there was a problem."**

**6.** What is the main difference in the way this story is written, compared to the other two about the same characters?

   _____ This story is told from Lee's point of view.

   _____ Sharla is not a character in this story.

   _✓_ It is not written as a journal entry.

**7.** How do you think Mrs. Holt feels about the girls solving their own problem? Explain.

   **Answers will vary.**

**8.** What is the setting for this story?

   **a school classroom**

**9.** The girls learned how to build a volcano by doing this project. What else do you think they learned?

   **Possible answer: They learned how to get along and work as a team.**

**233**

---

**I.** This story is mostly about

   _____ becoming best friends after working together.

   _X_ what the girls learned from their project.

   _____ how a teacher helped the girls get along.

**2.** How do the girls feel about their volcano project?

   **They are proud of it.**

**3.** When it is Lee's turn to speak, she feels

   _X_ nervous.

   _____ happy.

   _____ cross.

**4.** Why did Sharla's face turn red when Mrs. Holt asked about how they completed their project?

   **She was embarrassed.**

**5.** What experiences have you had working with other people? Were there times when you didn't agree or get along? Write about it.

   **Answers will vary.**

**6.** When it is Tess's turn to speak, what does she tell about?

   **a famous volcano and a town that got covered by mud and ash**

**7.** Make a check mark next to the thing that happened first.

   _____ Mrs. Holt had a question.

   _✓_ Lee said, "This is our volcano."

   _____ Mrs. Holt looked pleased.

**8.** If the girls had to work together again, how do you think they would do? Explain.

   **Answers will vary.**

**235**

# Reading Grade 3 Answers

---

In nonfiction writing, the author sometimes calls attention to words that the reader may not know. Those words appear in **bold** type. The author usually gives the meaning of the bold word in the same sentence.

Below are the bold words from the article. Write the meaning of each word.

1. molten **melted**

2. expand **get bigger**

3. fissures **cracks**

4. active **experience eruptions**

5. dormant **inactive**

Write **F** next to each sentence that is a fact. Write **O** next to each sentence that is an opinion.

6. **O** Volcanic eruptions are one of the most striking natural events.

7. **O** A volcanic eruption is more frightening than a hurricane.

8. **F** Volcanoes are located in many places in the world.

9. What does the illustration show?
**the inside of a volcano**

10. Trace with your finger the path that magma would take from under Earth's crust to the surface. Describe the path in your own words.
**Answers will vary.**

11. Write **C** next to the sentence below that is the cause. Write **E** next to the sentence that is the effect.
**E** Parts of Earth's crust open up.
**C** The molten rock gets very hot and expands.

12. What are scientists who study volcanoes called?
**volcanologists**

237

---

1. What four common characteristics do mammals have?
**warm blood, backbones, milk fed to babies, and hair or fur**

In the article, the author showed some words in bold type. The meanings of those words are given as well. Find the meanings of the words, and write them here.

2. habitat **natural conditions**

3. insectivores **insect eaters**

4. rodents **gnawing animals**

5. carnivores **meat eaters**

6. Hoofed animals are named for the kind of **feet** they have.

7. Give one example of each kind of forest dweller.
**Possible answers:**
insect eaters: **moles**    gnawing animals: **beavers**
hare-like animals: **rabbits**    meat eaters: **coyotes**
hoofed animals: **moose**

8. Why do you think a forest is a good habitat for many different kinds of mammals?
**Possible answer: There are lots of trees to provide shelter.**

9. Think about what you know about mammals. Name two kinds of mammals that are not mentioned in the article. **Possible answers:**
**dogs** and **dolphins**

10. **Meat eaters eat smaller mammals, such as rabbits, mice, and moles.** Is this sentence a fact or an opinion?
**a fact**

239

---

The author of this article chose to share her own point of view. Find a sentence in which the author uses the word *I*. What idea is the author sharing in that sentence?

1. The sentence begins with **Answers will vary.** .
The author is saying **Answers will vary.** .

2. Do you think the author likes snakes, dislikes snakes, or is neutral? Write a sentence from the article that supports your answer.
**Answers will vary.**

Write **F** next to each sentence that is a fact. Write **O** next to each sentence that is an opinion.

3. **O** People dislike snakes because they have no legs.

4. **F** Snakes control the rodent population.

5. **O** Not meeting many snakes is a good thing.

6. Name one difference between mammals and reptiles.
**Possible answer: Mammals are warm-blooded, and reptiles are cold-blooded.**

7. What is one way in which snakes are useful?
**They help control the rodent population.**

8. What is the main idea of paragraph 4?
_____ If you get bitten by a poisonous snake, seek medical help.
**✓** Some snakes are poisonous, but that's not a good reason to dislike all snakes.
_____ Poisonous snakes are very vicious.

9. Tell how you feel about snakes and why.
**Answers will vary.**

241

---

1. To see a redwood tree, you have to go to **Oregon or California**.

2. Why do redwoods grow there?
**They need moisture from the ocean.**

3. What might happen if someone tried to grow a redwood tree in Kansas or Missouri, for example?
**Answers will vary.**

4. What do you think is most special about redwood trees? Write why.
**Answers will vary.**

5. Why do you think the author chose to use questions for the headings?
**Answers will vary.**

6. If you want to find out what conditions redwoods need to grow, under which heading would you look?
**Why do redwoods grow there?**

7. If you wonder what the big deal is about redwoods, under which heading should you look?
**What's special about redwoods?**

8. What three objects are shown in the diagram?
**a building, a tree, and a van**

9. What is the author's purpose for writing this selection?
_____ to entertain
_____ persuade
**✓** to inform

10. About how long can a redwood live?
**as long as 2,000 years**

243

# Reading Grade 3 Answers

Complete each sentence with the correct word.

| author | dialogue | narrator |
|---|---|---|

1. When characters speak, their words make up the story's
   **dialogue**.

2. The person who wrote the story is the **author**.

3. Within the story, the person or character who tells the story is the
   **narrator**.

4. In most stories, the main character has a problem. Miss Eller's problem is that
   **she needs to find a topic that will make everyone happy.**

5. Look at the illustration. What did Miss Eller's students do during their study of redwood forests?
   **Answers will vary.**

6. Where did Miss Eller get the idea of how to solve the problem?
   **She saw a poster of a woodland scene on the wall.**

7. How do you think Miss Eller's class feels about the project?
   **✓** excited
   _____ worried
   _____ upset

8. The last paragraph says that the classroom had been transformed. What does this mean?
   **Possible answer: It has been changed to look like something else.**

9. Write **C** next to the sentence below that is the cause. Write **E** next to the sentence that is the effect.
   **E** Students raise their hands to answer the question.
   **C** Miss Eller asks what lives in a redwood forest.

**245**

---

1. This story is mostly about
   **X** two boys trying to do a magic trick.
   _____ a boy teaching another boy a magic trick.
   _____ how to do a magic trick.

2. Josh got wet because **the flower vase tipped and spilled**

3. Why was Josh under the table?
   **to pull the flower vase down; to make the flowers disappear**

4. Write **C** next to the sentence below that is the cause. Write **E** next to the sentence that is the effect.
   **E** The vase tipped and got Josh wet.
   **C** The bottom of the box got stuck.

5. Why were the boys so excited about the old table they found?
   **It was perfect for doing magic tricks because of the hole.**

6. Doing magic is (easier, (harder)) than the boys had expected.

7. Gary thinks that he and Josh need real things, so he tells Josh to go get a real
   **rabbit**.

8. Read the sentences below. Write **F** next to sentences that are facts and **O** next to sentences that are opinions.
   **F** Gary held his breath.
   **O** The boys should use real flowers.
   **O** Being a magician is hard work.
   **F** Josh's hair was wet.

9. What do you think will happen next?
   **Answers will vary.**

**247**

---

1. How was the magic trick supposed to work?
   **Josh would pull Wiggles down through the bottom of the box.**

2. What actually happened?
   **Wiggles actually got out without the boys noticing.**

Write the best word to complete each sentence below.

3. They should have thought of Wiggles **sooner**. (brighter, sooner, calmer)

4. The magic words made the boys **laugh** so hard. (laugh, lame, learn)

5. It made Gary feel like a real magician when he **waved** his arms. (waved, cried, tapped)

6. The boys couldn't **believe** Wiggles was gone. (agree, scramble, believe)

7. Write **R** next to the sentences that tell about something real. Write **M** next to the sentences that are about made-up things.
   **R** Rabbits eat lettuce.
   **M** Rabbits disappear and reappear.
   **R** Magicians say magic words.

8. In the story, who is the magician, and who is the assistant?
   **Gary is the magician, and Josh is the assistant.**

9. Do you think the boys were surprised that Wiggles was actually gone? Why or why not?
   **Answers will vary.**

10. Which words best describe the boys?
    **✓** good-natured
    _____ sneaky
    _____ irritated

11. What do you think will happen next in the story?
    **Answers will vary.**

**249**

---

1. The author wrote this article to
   _____ persuade.
   _____ make you laugh.
   **X** give you information.

Write **F** next to each sentence that is a fact. Write **O** next to each sentence that is an opinion.

2. **F** Harry Houdini died more than 75 years ago.

3. **F** Houdini could escape from handcuffs.

4. **O** Harry Houdini was the only "real" magician.

5. **O** Houdini's magic tricks were wonderful.

6. The article gives details about Houdini and his life. Number the details in the order in which the author tells about them.
   **3** He escaped from a straitjacket, hanging upside down.
   **1** Houdini had his first magic shows when he was 17.
   **4** Houdini exposed "fake" magicians.
   **2** Houdini's magic tricks became more showy and daring.

7. Which of these old sayings would Houdini have agreed with?
   **✓** Practice makes perfect.
   _____ You are what you eat.
   _____ A watched pot never boils.

8. **Houdini believed he had special powers and could talk to spirits.** Is this statement true or false?
   **false**

**251**

Spectrum Grade 3

# Reading Grade 3 Answers

**253**

1. David Copperfield is an __illusionist__.
2. What did he start doing at age 12?
   __performing magic__
3. What was he doing by age 16?
   __teaching college-level classes__

Check all answers that are correct.

4. Which of these words do you think best describe Copperfield?
   _____ thoughtless
   _____ lazy
   __✓__ hard-working
   __✓__ talented
5. What do you think a magician could learn from Copperfield's collection of old magic books and equipment?
   __Answers will vary.__
6. If you were a magician or an illusionist, what kinds of tricks would you like to do?
   __Answers will vary.__
7. The headings below belong in this article. To which paragraph does each heading belong?
   Copperfield's Beginnings __2nd__
   What Is an Illusion? __1st__
   Saving Magic for the Future __4th__
   Project Magic __3rd__
8. In your own words, explain what an illusion is.
   __Possible answer: An illusion is like a trick on the eyes or the senses.__
9. The youngest person ever to be allowed to join the Society of American Magicians was __David Copperfield__
10. Why do you think Copperfield believes that his best work is Project Magic?
    __Possible answer: It's something he has done that helps other people and makes a difference in their lives.__

**253**

---

**255**

1. Number the sentences to show the order in which events happened in the story.
   __2__ Gary laughed about their magic words.
   __4__ The boys heard Josh's mom.
   __5__ The boys discovered Mom and Wiggles.
   __3__ The boys figured out how to say the words backward.
   __1__ Gary felt great because their trick worked.
   __6__ The boys tried to make Mom's flowers reappear.
2. What problem do the boys have in this story?
   __They can't find Wiggles the rabbit.__
3. What problem does Mom have?
   __Wiggles has eaten her flowers.__
4. How do the boys try to help Mom? Do you think it will work?
   __They try to do a magic trick to make her flowers reappear.__
5. Who does Wiggles belong to?
   __Josh__
6. Do you think Wiggles has escaped before? What details in the story helped you answer this question?
   __Yes, because Josh's mom says, "Now how many times . . ."__
   __This sounds as though Wiggles has escaped and eaten flowers many times before.__
7. Do you think the boys will continue working on their magic tricks? Why or why not?
   __Answers will vary.__

**255**

---

**257**

Write the best word to complete each sentence below.

1. Up ahead, the line of cars went around a ___curve___.
   (curve, ledge, movement)
2. Jason was worried about the bus being ___late___. (hard, late, extra)
3. Steven wanted to ___count___ the cars. (spin, read, count)
4. Have you ever been stuck in traffic? Write about how it felt.
   __Answers will vary.__
5. What might cause a traffic jam? List as many reasons as you can.
   __Answers will vary.__
6. How do you think the bus driver feels about the traffic jam?
   _____ amused
   _____ joyful
   __✓__ frustrated
7. If the bus is late, what will the bus driver do?
   __radio the school to let them know__
8. Write **C** next to the sentence below that is the cause. Write **E** next to the sentence that is the effect.
   __C__ Lots of cars are on the highway at the same time.
   __E__ The cars are causing a traffic jam.

**257**

---

**259**

1. What kinds of things do we count? List two examples from the article.
   __Ex.: inches of rain, students, government spending, voters, traffic accidents, etc.__
2. What do we learn from counting things?
   __Ex.: to see how things need to change or how things are changing__
3. How do you think the information shown in this graph affects you and your community?
   __Answers will vary.__
4. What can the number of traffic accidents tell us?
   __where new stop signs and lights should go__
5. How many years does this chart cover?
   __40 years__
6. Why is the title of the chart important?
   __It tells you what the chart shows.__

Use the bar graph to answer these questions.

7. For each year, which is greater, the population or the number of cars?
   __the population__
8. If you want population data for 1950, would this graph help you? How can you tell?
   __No. The title says that the graph includes data only for 1960–2000.__
9. What was the population of the United States in 1970?
   __about 203.2 million, or just over 200 million__
10. How many cars were there in 1990?
    __about 133.7 million, or about 130 million__

**259**

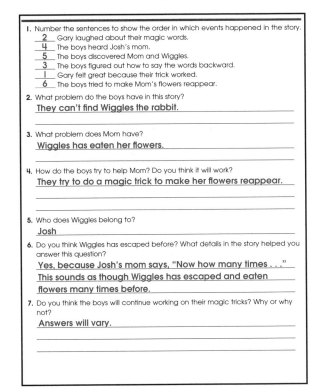

# Reading Grade 3 Answers

---

**1.** Tatsu is sitting in the shade on the front steps because
__it is a very hot day__.

**2.** Tatsu titles her drawing "Heat" because
__the sun is what is making her so hot__.

**3.** Write **R** next to the sentences that tell about something real. Write **M** next to the sentences that are about made-up things.
__M__ A person can make shade by drawing a picture of it.
__M__ A person can draw a picture of heat.
__R__ A person can draw a picture of the sun.

The **narrator** is the person who tells a story. Answer these questions.

**4.** Because the narrator is also a character, she uses the words *I* and *me* to tell her story. Find a place in the story where one of these words is used. Write the sentence here.
__Answers will vary.__

**5.** Where in the story do you discover what the narrator's name is?
__When her brother asks her a question.__

**6.** Do you think Tatsu and Fujio live in the city, in the country, or in a small town? Why?
__a city; Possible answer: They live in an apartment building.__
__The picture looks like a city, with lots of concrete.__

**7.** From whose point of view is the story told?
__✓__ Tatsu's ____ Fujio's ____ Not enough information is given.

**8.** The author uses lots of descriptions to tell how hot it is. List three details from the story that help you imagine the heat.
__Possible answers: Everything feels hot and sticky, including my own__
__skin; I feel like the glass greenhouse at the city park; I can count on__
__the fingers of one hand the number of leaves moving in the breeze.__

**9.** What do you like to do on a super hot summer day?
__Answers will vary.__

**261**

---

**1.** Why do Mario and Katie choose to draw pictures of cool water and a snow bank?
__because it helps them think about being cool on a hot day__

**2.** Why does Tatsu cross out her own picture of the sun?
__She thinks it might be making things feel hotter.__

**3.** Which word best describes the group of friends?
____ energetic
__✓__ creative
____ anxious

**4.** Mario doesn't use words to ask Fujio what he drew. How does he ask instead?
__He raises his eyebrows.__

**5.** What is the author's purpose in writing this story?
____ to teach ____ to persuade __✓__ to entertain

**6.** Why is the story titled "Wishes on the Sidewalk"?
__Possible answer: The kids draw pictures on the sidewalk of__
__things they are wishing for.__

**7.** Do you think that thinking about cool things can help a person cool down? Write why or why not.
__Answers will vary.__

**8.** Can you remember a hot day? How did it feel? Describe it so that someone else can imagine it easily.
__Answers will vary.__

**263**

---

**1.** This article is mostly about
____ animals that lived thousands of years ago.
__X__ early cave art.
____ how early people survived.

**2.** What did early cave artists use for paint?
__animal fat mixed with dirt or berries__

**3.** Where did early artists make their drawings?
__on walls deep inside caves__

**4.** Early cave art has been found in more than __130__ caves.

**5.** How do you like the cave art shown on this page? How is it the same or different from other drawings you have seen of mammoths?
__Answers will vary.__

**6.** Who is the author addressing, or talking to, in this article?
____ the reader
__✓__ the people who made the cave paintings
____ artists of today

**7.** Why is this an unusual way to write the article?
__Possible answer: Those people have been dead for__
__thousands of years. They are not reading the article.__

**8.** Most of the cave drawings have been found in __France__ and
__England__.

**9.** What is the main idea of paragraph 4?
__People drew what they saw around them.__

**10.** About how many years ago were the cave paintings made?
__about 17,000 years__

**265**

---

**1.** Number the sentences to show the order in which things happened.
__3__ Kyle gives Mom the phone message.
__4__ Mom goes to school on Thursday.
__1__ Mom goes out to mow the lawn.
__2__ Kyle takes a phone call for Mom.
__5__ Mrs. Essman asks Mom where the cake is.

**2.** Why does Mom take cookies to school on Thursday?
__She thought they were needed for a bake sale.__

**3.** While he is talking on the phone, Kyle is also __doing his homework__

**4.** What is the setting for this story?
__Kyle's kitchen__

**5.** What type of story is this?
__✓__ realistic fiction ____ science fiction ____ a tall tale

**6.** In paragraph 7, the author says that Mom is getting a little prickly. What does this mean?
__Possible answer: She is starting to sound irritated.__

**7.** What do you think Kyle will do the next time he answers the phone? Why?
__Possible answer: He will take a message and give it to his__
__mom. He learned from his mistake.__

**8.** Do you think it was fair for Kyle's mom to be frustrated with him? Explain.
__Answers will vary.__

**267**

# Reading Grade 3 Answers

**269**

1. What important parts of a phone message did Kyle forget the other day?
All four parts—name, number, write it down, and deliver the message

2. Look at the illustration. What do you think Mom is saying? Write the dialogue.
Answers will vary.

3. Why is Mom talking to the boys as though they are four years old?
Possible answer: She wants to be very clear with them about phone manners.

4. Look at the picture of Kyle and Anthony. What do you learn about the boys from the picture that isn't in the story?
They are probably twins.

5. How will the boys be tested?
They will be tested each time the phone rings.

6. Do you think Mom's phone class will be a success? Why or why not?
Answers will vary.

You have just attended the Phone Manners from Mom class. How should you respond to these telephone situations?

7. The phone rings. You answer it by saying, "Hello. (Last Name) residence. This is (First Name) speaking.

8. Your dad is reading a book on the porch. The phone rings and the person says, "May I speak to your father?" What do you say?
Yes you may. May I ask who is calling, please?

9. Your mom is washing her hair and can't come to the phone, so you must take a message. What are the four important parts of a phone message?
name, number, write it down, deliver the message

**271**

1. What surprised Kyle and Anthony about Uncle Dale's phone conversation?
_____ the fact that he had even answered the phone
_X_ the way he spoke
_____ the length of the conversation

2. Number the sentences to show the order in which events happened.
_6_ Uncle Dale gets a lesson on how to take phone messages.
_2_ Uncle Dale arrives.
_4_ Uncle Dale answers the phone.
_1_ Kyle takes a phone message.
_5_ Mom enters the kitchen.
_3_ Kyle greets Uncle Dale.

3. Why does Uncle Dale's face look a little pained in paragraph 11?
Possible answer: He realizes that he made a mistake.

4. Why are Kyle and Anthony not supposed to say "yeah" on the phone?
It is not good manners.

5. How are Uncle Dale and Mom related to each other?
They are brother and sister.

6. Do you think that Uncle Dale will use better phone manners in the future? Explain.
Answers will vary.

**273**

1. The article says it's not your voice, but __sound waves__ made by your voice, that enter the telephone's microphone.

2. When the current in a telephone wire is flowing smoothly, what does the person on the other end hear?
nothing

3. When sound waves interrupt the flow of current, what does the person on the other end hear?
the speaker's voice

4. How long ago did people know that sound could travel along a wire?
almost 400 years ago

5. How long ago did Alexander Graham Bell invent the telephone?
about 130 years ago

Write **F** next to each sentence that is a fact. Write **O** next to each sentence that is an opinion.

6. _F_ Sound waves travel along a wire with the help of an electrical current.

7. _O_ The telephone is the most important invention of the last 200 years.

8. _O_ Without the telephone, modern businesses would fail.

9. How does the computer know to connect you to the person you are trying to call?
When you dial the person's phone number, that tells the computer to connect your phone to theirs.

10. Telephones have been around for less than a hundred years. Is this statement true or false?
false

11. How do you and other members of your family use the telephone today?
Answers will vary.

12. What would it be like if you had to get along without telephones? How else would you communicate?
Answers will vary.

**Notes**

**Notes**

**Notes**

*Low-Cost*
# GREEN LUMBER CONSTRUCTION

# *Low-Cost*
# GREEN LUMBER CONSTRUCTION

by Leigh Seddon

GARDEN WAY  PUBLISHING
CHARLOTTE, VERMONT 05445

To Ann, whose early encouragement launched this project
and helping hand made it a reality.

*Illustrations by Bob Vogel*

**Library of Congress Cataloging in Publication Data**

Seddon, Leigh, 1951–
   Low cost green lumber construction.

   Includes index.
   1. Building, Wooden.   2. Barns—Design and
construction.   3. Lumber.   I. Title.
TH4818.W6S42          694'.2          81-2798
ISBN 0-88266-250-3                    AACR2

# Contents

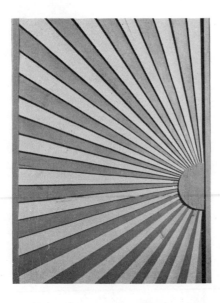

We live in an age of price shock. The price of goods and services is constantly rising due to dwindling natural resources and an economic malaise that is as widespread as it is entrenched. The price of food, which for many years remained stable, now jumps by monthly bounds, guaranteeing a shock every time we go to the market.

One of the most distressing results of inflation is the incredible price we must pay for housing. The median price for a new home in the United States is now $64,000. And assuming you are one of the small percentage of Americans who can qualify for a mortgage of that magnitude, you can expect your monthly payments to be over $700 because of high interest rates. Renters fare no better. In New York City, a single-bedroom apartment for $500 a month is a steal. Shelter, a basic necessity for us all, is quickly becoming a luxury item.

But economic pressure always breeds innovation and resourcefulness, and the housing crunch is no exception. Almost overnight, a new type of homeowner has appeared—the owner-builder. Building their homes from the ground up, or renovating worn out buildings and apartments, these new homeowners are challenging the notion that housebuilding is the exclusive (and expensive) domain of contractors. Today, using low-cost native materials such as green wood and recycled materials, elegant and efficient houses are being owner-built for as little as $10,000 in every part of the country.

Building with native green lumber is nothing new. It has gone on for centuries. The value of the local sawmill, the woodlot, and one's own labor are simply being rediscovered. The homeowner is becoming the owner-builder, a self-sufficient person who looks to the natural and human resources of their own communities in their fight against housing inflation.

When I first started this book, I thought there was just a handful of green wood homes in Vermont. But as I traveled the state, looking at different houses, I soon discovered how very wrong I was. In almost every town and village there were owner-builders at work building low-cost, attractive green wood homes. The same thing is true through much of the United States.

It is my hope that this book can further this quiet revolution, not only encouraging the use of native timber and other resources, but helping would-be homeowners gain enough confidence to pick up the hammer and do it themselves. It is not government, private industry, or new technology that will solve the housing problem in this country. It is a nation of owner-builders quietly helping themselves, and in the process helping us all.

# Acknowledgments

I would first like to thank all the green wood owner-builders who opened their houses to me and shared their building successes and failures. Their experiences fill the pages of this book and tell the real story of green wood building. I am indebted to them for the interest they showed in the project and the hospitality they showed to me.

I am also indebted to my partner in the building trades, Toby Talbot-Reid. Toby not only kept the business going during my frequent absences, but developed the photographs for the book as well. His perseverance on the job and in the darkroom is greatly appreciated.

I wish to thank Bob Vogel, whose illustrations are clearly worth a thousand words. Bob skillfully deciphered my rough drawings and corrected without complaint the details that I had overlooked.

Finally, I would like to thank my editor, Roger Griffith, for his enthusiastic support and knowledgeable advice. The one rule of writing I have always aspired to obey is William Strunk's famous exhortation, "Omit needless words!". Roger caught my frequent transgressions, and with a few skillful strokes of his editor's pen, transformed my ramblings into a readable manuscript. For his continued support and criticism I am most grateful.

# A Yankee Barn

*Sawing and scavenging can save a bundle*

A Yankee is by one definition an inhabitant of New England. The word is most often used, however, to describe a person with a high degree of resourcefulness, ingenuity, and independence.

Certainly not all modern-day inhabitants of New England possess these traits, but in every small New England village there are still a few Yankees who live up to the full meaning of the word.

## A Jack-of-all-Trades

Keith Gould is one such Yankee. He lives in Northfield, Vermont. In true Yankee fashion, Keith is a jack-of-all-trades. He is an English teacher at Norwich University, a part-time farmer,

and as that job requires, a logger, builder, and mechanic.

Several years ago, with little building experience but a good deal of patience and common sense, Keith set out to build a 30 x 50 barn to hold his animals and hay. Keith started from scratch, cutting all his own logs, sawing them into boards and timbers at a local mill, scavenging old building materials, and then raising the barn himself over a period of two years. The finished barn is a direct reflection of Yankee simplicity, resourcefulness, and craftsmanship.

While the building's shape, size, and construction are all fairly typical of other New England barns,

Keith's use of low cost and recycled building materials is not. By cutting his own timber and scrounging everything from used metal roofing to a hayloft ladder (this from an old railroad car), he was able to build the barn for only $1,800. That is less than one-quarter of what new materials and kiln-dried lumber for a comparable barn would cost.

Keith started by cutting about 7,500 board feet of hemlock from the woods behind his house. The trees were sawed by a friend at a local mill. By helping with the sawing, Keith was able to get his lumber milled for only six cents a board foot.

With his boards and timbers

ready, Keith laid out his new barn on foundations where a barn once stood. Using post-and-beam framing and learning as he went along, Keith built the entire barn by himself with only occasional help from friends to lift the larger beams in place.

**By cutting his own timber and scrounging everything from used metal roofing to a hayloft ladder, he was able to build the barn for only $1,800.**

The siding on the barn is vertical hemlock boards without battens. The boards, originally laid tightly edge to edge, now have ⅛- to ¼-inch cracks between them.

### No Problem with Cracks

"The gaps between the boards are no problem at all," Keith remarked. "The only place I have to seal is where the wind blows through on the animals, otherwise it's just as tight as I want it." Such gaps are common in many hay barns where ventilation is needed to eliminate moisture that could ruin the hay and might lead to spontaneous combustion and a fire. While not worrying about the lack of battens, Keith plans to finish the trim details such as corners and fascia boards.

The roofing is recycled galvanized metal that Keith was able to get at a fraction of the cost of new metal roofing. Because the sheets came off different roofs and had weathered differently, the barn roof has a slightly quilt-like appearance. Not being able to find enough old metal to completely cover the barn, Keith broke down and bought a few sheets of new metal roofing, which adds to the quilt effect.

*The trickiest part of the barn to build was this cupola.*

### Built Sliding Door

Using a recycled track and door hangers, Keith built a 10 x 10 sliding door for the main section of the barn.

"That was tough work, getting that door in place," Keith exclaimed. "It must have weighed close to a half a ton." He used a block and tackle, and, with the help of friends, slowly lifted the door into place and set it on its tracks. It now glides back and forth with only a slight push.

### Final Touch: A Cupola

Keith's final touch to his green wood barn was to build a cupola to allow air to circulate through the barn and be vented out the roof.

"The cupola was the trickiest part of the whole building," he said with a smile. "I studied other cupolas, made a few drawings, but still wasn't sure how to build it. Finally, I just started to build it and let it take shape as I went along."

On top of the cupola sits a large weathervane that completes the image of an old New England barn. I asked Keith where he had managed to scavenge such a nice weathervane.

"The weathervane? That's brand new." ❧

CHAPTER 1

# Green Wood Building

THROUGHOUT THE YEAR YOU HAVE BEEN PLAN-
ning an addition to your house, an attached barn about 20 by
24 feet, just big enough to hold the family car, your tools, and
perhaps a few chickens in a shed at the far end.

As spring approaches, you ask a local contractor for an estimate. After calculating materials, labor, and overhead, the
contractor informs you he would be happy to build it for only
$8,000.

$8,000?

That was more than twice what you had imagined. To fi-
nance that you would have to take out a new mortgage. As you
thank the contractor and tell him you will get back to him
soon, your dream of a new barn is fading away.

Such is the reality of conventional building today. The average new house in the United States costs well over $50,000,
putting a newly built home out of the reach of most Americans.
But a new approach to housing and house building is beginning to surface—owner-builders designing and building their
own homes, often using local resources and recycled materials.
For a mere $2,000 an owner-builder could erect the barn pic-
tured here. It is 20 by 24 feet, has an attached shed, and a
breezeway connects it to the house. It was built entirely with
green wood, freshly cut at a local sawmill, and has recycled
windows and doors. Homes can be built with similar savings.

While the owner-builder saves considerably by providing his

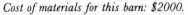

*Cost of materials for this barn: $2000.*

PHOTO BY TOBY TALBOT-REID

*Green wood (left) and kiln-dried lumber.*

or her own labor, the labor costs in a new home amount to only about 30 percent of the total cost. Material costs (excluding plumbing, wiring, etc.) account for a full 40 percent of the building costs. Thus it is imperative to reduce material costs as much as possible, and perhaps the easiest way is to use rough-sawn green wood.

## Wet and Heavy

Green wood is wood that has been freshly cut and that has not yet dried. Green lumber differs in many respects from commercially available kiln-dried lumber, lumber that has been dried in ovens to remove moisture and then planed to exact finish dimensions. The most obvious difference is that green wood is wet. Green hemlock, for instance, weighs almost twice as much as kiln-dried hemlock. Green wood is also rough-sawn, leaving a rough-textured surface and slight variations in dimensions.

## Less Expensive

If green wood is wet, heavy, and uneven, why build with it? The answer, of course, is price. Green lumber can be bought for as little as half the cost of kiln-dried lumber. Currently in Vermont, green lumber can be purchased for about twenty-two cents a board foot, while kiln-dried lumber costs about thirty-seven cents a board foot. With 40 percent of the cost of a building being in materials, building with green lumber can mean saving up to 16 percent on the entire cost of a commercially built house. And if we are talking about an owner-built barn, the savings are about 30 percent of the cost of building with kiln-dried lumber.

## Stronger

Green lumber may initially have only the strength of thinner kiln-dried lumber because of its moisture. But it is most certainly stronger after it has dried in place. It is rough-cut to approximately its stated dimensions (1 x 6, 2 x 4), but kiln-dried lumber is always ¼ to ¾ inch smaller than its nominal dimensions. This means a green 2 x 6 has a full 45 percent more wood in it than its kiln-dried counterpart, giving it extra strength.

Green wood is also exceptionally beautiful. Because it is rough-sawn, green wood has striking surface patterns and colors. If selected and used properly, rough-sawn lumber is one of the most attractive materials for exterior siding.

Green lumber is as readily available as kiln-dried for those

### Kiln-Dried Lumber

| SIZE | ACTUAL SIZE |
| --- | --- |
| 1 x 2 | ¾ x 1½ |
| 1 x 3 | ¾ x 2½ |
| 1 x 4 | ¾ x 3½ |
| 1 x 6 | ¾ x 5½ |
| 1 x 8 | ¾ x 7¼ |
| 1 x 10 | ¾ x 9¼ |
| 1 x 12 | ¾ x 11¼ |
| 2 x 4 | 1½ x 3½ |
| 2 x 6 | 1½ x 5½ |
| 2 x 8 | 1½ x 7¼ |
| 2 x 10 | 1½ x 9¼ |
| 2 x 12 | 1½ x 11¼ |
| 4 x 4 | 3½ x 3½ |
| 6 x 6 | 5½ x 5½ |
| 8 x 8 | 7¼ x 7¼ |

*Green wood adds beauty to this home.*

willing to seek out local sawmills. There are small sawmills in all parts of the country, with many in New England, the Southeast, and the Northwest. By buying green lumber from a local sawmill, you will be getting a bargain as well as using local resources and supporting the local economy.

## Disadvantages

Building with green lumber has distinct disadvantages. Green lumber is heavy and it will shrink and sometimes crack. You will probably have to truck it yourself to the building site or hire someone to do it for you. Because of the inevitable bad boards with 6-inch knots or large cracks, you will have to sort and grade the lumber after you buy it. And yes, some of the

boards will have to be discarded for kindling. Green wood must also be stacked properly so that it can air-dry if it is not used immediately. Above all, you will have to learn the art of working with green wood—a little common sense, a bit of patience, and a great deal of care.

## Can Cause Trouble

Builders or homeowners who have built with green wood have horror stories to tell about their or others' experiences. Some are scary (and expensive) enough to make you vow never to use green wood. While I have never heard of a green wood house self-destructing to the point of collapse, I have heard about floors with cracks large enough to resemble glacial crevasses, avalanches of Sheetrock as drying studs pull the nails right through the drywall, and snowstorms in living rooms because of cracks in the board-and-batten siding.

But these are all mistakes, examples of how *not* to build with green wood. There is no reason why an economical, energy-efficient, and attractive green wood house or barn cannot be built by an owner-builder. It is simply a matter of understanding green wood and why it is different from kiln-dried lumber.

Understanding green wood is what this book is all about. If you are just in the planning stages of building, it will help you decide whether green lumber would be practical and economical for your project. If you have already decided to build a green wood barn or house, you will find the necessary information to build a sturdy, economical structure.

# Green Wood Economics

Before building with green wood, give some thought to the comparative economics of green versus kiln-dried lumber. While building with green wood usually is considerably less expensive, this is not always the case when time, labor, and other economic factors are considered. Before deciding on green wood, make an analysis of the net savings.

The first and major factor to consider is the price of lumber. If you can buy green spruce for twenty-two cents a board foot and kiln-dried for thirty-seven cents, you can save 40 percent on your lumber costs. If green lumber costs twenty-eight cents and kiln-dried is thirty-five cents, the savings are cut in half to 20 percent. By checking with local sawmills and calling commercial lumberyards, you can find out these figures and determine your savings.

While the board foot is an ideal unit for comparative pricing and is still used by sawmills, unfortunately many commercial lumberyards are moving away from board feet to unit pricing. Thus a lumberyard may quote you a price of $2.95 for an 8-

foot 2 x 6 or $6.40 for a 12-foot 2 x 8. You will notice that the unit prices do not correspond to a given board-foot rate. In fact, the board-foot rate increases as the size of the piece increases. The reason for this is that it costs the lumber company more to get a straight 12-foot 2 x 12 than it does to produce three 12-foot 2 x 4s.

## Comparing Prices

Unit pricing may make sense for the lumber company, but it makes it more difficult for you to compare prices. The solution is to convert to board feet the major types of lumber you will be using. Thus if you are using 8-foot 2 x 6s for your stud walls and they cost $2.95 apiece, the board-foot cost is $2.95 divided by 8 board feet or about thirty-seven cents per board foot. Do the same for siding and any other types of lumber you plan to use, and then figure an average board-foot cost for the entire building. In this way you will be able to compare the cost of green and kiln-dried wood without having to figure the total material cost of the building each time you call a lumberyard.

## Transportation Costs

The next factor to consider in your net savings analysis is transportation. Kiln-dried lumber will arrive at your doorstep free of charge courtesy of the lumberyard. (The cost is included in the price of the lumber, of course.) You will have to haul green lumber yourself or hire someone to do it for you. Transportation can often be a major expense because green wood is so heavy. A 12-foot green hemlock 2 x 6, for instance, weighs about forty pounds. If you are building a large structure, using a small pickup may be out of the question. The most sensible solution is usually to rent a large truck so that the wood can be hauled in one or two loads, cutting down mileage and time.

There are several ways to figure the cost of transportation. One is the cost of hiring someone to do it. A medium-sized truck with driver will cost at least $30 an hour, and if the sawmill is 20 miles away, you can figure on an hour each way and two hours loading and unloading. The minimum cost for hauling the lumber needed for a 20 x 24 barn this way would be about $120.

A more economical method is to rent a truck and haul the wood yourself. A large U-Haul can be rented for about $40 a day plus mileage and gas. The total truck cost of this method for hauling the barn lumber would be about $60 or half the cost of hiring someone.

Don't forget to add an hourly wage for yourself. The time you spend hauling wood could be used earning money at a job,

> ## What's a Board Foot?
>
> Lumber is usually measured by the board foot (bdf), which is a volume measurement of 144 cubic inches.
>
> Thus a piece of 1-inch board that is 12 inches long and 12 inches wide is exactly 1 board foot.
>
> Similarly, an 8-foot board that is 2 x 6 measures 2 inches times 6 inches times 8 feet times 12 inches, or 8 board feet.

tending the garden, or simply relaxing, all of which have a certain value. Thus if you value your time at $5 an hour and you spend four hours hauling wood, you would add $20 to the $60 truck charge to arrive at a total transportation cost of $80.

Transportation costs become less significant as the size of the building project increases. If you are building a small front porch, your lumber savings may be $40 but your transportation costs $10, reducing your net savings by 25 percent. If you are building a house, however, your lumber savings may be $3,000 and your transportation costs $150, which only reduce your savings by 5 percent. Since transportation costs are the largest single extra cost of building with green wood rather than kiln-dried lumber, try to get a realistic figure for transportation expenses that will allow a fair comparison between the cost of green and dry lumber *at your doorstep.*

## Waste Lumber

Another cost is the inevitable rough or rotten lumber that comes from the local sawmill. While quality varies widely from mill to mill, all mills produce some lumber that is not up to building standards. This may be because of knots, cracks, rot, or other defects. When buying from a local mill, expect that up to 5 percent of the wood will have serious defects. Careful selection of wood (which is not always possible or advisable) can reduce this to around 1 percent. If you are buying without seeing the lumber first, I would count on 5 percent waste and subtract this from your calculated savings.

The other costs are what economists refer to as "intangibles." It's hard to put a dollar figure on them, but we intuitively know they are there. Some of the intangibles are the extra time spent sorting and looking through green wood piles for the "right" piece, the delay in building if you decide to air-dry your lumber, and other small inconveniences. While many people might dismiss these things as insignificant, they are real costs and should be considered by each prospective green wood builder.

| **Dry or Green Lumber** | | |
|---|---|---|
| | While building with green wood is possible, it is preferable to build with dry lumber, all other things being equal.<br><br>Green lumber is inexpensive because it comes from a local sawmill and has not been dried and processed. With a little planning and foresight, the owner-builder can purchase green lumber and | air-dry it before it is used. By doing this the owner-builder can take advantage of low-cost lumber but with few of the problems or precautions necessary for building with green lumber.<br><br>The savings come from buying green, not necessarily building green. |

## Calculating Savings

After adding up all of the extra costs of building with green wood, the comparative economics of green versus kiln-dried lumber can be seen. Using the 20 x 24 barn as an example, we can calculate the actual savings. If the initial price difference in wood is 40 percent, about $640 will be saved by buying green framing lumber and siding materials. Subtracting $80 for transportation costs and $30 for rough and rotten wood, the final savings on the entire material cost for the barn would be $530 or 22 percent. Even considering the intangibles, using green lumber is obviously wise in this case. If the initial price difference were only 20 percent, however, and the sawmill were twice as far away, the final savings might be 10 percent or less. In this case, you would do well to think twice about your choice of wood.

When considering whether to build with green wood, consider the type of structure being built. Because of the shrinkage and irregularities of green lumber, it is better suited for use in some types of buildings than others. Green lumber is excellent for barns or other outbuildings that are left unfinished on the inside and not heated. Green wood is less suitable in a northern climate for a year-round residence that must be airtight and heated most of the year. An attractive, energy-efficient home can be built with green wood but it will take a little more time and more care than building with kiln-dried lumber.

### Building Cost Breakdown

Where the money goes for a 1,000-square foot house built by a contractor.

| ITEM | PER-CENTAGE |
|---|---|
| General construction materials | 42 |
| Labor | 25 |
| Electrical, labor and material | 7 |
| Plumbing and heating, labor and materials | 10 |
| Overhead and profit | 16 |

### Green Wood Ecomonics

Comparison of material costs for a barn 20 by 24 feet built with green wood and built with kiln-dried lumber.

| ITEM | GREEN | KILN-DRIED |
|---|---|---|
| Lumber | $1000 | $1640 |
| Foundation | 125 | 125 |
| Roofing | 300 | 300 |
| Windows & Doors | 300 | 300 |
| Transportation | 80 | — |
| Waste: due to unuseable boards | 30 | — |
| Total Materials | $1835 | $2365 |

Overall savings by using green wood = $530 or 22 percent

This table is based on a cost of 22 cents/bdf for green lumber, 36 cents/bdf for kiln-dried lumber.

## Ideal for Barn

The barn is the ideal green wood structure. Because the inside walls are not finished with Sheetrock or some other wallboard, the minor irregularities in the width of the studs can be ignored. And because it does not need to be perfectly airtight, a simple board-and-batten siding will keep out the weather. If a metal roof is used, green wood boards spaced every 12 inches on the rafters are all that is needed to support the roof.

Studying the economics of the green wood barn shows that the large savings are due to using green lumber both for framing and for siding. We have already seen that green lumber can save 30 to 40 percent over the cost of kiln-dried framing material. The savings are even greater with siding. Clapboard siding with ½-inch plywood underlayment typically costs about $100 per square (10 by 10 feet). Green wood board-and-batten siding, such as on the green wood barn, costs $30 per square, a savings of 70 percent. Savings are even greater because clapboards require two to three times the labor of board-and-batten siding to install. Even if ½-inch plywood underlayment is used under the board and batten (which might be the case for a house), there would still be a savings of 40 percent.

## Save on Siding

Because board and batten is such economical siding, consider using it even when the rest of the structure will be framed conventionally, using kiln-dried lumber. With some house designs it may not be advisable to use green framing lumber. An example is a passive solar home that has extensive areas of glass that might be broken as the studs dry and shrink. The use of green board-and-batten siding should still be considered, however, since it can provide a durable, economical, and attractive exterior finish for the structure.

Deciding to use green wood as a building material requires economic, technical, and personal value judgments.

You should be sure that green wood will be less expensive, that it can be properly used in the structure you are considering, and that you like the looks and feel of rough wood.

If green wood passes these three tests, you are set for the next step—a trip to the local sawmill.

# Green Wood Post and Beam

*Robin Worn becomes her own contractor*

When Robin Worn bought her ten acres in Richmond, Vermont, the first order of business was to put in the vegetable garden. A house could wait, but with Vermont's short growing season, vegetables couldn't. With seeds safely planted, Robin started to plan her two-story green wood house.

"I was the general contractor for the whole house, but I didn't know a thing about building," Robin admitted as we talked about her house. "I consulted a few good books on designs for energy-efficient homes. They gave me an idea of what the house should look like. But I mostly relied on advice and help from my friends as to how to build it."

By acting as her own contractor, building with green wood, and using the resources of neighbors and friends, Robin was able to build her passive solar home for only about $10,000 in materials. That includes a full foundation and 8-foot basement.

Robin designed her house with large areas of glass on the south side for solar heating, and a clerestory which admits light and heat for the second floor. The house measures 32 by 24 feet with the kitchen, dining room, and living room on the first floor, and two bedrooms, a bath, and a plant area on the second floor. The basement area is reserved for storage and a large wood stove which heats both the house and hot water.

**Friends Helped**

While Robin designed the layout of the house, a friend, Terry Bachman, who is a builder and craftsman, did all the structural engineering for the house such as the sizing and placement of the beams. The house is a post-and-beam structure using 8 x 8 beams and 2 x 6 studs for the walls. Robin, together with Terry, Peter Paquette, and Andy Palmer (whose green wood house appears on page 78), framed the house in six weeks.

As with many post-and-beam houses, there was a daylong house-

*This window highlights jointry of 8x8 beams.*

siding has a slightly better R-value than regular board and batten because there is an inch of dead air space under the board between the 3-inch battens.

On the east, south, and west sides of the house, 1 x 8 hemlock was used. On the north side, pine was used since Robin felt it would withstand the severer weather conditions of that side better than hemlock. All the siding was purchased green, dried over the winter, and put on the following spring to avoid any problems of splitting and cracking.

**Robin designed her house with large areas of glass on the south side for solar heating.**

The interior walls are Sheetrocked. It was put up only two months after the house was framed, but Robin reports she has had no problems so far with moisture or shrinkage damaging the Sheetrock.

While it is a good rule to allow at least six months for green wood walls to dry before they are covered, Robin's experience shows that drying times vary tremendously and that, given the right conditions of warmth and humidity, green studs can dry in as little as two months.

### Kiln-Dried Flooring

The flooring is kiln-dried yellow pine, placed directly over the floor joists and beams. The first-floor ceiling was left unfinished, to expose the rough beams and flooring.

One problem Robin did encounter with the flooring was that it buckled and twisted in a few spots as the 8 x 8 beams dried and

raising. After all the beams had been cut to length and notched to fit together, Robin invited friends and neighbors to help lift the beams in place. In one day with everyone's help, the floor and wall beams and roof rafters were all set in place, and some of the pine flooring was laid.

### Green Lumber Studs

Once the beams were in place, the walls were studded in with green 2 x 6s 2 feet on center. To avoid any problem with Sheetrocking the interior, all the 2 x 6s and 2 x 4s were ripped down to exact dimension in Andy Palmer's woodworking shop next door. Ac-

cording to Robin, this took very little time and eliminated a lot of potential problems with the interior finish work.

The roof was framed with green 2 x 10 rafters, 2 feet on center, with ⅝-inch plywood decking. Standing-seam galvanized metal roofing was put on the plywood.

The exterior siding is rough-sawn hemlock and pine placed board on batten. This is in contrast to the usual board and batten, where thin battens are nailed over the boards. The siding here consists of 8-inch boards nailed onto 3-inch battens. This gives the house clean, well defined lines.

Theoretically, board-on-batten

*Plant area is directly above dining room on the south side of the house. Note use of yellow pine flooring laid directly over the 8x8 beams.*

*Robin Worn rests on the rear entry of her green wood house.*

shrunk. This could have been avoided by going to the extra expense of laying a rough wood or plywood subfloor which then could be covered with the finished flooring when the beams and subfloor had dried.

In order to keep down costs, Robin made extensive use of recycled windows and doors. Some were taken from old buildings, while others were purchased from contractors who had windows left over from jobs they had finished. They were willing to sell these new units at bargain prices.

According to Robin, $3,000 was

**By acting as her own contractor, building with green wood, and using the resources of neighbors and friends, Robin was able to build her passive solar home for only about $10,000 in materials.**

spent on green wood for beams, studs, rafters, and siding, about $3,000 for plywood, roofing, windows, and hardware, and about

$3,500 for foundation, slab, and basement walls.

The total cost for materials for the entire house, $10,000, figures out to about $12 a square foot. This is about one-half to two-thirds of what materials for a conventionally framed house would cost, and a price any contractor would envy.

While the average price of a new home in the United States is now up to an astounding $64,000, Robin Worn's green wood solar home shows what an enterprising owner-builder can do for a fraction of the cost. ✤

**Worn house floor plan**

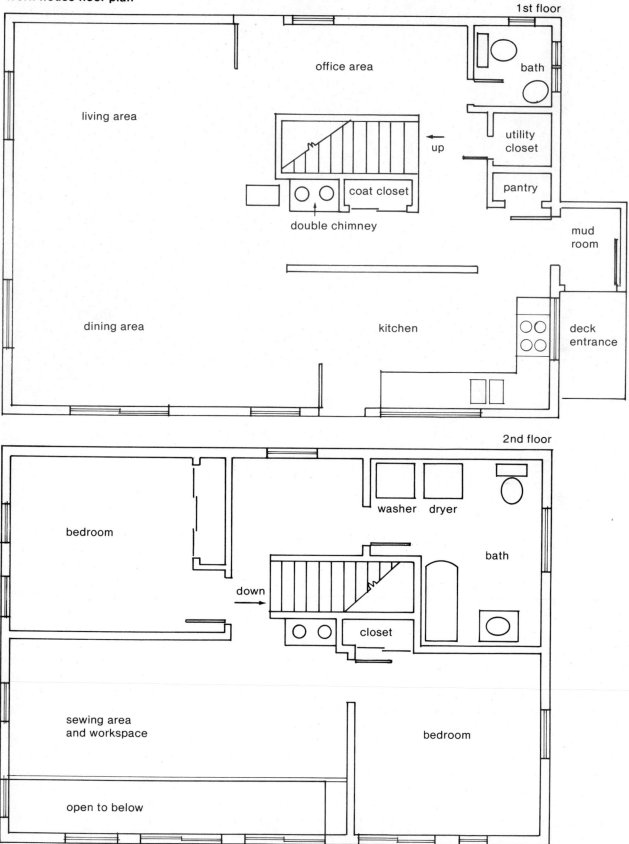

1st floor

living area

office area

bath

up

utility closet

pantry

coat closet

double chimney

mud room

dining area

kitchen

deck entrance

2nd floor

bedroom

washer    dryer

bath

down

closet

sewing area and workspace

bedroom

open to below

# CHAPTER 2

# Getting It Green

FINDING A SOURCE OF GREEN LUMBER IS THE first step for the prospective green wood builder. Green wood enthusiasts in Kansas may wonder where they are going to find green lumber in the corn and wheat belt of America. But even Kansas can boast of 1⅓ million acres of forested land and many small sawmills cutting sycamore, cottonwood, oak, and walnut. Almost every state in the nation can claim at least a half-million acres of forest, and where there are forests, there is green wood.

You can get green wood in several ways. The most common source is commercial sawmills, which abound in the Northeast, South, and Northwest. Another source is the small farm or home mill that produces lumber at certain times of the year to supplement the family budget. Finally, timber owners or homesteaders who are clearing their land can buy or rent portable sawmills and mill their own lumber.

Sawmills are located close to their sources of raw materials, the major forests of the United States. Many of these mills are owned by large corporations such as Weyerhaeuser, Boise Cascade, and Georgia-Pacific, with some of their more modern mills producing up to 100-million board feet of lumber every year. But the vast majority of sawmills in this country are small, independently run operations that produce less than a million board feet a year. It is from these small sawmills that the green wood builder can expect to buy lumber.

# Commercial Sawmills

## How to Find Them

Because many mills are small, backwoods operations, they are not always easy to find. Look in the yellow pages of the telephone directory. There you will find the larger mills in your area. Next, talk to someone at a local commercial lumberyard or a carpenter who has been building for some time in the area. These people will be able to tell you about smaller local mills, what kind of lumber they produce, and at what price. If you find several mills, try to find out a little about them. What is the quality of their lumber, will they sell to individuals at retail, and what is their reputation for filling orders promptly and correctly? Often there will be startling differences in price and quality among mills.

If there are several mills in your area and you're trying to decide which to buy from, here are some things to keep in mind. Find out whether the mill will sell to you as a retail customer and at what price. Then check the quality of the lumber.

One aspect of quality is the accuracy of the milling. Is the lumber dimensionally correct? By taking a few random measurements of the lumber in the yard, you can quickly find out how much boards vary from their nominal dimensions. Some mills, because of their machinery and quality control, can produce lumber that doesn't vary even ⅛ inch over or under the nominal dimension. Others produce lumber with much greater variations that can lead to problems when building.

Of greatest concern are variations in the widths of boards and timbers. If wall studs vary significantly in width, the wall will be uneven and wavy. There are ways to compensate for this, but, as a rule of thumb, don't accept lumber that varies more than ¼ inch over or under its nominal dimension since even this will produce a full ½ inch difference between pieces of lumber.

## Quality of Wood

Study the quality of the wood. Are the boards filled with large knots and other defects? Since knots, pitch marks, and checks lower the strength of wood, lumber should be compared for clearness and straightness of grain. While it is not possible to measure precisely differences in lumber quality unless you are a professional lumber grader, a general impression of the lumber quality of a mill can be gained by examining different pieces of wood in the yard. It should be noted, however, that since mills are continually buying new timber from different cutting sites, the quality will vary with each new load. What's in the yard might not be what you receive. When you are plac-

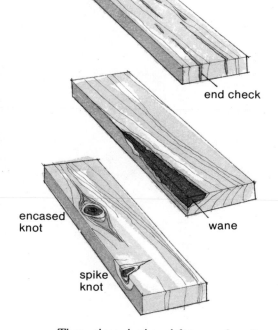

surface check

end check

encased knot

wane

spike knot

*These three lumber defects weaken the strength of a board.*

*The band saw at the Heath Mill in North Hyde Park, Vermont, is 42 feet long and the largest in the state.*

ing a large order, see what kind of lumber the mill is producing since this is most likely the quality of lumber you will receive.

## How is Lumber Stored?

A final thing to check is how the lumber is stored. Green lumber should be properly *stickered* so that it can dry. Stickering is separating each layer in a pile of lumber with inch-thick sticks so that air can circulate around the boards and dry them. Green lumber that is not stickered will begin to rot and warp.

A yard full of well-stickered piles is a sign that a mill operator cares about his finished product, and that air-dried lumber

*If boards vary more than ¼ inch over or under the nominal dimensions, beware.*

may be available at the same price as green lumber. This is often true at mills that keep a large inventory. A green wood buyer should be on the lookout for a forgotten stack of lumber that has been drying for a year and that the mill operator would just as soon sell to make more room.

Most sawmills cut all types of wood, from hardwoods like oak, maple, beech, and cherry to softwoods such as pine, spruce, and hemlock. Some sawmills may cut only softwoods for building construction lumber or only hardwoods for cabinetmaking. In the Northeast and Northwest, spruce and hemlock are the common building materials. In the South, pine and even oak are used for building. The softwoods, being cheaper and more readily available, make the most sense for green wood building, though the more durable hardwoods are often used for certain applications such as floors and trim. Often small sawmills cut what is available, whether it be spruce, hemlock, or pine. Certain species may not be available or available only a few times a year.

## Transportation

Consider how you are going to get green lumber to the building site. It is extremely heavy and transporting it can become a major cost depending on the amount of wood and the distances involved. For example, a 20 x 24 barn (Chapter 7) requires about 4,500 board feet of green lumber. Since green hemlock weighs about 3½ pounds per board foot, the lumber to

build such a barn would weigh nearly 16,000 pounds or eight tons. Hauling eight tons anywhere requires either a very large truck or many, many trips in a pickup.

When you are scouting mills for prices and quality, ask about the possibility of having your order delivered. Mills usually have several large trucks for hauling wood, and if your order is large enough the mill might deliver at a very small charge. If the mill will not deliver, the next step is to consider renting a truck from a friend or a commercial business such as U-Haul. Unless your order is very small, it usually pays to rent a large truck rather than haul your lumber in many small loads in your pickup or car. The greater the distance from the mill to your building site, the more a large truck will save you in gasoline and time.

## A Favor to You

When you buy green wood, remember that sawmills sell most of their lumber wholesale. Their business is to saw large volumes of lumber that are then kiln-dried and planed, and finally sold to commercial lumberyards. Unless you are building a large house or barn, your order probably won't amount to much in terms of the mill's overall volume. Since sawmills are generally not in the retail business, when an owner allows you to wander around the yard and select a few boards, he is doing

*Often sawmills have old boards like these. They are air-dried, but can be bought for the price of green lumber.*

you a favor. Repay that courtesy by remembering two things. First, restack a pile of boards that you've picked through. Second, pay by cash or check. A mill operator does not have the personnel to clean up the yard after customers or bill them at the end of the month. By sticking to cash and carry, individuals can buy green wood at wholesale prices without interrupting the operation of the mill.

# Portable Sawmills

If you're a green wood builder who has access to or owns forest land, you have another avenue for obtaining green lumber. Cut your own trees and mill them with a portable sawmill. Producing your own lumber from start to finish will save money and give you control over the quality of the lumber. A number of small portable sawmills are made, ranging in size from machines capable of turning out several thousand board feet a day to small chain saw mills capable of cutting several hundred board feet a day. (See Appendix 1 for manufacturers of portable sawmills.)

One of the most versatile of the larger portable sawmills is made by Mobile Manufacturing Company of Oregon. This mill was designed to salvage lumber from stumps left behind in logging operations because they were too large to move. Powered by a fifty-three horsepower industrial Volkswagen engine, the saw moves along a carriage that is mounted against the log. Unlike usual sawmills, which carry the log through the saw on a conveyor, the Mobile saw moves through the log and returns automatically when it has finished the cut.

The Mobile saw has three cutting blades—the main saw, which is 30 inches in diameter, and two edging blades 11½ inches in diameter that cut horizontally. The edging blades can be adjusted to cut any width board up to 12 inches wide. Because of these preset edging blades, the Mobile sawmill is capable of turning out dimension lumber with only one pass and with less than 1/16-inch variation in width.

One person operates the Mobile sawmill and can cut from 1,500 to 6,000 board feet a day depending on the size lumber being sawed. It uses only one gallon of gasoline to cut approximately 500 board feet of 1-inch stock. The sawmill weighs 700 pounds and is mounted on a trailer so that it can be easily moved by one person and hitched to the back of a truck and hauled to different cutting sites.

For the person who has a large woodlot from which lumber will be cut continually, a portable sawmill of this size makes considerable economic sense. This is especially true for a homesteader who wishes to clear some timber for a house site and then continue periodic cuttings. By using a portable sawmill to produce lumber right at the house site and then using the mill

*Marshall Webb of Shelburne Farms, Shelburne, Vermont, positions his portable Mobile Sawmill next to a log. The engine and saw assembly moves along a metal rail, cuts a board, then returns to its starting position. Marshall removes the board and loads it on a flatbed trailer.*

**GETTING IT GREEN**

to cut additional timber for sale, an operator could pay for the mill in several years.

## Hire a Mill Owner

For the homesteader who wishes to cut his own timber but can't afford or doesn't wish to invest in such a large lumber production capability, there is the possibility of hiring someone with a portable mill to cut the lumber on site. This has the advantage over having a local sawmill cut the lumber of eliminating the expense of hauling the logs to the mill and trucking the finished lumber back to the site. Your best bet in locating such a person would be a local county forester or Extension Service agent.

## Chain Saw Mills

At the other end of the scale of portable sawmills is the chain saw sawmill. Using a special ripping chain and powered by one or two large chain saw engines, these mills provide an inexpensive way to cut up trees right where they fall. Most chain saw mills are at least 36 inches wide and can cut large timbers as well as 2 x 4s. According to users, chain saw mills can cut up to 10 board feet of 1-inch stock per minute.

These sawmills operate with horizontal guide bars that roll along the top of the log, guiding the cutting bar. By adjusting the depth of the cut (by raising the guide bars) 1-inch, 2-inch, or larger timbers can be cut. Slabbing rails are used to make the first cut since the top of a log is irregular. These are pieces of wood nailed onto a log. The guide bars roll along on them to give a smooth and even cut. After the first cut, the guide bars roll along the surface of the previous cut.

Unlike the Mobile sawmill, chain saw mills don't trim the edges of the boards. Therefore, in order to produce dimension lumber it is necessary first to "square up" a log by slabbing the top and the bottom, rotating the log 90° and then starting the cuts of the desired thickness.

Whether it is economical to buy a portable sawmill depends on many factors. Most important is the availability and price of green lumber from local commercial mills. Portable mills make sense for the small woodlot owner who will mill his own lumber for a specific building project, then continue using the mill for lumber production at least on a part-time basis.

Logging and milling are strenuous, noisy, and hazardous operations that should only be undertaken with extreme care and the proper equipment. Only the exceptional logger or sawyer does not have battle scars to show.

*This Alaskan MK III chain saw mill is mounted on a chain saw, and will cut lumber from ½ to 13 inches thick, and as wide as 54 inches.*

While cutting your own timber and milling it with a portable saw may not provide the answer for every green wood builder, it is economical in many circumstances and provides the unique satisfaction of being able to partake in the entire building process, from forest to finished house.

## Checklist for Selecting a Sawmill

Will mill sell to you?     \_\_\_\_\_
What are its prices?     \_\_\_\_\_

*Quality of lumber*
Can mill cut various sizes you want?     \_\_\_\_\_
Is lumber in yard cut to proper dimensions?
   (Within ¼ inch)     \_\_\_\_\_
Is lumber cut squarely? (Not like this ⬜ )     \_\_\_\_\_
Are boards fairly free of knots, other defects?     \_\_\_\_\_
Is lumber cut from species of trees that you prefer?     \_\_\_\_\_
Are boards straight?     \_\_\_\_\_
Is lumber stickered to avoid warping?     \_\_\_\_\_

Will mill deliver lumber?     \_\_\_\_\_
Can mill furnish any special milling?     \_\_\_\_\_

# Further Reading

*Knowing Your Trees,* G. H. Collingwood and Warren D. Brush, Revised 1978, 389 pp. Available from the American Forestry Association, 1319 18th St. NW, Washington, D.C. 20036. This is the encyclopedia of American trees, a standard text for forestry students.

*Axes & Chain Saws, Use & Maintenance,* Garden Way Country Wisdom Bulletin A-13, 32 pp. Available from Garden Way Publishing, Charlotte, VT 05445.

*Barnacle Parp's Chainsaw Guide,* Walter Hall, 1977, 288 pp. Rodale Press, Emmaus, PA 18049.

*Chain-saw Lumbering,* Robert Sperber, Fine Woodworking Magazine, Vol. 2 No. 2, Fall 1977, pp 50–52. Tauton Press, Newton, CT 06470. An article by the manufacturer of Sperber chain saw mills, showing its operation and useful hints.

*Sawmilling: How One Small Mill Works,* Dwight Gorrel, Fine Woodworking Magazine, July-August 1979, Vol. 17, pp. 36–42. Tauton Press, Newton, CT 06470. An account of a Centerville, Kansas, sawmill, explaining the parts and operation of a small family-run mill.

# Green Lumber
# (and Green Builders)

*$5,000 is all the Scatchards needed to build their first home*

In the summer of 1976, Tom and Ebeth Scatchard, on vacation from their jobs as elementary school teachers, designed and built their own green wood house in Charlotte, Vermont.

Starting in mid-July, they finished the frame, roof, and exterior sheathing of their 30 x 32 two-story home by October. Their total cost for all the wood was $3,600.

The house is a model of how simple and economical green wood building can be.

## Open Area

The house has an open first floor, which includes a living room with cathedral ceiling, a kitchen and an adjacent dining room area, plus a bathroom.

The open area, combined with large windows on three of the walls, gives the house a very light, airy atmosphere despite its massive beams and planks. Two bedrooms on the second floor are over the kitchen and dining areas, with a small sundeck off the front bedroom.

## Solid Structure

The first impression you receive when entering the house is how solid the structure is. Tom explained that the walls are made out of pine 4 x 12s stacked on edge and held together by 8-inch spikes interlocking the 4 x 12s every few feet.

The house is basically a green wood log cabin, a design that both Tom and Ebeth felt was simple enough for them to build since neither had advanced carpentry skills. "For framing the entire

house, all we needed was a three-pound hammer, a drill, and a chain saw," Tom explained.

### Concrete Piers

The house is built on a concrete pier foundation, which they put in at a cost of $200. Twenty-four 12-inch piers laid out on 6-foot centers support the 6 x 8 hemlock sills.

Using a hose and the water-leveling technique, the Scatchards were able to get all twenty-four piers the same height, providing a level platform on which to build and eliminating the time and frustration of shimming up all the foundation beams. Six-inch fiberglass insulation was laid between the 6 x 8 sills, supported by heavy cardboard obtained free from a local packing company.

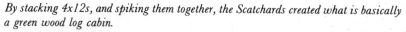

**The Scatchard house is a model of how simple and economical green wood building can be.**

On top of the 6 x 8 sills and joists, 4 x 12s were laid edge to edge for the first-floor decking. This saved the expense of framing in the joists every 2 feet to support a subfloor and finished floor, but it also led to a problem. The green 4 x 12s shrank up to ½ inch in width as they dried, leaving large cracks between the floor timbers.

While the Scatchards joke about the wonderful ventilation this provides for their wood heat, they eventually plan to lay hard-wood flooring at least on the first floor. The Scatchards' experience points out that finished-flooring must be dry before it is laid.

### Wall Timbers Interlocked

The 4 x 12 walls were laid directly on top of the first floor deck with cutouts for the windows. By drilling the 4 x 12s from the top and driving an 8-inch spike through 4 inches into the lower timber, the wall timbers were interlocked and held together.

The second floor boarding is laid on the diagonal, bracing the outer walls and giving more structural rigidity to the house. On the exterior, the walls were finished with ½-inch insulating Homasote board and vertical shiplapped hemlock.

*By stacking 4x12s, and spiking them together, the Scatchards created what is basically a green wood log cabin.*

### Let Walls Dry

During the first winter, the inside walls were left unfinished to allow the 4 x 12s to dry and settle. Measuring the walls next spring, the Scatchards found they had shrunk a full 4 inches vertically. This is much more than a green wood house with conventional stud framing would shrink, since studs shrink very little along their vertical dimension.

When the walls had dried, 1½-inch thick nailers were added on the inside to create a cavity for fiberglass insulation. Over this

---

**The first impression you receive when entering the house is how solid the structure is.**

---

went a vapor barrier and then shiplapped pine. The total insulating value or R-value of the wall is 14.6 which compares favorably to an R-value of 15.5 for a conventionally framed 2 x 4 wall with fiberglass insulation.

Tom and Ebeth are very satisfied with what they accomplished. Not only did green lumber allow them to build a house they could afford, but it also allowed them to use their log cabin design which was simple to erect and could be lived in and finished gradually as time and money permitted.

Would they use the same log cabin technique again?

Probably not, they explained. They're more accomplished builders now, and so they would try the post-and-beam technique, since it allows for better insulation in the walls.

### Insulation

One misconception they had when they built the house was that pine was a good insulator and that

*Tom and Ebeth Scatchard enjoy the comfort of the 4x12 furniture they built for their living room.*

*Laying flooring on the diagonal helps brace this house.*

the 4 x 12s would offer adequate insulation. After the house was finished, they found that pine has only one-third the R-value of fiberglass insulation of the same thickness, and so they added the layers of insulation and Homasote.

## Problem with Rafters

Another problem the Scatchards ran into was using green lumber for roof rafters. Since the house has a cathedral ceiling, the roof deck needed to be straight both inside and out so that it could be finished on both sides. But since their rafters varied in dimension up to ½ inch, they ended up with a slightly wavy roof deck. This is a typical problem with green lumber and is more aesthetic than structural. It can be solved by some of the techniques suggested in Chapter 4.

Tom suggested a simple solution: "Buy kiln-dried rafters and save yourself the hassle."

## Learned while Building

The Scatchard house shows what persons who are constructing their first house on limited funds can accomplish. Building on a budget of around $5,000, they not only created an extremely functional and attractive home, but learned the ins and outs of house building as well.

"The walls were a challenge," Tom remembered. I understood as I looked at pictures of them lifting 12-foot 4 x 12s to build a wall 19 feet high. ❦

**Scatchard house floor plan**

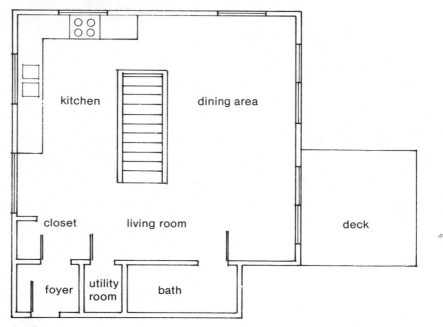

kitchen    dining area

closet    living room    deck

foyer    utility room    bath

1st floor

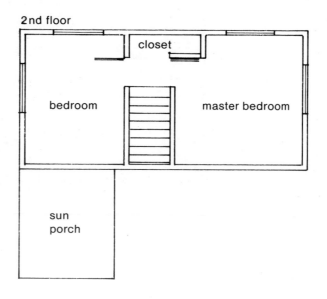

2nd floor

closet

bedroom    master bedroom

sun porch

CHAPTER 3

# Drying Green Lumber

GREEN LUMBER, CUT BY YOU OR PURCHASED from a sawmill, can reduce your building materials cost by as much as 30 to 40 percent. But buying green lumber does not necessarily mean that you must build with it green. If you buy green lumber and dry it yourself, you will save money and have the benefit of building with dry wood that will not shrink after it is in place.

While it is possible and often desirable to build with green lumber that is fresh off the stump, it is always easier to build with lumber that is dry. Dry wood is lighter, easier to work with, and for some items such as flooring it is an absolute necessity. So if you have the time, buy your lumber at least three months before you are going to use it, so that it can have time to air-dry properly. By buying green lumber and drying it yourself, you can enjoy the best of both worlds—dry lumber at a price you can afford.

If you are using large beams, such as for post-and-beam construction, it is not necessary to air-dry them first, since they take so long to dry, and will dry perfectly well in place.

In order to understand the drying process, you must know a little about the structure of wood. Wood is composed of tube-like cells that are aligned parallel to the trunk of the tree. If you cut across the trunk of a tree, you expose several different kinds of wood, each of which has a specific function. On the outside of a tree is the outer and inner bark, and then, moving inward, the cambium, sapwood, heartwood, and pith.

Of particular importance is the difference between sapwood and heartwood. The sapwood forms part of the living section of the tree. Inside of this is the heartwood, composed of dead cells that help support the tree. In general, sapwood is lighter than heartwood and it contains more moisture. The deeper heartwood dries more slowly than sapwood because it is less permeable to moisture.

The moisture content of green lumber varies widely among species. The accompanying table gives the moisture content for some North American wood species. (For a more complete listing, see Appendix 3.) Moisture is expressed as a percentage of the wood's oven-dry weight. This means that a tree that has a moisture content of 100 percent contains water equal in weight to that of the dry tree. A moisture content of 50 percent would indicate that water equal to one-half the weight of the dry wood is present in the green wood. As can be seen from the table, spruce has the lowest and hemlock the highest moisture content of the most commonly used lumber.

# The Properties of Wood

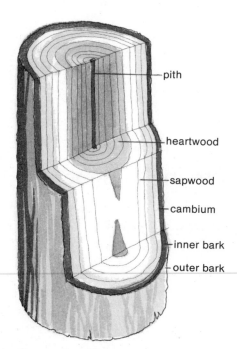

*Cross-section of a tree.*

pith

heartwood

sapwood

cambium

inner bark

outer bark

## Average Moisture Content of Green Wood
### (based on oven-dry weight)

Figures are percentages

| SOFTWOODS | HEARTWOOD | SAPWOOD | MIXED HEARTWOOD AND SAPWOOD |
|---|---|---|---|
| Cedar, northern white | — | — | 55 |
| Fir, Douglas | 30 | 140 | — |
| Hemlock, eastern | 97 | 119 | — |
| Pine, eastern white | — | — | 68 |
| Pine, sugar | 98 | 219 | — |
| Pine, red | 32 | 134 | — |
| Redwood, young growth | 100 | 200 | — |
| Spruce, red and white | — | — | 55 |
| **HARDWOODS** | | | |
| Ash, white | 46 | 44 | — |
| Beech, American | 55 | 72 | — |
| Birch, yellow | 74 | 72 | — |
| Butternut | — | — | 104 |
| Cherry, black | 58 | — | 65 |
| Hickory | 71 | 51 | — |
| Maple, sugar | 65 | 72 | — |
| Oak, northern red | 80 | 69 | — |
| Oak, northern white | 64 | 78 | — |
| Sycamore, American | 114 | 130 | — |
| Walnut, black | 90 | 73 | — |

From: Air Drying of Lumber, Agriculture Handbook No. 402, U.S. Department of Agriculture.

# Drying Lumber

Lumber is dried by evaporating water from its surface area. During this process, moisture moves from the inside of the wood to the surface or from zones of high moisture content to low ones. As water evaporates off the surface, it pulls the interior water out, gradually bringing the wood's moisture content into equilibrium with the atmospheric moisture.

In drying lumber, two types of moisture are distinguished. The first is called *free water,* which is moisture in the cell cavity. This free water is not tightly bound in the wood and evaporates relatively easily. The second is called *bound water,* which is moisture trapped in the cell wall and is harder to remove. When wood reaches a moisture content of about 30 percent, all

the free water has evaporated. This is called the *fiber saturation point* since all water is now held in the cell walls. In the drying process, the fiber saturation point marks the start of wood shrinkage since water is now being removed from the cell walls, causing them to shrink.

## Why Lumber Warps

As lumber progresses from a moisture content of 30 percent down to the usual 15 percent for dry softwood and 7 percent for dry hardwood, it shrinks, often causing various types of distortions. These distortions or warps, which can be controlled by proper drying techniques, occur because wood shrinks at different rates across its three dimensions. It shrinks most across the grain (tangentially), about half as much perpendicular to the grain (radially), and only very slightly with the grain (longitudinally). The illustrations show the three different directions of shrinkage, and depict how boards would shrink cut from various parts of a log.

Uneven shrinkage causes four kinds of warps:

*Cup.* This is probably the most common way boards warp, and is caused by the position of the annual growth rings. Since greater shrinkage occurs across the outer face of a board (where

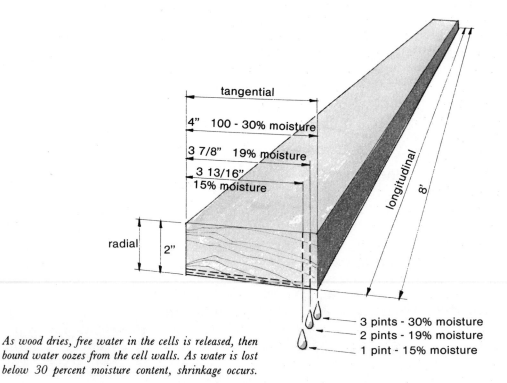

*As wood dries, free water in the cells is released, then bound water oozes from the cell walls. As water is lost below 30 percent moisture content, shrinkage occurs.*

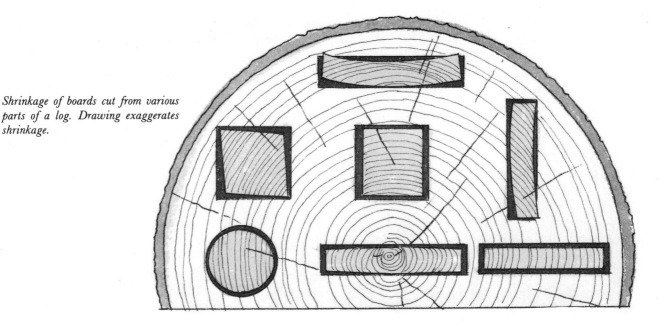

*Shrinkage of boards cut from various parts of a log. Drawing exaggerates shrinkage.*

the growth rings are tangential) than across the inner face (where the rings are more radial), the board tends to become concave.

**Bow.** Bow refers to a bend in the edge of a board caused by spiral or changing grain patterns. This is the most serious defect from a carpenter's point of view since a badly bowed piece of lumber cannot be used for sill plates, rafters, or studs.

**Twist.** Twist refers to a bend in the plane of a board so it no longer lies flat. Twisting is a problem encountered when installing flooring or paneling.

**Crook.** A crook is a bend in a board when viewed on edge. Again this may be caused by irregularities in the grain.

### Shrinkage

Wood species vary in shrinkage as they dry. In general, shrinkage is considered to be proportional to the amount of moisture removed under 30 percent, the fiber saturation point. The table gives the amount of shrinkage for some North American woods. (See Appendix 3 for a complete listing.) For anyone wishing to calculate what fraction of an inch a given piece of lumber will shrink when dried to a certain moisture content, Appendix 3 gives a formula for calculating such dimensional changes. As a rule of thumb, you can expect up to ¼-inch shrinkage on 6-inch wide spruce or hemlock that has been dried to a 15 percent moisture content.

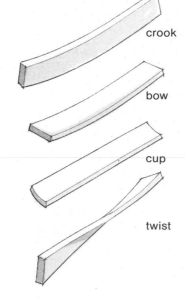

crook

bow

cup

twist

*Four types of warps.*

## Approximate Shrinkage
### (as percent of green dimension)
### from green to 0 percent moisture content

| SOFTWOODS | TANGENTIAL | RADIAL | T/R* |
|---|---|---|---|
| Cedar, northern white | 4.9 | 2.2 | 2.2 |
| Fir, Douglas | 7.6 | 4.8 | 1.6 |
| Hemlock, eastern | 6.8 | 3.0 | 2.3 |
| Pine, eastern white | 6.0 | 2.3 | 2.6 |
| Pine, sugar | 5.6 | 2.9 | 1.9 |
| Pine, red | 7.2 | 3.8 | 1.9 |
| Redwood | 4.4 | 2.6 | 1.7 |
| Spruce, red | 7.8 | 3.8 | 2.1 |
| **HARDWOODS** | | | |
| Ash, white | 7.8 | 4.9 | 1.6 |
| Beech, American | 11.9 | 5.5 | 2.2 |
| Birch, yellow | 9.5 | 7.3 | 1.3 |
| Butternut | 6.4 | 3.4 | 1.9 |
| Cherry, black | 7.1 | 3.7 | 1.9 |
| Hickory | 11.5 | 7.2 | 1.6 |
| Maple, sugar | 9.9 | 4.8 | 2.0 |
| Oak, northern red | 8.6 | 4.0 | 2.2 |
| Oak, northern white | 10.5 | 5.6 | 1.9 |
| Sycamore, American | 8.4 | 5.0 | 1.7 |
| Walnut, black | 7.8 | 5.5 | 1.4 |

* T/R is the difference between tangential and radial shrinkage. Thus white ash shrinks 1.6 times as much tangentially as it does radially.

# Air-Drying Green Lumber

Air-drying involves exposing piles of green lumber to air that can carry off moisture. It is an extremely simple and economical process that can produce construction grade lumber at 12 to 15 percent moisture content. Despite its simplicity, there are a few details that must be understood in order to dry wood without defects.

Most important is correct piling of the green lumber. Lumber of the same dimension should be stacked in layers that are separated by stickers. Stickers are small pieces of wood that allow air to flow around the boards. Proper stickering is extremely important, since, if it is not done right, air flow will be impeded, drying time slowed, and the lumber may be damaged.

The illustration shows a properly stacked pile of green lumber. Notice that the stickers (usually 1 inch thick and 1 to 2 inches wide) are all aligned vertically and are placed about 2 feet apart. Vertical alignment is necessary to provide proper support as the weight of the pile is transmitted from board to

board. Stickers should also be placed fairly close to the ends of the boards for support and to prevent the ends from cracking. Since stickers are compressed against the board surface, they will leave a dent if they are too narrow, and leave a stain if they are not completely dry. Therefore, it is best to use stickers that are at least 1 inch wide and are kiln-dried or completely air-dried. If the stickers are going to be used again, use of more durable hardwood stickers should be considered.

## High, Open Pile

In order to facilitate air movement and speed up drying, a high and fairly open pile is the best. Boards are usually laid edge to edge and a *chimney* is left in the center to promote downward air flow. The boards can also be laid with a gap between their edges to allow air to move downward, without a chimney. In a well-built pile, warm air enters at the top, circulates around the boards, absorbing moisture and cooling, and then drops through the pile and out the bottom. The foundation of a pile is also critical since there is considerable moisture and little air flow at ground level. By starting the first layer of boards at least 6 inches off the ground and keeping surrounding vegetation cut back, you can minimize absorption of ground moisture and maximize downward air flow through the pile.

The location of drying lumber piles is also important. While an empty garage or barn makes an excellent place, piles can also be stacked outdoors as long as they are covered. Used

*In this pile the stickers are correctly aligned vertically so they, and not unsupported sections of boards, carry the weight of the pile. Stickers are placed close to end of boards to minimize checking, and boards are separated to facilitate air movement.*

LOW-COST GREEN LUMBER CONSTRUCTION

metal roofing, discarded plywood or paneling, or any other stiff panel material is an adequate cover as long as it forms a waterproof roof. Stiff panels should be used since weights must be placed on top of the pile to keep the top layers of lumber from warping. The roof should be at least 2 inches off the pile, to permit air flow. This can be done by using 2 x 4s for stickers on top of the last layer of boards.

Lumber piled outdoors should be oriented to take advantage of the sun and prevailing winds. Piles should be stacked with a good southern exposure that will allow the sun's rays to hit the pile and warm it. By stacking piles with the stickers parallel to the prevailing wind, air flow can be encouraged across the surface of the boards.

## Drying Defects

Air-dried lumber is subject to several types of defects that can be avoided by using proper drying techniques. Green wood is an excellent growing surface for fungus which can often stain the wood. "Blue" stains are the most common type of fungus, turning wood blue to black in color. Blue stains usually occur because the drying process has been stopped due either to constant rewetting by rain or by impeded air flow. While these stains do not affect the structural soundness of the wood, they do affect its quality where color is important.

Another drying defect is checking, which causes splits along the grain of the wood. There are three types of checks—end, surface, and honeycomb. These are structural failures in the

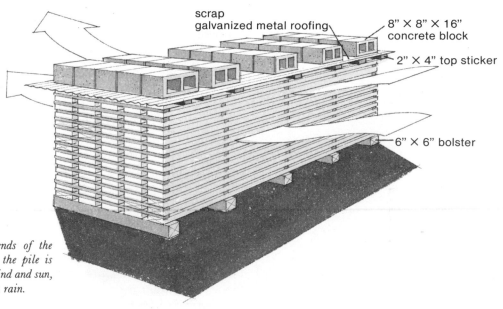

*To insure proper drying, the ends of the boards are sealed with varnish, the pile is placed to take advantage of the wind and sun, and it's covered to protect it from rain.*

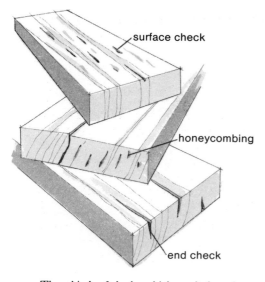

*Three kinds of checks which result from drying stresses.*

wood caused by excessive drying stresses and will often grow into large cracks. A final drying defect is warp, which, as discussed before, is caused by unequal rates of surface shrinkage.

## Avoiding Defects

In order to avoid these drying defects, several precautions are necessary. First, all lumber must be restrained to prevent warping. On the lower layers of the pile, this is accomplished by the weight of the upper layers transmitted through the stickers. In order to restrain the upper layers, weights must be placed on top of the pile. A cover of cinder blocks or equally weighty objects placed on the roof of a pile over the lines of the stickers will keep the top boards flat.

A second precaution to take, especially if you are drying hardwood or lumber to be used for cabinet-grade work, is to seal the ends of the boards with polyurethane or varnish. This will help prevent end-checking, caused because end grain loses moisture twelve times faster than the side grain, setting up large stresses in the wood. Coat the end grains as soon as possible after cutting to minimize this possibility.

## Slow Drying

Because rapid drying sets up stresses in lumber that can cause surface checks and honeycombing, start the drying process slowly, if possible in early spring or late fall when temperatures are cool and moisture is high. Spring is ideal since it allows final drying to take place in the hot, dry summer months.

Mark on the pile the date and where the wood came from, so you won't forget when the wood started drying. It is now ready to dry for a month, a year, or until you need it. The table gives the air-drying time for some common woods. Even if you cannot afford the time to air-dry your wood completely, green wood should be stacked in this manner from the moment it is delivered to prevent rot and decay. A great deal of moisture can be eliminated from green wood that is stickered for only a few weeks since drying takes place rapidly at first and then slows down.

## Determining Dryness

The most accurate way to determine whether your wood is dry is to use a moisture meter. Through means of a metal probe, this meter measures the moisture content of the inside of a board.

## Air-drying Times

Approximate time to air-dry green 1-inch lumber to 20 percent moisture content.

| SOFTWOODS | DAYS |
| --- | --- |
| Douglas fir, coast | 20–200 |
| Hemlock, eastern | 90–200 |
| Pine, eastern white | 60–200 |
| Pine, red | 40–200 |
| Pine, sugar, light | 15–90 |
| Redwood, light | 60–185 |
| Spruce, red | 30–120 |

| HARDWOODS | |
| --- | --- |
| Ash, white | 60–200 |
| Basswood, American | 40–150 |
| Birch, yellow | 70–200 |
| Cherry, black | 70–200 |
| Elm, American | 50–150 |
| Maple, sugar | 50–200 |
| Oak, northern red | 70–200 |
| Oak, northern white | 80–250 |
| Poplar, yellow | 40–150 |
| Walnut, black | 70–200 |

From: Air-drying of Lumber, Agriculture Handbook No. 402.

Since most of us don't have moisture meters, a more practical way to determine whether your lumber is dry is to weigh it. Most green wood is at least half water by weight, and as it dries it will lose a considerable amount of weight. By periodically weighing a few boards (a bathroom scale is accurate enough), you can determine how fast your wood is drying. When it no longer loses weight, it has reached equilibrium with the surrounding air and is *air dry*. In the Northeast, with a relative humidity of 75 to 80 percent, green lumber will dry to 12 to 14 percent moisture content.

When your lumber is dry, it should be stored inside to prevent any further degradation due to rain, sun, or snow. At moisture levels of 15 percent or below, lumber can be stored in a dry area without warping, further shrinkage, or growth of fungus.

While air-drying can produce lumber with a moisture content of 12 to 14 percent in a matter of months, for the builder or wood worker who wishes to dry large quantities of green wood regularly, an inexpensive solar kiln may be a good investment.

# Solar Kilns

Using only the sun's energy, a solar kiln can dry a load of softwood in a month or a load of hardwood stock in two months. A solar kiln, too, can produce lumber with a moisture content of 7 to 8 percent, which is necessary for cabinet-grade hardwoods and is not possible by simply air-drying.

## Johnson Kiln

Over the years, several kinds of solar kilns have been built in the United States. One of the first was designed and built by Curtis Johnson, a retired Forest Service employee in Madison, Wisconsin. Mr. Johnson's latest kiln is built out of wood, measures 10 feet wide and 12 feet long, and holds about 800 board feet of lumber. The south side of the dryer is enclosed with glass panels mounted at 40°. The hot air collectors consist of a framed box with a back of sheet metal painted black to absorb the sun's energy, a 1½-inch air space, and a glass cover. The top and the bottom of the collectors are open so that air can enter from the bottom, be heated, and then be drawn out of the top. Two overhead fans circulate 1,200 cubic feet of hot air per minute downward between the two lumber piles.

According to Paul Bois, a wood-drying specialist with the Forest Service, the kiln heats up to 130° F. in the summer and 90° F. in the winter. It can dry hardwoods to 8 percent moisture content or less in 80 days during the summer (assuming 70 days of sunshine), and can do the same in 150 to 200 days during the colder and cloudier winter months.

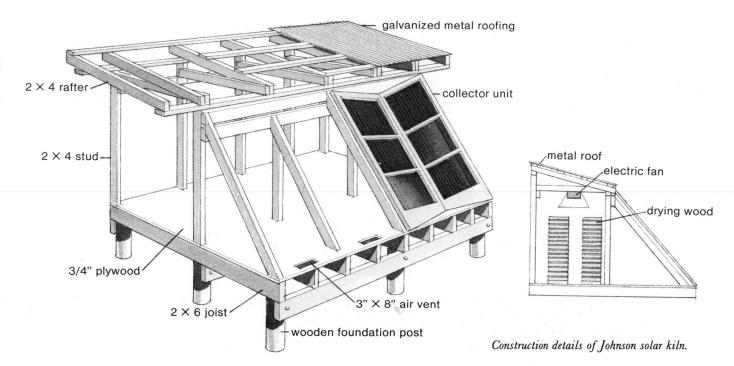

*Construction details of Johnson solar kiln.*

**LOW-COST GREEN LUMBER CONSTRUCTION**

*The Johnson solar kiln can hold about 800 board feet of lumber.*

## Materials List for Johnson Solar Dryer

### Structure

| | |
|---|---|
| Treated posts 5 inches top, 42 inches long | 9 pieces |
| 4 x 6, 10 feet long, Douglas fir | 2 pieces |
| 2 x 6, 10 feet long, Douglas fir | 2 pieces |
| 2 x 6, 12 feet long, floor joists | 8 pieces |
| 2 x 4, 10 feet long | 5 pieces |
| 2 x 4, 6 feet long | 12 pieces |
| 2 x 4, 7 feet long | 6 pieces |
| 2 x 4, 8 feet long | 14 pieces |
| 2 x 4, 12 feet long | 4 pieces |
| 4 x 8, ¾ inch plywood underlayment | 4 sheets |
| Pedestrian door, 2 feet 6 inches by 6 feet plus | 1 |
| 1 x 8 boxcar siding | 300 board feet |
| 1 x 4, 8 feet long trim | 8 pieces |
| 1 x 6, 12 feet long trim | 6 pieces |
| 25/32-inch standard sheathing, for inside lining | 6 sheets |

### Roof

| | |
|---|---|
| Rigid-rib metal roofing, 8 feet | 5 sheets |
| Foil-faced insulation | 1 roll |

### Solar Collectors

| | |
|---|---|
| 24-inch roll of valley tin for heat collector | 25 feet |
| 1 x 6 frames for heat collector | 32 lineal feet |
| 5/4 x 6 pine for sash | 24 lineal feet |
| 1 x 6 pine for sash | 24 lineal feet |
| Glass | 48 square feet |
| 4 x 8 sheets, ⅛-inch tempered hardboard | 2 sheets |
| 4 x 8 sheets, ⅜-inch exterior plywood | 1 sheet |

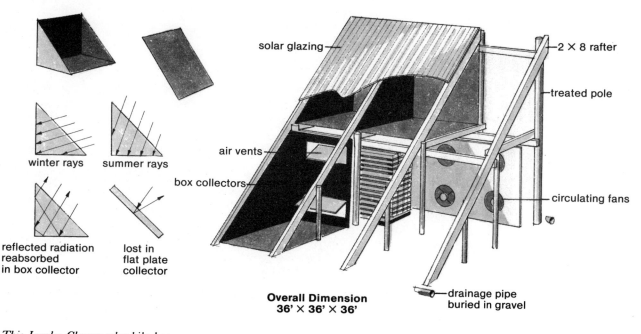

solar glazing

2 × 8 rafter

treated pole

air vents

box collectors

circulating fans

winter rays

summer rays

reflected radiation
reabsorbed
in box collector

lost in
flat plate
collector

drainage pipe
buried in gravel

**Overall Dimension
36' × 36' × 36'**

*This Lumley-Choong solar kiln has a capacity of 25,000 board feet. Box-type collectors continue to collect the sun's rays even when the sun's position changes during the day and throughout the seasons.*

### Lumley-Choong Kiln

A larger and more sophisticated solar kiln has been built by Timothy Lumley and Elvin Choong of Louisiana State University. The big differences in their kiln are the collector arrangement and that it does not vent air to the outside.

The kiln uses two box-type hot air collectors that are mounted in front of and over the lumber pile. These collectors have the advantage of having four absorption surfaces instead of only one as in a flat plate collector. According to the designers, this effectively doubles the absorption area while keeping the glazed area (and therefore the cost) the same. Another advantage of the box-type collectors is that the four surfaces can effectively pick up solar radiation from different angles as the sun's position changes during the year.

By using a closed-air system, this kiln conserves the solar energy it receives since none of the warm air is vented outside. The kiln uses condensation rather than venting to control moisture build-up. Because of daily temperature fluctuations, solar kilns naturally lose their moisture at night as the chamber cools and moisture condenses on the coolest surface, which is the floor. In the Lumley-Choong kiln, moisture condenses on a gravel floor and is carried away by drainpipes under the gravel. This condensation cycle is at work even during the day as warm air passes over the cooler gravel floor and the moisture condenses.

## Minimize Defects

Solar kilns have a distinct advantage in minimizing checking and other drying defects. Because solar kilns cool off at night, the relative humidity inside the kiln rises and relieves some of the drying stresses in the lumber. In effect, solar kilns allow boards to "rest" at night, giving them a chance to equalize their interior and exterior moisture contents. The color and "brightness" of solar-dried lumber are also reported to be superior to lumber from conventional kilns.

When one considers that two-thirds of the energy used to manufacture lumber is used to dry it, the importance of air-drying and solar kilns becomes apparent. It is the kiln-drying operation that accounts for the high price of commercial lumber. By buying green and drying lumber yourself, you can save money and with a little care produce lumber that is superior in quality to that found in lumberyards.

# Further Reading

*Wood Handbook: Wood as an Engineering Material,* Forest Products Laboratory, Agriculture Handbook No. 72, Forest Service, USDA. The definitive text on wood's structural, machining, and building properties. Available from the Superintendent of Documents, U.S. Government Printing Office.

*Air Drying of Lumber: A Guide to Industry Practices,* Raymond C. Rietz and Rufus H. Page, Agriculture Handbook No. 402, Forest Service, USDA., July 1971. This is the most complete and useful text available on drying wood. Also available from the Superintendent of Documents, U.S. Government Printing Office.

*Constructing and Operating a Small Solar Heated Lumber Dryer,* Paul J. Bois, Forest Products Utilization Report No. 7, Forest Service, USDA. A technical description of the Johnson solar kiln with plans and a list of necessary materials. Available from the Superintendent of Documents, U.S. Government Printing Office.

*Fine Woodworking Magazine,* The Taunton Press, Newton, Connecticut. Several articles on wood drying have appeared in *Fine Woodworking:*

*Alternative Wood Drying Technologies,* No. 22, May/June 1980.

*Drying Wood: The Fundamental Considerations,* No. 5, Winter 1976.

*Water and Wood: The Problems of a Difficult Pair,* No. 4, Fall 1976.

# Green Wood Solar Home

*A greenhouse and green wood for energy and savings*

"Green wood houses all look alike."

This is a common complaint I hear from people when they are discussing the merits of building with green wood. The Rood house in Warren, Vermont, framed entirely with green wood, clearly puts this contention to rest. The house looks very little like the conventional barn structure associated with green wood, and it is a passive solar house as well.

In the Rood house, neither architectural design nor energy efficiency has been sacrificed by using green wood.

Designed by Mac Rood, a house designer and builder by trade, the house is a home for Mac and his wife, Bobby, and contains a separate apartment for his parents as well. The house is built around a large solar greenhouse, which forms a courtyard onto which all the rooms of the main house open. The greenhouse heats the main house and apartment and also gives an air of spaciousness to the compactly designed house.

## Clapboard Siding

Mac and several friends built the house in 1978, framing it with green 2 x 6s. The exterior of the house was sheathed and then cov- ered with clapboards. The interior walls are covered with Sheetrock and pine paneling.

An interesting detail is the first floor ceiling, which was left unfinished in order to expose the rough wood joists and subflooring above. The rough wood contrasts nicely with the white Sheetrocked walls, tile, and hardwood floors downstairs.

The finished flooring for most of the house is birch hardwood, laid over composition board in order to smooth out the irregularities of the green wood subflooring. In the kitchen, the finished floor is ceramic tile. This is easy to maintain

and adds thermal mass to absorb heat from the greenhouse and wood stove.

The greenhouse is the focal point of the main house, with all the rooms overlooking it. Heat is stored in a rear Trombe wall built of two concrete block walls with 4 feet of rocks between them. Hot air from the greenhouse rises naturally to heat the second-floor bedrooms and excess heat is collected in the cupola area and then blown by small fans down through the rocks for storage.

---

## "Why cut wood in Oregon and truck it all the way here when it grows in your own backyard?"

---

The Trombe wall in the greenhouse also serves as the rear wall of the apartment and radiates heat into it. In the summer, excess heat is vented out the cupola.

The greenhouse is covered with 900 square feet of Kalwall solar glazing. This is the only part in the house that was not framed with green wood. Because green wood rafters would have shrunk and twisted slightly, damaging the glazing and its waterproof joints, kiln-dried lumber was used.

I asked Mac why he had bothered to use green wood, considering the design of the house and the fact that clapboards were used on the outside. He gave several specific reasons. "First of all and most importantly, green wood is inexpensive. The wood for this house was about 18 cents a board foot from a local mill. Secondly, I like the looks of rough wood and the feeling it gives to a house. Finally, I believe you should use local resources whenever possible. Why cut wood in Oregon and

*This solar greenhouse is the focal point of the house. Greenhouse rafters are the only structural members that were not green.*

*Inside the kitchen/living room, looking into the greenhouse.*

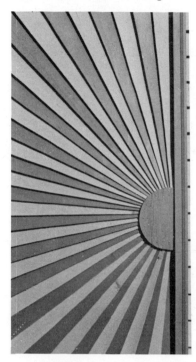

*Design on side of Rood house suggests builder's interest in solar heating.*

*Inside the greenhouse. Arched roof covers corner of kitchen.*

*South side of house. Light enters the greenhouse through translucent Kalwall roof glazing and the vertical sliding glass doors.*

truck it all the way here when it grows in your own backyard?"

## Dried Framing

When he built the house, Mac was well aware of the need to let green wood framing dry before the interior was closed up. While the exterior sheathing and clapboards went on right away, the interior Sheetrock, paneling, and finished flooring were not installed for about nine months. Even after this lengthy drying time, Mac still had a few problems with Sheetrock nails popping and pulling through.

## Used Sheetrock

While the interior walls looked very smooth and well finished to me, Mac, as the designer, builder, and resident of the house, voiced some dissatisfaction with the way the Sheetrock went over the green studs. "If I built with green wood again," Mac said, "I'd be sure to either dry it or use kiln-dried wood in the corners and other places where the finish must be perfect. Wood paneling goes on fine over green wood, but Sheetrock shows every little irregularity."

---

## Green wood can be used attractively and economically in any house design.

---

Considering that the green wood studs Mac had to work with varied by as much as ¼ inch in width and that he had taken no precautions to even out the wall surface, I was impressed by how well he had dealt with the green wood and Sheetrock problem.

## Attractive, Economical

While the Rood house is certainly not typical of other green wood houses, it shows that green wood can be used attractively and economically in any house design.

By using green wood for framing, Mac saved a considerable amount of money—money that could then go into a solar greenhouse, clapboard siding, and interior trim detail. And by leaving the heart of green wood exposed in the rough wood ceilings, the modern finish and angular aspects of the house are tempered with a bit of rustic charm that goes a long way toward connecting and linking the house with its rural environment. ☘

**Rood house floor plan**

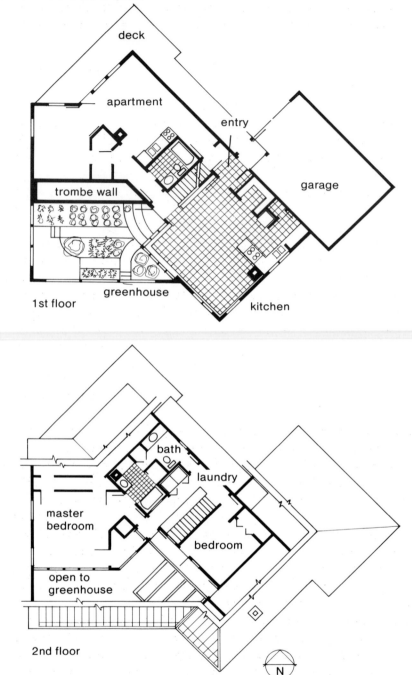

# CHAPTER 4

# House Framing, Past and Present

## "YOU CAN'T BUILD WITH GREEN WOOD."

This is the advice I often receive from friends including knowledgeable carpenters. The reasons given are that green wood is too uneven, too weak, and will warp, split, and check. The truth is that green wood has been a standard building material from medieval times right up through the last century. It was not until the late 1800s, when kiln technology and commercial lumber operations came of age, that planed, kiln-dried lumber became commonplace. And far from being inferior buildings, green wood post-and-beam structures of medieval England are still standing 500 years later.

# Framing History

From those early days through the last century, green wood post-and-beam framing was the common construction method for wooden buildings. While wood for finish work such as paneling and flooring was usually air-dried, buildings were framed out of green wood that was allowed to dry in place.

Not surprisingly, the architecture and construction methods that evolved from green wood framing were as much a response to the nature of the building material as they were to artistic and social ideals. From the earliest times, carpenters recognized that green wood beams would shrink, check, and twist as they dried. Wood jointry evolved to deal with these problems, reaching its peak in sixteenth century Europe. The wood jointry of this era shows remarkable engineering knowledge and attention to detail. Joints were made that would last centuries, resisting shrinkage and twisting, and were of great beauty.

*This intricate and beautiful scarf joint was carved in the early fifteenth century in England.*

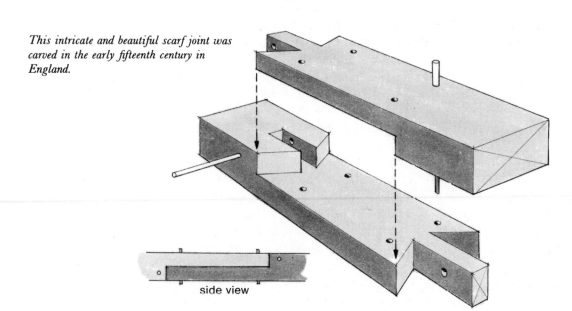

side view

*Georgian paneling with ornate edge molding that hides the shrinking and swelling of the boards.*

## Georgian Architecture

From the point of view of craftsmanship and attention to detail, the pinnacle of wooden architecture in this country was perhaps the Georgian era (1750–1800), the final development of the colonial style. Georgian architecture is noted for its use of elaborate millwork and decorative trim. While these decorations served an artistic purpose, they also were functional, hiding the inherent movement of wood as it shrank and swelled with the changing relative humidity.

A good example of this is the treatment of paneling in Georgian architecture. Wooden paneling was often milled with one or more rounded edges on its side where the boards overlapped. This sculpturing of the edges served to break up visually the vertical lines between panels so that as the boards shrank or expanded the difference in the gaps between the pieces of paneling was not noticeable.

Small but important details such as this were not only a response to building with wood that was often green, but also to the recognition that wood is a "living" material that changes dimensions with the seasons because of different levels of humidity. Today we build with wood as if it were an artificial material that comes to us milled to exact dimensions and supposedly never changes. The fallacy of this view is apparent to anyone who has struggled with a swollen door or window due to humid summer weather. To colonial builders this movement was natural and unavoidable, something to be planned for, not ignored.

## Dimensions Uneven

Colonial builders also had to deal with the uneven dimensions of green, rough-sawn lumber. The beams and posts that framed the house would often vary ½ inch or more in dimension. To get a smooth and true wall surface from this crude and uneven frame, a combination of lath and plaster was used.

Thin wooden strips called laths were nailed to the wall frame with gaps left between them. The laths held the plaster that squished through the opening between strips, forming a "key," and it also smoothed out the wall surface. Plaster was applied over the laths in thicknesses varying from ¼ to ¾ inch to get a smooth, finished wall. By gradually building up a wall or ceiling from uneven rough wood to a smooth plaster finish, the inherent difficulties of building with green, rough-sawn wood were overcome.

Such construction methods required skilled labor and a considerable amount of time. Even in colonial America, labor was scarce and expensive when compared to materials, and soon

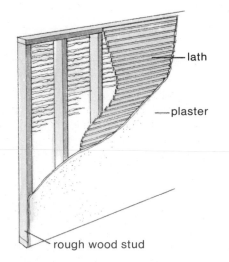

— lath

— plaster

rough wood stud

*House walls once were built up slowly from rough and uneven studs to a smooth and even plaster finish.*

time-cutting innovations were introduced that allowed a house to be framed by less-skilled craftsmen and in less time.

## Balloon Framing

The principal change took place in the 1800s when post-and-beam framing was replaced by *balloon* framing which uses milled lumber, such as 2 x 4s and 2 x 6s, rather than large timbers.

Despite the change in framing techniques, green lumber was still used extensively and its limitations overcome by the use of plaster walls and ceilings, and decorative moldings.

## Wood Frame Construction

Today we build houses by what is called *wood frame construction,* but it bears little resemblance to the practices of past centuries. While houses are built with wall studs much as they were 100 years ago, today those studs are all planed to exact dimensions and kiln-dried to prevent shrinkage. Walls are no longer carefully built up from rough to smooth. With kiln-dried, planed lumber, the studs themselves form a perfectly true surface; all that needs to be done is to place Sheetrock or paneling directly over them. Plywood or composition board is used to cover the exterior walls and then wood clapboards or more likely vinyl or aluminum siding is applied. It is all de-

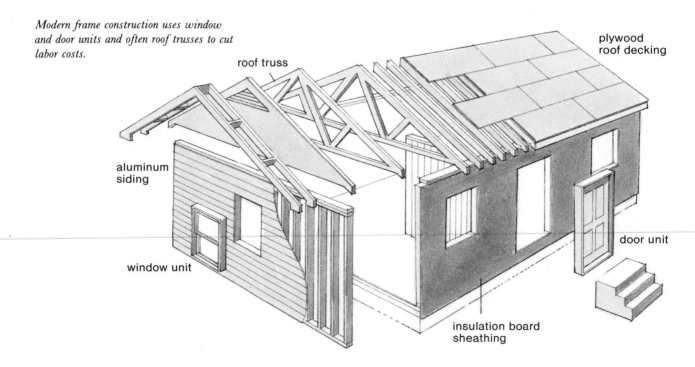

*Modern frame construction uses window and door units and often roof trusses to cut labor costs.*

roof truss

plywood roof decking

aluminum siding

window unit

door unit

insulation board sheathing

signed to save labor and allow the use of less-skilled workers, but the material costs are high.

In the past fifteen years, as the cost of an average home in this country has climbed from $25,000 to $50,000 and now well beyond that, many architects, builders, and homeowners have been reassessing the practicality of modern construction methods. Not only have labor costs been skyrocketing, but material costs have gone up as well, often at a faster rate than labor costs.

In an attempt to get affordable housing, many people have taken to designing and building their own homes. Having substantially lowered their labor costs of building, these owner-builders are eager to reduce material costs as well, often using recycled and low cost native materials such as green wood. By building green, these owner-builders can not only reduce material costs substantially, but they can also afford the time and attention to work with it properly because they are supplying their own labor.

## Back to Post and Beam

In states such as Vermont that have an abundance of local sawmills, the building cycle has come full circle back to green wood post-and-beam construction. Rather than being the exception, green wood building is becoming the rule among owner-builders. Even contractors, when they have access to local mills, are turning to green wood because of its lower costs and acceptability in terms of contemporary aesthetics.

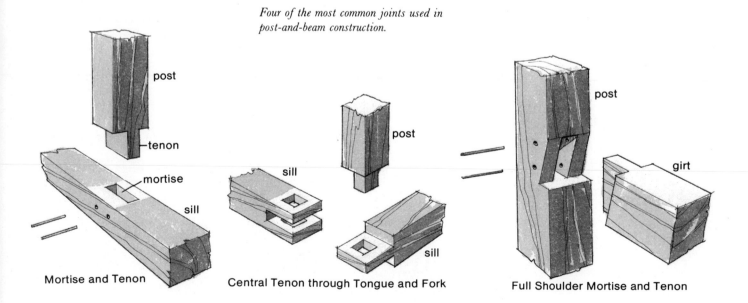

*Four of the most common joints used in post-and-beam construction.*

LOW-COST GREEN LUMBER CONSTRUCTION

While building with green wood can save considerable amounts of money, it is inherently more difficult to work with than kiln-dried lumber. The basic construction techniques are the same whether you are using green or dry lumber, but with green lumber special considerations are necessary to achieve satisfactory results. Green lumber is wet, heavy, uneven, and will shrink after it is in place. While these factors pose certain problems, they are not insurmountable obstacles, and they can be overcome using a number of simple techniques. When people tell me, "You can't build with green wood," I think what they are really saying is that it takes care, understanding, and patience to build with green wood. There's a big difference.

# Framing Fundamentals

The two principal methods of framing a house practiced today are post-and-beam framing and stud or "platform" framing. Post-and-beam framing relies on the use of large beams, usually 6 x 6s, 6 x 8s, and 8 x 8s, while stud framing uses milled lumber 2 inches in thickness and from 4 to 12 inches in width for floor, wall, and roof supports. Modern residential houses are almost always stud framed, although post-and-beam construction is making a comeback in rural parts of this country.

Post-and-beam or "timber" framing has been practiced for centuries and was not replaced by stud framing until the late 1800s. The structure of a colonial New England house offers an excellent example of post-and-beam framing and is often copied today for modern post-and-beam houses because of its simplicity and economy.

The sills, usually 8 x 8 green hemlock, spruce, or hardwood, sit on the foundation wall. Wall and corner posts are set into the sill and support the top rafter plate. Girts are notched into the sill and rafter plates to carry the floor. Summer beams run between the girts to break up the long flooring spans, and floor joists are framed in between the girts to support the flooring.

## Two Roofing Systems

Two types of roofing systems are used, the common rafter and the principal rafter-and-purlin. The common rafter system consists of 4 x 6 rafters set 3 to 6 feet apart with the roof sheathing laid perpendicular over the rafters. The principal rafter-and-purlin system uses larger rafters, 6 x 6 or larger, spaced up to 9 feet apart, with purlins (usually 4 x 4s) running between them at 3- to 4-foot intervals. The roof sheathing is laid across the purlins and parallel with the rafters. Finally, the collar ties hold the rafters in place and keep them from either bowing in or spreading out at the top plate.

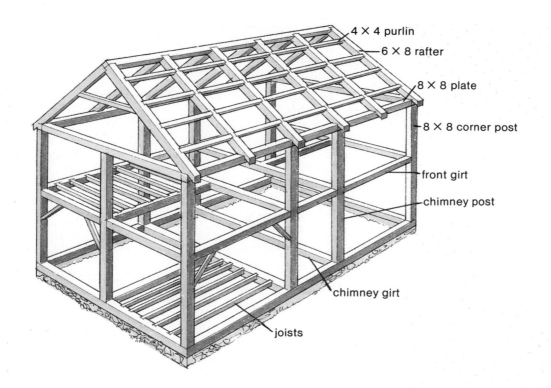

4 × 4 purlin

6 × 8 rafter

8 × 8 plate

8 × 8 corner post

front girt

chimney post

chimney girt

joists

*Framing detail of an early New England post-and-beam colonial.*

## Platform Framing

Stud or platform framing uses 2-inch lumber to replace the posts and beams. A 2 x 8 sill plate is laid on the foundation wall, joist headers and joists are framed on top of this, and sub-flooring, either boards or plywood, is laid on top of the joists to form a platform. A 2 x 4 or 2 x 6 plate (depending on thickness of the wall) is laid on the subflooring, studs are nailed on top of it, either every 16 inches for 2 x 4s or every 24 inches for 2 x 6s, and two overlapping top plates are nailed on top of the studs to form a wall. Joists are again laid on top of the double plate and the process begins again for the second floor. The roof is framed in much the same way as the common rafter system of post-and-beam construction, although the rafter size usually ranges from 2 x 6 to 2 x 12 and they are framed closer together, either 16 inches or 24 inches on center.

This method of stud framing is called "platform" framing for the obvious reason that it forms individual platforms from which the next floor can be built.

## Balloon Framing

The first type of stud framing that evolved from post-and-beam construction was balloon framing. The unique feature of this method is that the studs are continuous from the sill plate

to rafter plate, and the joists are supported on a wooden ribbon notched into the studs. This method is seldom used today because its construction takes more time and it is often hard to get good quality lumber that can span all the way from foundation to roof.

## Advantages of Post and Beam

Both framing methods offer distinct advantages and disadvantages. Post-and-beam framing requires more material and more skilled labor. These are the two principal reasons it was replaced by stud framing. However, post-and-beam construction offers much greater flexibility in design than stud framing. Because wall sections are supported by the overhead beam, window walls, large doorways, and other details can be framed in without worrying about the supporting studs and headers that would be necessary with stud framing. This makes post-and-beam construction particularly desirable for passive solar homes where the entire south wall might be filled with glass or some other non-structural glazing material.

While the wood jointry in post-and-beam construction requires more labor and skill, post-and-beam houses are perfectly suited for the old-fashioned community house raising. Once the posts and beams have been cut to length and notched out, the frame of an entire house can be raised in a single day with the help of friends and neighbors. Robin Worn's house (p. 11) is a solar post-and-beam structure that was raised by a small army of friends in a day of hard work and celebration. Finally, post-and-beam houses are strong, some having been standing for

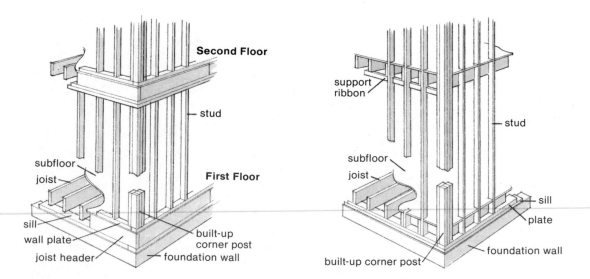

*Platform framing*

*Balloon framing uses studs reaching from the sill plate to the rafter plate.*

over 500 years, and extremely fire resistant since it takes a long time to burn through the large timbers.

## Stud Framing Advantages

Stud framing is considerably simpler, taking less time and skill in the preparation of joints and framing members. The only woodworking joint that might be required is a simple shiplap. All other joints are butted and nailed together or secured with metal fasteners. Stud framing components are also lightweight and can be easily moved and handled by one person. For this reason, owner-builders who are working alone will often choose to stud frame their houses. A final advantage of stud framing is that all modern building materials such as plywood and Sheetrock come in modular sizes based on 4-foot squares designed to fit framing that is either 16 inches or 24 inches on center. While these materials can easily be worked into post-and-beam designs, they were made specifically for stud framing.

Those starting to build a house for the first time need to gather and consider a tremendous amount of information before any design decisions are made, and most certainly before construction is started. While it is fairly easy to build a house that will keep out the wind and rain, it is much more difficult to design and build a house that meets your particular needs in an economical and aesthetically pleasing way. To do this one

*Green, rough lumber, plain lines—a beauty of a barn.*

needs to be knowledgeable about a wide variety of construction methods and materials. For every way of building something, there are at least five others. And there is no "best" way. It all depends on what your particular circumstances and goals are. So where to start? The further reading section that follows will help you on your way.

# Further Reading

*Modern Carpentry*, Willis H. Wagner, Goodheart Wilcox Co., Inc. South Holland, Illinois. This is *the* carpentry book. Not flashy, but complete and well illustrated, this is the standard text for high schools, vocational schools, and trade unions. It is the first construction book I owned and is still my most used reference.

*The Natural House*, Frank Lloyd Wright, Horizon Press, New York, N.Y., 1970. Sensible thoughts on housing design and building techniques by the most famous architect of this century. A good foundation on which to base your housing ideas.

*Architectural Graphic Standards*, Charles Ramsey and Harold Sleeper, John Wiley and Sons, Somerset, N.J., 1970. If, after reading *Modern Carpentry*, you have the idea but still aren't sure of the specifics, consult this book. *Standards* will show you how to build anything you ever dreamed of and more. The only drawback to this bible of building is its incredible price tag, $65. Check the local library first.

*Building The Timber Frame House (The Revival of a Forgotten Craft)*, Ted Benson and James Gruber, Charles Scribner's Sons, N.J., 1980. Post-and-beam framing well illustrated.

*Wood Frame House Construction*, L. O. Anderson, Agriculture Handbook No. 73, U.S. Department of Agriculture, 1975. A straightforward, no-nonsense book on wood house building using platform framing. A real good buy from the U.S. Printing Office and recently republished by several commercial concerns at a slightly higher price.

*The Barn (A Vanishing Landmark of North America)*, Eric Arthur and Dudley Whitney, A & W Publishers, New York, N.Y., 1975. A beautiful and well-researched book on barns, the original green wood structures. The photography will give you a sense of the aesthetics of green wood, while the text and appendices will show you the evolution of barns in this country and Canada.

*Handmade Houses (A Guide To The Woodbutcher's Art)*, Art Boericke and Barry Shapiro, A & W Publishers, New York, N.Y., 1973. A picture book of wonderful owner-built homes, mostly out of rough-sawn native wood. An inspiring look at the possibilities of green wood building.

# Plainfield Pioneers

*Breaking away from convention isn't always easy*

In my search for contemporary green wood houses, rarely have I found one that was built before 1970. This seems to be the time when use of native resources was being rediscovered on a wide scale.

Since the Civil War, when kiln-dried lumber became the predominant building material, use of rough-cut native wood has been on the decline. Only in recent years has it staged a comeback in rural parts of the country.

### Rebirth in Interest

The renewed interest in green wood seems to be a function of both economics and a new awareness of the importance of using local resources.

The beginning of the 70s marked the start of rising lumber prices and the maturing of environmental consciousness, and not surprisingly the rediscovery of the value of the local sawmill. As the price for kiln-dried lumber rose from fourteen cents to twenty-two cents a board foot in the early 70s, green wood building came of age.

One of the early green wood houses built in 1970 is nestled into the side of East Hill in Plainfield, Vermont. It is the home of Michael Birnbaum and his daughter, Corrina. While Michael helped frame the original structure and has been working part-time on the house for nearly ten years, the house was originally designed by Steve Jacob, a local designer-builder who challenged the world of conventional construction in the late 1960s with his attempts to build houses for as little as $10 a square foot by using native materials.

Before he moved to British Columbia, Steve built several low-cost green wood houses in the

Plainfield area and had achieved some national recognition for the benefits of using native lumber.

### Sod Roof Replaced

When Michael bought the house from Steve Jacob, it was not as large as it is today and was considerably different inside and out. One of the most unusual aspects of the original house was its sod roof, 6 inches of soil and grass that covered the entire house. While the idea of an insulating and maintenance-free sod roof was good, the roof beams were not designed to hold that much weight.

After shoveling snow off it for

---

**The beginning of the 70s marked the start of rising lumber prices and the maturing of environmental consciousness, and not surprisingly the rediscovery of the value of the local sawmill.**

---

several winters and watching it slowly rot the top of the siding boards, Michael decided to remove it and replace it with a covering of roll roofing and tar. According to Michael, Steve was a better builder than an engineer.

The house is framed out of green 8 x 8s and smaller beams, with wide hemlock board-and-batten siding.

While the wall framing is fairly conventional post and beam, the roof framing is unique. Rather than framing a straight-pitched roof with rafters running with the slope from top to bottom, Steve designed a curved roof system with rafters running level across the house at different heights. To achieve a curved wave-like roof,

4 x 8 roof beams were supported between wall studs at different heights that traced out a curving pattern. With this system, both roof and interior ceiling lines curve and undulate gracefully, mimicking the contour of a rolling field.

The interior ceiling was finished with ⅜-inch Sheetrock that could be bent to match the curve of the roof beams.

### Enlarged House

Michael has enlarged the house to include two new bedrooms, a darkroom for his photography work, and a utility room. The two bedrooms are set into the hillside about 4 feet deep into the ground. Where earth covers the siding, the wood has been treated with creosote and covered with metal flashing about half way up the wall to prevent water infiltration and rot.

### Roof too Heavy

As Michael showed me the additions and changes to the house, he explained problems he had encountered. The first was the sod roof. It was just too heavy, when covered with wet, heavy snow, for the framing to support. The roof was also damaging the siding boards because inadequate eaves and flashing allowed the roof water and soil to come into contact with the wood.

He also found that the unstained hemlock siding provided a home for carpenter ants. To eliminate the water and insect problems, he stained the entire house with creosote.

### Windows Leak Heat

The windows are another problem area that Michael plans to deal with soon. While Steve's window details were artistic, they weren't particularly energy-efficient. Built out of single panes of glass with no weatherstripping or

*Michael Birnbaum relaxes in his living room while telling the history of his green wood house.*

*A door with the simplicity of the Shaker style was made using tongue-and-groove 2x6s and a Z-frame.*

caulking, they lose heat. Michael's plans are to double glaze and weatherstrip them.

---

**One of the most unusual aspects of the original house was its sod roof, 6 inches of soil and grass that covered the entire house.**

---

When I asked Michael if he would build anything differently if he were starting all over again, he replied quickly, "There is absolutely no closet space in the house. You can't believe what it's like not to have any storage space. If I were building again, I'd put closet space in every room."

While architects always include closet space by habit and training, many owner-builders forget about this basic necessity. In some large houses, closets can easily be fitted in as an afterthought, but in a house as compact as Michael's, finding enough room to add a closet can be nearly impossible.

### Pioneering Effort

As one of the first wave of alternative houses, built at a time when domes, zomes, and other innovative house designs were being explored, Steve Jacob's East Hill home is a good example of the pioneering effort to break away from conventional architecture with its ever-inflating price tag and wasteful use of resources.

While many of the features had to be changed by Michael because of technical problems, the basic design of the house with its sod roof, orientation to the south, and protecting earth hillside to the north clearly anticipated passive solar and underground housing which is just beginning to be accepted nearly a decade later. ❦

CHAPTER 5

# Green Wood Techniques

BUILDING WITH GREEN WOOD IS AN ART BECAUSE you must understand the nature of the material you are working with to get good results. Construction-grade kiln-dried lumber is dry, straight, and true; it is used almost as if it were an inert piece of plastic or steel. Green wood is wet, roughly cut, and dimensionally uneven. Each piece must be given individual attention. Understanding this difference and coping with it is the art of green wood building, and like any craft there are techniques or "tricks of the trade" that will help you get around the inherent problems of green wood.

## Storing Lumber

The first step in green wood building, and something that is often ignored, is the proper storage of lumber. Lumber, after it has been transported from the mill to the building site, will often sit for weeks before it is used. Because green lumber goes through its fastest drying period right after it is cut, it should be stacked with stickers to aid the drying process and minimize twisting and checking (see Chapter 3). This is especially true of siding boards, which will be used last and are extremely susceptible to drying defects. By stacking your boards from the moment they leave the mill, you can minimize these defects and have fairly dry lumber when it is time to put on the siding. The drier the siding, the less the boards will check and split after they have been nailed in place.

A possible exception to this rule is when using green oak. Green oak is easy to cut and nail, but dry oak is like a rock, making it a very difficult framing material. One builder of green oak houses recommends piling the oak without stickers, soaking it with water, and then covering it with a tarp until it is used. This will certainly keep the oak from drying, but it might

*Two ways of piling green lumber. There's no doubt which lumber will crack and warp.*

also promote the growth of fungus which can give lumber blue stain or off colors. While this isn't a problem for framing material which will be covered, it could become one where the oak will be exposed as a finished surface.

Always sticker green softwood lumber so it will begin drying immediately. This will cause fewer problems after the wood is in place, and it will save wear and tear on your muscles. When putting large rafters or beams in place, you will often be lifting over 100 pounds of pure water. A few weeks of air-drying can reduce that substantially.

# Dealing with Dimensions

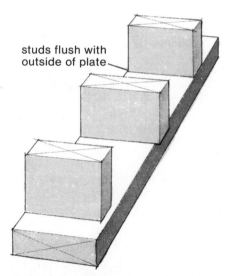

studs flush with outside of plate

*In framing a green wood wall, line up the studs flush with the outside of the plate. The inside can be smoothed out later for Sheetrock or paneling.*

The first difficulty you will encounter in green wood building is the uneven dimensions of the lumber. As you start laying down sill plates and framing in the walls, you will notice that none of your lumber is the same size. Going over to the lumber pile to measure a few of your 2 x 6 wall studs, you may find that they range from 5¾ inches to over 6¼ inches in width. And some pieces that start out as 6 inches on one end are only 5¾ inches at the other end. The thicknesses are no better.

If you put up these pieces as they come off the pile, the walls and ceilings of your house will resemble a roller coaster ride, impossible to finish, let alone live with.

What to do?

The answer depends on what type of structure you are building. If you are building a barn or outbuilding that will not be finished on the inside, there is no problem. Line up all the studs and plates flush with the outside of the wall so that your have a smooth surface on which to apply the siding, and let the inside be as it may. Since no wall covering will be applied on the inside, the unevenness of the wall studs will not cause any problem.

If you are building a house that will be finished on the inside, you have a problem. There are several ways out of it.

## Remilling

Your first option is to remill all the lumber down to the same size, usually the dimension of the smallest piece. Thus if you were working with 2 x 6s, you would mill all the lumber down to 5¾ or even 5½ inches.

If you have access to a good table saw or commercial woodworking shop, this is not an unreasonable task. This was done in the building of Robin Worn's house (p. 11) with very little extra effort, at a shop next door. By remilling all their framing lumber, the builders eliminated slowdowns in framing, flooring, roofing, and Sheetrocking, thus saving considerable time and headaches.

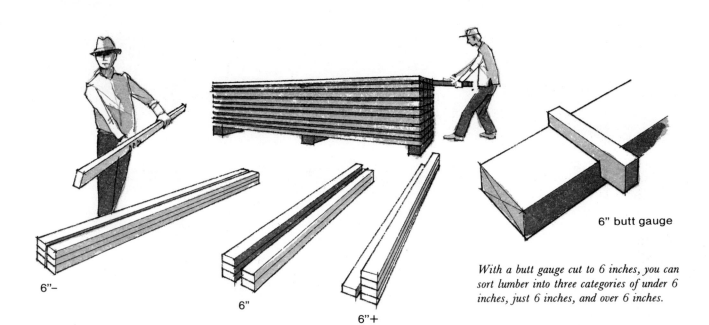

6"–

6"

6"+

6" butt gauge

*With a butt gauge cut to 6 inches, you can sort lumber into three categories of under 6 inches, just 6 inches, and over 6 inches.*

## Sorting

Another solution is to sort green lumber before it is used. By sorting studs, joists, and rafters into size categories, such as 5¾ inches, 6 inches, and 6¼ inches for 2 x 6s, you can eliminate large jumps in size between adjacent studs or joists. With the lumber sorted, start at one end of the wall, floor, or roof with the smallest pieces and work up to the largest as you frame to the other end. Using this method, you can keep wall variations down to ⅛ inch if you are careful. This is more than adequate for Sheetrock or any other wall covering.

If you are platform framing, select the *smallest* pieces for both the bottom and top plates of the wall. This will ensure they do not stick out beyond the studs and interfere with the wall covering.

## Shimming

A final solution is not to worry about the different widths of the lumber, build the wall, and then shim it out with furring strips and shim shingles. The easiest way to do this is to use pieces of 1 x 3 strapping set horizontally at 2-foot intervals up the wall. Nail the strapping onto the high points of the wall, and, using a long straightedge such as a straight 8-foot 2 x 4, slip shim shingles behind the strapping at the narrow studs until the strapping is flush with the straightedge. A string guide can be used in place of a straightedge. While this method is time-consuming and uses more materials, it can give a perfectly true wall surface regardless of the unevenness of the wall studs.

Insulate the wall before the strapping is applied so you won't have to fish the insulation behind the strapping.

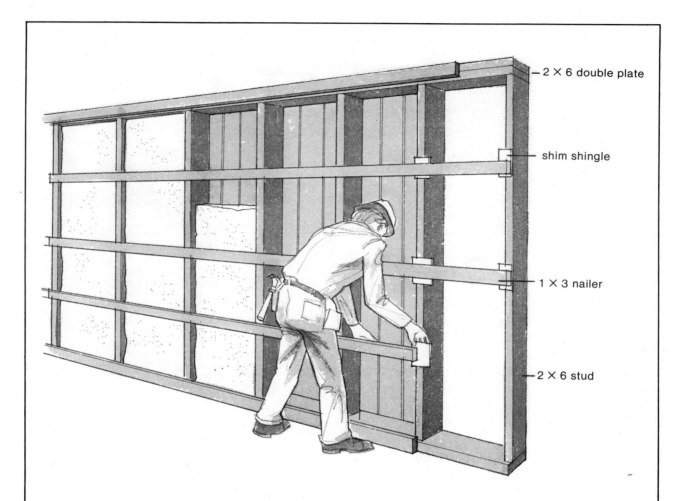

- 2 × 6 double plate
- shim shingle
- 1 × 3 nailer
- 2 × 6 stud

## The Indispensable Shim

The life of a carpenter would be dismal indeed without shim shingles. These thin wedges of wood take up the gap in ill-fitting joints, smooth out bumps in a wall, and level door and window jambs. They have a thousand uses, and, far from being a sign of sloppiness or incompetence, are a necessity if finish work is to be straight and true. And this is especially true if you are framing with green lumber.

Shim shingles come in bundles like regular shingles, but they are reject cedar or spruce shingles that have knotholes, pitch marks, and other defects that make them unsuitable for siding. These defects don't affect their shimming ability, however, and they lower the price to a fraction of what good cedar shingles cost. At the lumberyard make sure you ask specifically for "shim" shingles, otherwise you might end up taking home a $20 bundle of grade As.

When shimming behind a piece of wood, break the shingle in half so that you have two wedges. Drive the thin edges under the board from opposite sides. This will ensure that the bevel of the shingle does not twist the piece of wood. Push the shingles together until the shim is the proper thickness, then nail the board and shingles in place. With a hatchet or saw cut away the excess shingle on either side of the board and voilà—a perfect fit!

Whether you are framing walls, putting in floor joists, or setting rafters, the problem of uneven dimensions is always present in green wood building. By using one or all three of these methods, problems can almost always be dealt with satisfactorily.

Keep in mind how a particular section of a building is going to be finished when you are framing it because different finishes will require different degrees of trueness of the wall surface. For example, wall boards can be put over almost any surface and look fine; Sheetrock is a little more fussy and requires a fairly true wall; ceramic tile, glass, and other unforgiving materials require an absolutely true surface. The amount of care and fussing over the framing depends ultimately on the finish details. By knowing the finish details ahead of time, unnecessary work and the frustration and expense of rebuilding can be avoided.

# Moisture and Movement

Another major problem with green wood is its moisture content. A green 2 x 6 8 feet long contains over twenty-five pounds of water. As it dries, it releases this water, shrinking up to ¼ inch in width. This release of water and shrinkage puts some limitations on the use of green wood.

Because green lumber contains so much water, the interior walls of any green wood building should be left uncovered for at least three to four months after it has been framed. If a green wood wall is Sheetrocked immediately after framing, two things happen. First, the studs shrink, pulling away from the Sheetrock and causing it to crack and the nails to pull through. Second, all the water being released by the studs is trapped in the wall and can damage the insulation and rot the wall. For these reasons, green wood walls are normally insulated and left open on the inside to dry. When insulating the wall, don't staple the kraft paper edge of the insulation over the stud. Place the fiberglass between the studs, leaving the edges of the studs uncovered and able to breathe. The rough surface of the studs should hold the fiberglass in place without any staples. When the wall has dried the Kraft paper can be stapled over the studs, forming a tight seal.

I have seen walls that were immediately Sheetrocked with no problem, and I have also seen Sheetrock destroyed by the drying studs. The action of a green wood wall can vary tremendously depending on the original moisture of the studs, the wall covering, and the relative humidity in and outside the house. Because the action is so unpredictable, the wisest and safest thing to do is wait a few months before finishing the inside of a green wood house.

The exterior siding can and should be put on immediately

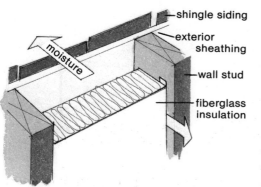

*The interior of a green wood wall should be left open to dry for several months. If it is insulated, don't staple the kraft paper edge of the insulation until drying is completed.*

after the house is framed in order to keep out the weather. Regardless of whether you are using green board-and-batten siding or clapboards with plywood sheathing, the siding can be put on immediately without problems. This means that while the interior walls must be left open, the exterior can be sealed and made weatherproof, the walls insulated, and the house made inhabitable even during winter. Because the exterior surface of a properly built wall will "breathe," letting moisture slowly escape, there is no danger of moisture accumulation in a green wood wall that is open on the inside but sheathed on the outside.

## Shrinkage

Another problem caused by the moisture in green wood is shrinkage as it dries. While the final amount of shrinkage depends on many factors, such as the type of wood, its moisture content, and the run of the grain, all green wood will eventually shrink. Accompanying this shrinkage is the tendency of green lumber to twist, warp, and check if it is not restrained. This movement is the real limiting factor in green wood building. While other problems such as the unevenness of dimensions can be dealt with fairly easily, shrinkage must simply be recognized and accepted. For this reason, green wood is suitable for only certain uses in house building. In general, green wood is acceptable for framing and rough carpentry but should not be used for finish work or cabinetry.

In framing a house, the shrinkage of green wood is relatively unimportant. Since all the wood is shrinking together at roughly the same rate, wall studs or floor joists simply move a fraction of an inch as a unit. This movement, however, is enough to damage interior finished walls or flooring. Unless the framing has dried completely, a finished surface such as a Sheetrocked wall will crack, and finished flooring will buckle.

## Twisting Beams

One problem that is often encountered in post-and-beam framing is that the beams twist and check as they dry. Checking can severely cut the strength of a beam, especially if large checks are near joints. While checking cannot be totally eliminated, it can be controlled through proper drying, usually by slowing down the drying process so that stress does not build up in the beam. This can be done by keeping the house humidity high or periodically wetting the beams. Perhaps the worst enemy of green beams is the wood stove, whose direct radiation and dry heat can send a beam into contortions.

Twisting, or warping, is another drying defect that can heave floors, skew doorway frames, and bulge walls. Twisting is a natural reaction of certain types of grain to drying stresses. To see how great these stresses are, leave a piece of green 1 x 6 in a corner for a few weeks. You'll hardly recognize the contorted result.

The solution to twisting is to restrain any possible movement in a beam or piece of wood. In stud framing, this is done by securely nailing the top and bottom to the wall plates with galvanized nails. In post-and-beam framing, restraint is achieved by the interlocking joint that connects a beam with a post or another beam. The most common reason beams twist after they are in place is that the joint is not designed or cut to restrain the beam. Often joints are made with only the thought of keeping the beam from falling down rather than restraining it from all possible angles of movement.

A study of post-and-beam jointry, at its prime around 1500 A.D., will show that such movement was clearly recognized and dealt with by the development of intricate joints. Those who have the time and skill can cut these joints and modern variations of them so that they will hold a beam securely and keep it from twisting. For those looking for strength, but not necessarily beauty, an alternative is the use of steel plates. Where beams are joined, steel plates can be used to overlap the joint and bolt the beams together.

*This wood joint wasn't strong enough to restrain the beam from twisting.*

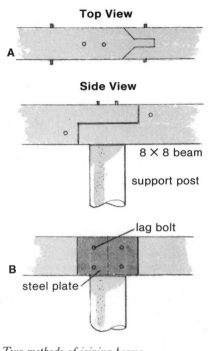

**Top View**

A

**Side View**

8 X 8 beam

support post

lag bolt

B

steel plate

*Two methods of joining beams.*
*A   A properly cut scarf joint*
*B   Steel plates and bolts*

## Lack of Strength

A final problem due to the moisture in green wood is its lack of strength. Green wood is not as strong as dry wood because its cells are much more supple and susceptible to bending pressures. Carpenters take advantage of this by steaming or soaking a dry piece of wood in water in order to bend it into a particular shape. Because green wood is rough cut, however, it is thicker and wider than kiln-dried lumber of the same nominal dimension. A green 2 x 6 is really 2 inches by 6 inches whereas a kiln-dried and planed 2 x 6 is only 1½ inches by 5½ inches. The green 2 x 6 has 45 percent more wood in it, and this helps offset the weakness of its fibers. When it has dried, of course, it is much stronger than a kiln-dried 2 x 6.

The weakness of green wood is never a problem in stud framing, but it can be a problem in post-and-beam framing. Beams that are slightly undersized or sized according to a table of dry wood strengths can sag if they are fully loaded when still green. For this reason, care must be taken when designing green post-and-beam structures that the spans are designed for green lumber. Usually post-and-beam framing is sufficiently oversized and overbuilt that the beams can carry the load, green or dry. If there is any indication of a sag in a beam, a temporary post can be placed under it until it has dried and hardened.

### Safe Loads for Kiln-Dried Girders

| GIRDERS | SAFE LOAD IN POUNDS FOR THESE SPANS | | | | |
|---|---|---|---|---|---|
| Size | 6 Feet | 7 Feet | 8 Feet | 9 Feet | 10 Feet |
| 6 x 8 solid | 8,306 | 7,118 | 6,220 | 5,539 | 4,583 |
| 6 x 8 build-up | 7,359 | 6,306 | 5,511 | 4,908 | 4,062 |
| 6 x 10 solid | 11,357 | 10,804 | 9,980 | 8,887 | 7,997 |
| 6 x 10 built-up | 10,068 | 9,576 | 8,844 | 7,878 | 7,086 |
| 8 x 8 solid | 11,326 | 9,706 | 8,482 | 7,553 | 6,250 |
| 8 x 8 built-up | 9,812 | 8,408 | 7,348 | 6,544 | 5,416 |
| 8 x 10 solid | 15,487 | 14,732 | 13,608 | 12,116 | 10,902 |
| 8 x 10 built-up | 13,424 | 12,768 | 11,792 | 10,504 | 9,448 |

From: Modern Carpentry, Willis H. Wagner, Goodheart Wilcox Co., Inc.

# Where to Use Green Wood

While green wood makes an economical framing material, it can also be used for exterior siding at a fraction of the cost of conventional materials. Vertical board-and-batten siding, with 1- to 2-inch battens covering the joints between boards, is the green wood siding that has been used for centuries. As the

boards dry, the battens effectively cover any gap that develops between the boards, keeping the siding weathertight. Vertical shiplapped boards can also be used without battens for siding since the ½-inch overlap will prevent any gap between the boards. Several other green wood sidings are illustrated in Chapter 6.

## Interior Paneling

Green wood can be used for interior paneling but shrinkage must be expected. Shiplapped paneling is most commonly used since battens make a rough wall surface. Usually interior paneling is planed smooth on one side to avoid splinters and to make it easier to clean. Rough wood will accumulate dirt and odors very quickly. Most often, however, interior wood paneling is air-dried. Since the interior walls are left unfinished for several months to facilitate drying of the green wood frame, there is time to stack and air-dry the paneling.

Green lumber should never be used for finished flooring. Because green boards shrink and twist as they dry, green wood floors are invariably uneven and have large gaps between the boards where dust and dirt can accumulate. Finished flooring must be dry when it is installed. Preferably, it is stacked in the rooms where it will be used for at least a month before it is installed so it can adjust to that room's particular humidity.

*These floor boards were put down green. The ½-inch cracks developed during drying.*

## Laying Subflooring

Rough wood subflooring can be laid green. If you are building a house entirely out of native wood, you can put down green wood subflooring to walk on while the house is drying and while your finished flooring is drying. As the house dries, so will the subflooring, developing gaps and perhaps some buckles and twists. This is no problem since it can be renailed flat and covered with finished flooring. Plywood can also be used for subflooring. While it is more expensive, it can be installed very quickly, is stronger than board subflooring, and provides a splinter-free surface to walk on.

Do not use green wood around glass, Plexiglas, or other glazings. Because green wood shrinks and twists, using window sash made from green wood is the perfect way to break glass. While rough openings for windows and even the window trim can be made of green wood, the window sash, or wood that holds the glass, should be dry. Where large panes of glass such as patio doors or plate glass windows are being used, it is often advisable to use dry wood for even the rough framing.

A good example of where green wood should be used with

caution, and one that is becoming much more common today, is the south wall of a passive solar building with large areas of glass and very little solid wall. Because of the expense of glass and other glazings and the unpredictability of movement in green wood, it often makes sense to frame the entire wall with air-dried or kiln-dried lumber. Another approach is to let the green wood dry and settle before installing large panes of glass. This, of course, would take several months and necessitate the use of plastic sheets to cover the window openings in order to keep the rain and wind out.

*The Plexiglas windows on this house have leaked because they were set in green wood.*

LOW-COST GREEN LUMBER CONSTRUCTION

The Rood house (p. 46) is a good example of the sensible use of dry wood. The entire house, except for the roof of the solar greenhouse, was framed in green wood. Here kiln-dried lumber was used to minimize any movement and damage to the solar glazing material. The Gruvin house (p. 105), however, was built with Plexiglas roof windows framed in green wood. The result has been water leaks in nearly all of these windows.

It is often hard to say when and where green wood will cause problems with windows. Where there is the least doubt about the results, it is best to err on the side of caution and use dry wood. Discretion is the better part of valor. As the size of your window panes grows, so should your discretion.

## Where to Use Green Lumber

| ALWAYS | WITH CAUTION | NEVER |
|---|---|---|
| Sills | Trim (on barns, etc.) | Finished flooring |
| Beams | Interior paneling | Window sash |
| Stud walls | Door and window | Panel doors |
| Joists |    jambs | Cabinet work |
| Rafters | Framing for solar | |
| Subflooring |    glazing or | |
| Exterior sheathing |    greenhouses | |
| Siding | Roof decking for | |
| Roof decking for metal |    asphalt shingles | |
|    and wood shingles | | |

GREEN ⟶ DRY

Above 30 percent moisture        8 percent moisture

# Green Wood Art

*Imagination surmounts a tight budget*

In 1972 when Andy and Onni Palmer set out to build their house in Huntington, Vermont, they had a budget of only $10,000. With that amount they had to build a road into their property, bring in electric power, and build a house. Even in 1972 when a dollar still bought something, it was a very tight budget. But by using native wood, recycled materials, and a lot of imagination, Andy and Onni designed and built a house that is a unique work of green wood art.

Andy, a woodworker by profession, designed the house to recapture the air of summer homes he had grown up in. The Palmers' green wood house with its open wood walls and ceilings reminds one of exactly that, a vacation home of the 1920s, informal and relaxing but with great attention to detail. Everywhere are stained glass windows, curved doorways, woodworking details, and decorations that display the artistry of both Andy and Onni. And though the house was initially built over eight years ago, it is still evolving and changing as finishing touches are completed and new details added.

The house is on the edge of a clearing, tucked into a wooded hillside. Facing south, the house overlooks the adjacent river valley and the Green Mountains.

## Wall to Wall Windows

To take advantage of the southerly exposure and tremendous views, the first floor of the house is almost wall-to-wall windows on this side, many of them stained and leaded glass.

The house is built entirely with green lumber from a local mill. They used 8 x 8s for the sills and floor joists, 4 x 4s for the wall framing, placed 4 feet on center,

and 2 x 6 tongue-and-groove spruce for the flooring, laid directly over the beams.

### Open Interior Walls

Of particular interest is how the walls were framed, insulated, and sheathed. In order to achieve the look of summer homes that Andy liked, he left the interior walls and ceilings completely open, exposing the rough wood post-and-beam structure.

---

**Everywhere are stained glass windows, curved doorways, woodworking details, and decorations that display the artistry of both Andy and Onni.**

---

This left the problem of how to insulate the walls. While Andy liked the openness of a summer home, he certainly didn't want to be frozen out of his home in mid-February when the temperature dropped to −40°.

### Insulation on Outside

His solution was to apply 2 inches of foam insulation to the outside of the house. The 4 x 4 wall frame was sheathed with 1 x 8 hemlock laid diagonally to brace the walls. Two-inch nailing strips were applied horizontally over the boards on the outside of the house. Foam insulation was then blown between the nailers, and finally 1 x 8 hemlock was applied vertically onto the nailers to cover the foam.

This unique method of wall construction has several points to recommend it, but it also has some potential drawbacks. The best thing about this method is that the interior walls do not need to be finished. This is important in a green wood structure where varia-

tions in the thickness of wall studs can play havoc with Sheetrock or other interior wall coverings. By eliminating Sheetrock and the studding necessary to hold it, considerable money, time, and frustration can be saved. Another benefit to this method is that if the interior wall is finished for some reason, extra insulation can be put in to enhance the R-value of the wall.

While there are benefits, there are also drawbacks. Because the nailers and foam insulation are only 2 inches thick, the R-value of the wall is only equivalent to a stud wall with 3½ inches of fiberglass. This used to be the standard, but now in northern climates 2 x 6 walls with 5½ inches of insulation are considered to be the minimum standard. In order to achieve a similar R-value with foam, the

**Below,** *arched doorway and stained glass windows make this an inviting front entrance.* **Bottom,** *art in the kitchen. This is a sculptured sink unit, one of Andy's many pieces of woodworking that decorate the house.*

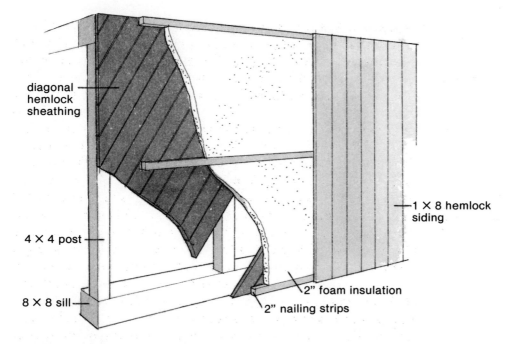

diagonal hemlock sheathing

4 X 4 post

8 X 8 sill

1 X 8 hemlock siding

2" foam insulation

2" nailing strips

*The three layers in the exterior walls include the 1x8 hemlock laid diagonally, 2-inch nailing strips with foam insulation between them, and 1x8 hemlock applied vertically for the exterior siding.*

nailers would have to be at least 3½ inches thick. While this can be done, such nailers are hard to attach properly.

### Insect Problem

Another problem is that exterior foam is subject to attack by rodents and insects. The Palmers have had some problems with both mice and ants finding the foam a perfect place to live. This problem can be minimized by making sure the bottom of the siding boards and foam are sealed by the bottom nailer.

A final problem is that all plumbing and wiring must be boxed in to be concealed. The best way to deal with this is to make sure the major plumbing and wiring runs are centralized into one wall which can then be covered.

A unique aspect of the Palmer house is the many different win-

**Andy and Onni's work is first-hand proof that a tight budget does not mean much when it comes to green wood building.**

dows of varying shapes, sizes, and materials. According to Andy, about 90 percent of these were recycled from old buildings. While Andy feels that new commercial window units are "ugly, characterless, and expensive," he still installed a few new units so that he could have adequate ventilation in the summer.

Despite their beauty, the recycled windows, which are fixed panes of glass, present a severe heat loss problem.

The windows are single-paned,

without storms, and are not as airtight as modern window units. Luckily most of these windows are on the south side of the house, so that the solar heat gain during the day helps balance their heat loss at night.

Because Andy and Onni heat with wood, their heating costs are still much lower than the average homeowner's despite those old windows.

While most prospective ownerbuilders would not set out to build a house like the Palmers', Andy and Onni's work is first-hand proof that a tight budget does not mean much when it comes to green wood building. The Palmer house with its stained glass windows, hobbit-like arches, and unique details, shows that it is not money but only one's imagination and resourcefulness that are the limits to building your own home.

CHAPTER 6

# Green Wood
# Building Systems

AS YOU KNOW IF YOU HAVE SET OUT TO DESIGN your own house from scratch, it is a time-consuming and often confusing undertaking. What will the floor plan look like? What kind of roof will it have? How will it be insulated and heated? These and a thousand more questions must be carefully considered and answered before a final plan is drawn up. And to make matters worse, there is always the constraint of a tight budget hanging over your head.

Using green wood can ease your budget restrictions somewhat and make available new building options, but it can't take the place of the planning and detailing needed to translate your original idea of a house into reality. In fact, green wood house building often entails greater planning and thought because of the inherent problems of working with green, rough-sawn wood.

By understanding the different wall, floor, and roof systems that are commonly used for green wood buildings, you can design and build a house that suits your particular tastes and needs. While different methods are often chosen for aesthetic reasons, in many cases there are structural as well as energy and economic differences between systems that are important to consider.

In terms of saving money, green wood cannot be beat for use as exterior siding. It can be installed for as little as one-half to two-thirds the cost of conventional clapboard siding. There are several types of siding and siding materials to choose from, each with its distinct appearance and advantages.

## Board and Batten

Board and batten, the traditional green wood siding, consists of 1 x 6 or wider boards covered with 1- to 2-inch battens where the boards are butted together. The boards are nailed onto *cats* or blocks set between the studs at 2- to 4-foot intervals, into furring strips set into the studs, or simply nailed onto sheathing boards or plywood. Galvanized nails are always used to prevent corrosion and staining of the wood, and are normally eight penny common nails. Galvanized nails also hold better and keep the boards from twisting as they dry.

There are several variations on board and batten. These are the reverse batten and board and the board and board. Batten and board puts the batten behind the boards, and changes the appearance of the siding considerably. Board and board dispenses with the batten altogether.

# Exterior Walls

board and board

board and batten

batten and board

*Three styles of vertical board siding.*

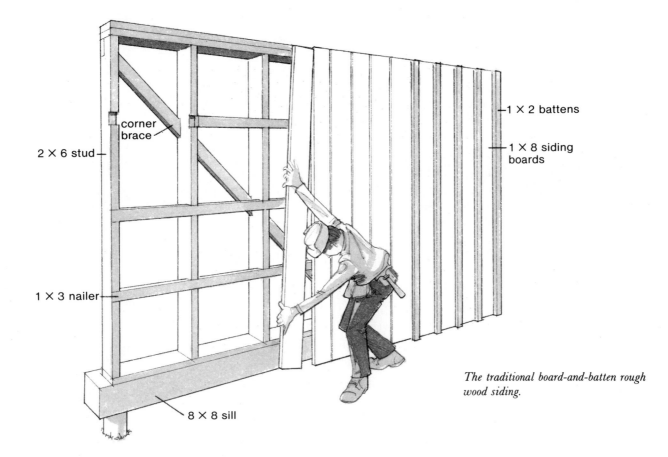

corner
brace

2 × 6 stud

1 × 3 nailer

8 × 8 sill

1 × 2 battens

1 × 8 siding
boards

*The traditional board-and-batten rough
wood siding.*

## Shiplapped Boards

Another type of vertical siding is shiplapped boards. These are boards that have a ½- to ¾-inch half-lap on their edges, allowing the boards to overlap and shrink without creating an air gap. Where shiplap or any other type of vertical siding is joined end to end, a 45° bevel lap is cut to insure that water dripping down the siding is not trapped and that as the boards shrink vertically an air space does not open up. These butt joints are usually staggered vertically for appearance's sake.

Another method of joining vertical siding is to use a drip cap, which is a piece of wood that overhangs the siding below it and keeps water from getting behind the boards. With a drip cap, all the joints are lined up at the same height and the cap is placed over the ends of the boards running horizontally across the building. The upper boards are then butted tight against the top of the drip cap, which has a slight bevel to drain water.

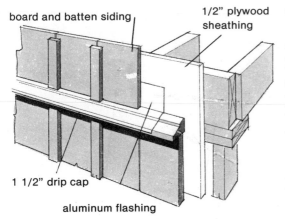

board and batten siding

1/2" plywood
sheathing

1 1/2" drip cap

aluminum flashing

*A drip cap covers joints in board-and-batten
siding.*

## Horizontal Siding

There are several types of horizontal siding. The most common are bevel siding or clapboards, drop siding, and shingles. Bevel and shingle siding, because of the thinness of the boards,

**LOW-COST GREEN LUMBER CONSTRUCTION**

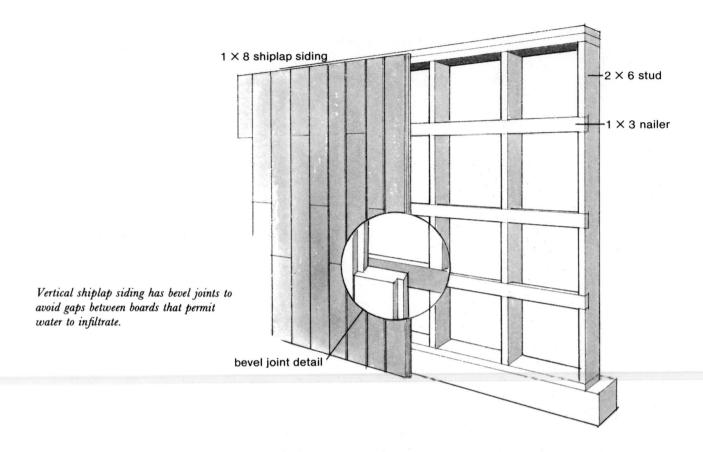

1 × 8 shiplap siding

2 × 6 stud

1 × 3 nailer

bevel joint detail

*Vertical shiplap siding has bevel joints to avoid gaps between boards that permit water to infiltrate.*

are usually dried before they are installed. Drop siding, with its tongue-and-groove overlaps, can be installed green or dry.

Clapboards and shingles must be installed over sheathing which can either be 1-inch green wood boards, ½-inch plywood, or composition board, which is made of recycled wood fibers. Each of these sheathings has certain advantages. Green wood boards are inexpensive, fairly strong, and help brace the wall if applied diagonally. Plywood is expensive, but it is extremely strong and lightweight, goes on very quickly, and eliminates the need for wall bracing because of its rigidity. Composition board is like plywood, but a little less expensive and not quite as strong.

While board-and-batten and drop siding don't require any sheathing on houses, it is often advisable to use some wall covering underneath it to stop possible air infiltration. Use of plywood or composition board can eliminate the need for wall blocking to nail the siding onto, and it can also eliminate the need for wall bracing. If only insulating fiberboard is used, siding nailers must be set in the wall and diagonal braces set into the studs at the corners of the building.

Several different kinds of wood are used for siding. The most common are spruce, hemlock, pine, and cedar. Cedar is undoubtedly the best because of its resistance to water and decay. Unfortunately it is also the most expensive and is usually avail-

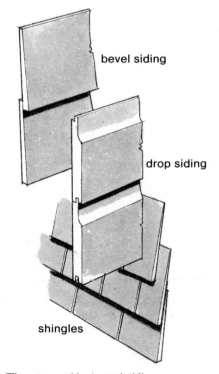

bevel siding

drop siding

shingles

*Three types of horizontal siding.*

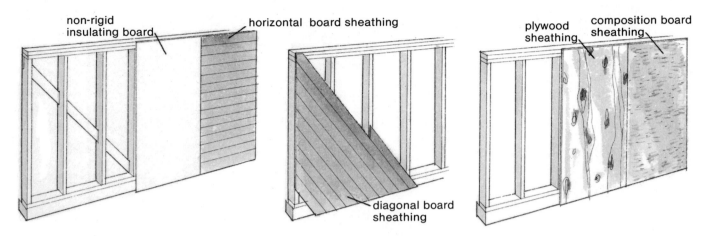

*Three methods of sheathing and bracing a wall.*
*A   Walls with horizontal board or insulating board sheathing need diagonal corner braces.*
*B   Rough wood boards laid on the diagonal also serve as bracing.*
*C   Plywood and composition board sheathing are rigid enough to brace a wall.*

able as a green wood only in the Northwest, where it is harvested commercially. In many parts of the country, especially the Northeast, spruce, hemlock, and pine are the common green wood siding materials.

All of these woods show fairly good resistance to weathering, but each has unique characteristics. Eastern white pine is usually considered the best because of its resistance to splitting and warping. Hemlock and spruce are about equal, except that hemlock is susceptible to grain separation, causing large layers to split and separate from a board much in the same way a piece of plywood will delaminate under adverse conditions.

## Protecting the Siding

Almost any natural wood siding, with the exceptions of cedar and redwood, will degrade fairly rapidly if left unprotected. For this reason, green wood siding should be protected, preferably with linseed oil, a natural, non-poisonous wood preservative and conditioner. Unless you are a millionaire or a glutton for punishment, you should avoid painting a house. It is time-consuming, extremely expensive, and, in a climate such as New England's, needs to be repeated at least every four years. It is a maintenance burden most homeowners can't afford.

Oiling a house, by contrast, is quick, easy, and considerably less expensive in the long run. Stains are available, ranging from natural wood colors to bright paint-like colors that can be mixed with linseed oil or bought mixed. Oiling green wood

siding also helps prevent drying defects such as splits and checks.

Chemical wood preservatives, such as pentachlorophenol, zinc naphthenate, and creosote, are usually not necessary if a house is built properly. Products containing pentachlorophenol should never be used since they contain dioxins, very toxic chemicals that have been linked to cancer and birth defects in laboratory studies. Zinc naphthenate, sold under the trade name of Cuprinol, is a good wood preservative that is safer to use but is toxic. Creosote is the least expensive wood preservative and comes as a dark brown stain with a strong tar-like odor. Creosote will burn the skin upon contact.

Toxic wood preservatives are not needed in house building if the foundation sills are kept out of contact with the soil, the roof overhangs are adequate to keep water off the siding, and the window sills and other flat wood surfaces drain well. The only real need for wood preservatives is when wooden poles are used for foundation supports and buried in the earth. It is also advisable to preserve outside deck framing since water will sit

*The siding on this house had to be creosoted because of lack of roof overhangs and the moist forest environment.*

on top of the joints. Only linseed oil should be used on the deck flooring, since people, especially small children, and animals will be in close contact with the surface.

## Weathering Characteristics of Wood

| SOFTWOODS | RESISTANCE TO CUPPING 1 = Best 4 = Worst | CONSPICUOUSNESS OF CHECKING 1 = Least 2 = Most | EASE OF KEEPING WELL PAINTED 1 = Easiest 4 = Hardest |
|---|---|---|---|
| Cedar, Alaska | 1 | 1 | 1 |
| Cedar, white | 1 | — | 1 |
| Redwood | 1 | 1 | 1 |
| Pine, eastern white | 2 | 2 | 2 |
| Pine, sugar | 2 | 2 | 2 |
| Hemlock | 2 | 2 | 3 |
| Spruce | 2 | 2 | 3 |
| Douglas fir | 2 | 2 | 4 |
| **HARDWOODS** | | | |
| Beech | 4 | 2 | 4 |
| Birch | 4 | 2 | 4 |
| Maple | 4 | 2 | 4 |
| Ash | 4 | 2 | 3 |
| Chestnut | 3 | 2 | 3 |
| Walnut | 3 | 2 | 3 |
| Elm | 4 | 2 | 4 |
| Oak, white | 4 | 2 | 4 |

From Table 16-1, Wood Handbook, Agriculture Handbook No. 72, Forest Products Laboratory, U.S. Department of Agriculture.

# Interior Walls

Interior wall coverings are almost as varied as exterior ones. The two common materials used are Sheetrock and wood paneling. Sheetrock, often called drywall, comes in 4 x 8 sheets and longer, and thicknesses from ⅜ inch to ¾ inch. Normally ½-inch Sheetrock is used for residential construction. Wood paneling is available in many different shapes and sizes, although green wood paneling that is available at local mills is usually limited to shiplap and V-groove boards 6 to 8 inches wide. Plywood and plastic paneling are also available in 4 x 8-foot sheets, but they tend to be expensive and not very attractive.

Green wood walls should be thoroughly dried before you install Sheetrock, otherwise nails will pop and seams will crack as the wall dries. Green wood walls must also be "rectified," or evened out, before they are Sheetrocked, using one of the three methods listed in Chapter 5. Once the walls are dry and true,

Sheetrock will go on as easily as with a conventionally framed house.

## Vapor Barrier

Before the walls are Sheetrocked or paneled, a 4 mil plastic vapor barrier should be put on over the studs. This plastic can be bought in 100-foot rolls. It will prevent moisture inside the house from entering the walls and damaging the insulation or framing. Vapor barriers are always put on the inside of a house, never the outside, since moisture moves from the inside to the outside. A vapor barrier on the outside of a house would only trap moisture by preventing it from escaping from the wall. For this reason, only pink felt building paper and never tar paper or plastic is used as a windbreak over the sheathing of a house.

*Interior wall coverings.*

## Installing Paneling

In order to install paneling, nailers must be placed in or on the wall to hold the individual boards. If the wall has already been blocked for vertical board siding, these blocks can double for use with the paneling. If the wall hasn't been blocked, 1 x 3 furring strips can be nailed on the wall horizontally every 2 feet. The use of furring strips has the advantage of smoothing

2 × 6 stud

1 × 3 nailer

insulation

polyethylene vapor barrier

*The vapor barrier is placed behind paneling or Sheetrock to prevent moisture from entering the walls and damaging the insulation.*

out the wall surface by evening out the abrupt changes in width among studs. If the wall is particularly wavy, the furring strips can be shimmed out with pieces of wood shingles as would be done if the wall were to be Sheetrocked.

While paneling takes longer to install and finish than Sheetrock, it has the advantage of hiding the unevenness of a green wood wall much better than Sheetrock. Also, it won't crack if the wall should happen to move after the paneling has been installed.

Two things to be careful about when using paneling are the surface texture and the color. Paneling should be planed on one side if it is possible. Rough wood paneling will give you splinters, get dirty, and pick up odors quickly, and is impossible to clean. Also, the color should be light if paneling is used to cover an entire wall. Dark paneling will make a house gloomy

*Note the difference in atmosphere created by the light and dark paneling in these two homes.*

**LOW-COST GREEN LUMBER CONSTRUCTION**

and dark. Dark paneling such as cherry or stained pine should be used sparingly, to form small details and to give visual relief from the main backdrop of lighter paneling or painted Sheetrock.

## Dry Paneling

While paneling can be bought green at considerable savings, it should be air-dried. If it is dry before being installed, it is less apt to shrink, warp, or crack. And since the green wood wall itself should be dried first, the paneling can be purchased at the same time as the framing materials, stickered, and left to airdry. When the wall is dry, so will be the paneling.

# Flooring Systems

Laying a wood floor that is sound, good looking, and won't buckle with the changing seasons is one of the hardest parts of building a house. And not surprisingly, it is the one area where owner-builders have the most problems. I have seen wooden floors in green wood homes that have been described as everything from "gently undulating" to "a sea of deadly crevasses." By doing some planning and thinking, and by careful workmanship, the inherent problems of laying a wood floor can be avoided.

There are several floor framing techniques, and the problems you will encounter depend on which you use. Post-and-beam framing allows the greatest flexibility with floor systems, since the floor supports can be either 6 x 6 or larger beams, 2 x 6 or larger floor joists, or a combination of the two. With post-and-beam construction, the finished floor is often 2 x 6 tongue-and-groove planks laid directly over the beams. The underside of the planks, usually cut with a decorative V-groove, forms the ceiling below.

This method of floor framing and flooring is by far the easiest and most economical since it eliminates the need for subflooring and a finished ceiling below.

It also has several drawbacks. First, the 2 x 6 planks must be dry before they are put down. Since the flooring must be installed as the house is framed (so there is something to walk on), the flooring must either be bought kiln-dried or else air-dried in advance of framing the house.

A second problem is acoustical. Because there is no dead air space between the two floor levels, sound will travel readily from the first to second floor, diminishing privacy.

A final problem presents itself when you are ready to wire the house. Any wires or light fixtures put in the ceiling would have to be exposed. While this problem can be overcome by either eliminating overhead wiring and lighting or using sur-

face mounted wiring (conduit or armored cable), this flooring system does limit the wiring options in a house.

## Laying the Subfloor

If joists are used between the floor beams, a subfloor of 1 x 6 boards or plywood and a finished floor over that can be laid. This eliminates the problem of having to buy kiln-dried flooring, since the subfloor can be laid green and walked on while the finished flooring is air-drying. Often the subflooring is left exposed in the ceiling below just as the 2 x 6 planks are.

"One man's ceiling is another man's floor," or so the song goes, and it's a good thing to keep in mind when you are framing your house. Floors and ceilings are very much interrelated and dependent on the method of framing used.

For example, if a floor is framed with 6 x 6 beams every 4 feet, then in order to install a ceiling of either Sheetrock or boards, nailers must be installed between the beams every 2 feet to support the ceiling. If 2 x 4 nailers were used, the ceiling could be recessed between the beams; if 2 x 6 nailers were used, the ceiling would cover the beams. If the floor framing was 8 x 8s with 2 x 6 joists running between the beams, the ceiling could be applied directly to the joists or over furring strips if the joists were too uneven.

The important thing to remember is that a floor, floor supports, and ceiling are interrelated, especially in post-and-beam framing. Think the whole system through before you start hammering nails.

If a green wood house is being platform or stud framed, the problem of uneven dimensions in the floor joists often occurs. Because the joists are not all the same size, they can only be

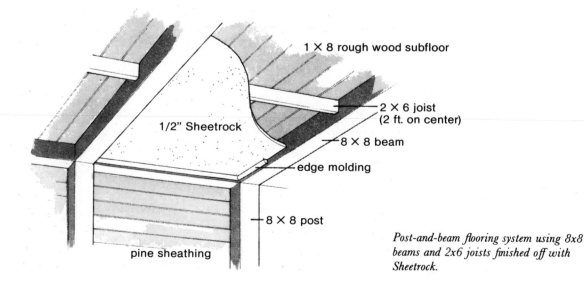

1 X 8 rough wood subfloor

2 X 6 joist (2 ft. on center)

8 X 8 beam

edge molding

1/2" Sheetrock

8 X 8 post

pine sheathing

*Post-and-beam flooring system using 8x8 beams and 2x6 joists finished off with Sheetrock.*

**LOW-COST GREEN LUMBER CONSTRUCTION**

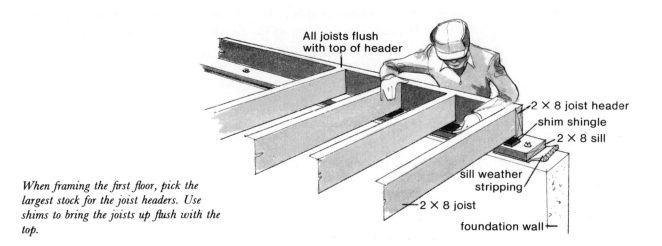

All joists flush with top of header

2 X 8 joist header

shim shingle

2 X 8 sill

sill weather stripping

2 X 8 joist

foundation wall

*When framing the first floor, pick the largest stock for the joist headers. Use shims to bring the joists up flush with the top.*

lined up on the top or bottom, not both. When framing the first floor, this is no problem since underneath is either a basement or crawl space, neither of which usually has a finished ceiling. On the first floor, all the floor joists should be lined up even with the top of the outside joist headers and shimmed underneath off the sill plate, if this is necessary. Remember to select the *widest* of the joist stock for the headers so that none of the joists will stick up above the header when it is resting on the sill plate. Using this method you can get a perfectly even first floor with very little trouble.

If the first-floor ceiling is to be left exposed, the same technique can be used for framing the second-story floor. If the ceiling is to be covered, you've got some problems. As in building green wood stud walls, there are three methods you can use to even out both surfaces of green wood framing (see Chapter 5).

The first method is to mill all the joists and headers down to the smallest dimensions of any of the pieces, usually 5¾ inches for rough 2 x 6 stock, then build as if you were using kiln-dried lumber.

## Sort Joists

If this isn't practical, you can use the sorting method, separating the joists into bundles of increasing sizes. The joists can then be laid on the wall plates in ascending order of size, forming a perfect ceiling surface and a floor surface that is fairly even but slightly sloping. At most the slope will be ½- to ¾-inch over the entire width of the floor. This is not enough to worry about. When using this method, select the *smallest* stock for the joist headers so they will not stick up above the floor joists and interfere with putting down the floor plates or subflooring.

**GREEN WOOD BUILDING SYSTEMS**

A final method is to set all the joists even with the top of the header, as was done on the first floor, using the largest stock for the headers and shimming up joists where necessary. The ceiling below must then be evened out with 1 x 3 furring strips and shim shingles before it is covered.

## Avoid Green Flooring

Aside from the problems of getting a smooth surface for the finished flooring and ceiling, the most common problem in owner-built green wood homes is that the finished flooring was laid green or semi-green. The obvious result is a floor with large cracks between the boards, often accompanied by some twisting and warping. Green wood should never be considered for finished flooring in a house. For the barn, woodshed, or chicken coop it's fine, but in a well-finished house, green flooring is not only unattractive but downright hazardous as well.

Buy your finished flooring from the mill when you buy your framing lumber, sticker it in piles, and let it dry for six months or longer. In the meantime, put down rough wood subflooring or plywood for a temporary floor. It may be a bit bouncy, but it will hold you and take all the dust and grit of construction, saving your finished floor from being scratched and gouged.

Finished flooring ranges from hardwood boards to linoleum, carpeting to quarry tiles. Linoleum is definitely the least expensive to install, followed by carpeting, softwood and hardwood flooring, and then stone or tiles. If you get your hardwood flooring green from the mill, air-dry it yourself, and install it yourself, you may well find it is the least expensive choice.

# Roofing Systems

Roofing systems in green wood houses vary as much as wall and flooring systems do. Each builder has a preference, either because of aesthetics, cost of materials, or energy efficiency. Nevertheless, several principal framing methods are commonly used, most others being variations on these.

The simplest roofing system is the common rafter system used in stud framing. Rafters ranging in size from 2 x 6 to 2 x 12, depending on their span and spacing, are run from the top wall plate to a ridge plate at the peak of the roof. The rafters overhang the edges of the building forming eaves which keep water off the siding and away from the house foundation, and can also serve as shading devices for solar-heated buildings.

The two roof framing methods used in post-and-beam construction, as mentioned in Chapter 4, are the common rafter and the principal rafter-and-purlin systems.

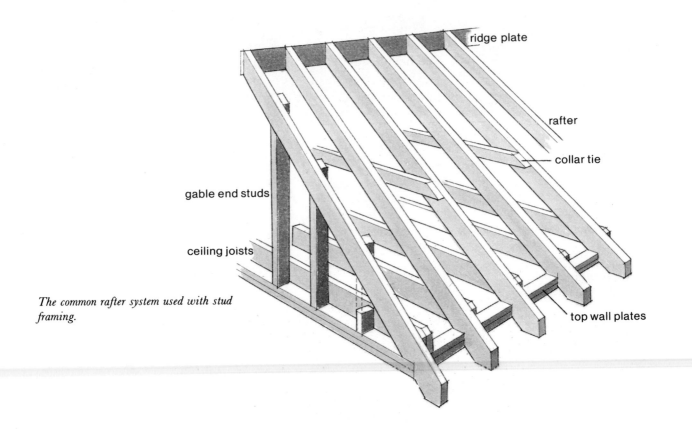

ridge plate

rafter

collar tie

gable end studs

ceiling joists

top wall plates

*The common rafter system used with stud framing.*

The common rafter system is similar to that used in stud framing, except that the rafters are larger, usually 6 x 6 or more, and are spaced wider apart.

The principal rafter-and-purlin system uses larger rafter beams spaced up to 9 feet apart with smaller purlins (usually 4 x 4) running between them. The roof sheathing is laid horizontally across the common rafters, but vertically across purlins, parallel with the rafters.

## Energy Efficiency and Ventilation

Insulation and ventilation are important in all roof systems and often determine their design and suitability for certain locations. After windows and doors, the greatest heat loss from a house is through the roof. Because of the rising cost of energy, R-38 roof insulation, or a roof with the equivalent of 10 inches of fiberglass insulation, 5 inches of rigid foam board, or 6 inches of blown-in polyurethane foam, is recommended for northern or "snow" climates.

Roofs must also be adequately ventilated since most of the moisture in a house is also lost through the roof. Even with vapor barriers on the walls and ceilings, moisture will tend to condense on the cold side of the insulation in a roof, lowering its R-value and in extreme cases rotting the structural members

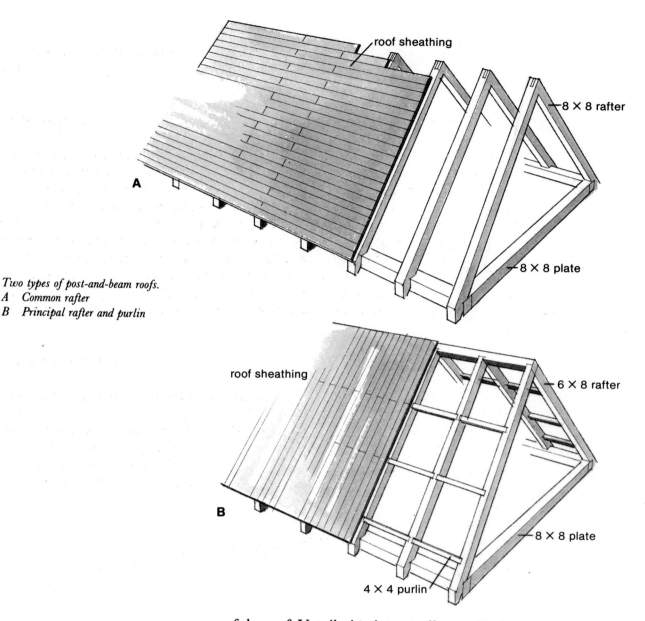

roof sheathing

8 × 8 rafter

8 × 8 plate

roof sheathing

6 × 8 rafter

8 × 8 plate

4 × 4 purlin

A

B

*Two types of post-and-beam roofs.*
*A Common rafter*
*B Principal rafter and purlin*

of the roof. Ventilation is normally provided to carry away this moisture by placing air vents in the eaves and leaving an air channel between the insulation and roof deck so air can enter the eaves, flow over the insulation, picking up moisture, and exit through a vent placed over the ridge. This ventilation also carries away heat lost from the house, thus keeping the roof cold and helping to prevent formation of ice dams on the edges of roofs that can damage shingles and lead to leaks.

A typical common rafter system for a northern climate uses 2 x 12 green wood rafters spaced 24 inches on center, plus 10 inches of fiberglass insulation. This leaves a 2-inch air space for roof ventilation.

Rafters usually are cut from a pattern that has been laid out with a framing square. The rafters are cut with a *bird's mouth* that fits over the top of the wall plate and a plumb cut that fits against the ridge plate.

**LOW-COST GREEN LUMBER CONSTRUCTION**

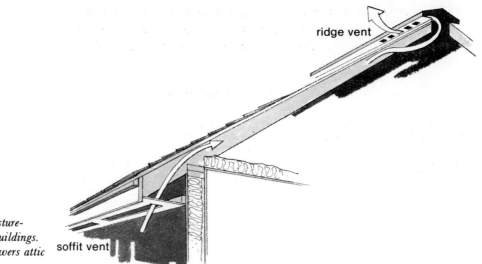

ridge vent

soffit vent

*Eave and ridge vents permit moisture-laden air to move out of heated buildings. Such moisture, if it condenses, lowers attic insulation R-value.*

Because the widths of green rafters will vary, it makes a big difference which edge of the rafter you line up with the pattern. If you line up the lower edge flush to mark your lines, this will be the surface of the rafters that will be even in the finished roof. This would be the edge to line up if you wished to put Sheetrock directly on the rafters to form a cathedral ceiling and were going to strap the top side of the rafters in order to put on metal roofing. If you wanted the roof deck to be smooth, you would line up the top edge of the rafter and pattern.

Which edge of the rafter you line up with the pattern depends on how both surfaces are to be finished. If the rafters simply enclose an unheated attic space, for example, you would line up the tops to get a smooth roof deck since there would be no interior finish to worry about. If the interior is to be a cathedral ceiling, you have to make a choice. If you are using asphalt shingles, you would probably line up the tops of the rafters and shim the ceiling. If you are using metal roofing, which goes on over strapping and doesn't need a smooth surface, you would line up the bottoms, making the ceiling surface even. Before you cut your rafters, think about how you are going to finish both inside and out.

## Roof Sheathing

What kind of roof sheathing you choose depends on what kind of roofing material you are using. For asphalt shingles, which are thin pieces of asphalt with a surface of mineral granules, it is important to have a smooth, strong deck. CDX plywood or composition board are the most common decking materials and offer the advantages of easy installation and a very smooth surface.

Rough green wood boards can also be used under asphalt shingles but have the disadvantage of forming small bumps in the finished roof because of their different thicknesses. Rough wood boards are fine for decking under wood shingles or shakes which hide the imperfections much better. For metal roofing, rough wood boards can be laid across the rafters and spaced 12 inches apart.

## Galvanized Metal

The choice of roofing material is both an aesthetic and an economic judgment. Galvanized metal roofing is certainly the most durable and economical choice. While galvanized metal roofing costs a little more per square foot than asphalt shingles, it requires only strapping for underlayment and goes on more quickly than any kind of shingle. It is also very durable, and in northern climates where snow and ice can ruin shingles, it is often the most sensible material to use.

Post-and-beam roof framing systems are a bit more complicated than conventional stick framing and usually require more materials. If the roof encloses an unheated attic, things are simplified. Because the insulation is put between the floor joists, the problem of insulating and ventilating the beam system is avoided, and the roof can be framed, decked, and covered.

If the roof forms the ceiling for the upper story, the roof must be insulated. This creates some problems. Usually in post-and-beam systems, the roof beams are left exposed and the sheathing over them forms the interior ceiling.

To form a cavity for insulation and a nailing surface for the top roof deck of plywood or boards, 2 x 6s are laid on edge over

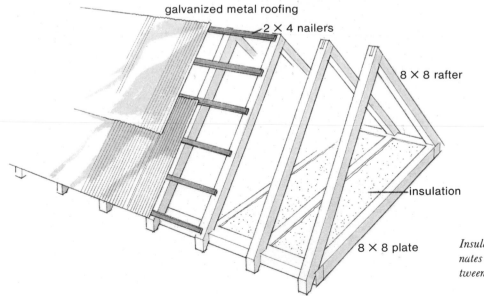

*Insulating between attic floor joists eliminates the problem of having to insulate between rafters in a post-and-beam roof.*

**LOW-COST GREEN LUMBER CONSTRUCTION**

the sheathing boards, running from the eaves to the ridge. These cavities are then insulated with fiberglass or foam, and the roof deck and finished roofing are applied over that. To achieve a high R-value for northern climates, blown-in or rigid foam should be used for the insulation. Five inches of blown-in polyurethane rigid foam will equal 10 inches of fiberglass, giving approximately an R-38 roof. Only 5 inches of foam are placed between the 6-inch deck rafters in order to leave a 1-inch air space for ventilation.

If the cathedral ceiling of a post-and-beam structure will be covered with Sheetrock or paneling, the insulation can be placed on the inside between the purlins. The purlin system is used when the interior ceiling is to be covered since it provides nailers for either Sheetrock or boards. Because the ceiling will be insulated and covered, there is no need for roof decking

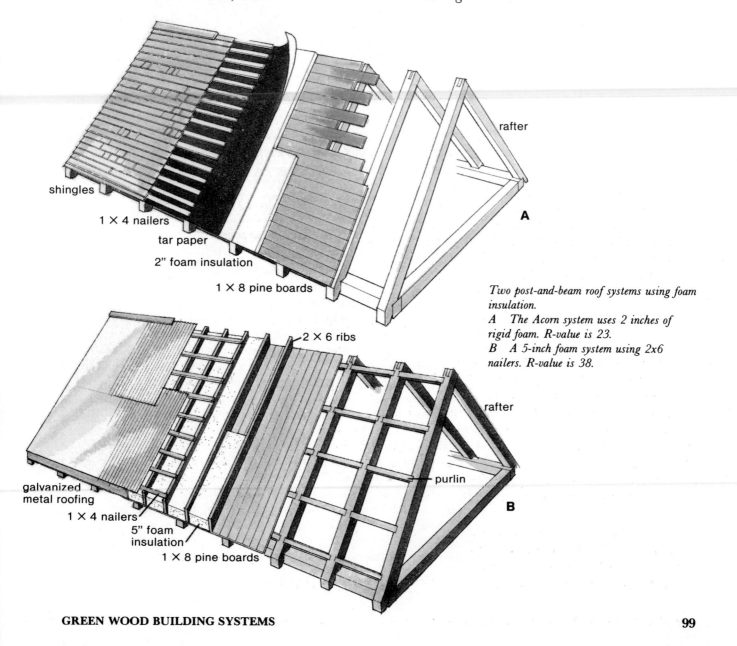

Two post-and-beam roof systems using foam insulation.
A   The Acorn system uses 2 inches of rigid foam. R-value is 23.
B   A 5-inch foam system using 2x6 nailers. R-value is 38.

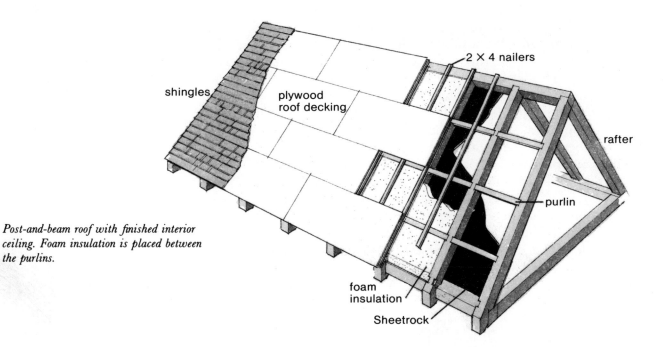

shingles

plywood
roof decking

2 × 4 nailers

rafter

purlin

foam
insulation

Sheetrock

*Post-and-beam roof with finished interior
ceiling. Foam insulation is placed between
the purlins.*

directly on the purlins. Instead 2 x 4s are laid on face vertically over the purlins every 2 feet to create an air channel above the insulation and to provide a nailing surface for the roof decking. Again, the purlins must be insulated with at least 5 inches of foam if an insulating value of R-38 for the roof is to be achieved.

## Foam, Flames, and Fumes

Foam is often the choice for insulating roof systems because of the need for a high R-value within a limited space. Some foams have up to twice the R-value per inch of fiberglass insulation and are impervious to damaging water and insects. (Fiberglass with 1 percent moisture by volume can lose up to 50 percent of its insulating value.) While foam is a good, sturdy insulator, it also has its drawbacks.

All rigid foams such as polyurethane, polystyrene, and polyisocyanurate are extremely flammable, and give off toxic fumes as they burn. For this reason, when foam is used on the interior of a house it must be covered with ⅝-inch fire-rated Sheetrock to meet building codes. Before you design

a foam wall or roof system, get the approval of your fire marshal.

Urea-formaldehyde, which is a blown-in foam, is not as combustible as the rigid foams but is still flammable. While it is less expensive than other foams, it also has a lower R-value which can shrink to that of fiberglass if installed incorrectly. Urea-formaldehyde's biggest drawback, and the reason the U.S. Government is considering banning it, is that it can give off noxious and toxic fumes. Many instances of houses having to be abandoned because of high levels of formaldehyde gas have been reported. If it is used in a vented roof system, this problem should not occur.

## Foam Comparison Chart

| RIGID FOAM BOARDS | R-VALUE PER INCH 0°F. | COST | CHARACTERISTICS |
|---|---|---|---|
| Molded Polystyrene "bead board" | 4.17 | medium | combustible water permeable |
| Extruded Polystyrene "blue board" | 4.55 | high | combustible impermeable |
| Polyurethane | 5.88 | high | combustible impermeable |
| Polyisocyanurate ("Thermax") | 7.4 | high | combustible impermeable |
| **BLOWN-IN FOAM** | | | |
| Polyurethane | 5.88 | high | combustible impermeable |
| Urea-formaldehyde | 4.2 | medium | combustible impermeable possible odor |

Source: ASHRAE Handbook, 1972, Cornerstone Energy Audit.

## Choosing the Right Roof

There are many variations on these basic techniques of roof framing, and several others that haven't been mentioned, such as steel, concrete, and sod roofs. Roof design ultimately depends on the local climate, building materials, and the aesthetic desires of the owner-builder.

By far the most common and economical roof is the common 2 x 12 rafter system with galvanized metal roofing. This system is not only used on many stick-framed houses but post-and-beam houses as well, such as Robin Worn's house on page 11. Because the 2 x 12 rafter system is the simplest, the easiest to install, and the most economical in terms of insulating value per dollar spent, it is what most owner-builders who are building their first home should consider. When your carpentry skills and pocketbook grow, you can try the more challenging post-and-beam systems.

# Foundations

Regardless of whether a house is built with green or dry lumber, steel or stone, it must have a strong, solid foundation. Like every other facet of building, there are several alternatives.

The most common (and expensive) type is the full basement foundation with 8-foot walls of either cement blocks or poured concrete and a concrete slab floor. This type of foundation can cost thousands of dollars and should only be considered if a full basement is really needed for a shop, root cellar, or storage.

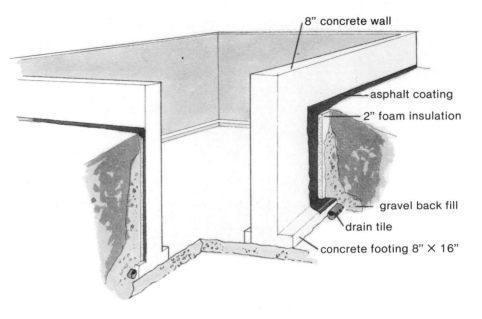

*Full basement foundation.*

8" concrete wall

asphalt coating

2" foam insulation

gravel back fill

drain tile

concrete footing 8" × 16"

While full basements are expensive, they are cheaper per square foot of space than additions to the above-ground part of a house, or building a separate outbuilding that must be heated.

## Concrete Piers

If you have no need for a full basement, consider using concrete foundation piers. A pier foundation saves the labor of full excavation and an enormous amount of materials, and can save you thousands of dollars. If you need a small cellar area for a furnace or root cellar, you can combine a small cellar foundation with concrete piers under the rest of the house. The minimum size of concrete piers or tubes is usually 8 inches in diameter, and the piers are spaced 4 to 8 feet apart, depending on the size of the building and the sill beams that are used. You can lay 8 x 8 beams directly on top of the piers and fasten them with anchor bolts. Likewise, a platform of 2 x 8 joists can also be framed and set directly on the piers.

In many building situations a concrete pier foundation is not only the most economical foundation, but it is the only one that can be put in. At a remote building site, one without an access road, or one with vegetation and trees that prohibit the use of earth-moving machinery, a concrete pier foundation dug by hand with a posthole digger may be the only solution. Despite the hand work involved, concrete pier foundations are often quicker to install than wall foundations because there is less earth moving, no need to build concrete forms, and less concrete to mix and pour. The pier foundation for the green wood barn in Chapter 7 took only two days and two people to lay out, excavate, and pour.

*Left*, framing a gambrel roof with green rafters and plywood gussets to form a roof truss. *Below*, a green wood house going up on an inexpensive concrete pier foundation.

**GREEN WOOD BUILDING SYSTEMS**

## Wood Foundation

A final foundation alternative to consider (especially if you are a green wood purist) is using wood. Set on rock or concrete footings below the frost line, pressure-treated wood can be used to build foundation walls or simply used as posts similar to concrete pier foundations. While pressure-treated wood foundations are still considered somewhat experimental, creosote-treated logs have long been used for post foundations under cabins. They are inexpensive and can be easily replaced if they fail.

If you decide to use a concrete or wood pier foundation for your house, make sure you can adequately insulate between the floor joists since the underside of the house will be directly exposed to cold air. Water and drain pipes must also be boxed in and insulated to keep them from freezing in the winter.

# Prickly Mountain Architecture

*A green wood tree house*

"It's definitely pure Prickly Mountain architecture," said Pat Bates with a smile as she showed me the rough wood beams, curved Plexiglas windows, and unusual layout of Joan and David Gruvin's green wood home in Warren, Vermont.

Prickly Mountain, as an enclave of young architects and designers, has gained a reputation for an architectural style that emphasizes the integration of buildings into the landscape and environment, relying on imaginative and organic architectural forms, the use

of native wood, and renewable energy resources.

While it may be a bit presumptuous to call the free-ranging designs of Prickly Mountain an "architectural style," there are common elements of an emerging green wood architecture that are apparent in the houses that flank Prickly Mountain.

## Part of Landscape

The Gruvin house, started by Joan Gruvin in 1974 and built with the help of many friends, is a good example of this eclectic ar-

chitecture. Nestled carefully into the woods, with large trees rising through the deck and branching over it, the house is an integral part of the landscape. Its four floor levels rise naturally among the trees as if it were a large tree house. The curved Plexiglas windows accent this feeling as they rise, connecting wall and ceiling, earth and sky.

The house is an imaginative post-and-beam structure that breaks away completely from traditional barn-like buildings.

Built with 8 x 8 beams laid on a

concrete pier foundation, the house has four floors that divide the major areas of the house. Starting from the living room with its outside deck, the house rises 4 feet to the kitchen and dining area and upper deck. A ladder stairway leads to the second floor with its bedroom, bath, and study. A second ladder leads to the third floor and the master bedroom that sits in the treetops.

## Used Green 2 x 4s

The post-and-beam frame of the house was studded in with green 2 x 4s and blocked with horizontal nailers to hold the interior paneling and exterior board-and-batten siding.

The interior paneling is 1 x 3 green wood strapping that was planed on one side. The strong vertical lines of the paneling form a unique and very attractive architectural feature that adds to the vertical element in the house.

Another distinctive feature are the Plexiglas windows, some of which form curved arches that join wall and ceiling, while others form skylights in the cathedral ceilings.

The roof system is a double-insulated deck which is common to many new post-and-beam houses. The finished ceiling of the house consists of exposed rafters covered with rough-cut sheathing boards. On top of this 2 x 4s were laid on edge, 3½ inches of fiberglass insulation placed between them, and sheathing boards laid over this for the roof deck. Galvanized metal roofing was then laid over the boards.

Many people in the Warren area helped to build the house. They included Carl Bates, who with his wife, Pat, are the current residents of the house. John Barkhausen, Joan Gruvin's brother and a local woodworker, has also been

*Set in green wood, this curved Plexiglas window has created problems by leaking.* **Opposite**, *John Barkhausen created these kitchen cabinets.*

involved in building the house since it was begun in 1974. Carl, who helped frame the house, and John, who did the interior finish

---

**It represents an important architectural effort to break away from the confines of traditional post-and-beam structures and to integrate housing into its natural environment.**

---

work and cabinetry, showed me around the house, pointing out its unique features and also some of its problems.

## Curved Plexiglas

The most distinctive feature of the Gruvin house and Prickly

Mountain architecture is the use of curved Plexiglas windows and skylights. While these custom-made windows perform specific architectural functions that normal windows can't, such as visually connecting the wall and roof elements of the house, elevating the field of vision, and opening the house and its inhabitants to the outside environment, they also present problems. Most notably, they have a tendency to leak.

## Difficult to Seal

While Plexiglas is the perfect glazing material for the imaginative builder, with its great flexibility and ease of cutting and handling, it is also a very difficult material to seal properly.

When heated or cooled, Plexiglas expands or shrinks considerably and can actually break the waterproof seal on the edge of the

window. And when Plexiglas is set in green wood, which is shrinking as it dries, this problem is compounded.

According to John, most of the roof-mounted Plexiglas has leaked at one time or another, and only now, with the wood finally dry, have he and Carl been able to seal the windows. While roof-mounted Plexiglas can be sealed, using care and the proper techniques, a good rule of thumb is never to use green wood for any type of window frame, especially when using Plexiglas.

**Poor Insulation**

Another problem with the Plexiglas is its poor insulation value or low R-value. While a typical glass Thermopane window or single-pane window with a storm has an R-value of 1.5, a single pane of Plexiglas as on the Gruvin house has an R-value of 0.86, or only a little better than half the insulation value of a standard glass window.

In order to make an energy-efficient Plexiglas window the panes of Plexiglas must be doubled, leaving an insulating air space between them, or insulating window quilts that cover the window at night can be installed.

Another design feature that has resulted in problems is the lack of adequate roof overhangs, which keep water off a building and away from the foundation.

On houses without roof overhangs such as the Gruvins', water tends to run directly off the roof onto the siding, causing discoloration and deterioration of the wood.

The week before I visited the house, Carl had covered the house with creosote, a powerful wood preservative and stain often used on telephone poles. According to John and Carl, it was essential, since the hemlock siding had begun to peel and split and had turned a lovely shade of green due to a covering of fungus.

**Northern Side Protected**

With most of the windows on the south-facing portion of the house, a large garage/woodshed that protects the northern side, and a compact floor plan that is easily heated with wood, the Gruvin house is as practical as it is imaginative. Despite a few technical flaws in the construction of the house, it represents an important architectural effort to break away from the confines of traditional post-and-beam structures and to integrate housing into its natural environment. ❦

CHAPTER 7

# The Green Wood Barn

BARNS, SHEDS, AND OTHER OUTBUILDINGS ARE the ideal candidates for green wood building. The rough wood fits in perfectly with the rustic, utilitarian nature of barns, and because the inside walls and ceilings are not finished, there is no problem with the uneven dimensions of green lumber. By using stud framing and board and batten for siding, green wood barns can be built as easily as planed, kiln-dried lumber barns, and at a fraction of the cost.

My partner and I built the barn pictured on page 112 for Scott and Mary Skinner of Middlesex, Vermont. Designed by the Skinners and built in 1979, the addition serves as a garage, workshop, and woodshed, and is connected to the main house by a breezeway. The cost for the project, including both labor and materials, was well under $5,000.

For owner-builders who plan to build a house, building a small barn first is often a smart way to start. The barn will house you and your tools while your house is going up, and it will give you some practice working with green wood. Besides being inexpensive, barns go up quickly. The Skinner barn, which measures 20 x 24 with an 8 x 10 gable woodshed and breezeway roof, took two people only four weeks to complete, start to finish.

# Getting It All Organized

When setting out to build a barn or an addition, the first thing to consider is the design and layout of the building. Barns range in size from mammoth post-and-beam structures to small stud-framed garages. The size of your particular barn will depend on two factors, its function and your budget.

Consider all of the functions the barn should serve, such as storage for machinery and tools, housing for livestock, or work space. Make sure to measure each piece of large equipment that will be used or stored in the barn so you know its space requirements. There is nothing quite as embarrassing as discovering that the rear end of your car sticks out through the garage door by a good 6 inches.

## Estimate Costs

Once you have designed the barn and its individual spaces for specific functions, think about your budget. More often than not, there won't be enough money to do all you wanted, so a process of scaling down and elimination must take place. Often, if there is not enough money to do the whole project at once, a part of the building, such as an end shed or finished second floor, can be postponed until there is enough money to complete it. Try to design your barn so that the basic structure

## Materials List for Skinner Barn

**1. Foundation:**
16—6″ Sonotubes (14 for barn, 2 for shed)
1 cubic yard concrete
60 ft. #4 reinforcing bar
20—⅝″ anchor bolts

**2. Walls (excluding shed):**
4—12′ 6 x 6 hemlock (sills)
4—10′ 6 x 6 hemlock (sills)
8—12′ 2 x 6 hemlock (plates)
18—10′ 2 x 6 hemlock (plates)
50—8′ 2 x 6 hemlock (studs)
120—8′ 1 x 8 hemlock (siding)
30—12′ 1 x 8 hemlock (siding)
40—8′ 1 x 8 hemlock (battens)
15—8′ 1 x 6 hemlock (nailers)
50 lbs. 12d galvanized nails
50 lbs. 8d galvanized nails
12 ft. ⅜″ threaded rod (corner ties)
8—nuts and washers (corner ties)

**3. Roof (excluding shed):**
21—bundles asphalt shingles (700 sq. ft. coverage)

23—4 x 8 x ½″ CDX plywood (roof deck)
42—14′ 2 x 8 hemlock (rafters)
4—rolls 15 lb. roofing felt
110 ft. 3″ galvanized metal drip edge
10—16′ 2 x 6 hemlock (collar ties)
50 lbs. 1¼″ galv. roofing nails

**4. Shed (8 x 10):**
1—10′ 6 x 6 hemlock (sill)
8—8′ 2 x 6 hemlock (studs)
4—10′ 2 x 6 hemlock (plates)
22—8′ 1 x 8 hemlock (siding)
6—8′ 1 x 8 hemlock (battens)
10—12′ 2 x 8 hemlock (rafters)
4—4 x 8 x ½″ CDX plywood (roof deck)
3—bundles asphalt shingles
40′ 3″ galv. drip edge
1—roll 15 lb. roofing felt.

**5. Breezeway:**
12—10′ 2 x 8 hemlock (rafters)
14—12′ 1 x 8 hemlock (ceiling boards)

5—4 x 8 x ½″ CDX plywood (roof deck)
4—bundles asphalt shingles
1—roll 15 lb. roofing felt
20 ft. 3″ galvanized drip edge
Aluminum flashing (roof joint w/house)

**6. Doors, Windows, and Trim:**
1—3′ x 6′-8″ exterior door w/4 window lights
2—double-hung windows
1—stained glass window
4—10′ 2 x 6 hemlock (sliding door frame)
2—8′ 2 x 6 hemlock (sliding door frame)
18—8′ 1 x 8 hemlock (sliding door boards)
18—12′ 1 x 6 hemlock (soffit boards)
9—12′ 1 x 8 hemlock (fascia)
10—8′ 2 x 4 hemlock (nailers)
2—10′ section steel track (sliding door)
2—sets door rollers (sliding door)
1—2 x 2 cellar window (sliding door)

can be built within your budget, and so that it can also be improved and expanded as money becomes available.

The next step is to locate it on your property. If the barn will house animals, you may want to locate it away and downwind from the house; if it is a garage you will probably want it to be next to the house. If it is at all possible, the barn should be south-facing along its longest axis, with most of its windows on the south side, to take advantage of the sun's heat.

The Skinner barn is an addition to an old Vermont farmhouse. Because it is used as a garage, the barn was built close to the main entrance of the house, running parallel to its main axis. While the barn could not be oriented to the south, it nevertheless helps conserve energy in the main house by shielding the north wall of the house from the cold winter winds.

The barn is framed with green 2 x 6s spaced every 2 feet on center. The 2 x 6s were chosen over 2 x 4s for studs for several reasons. First, 2 x 6 walls can be insulated with 6 inches of fiberglass if the barn is ever converted to a heated structure. And 2 x 6 walls require less framing time since there are fewer studs to cut and nail than in a 2 x 4, 16-inches-on-center wall. Finally, building a 2 x 6 wall requires only about 12 percent more board feet of lumber. If you are using green lumber, this amounts to an insignificant extra expenditure.

## Concrete Pier Foundation

The foundation for the barn is an inexpensive concrete pier system, and the floor was left as dirt, saving considerable expense. All the windows and doors (except the sliding garage door which was built on site) are recycled, bought by the Skinners at house sales and auctions. The most expensive part of the building is the roof, which is composed of black asphalt shingles on a plywood deck. Galvanized metal roofing would have been less expensive, but the shingles were used to match the color and style of the main house roof.

The siding is 8-inch hemlock boards covered with 1½-inch battens. The wood was left its natural color, and protected with a coat of linseed oil. Because the siding was air-dried for several weeks while the building's walls and roof were being framed, it showed almost no signs of splitting or cracking after it had dried in place for a year.

## Materials List

Once you have designed your barn and made a sketch that details the dimensions of all the walls, doors, and windows, you should make up a materials list. Itemize everything you need to

## Estimating Concrete

When you order concrete by the truck, it is measured in yards. A yard is 27 cubic feet or a volume measuring 3′ x 3′ x 3′. When figuring the amount of concrete needed to fill any square or rectangular area, the following formula can be used if all the measurements are in feet:

$$\text{Cubic yards} = \frac{\text{width x length x thickness}}{27}$$

For example, the concrete needed to pour a slab 9 x 18 feet and 4 inches thick would be:

$$\text{Cubic yards} = \frac{9 \times 18 \times \frac{1}{3}}{27}$$

$$= \frac{9 \times 18}{27 \times 3}$$

$$= \frac{6}{3} = 2 \text{ cubic yards}$$

If you are trying to figure the volume of a Sonotube foundation, you need to substitute the cross-sectional area of the Sonotube for the length x width measurements. The area of a circle is pi x radius$^2$. Thus the concrete needed for one 6-inch Sonotube that is 4 feet deep would be:

$$\text{Cubic yards} = \frac{3.14 \times 0.25^2 \times 4}{27}$$

$$= \frac{0.785}{27}$$

$$= 0.029 \text{ cubic yards}$$

You would need 34 Sonotubes just to use up one yard of concrete!

---

buy, from lumber to hardware to nails. Start from the foundation and work up, breaking everything down into individual size categories, so many 2 x 6 x 8s, 2 x 6 x 12s, etc. After you have figured up your lumber needs for plates, studs, rafters, and boards, add 5 to 10 percent extra for waste, rotten pieces, and small framing members you inevitably forget to count.

### Three Lists

Make three lists, one for green lumber, one for windows, doors, and hardware, and one for roofing and foundation materials. These groups of items will often be purchased from different sources. With the lumber list you can get quotes from local mills for cutting your order. With the list for windows, doors, and hardware you can scout out auctions, house sales, and newspaper ads for low-cost units. And with the list of roofing and foundation materials you can talk to the lumberyards and concrete suppliers about prices.

Lists are important. They tell you what to buy, and, by keeping them up-to-date, they can tell you what you still need to order and whether you're still meeting your budget. Don't throw away lists after you have ordered; you'll be mighty thankful to have them when the mill delivers 300 2 x 6 x 8s and you thought you only ordered 200 but can't quite remember. Let your lists do the remembering so you can do the thinking.

### Will Mill Deliver?

When you are checking local mills for green lumber prices, ask about the possibility of delivery. Scott and I loaded and hauled the tons of lumber needed for the Skinner barn. One day, while I was picking up the last few pieces, the mill owner asked where I was building.

"Why didn't you tell me this was for Scott?" he asked when I told him. "I would have been glad to put it on my truck for you."

True? Maybe, maybe not, but I certainly should have at least asked before I went to the expense and back-breaking labor of hauling it myself.

### Building Permit

A final thing to check before starting your building project is the law. Most states have building codes and most localities will require that you get a building permit before you start construction. The person to ask is the town clerk, town manager, or building inspector, who can steer you in the right di-

rection so you have all the necessary information you need about building codes, zoning and subdivision laws, and local ordinances of your community.

Depending on the scope of your building project, you may need to get approval only from the local zoning board or you may have to submit detailed plans and specifications and go before several boards. Regardless, getting a building permit always puts you face to face with a bureaucracy that moves at its own frustratingly slow pace and always requires more paperwork than you ever thought was possible. Don't despair and don't rebel. You have to have that piece of paper displayed at the construction site. Just grin and bear it, put your best foot forward, and you may even find they'll lend a helping hand.

# Putting in the Foundation

A foundation is the most important part of a building. A good foundation will keep a building straight and true for as long as it stands; a bad one will heave a building in a few years. Even though the foundation is underground and will never be seen once it has been built, it is the last place you want to scrimp on materials or construct hastily.

The Skinner barn has a concrete pier foundation, often called a Sonotube foundation after the brand name of the cardboard forms used to hold the concrete. It is by far the most economical foundation in terms of both labor and materials, and is perfectly suited for building both barns and houses unless a concrete slab floor is required, in which case a full concrete wall foundation must be built.

The first step in putting in a pier foundation (or any type, for that matter) is to lay out the lines of the building. This is done with batter boards, heavy string, a 50-foot steel tape measure, and a compass if you are trying to orient the building to the south for solar heating. A large framing square and level will also come in handy for the initial layout of the batter boards.

Batter boards are boards nailed onto stakes. The boards hold strings that mark the outside lines of the building. These boards are placed at least 4 feet outside the corners of the building so that the foundation trenches or holes can be dug without disturbing them, forcing you to lay out the building lines all over again. Four feet is adequate for foundation holes; if you are building a full cellar and in sandy soil, you will be wise to place the batter boards as much as 7 feet from the corners.

## Placing Batter Boards

To put the batter boards in place, first locate one corner of the building where you want it, and drive a stake in place

there. Now measure with the steel tape the four sides of the building, marking corners with stakes, and making the right angles as accurate as possible, using a large framing square.

Place the batter boards (use 1 x 6 lumber) on stakes 4 feet out from each corner and parallel with the sides of the building. As shown on page 118, you now have a wooden fence corner set 4 feet out from each corner of the building location.

To outline the outside dimensions of the foundation, tie strings from batter board to batter board so that each intersection of two strings is above one of those stakes you drove to mark the location of the building corners. Measure from line to line to make certain the measurements are correct.

Now it's time to check your accuracy, to see whether you have right angles at each corner. Measure from one intersection of two strings (*not* from the batter board corner) diagonally to the other intersection. Measure the other diagonal. If the two measurements are the same, you have right angles, and all is well. They should be within an inch of each other. If you have to adjust the strings to get a right angle, remember that you will have to move *two* strings; otherwise you will upset your measurements for the building.

Say, for example, that the angle of the *southwest* corner of your building is a tad more than 90°, because the *SW–NE* diagonal is a bit shorter than the other diagonal. Walk over to the *southeast* corner and move that end of the *south* string a bit north. Walk up to the *northeast* corner and move that end of the *north* string the same distance north. Now you've tightened the

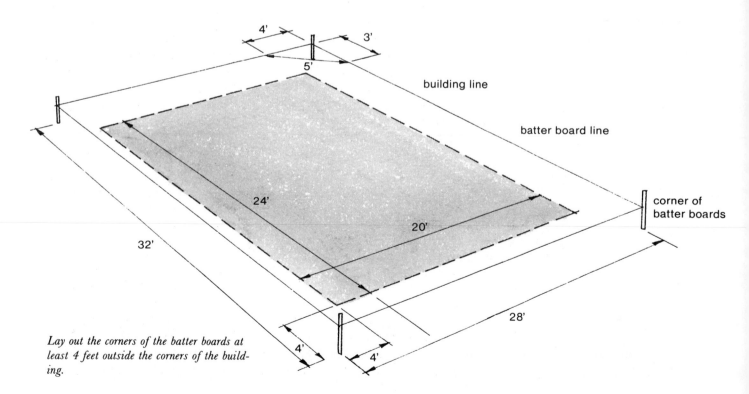

*Lay out the corners of the batter boards at least 4 feet outside the corners of the building.*

angles at both the SW and NE corners, but haven't changed the dimensions of the building.

When you're satisfied that the diagonal measurements are the same, so that all corners are right angles, make one final check of the building dimensions with your steel tape. It's far easier to correct any mistakes now, by moving strings, than it is when concrete piers or a foundation is in place.

## Another Check

There's another method used for checking right angles. If you remember back to high school geometry, you'll recall that a triangle with sides measuring 3-4-5 (or their multiples) forms a right angle. Mark off 3 feet from the corner post on one line, 4 feet on the other line, and then adjust the angle of the lines until these points are exactly 5 feet apart. You will then have a right angle. This method is accurate enough for small buildings, but, because any small error is multiplied over the area of the building, is not recommended for longer distances.

Having placed the strings so that they outline exactly the outside dimensions of the foundation for your building, take one final step. Using a saw or hatchet, mark the top edge of each batter board, exactly where the string is tied. This means you have insurance—you can take down the strings, or someone can trip over and snap them, and at any time you can tie up new strings to give you the exact location of your building's corners.

## Marking Location of Piers

With the building lines in place, you can mark the location of the center of each foundation pier. The piers for the Skinner barn were 6 inches in diameter, and thus the center of each hole was 3 inches inside the building lines. Use stakes and mark the center of each foundation tube. The layout strings can now be removed so the holes can be dug. The foundation holes can either be dug with a backhoe or by hand with a posthole digger. If you are digging by hand, the holes should be approximately twice the diameter of the foundation tubes. If they are dug with a backhoe, they will be quite a lot larger due to the size and operation of the backhoe bucket. While it is certainly cheaper to dig the holes by hand, the soil conditions may necessitate the use of machinery. The Skinner barn site, for instance, was filled with heavy boulders that could only be moved by a backhoe. If you try digging one test hole, you will know whether you want to hire a backhoe to do the rest.

Foundations must extend below the *frost line*. This is the

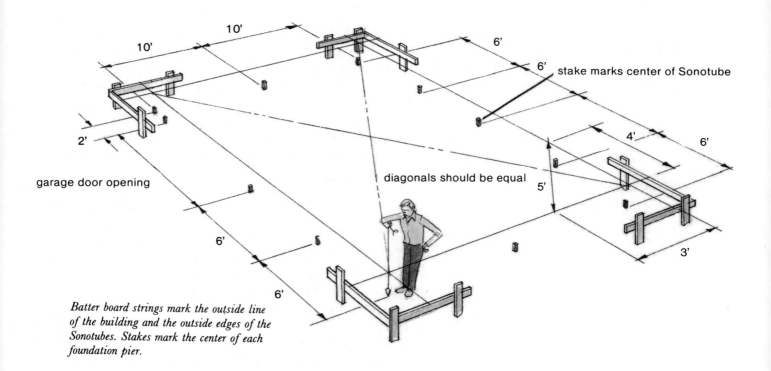

10'   10'   6'

6'   stake marks center of Sonotube

4'   6'

2'

garage door opening

diagonals should be equal   5'

3'

6'

6'

6'

*Batter board strings mark the outside line of the building and the outside edges of the Sonotubes. Stakes mark the center of each foundation pier.*

depth to which the ground freezes, and varies from locality to locality. In Vermont, the frost line is 4 to 5 feet deep. The frost line for any region can be obtained from either the National Weather Service or a knowledgeable builder. If the foundation is not extended below the frost line, it may heave and crack due to the powerful action of the freezing soil.

## Pouring the Footings

Once the holes are dug, the *footings* for the foundation can be poured. A footing is a large mass of concrete that supports the foundation pier. It should be twice the diameter of the pier and about 6 to 8 inches thick. Because of the small amount of concrete needed, footings are usually mixed by hand from bags of ready-mix concrete. Before you pour the concrete into the holes, be sure the bottom of the hole is really where it should be and is free of all loose dirt. Reattach the strings and, using a plumb bob, see that 6-inch piers can be put down the hole so they line up with the outside wall of the building.

In order to tie the footings and the concrete piers together and to strengthen both, ½-inch metal reinforcing bars are used. These are often called *rebar* and come in 20-foot sections that can be cut to size with a hacksaw. At least one piece of rebar should be put in every foundation pier. These should be cut to length before or right after the footings have been poured and

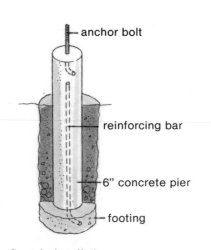

anchor bolt

reinforcing bar

6" concrete pier

footing

*Sonotube installation.*

placed in the footings before they harden. The bar should be formed with a J hook on the bottom and be cut short enough so it won't stick out of the top of the foundation tube.

## Pouring the Piers

Now you can get ready to pour foundation piers. You will usually want to hire a concrete truck. This will save time, effort, and money if you are using a cubic yard or more of concrete. Before the truck arrives, make sure you have everything ready. The last thing in the world you want to do is hold up the truck at $30 an hour. So, using the layout lines as a guide, place the cardboard tubes on top of the footings and carefully backfill them with earth until they are braced, making sure they are plumb with the outside lines of the building.

Mark the height the concrete will be poured to in each tube. There are several ways to do this. One is to use a string and line level that rides on the string. Starting in the corner where the ground is highest, make a mark 6 inches off the ground on the tube. This will be the top of the foundation and the bottom of the sill. With the line level attached, take the string from corner to corner, marking the foundation tubes where the level string crosses them. Because line levels are sometimes inaccurate and hard to read, a better way to check level is with a water hose and a bulb attachment at each end. Using a water level as il-

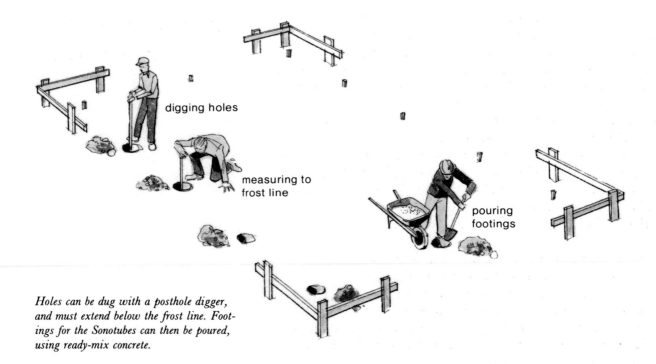

digging holes

measuring to
frost line

pouring
footings

*Holes can be dug with a posthole digger, and must extend below the frost line. Footings for the Sonotubes can then be poured, using ready-mix concrete.*

**THE GREEN WOOD BARN**

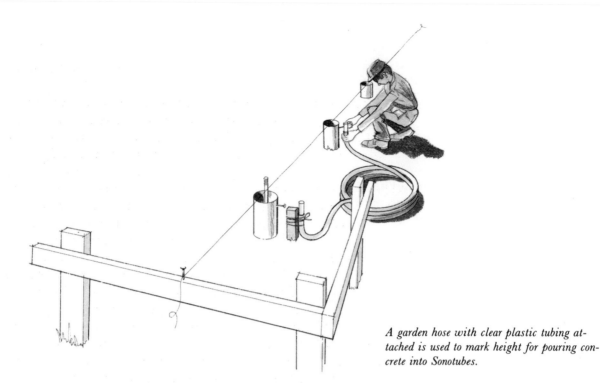

*A garden hose with clear plastic tubing attached is used to mark height for pouring concrete into Sonotubes.*

lustrated here, you can mark the tops of all the foundation tubes exactly and quickly. When marking tubes I usually drive a nail through at the correct height. Cut off the tubes a few inches above the nail marks and you are all set to pour. The concrete truck can simply back up to each tube, and, using a chute, fill it up.

## Anchor Bolts

Once the concrete has been poured, place anchor bolts in the tops of the tubes, to bolt down the sill. These bolts come 8 to 16 inches long to accommodate different sill thicknesses, and have a J hook at the bottom and threads on top. One should be placed in the center of each tube, and high enough so it will stick up an inch above the sill so a washer and nut can be put on. The only exception is the corner piers where the two sills will come together with a 45° bevel cut. There, two anchor bolts should be imbedded in the pier to hold both pieces of wood.

If putting in a foundation sounds like a lot of work, it is. But it is the most critical part of a building, something you don't ever want to fool with again or replace. By spending some time and effort on a foundation, making sure it is square, level, solid, and the right dimensions, you can save a lot of time and frustration when it comes to framing the building. You will have a level surface to build on, and you can proceed with confidence,

knowing that the time and money you are putting into the building will not be undermined by a crumbling foundation.

Rough framing is one of the most enjoyable activities of building. After digging foundations, mucking in the mud, and working with concrete, framing is pure joy. It is both physically and psychologically satisfying. At the end of a day you can see your accomplishment standing in front of you and feel it in your aching muscles.

## Framing the Walls

### The Sills First

Once the foundation piers have hardened (usually a day or two after they have been poured), the sills can be cut and put in place. In the Skinner barn, 6 x 6 hemlock beams were used for the sills to provide solid support between each of the foundation tubes. The beams were bought in 12- and 10-foot sections and then joined on the center foundation pier with a simple lap joint.

The length of the beam is measured from the outside corner to 1½ inches past the center of the concrete pier. The beam is then cut with a 45° bevel at one end and a 3-inch half-lap joint at the other. The illustration shows the right and wrong way to make half-lap joints on a foundation pier. After the beam has been cut, the spacing of the anchor bolts is measured, marked on the beam, and drilled. Cut several 6 x 12 pieces of asphalt shingle, fold them in half, and place them on top of the concrete piers. This will stop moisture that is absorbed by the concrete from the ground from reaching the sills and rotting them. When all the beams have been cut, notched, drilled, and put in place, and all fit snugly together, they should be bolted down with washers and nuts. The corner beams should also be tied together with either 30d spikes or, better yet, with a threaded rod drilled through the beams.

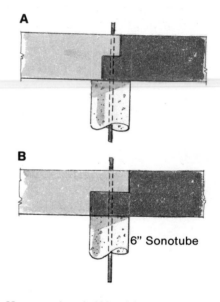

How to make a half-lap joint on a concrete pier.

A   The right way, with beams having 2 inches of bearing surface at their full 6-inch thickness.

B   The wrong way, with beams' strength cut in half.

### Building the Walls

The walls can now be framed. The easiest way to do this for a small building is to build on the ground and then lift the completely framed wall into place. If a wall is over 16 feet long, it should be built in two or more sections with the joints placed on the center of a stud. A 16-foot green wood wall is about all two strong men can wrestle into place.

First, two very straight pieces of lumber should be selected

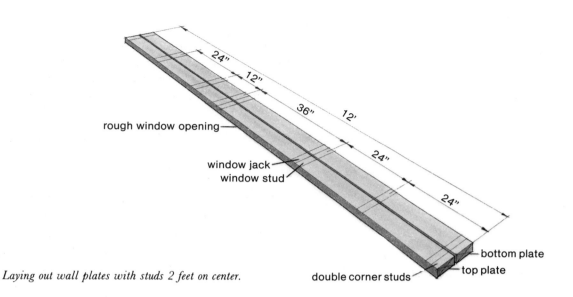

*Laying out wall plates with studs 2 feet on center.*

for the top and bottom plates. It is very important to have straight plates so that the finished wall will be straight. The plates are laid out with pencil marks showing the location of the studs every 2 feet on center, the window and door openings, and the placement of the jacks which support the window and door headers. Notice how the plates are laid back to back for easy marking.

Studs, jacks, and headers are cut to the appropriate length and nailed in place. All the framing members should be lined up flush with the *outside* edge of the plates so you will have a smooth exterior wall surface for the siding. I use 12d galvanized nails for putting the studs in place and 8d galvanized for toenailing. Use only galvanized nails when building with green wood because of their superior holding power and rust resistance. Ordinary nails rust quickly in green wood because of the high moisture level.

## Diagonal Braces

With the wall framed and still on the ground, diagonal braces should be built in the corners. Braces can be made from 1 x 6 boards ripped in half to 1 x 3 inches. First, square up the wall, using a large framing square in the corners and adjusting them until each reads square. Then lay the brace at a 45° angle across the corner studs on the inside of the wall. Make pencil marks on each side where the brace crosses a stud or plate. These marks will show you where to cut notches to let the brace into the studs and plates. Cut with a Skilsaw set to a depth of 1 inch. Make several passes with the saw and then knock out the waste wood with a chisel. The brace can then be nailed with 8d nails into the studs and plates.

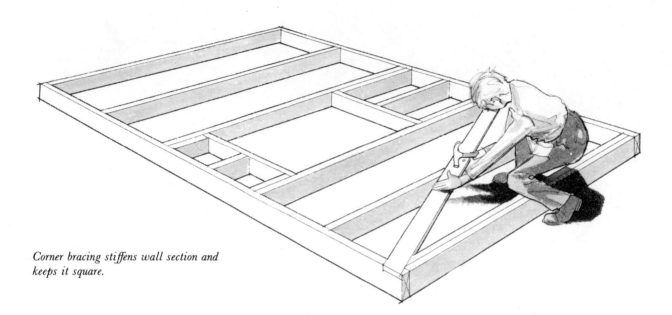

*Corner bracing stiffens wall section and keeps it square.*

Before the wall is put in place, put nailers on the outside to hold the board-and-batten siding. The simplest way to do this is to use 1 x 3 strips nailed horizontally every 2 feet to the outside of the studs. I prefer to let the nailers into the studs as was done with the braces and then use the bottom sill and top plate for nailers, but this is not absolutely necessary. Remember there is an inside and an outside to green wood walls. Nailers must go on the outside.

## Put Up the Wall

The wall can now be placed in position. Set the bottom of the wall up on the 6 x 6 sill and then slowly lift the wall up until it is vertical. Line up the outside of the bottom plate with the outside of the sill and set it in place with a few nails. Tack two temporary braces on the ends of the wall, then nail each one onto a post driven into the ground. This will hold the wall upright. One person should hold a level to the studs and make sure the wall is plumb, while another person nails the braces to the posts. When the wall is plumb and the bottom plate is lined up exactly where it should be, the wall can be secured with two 12d nails driven through the plate every 2 feet.

All the walls are built in this manner, with only a single top plate, then are set in place and temporarily braced. When all four walls are up, the top plate can be doubled up, using the top piece to overlap the corners and joints in the lower plate, securely tying the wall sections together. When the top plate is on and the corner studs are nailed together, the temporary bracing can be removed.

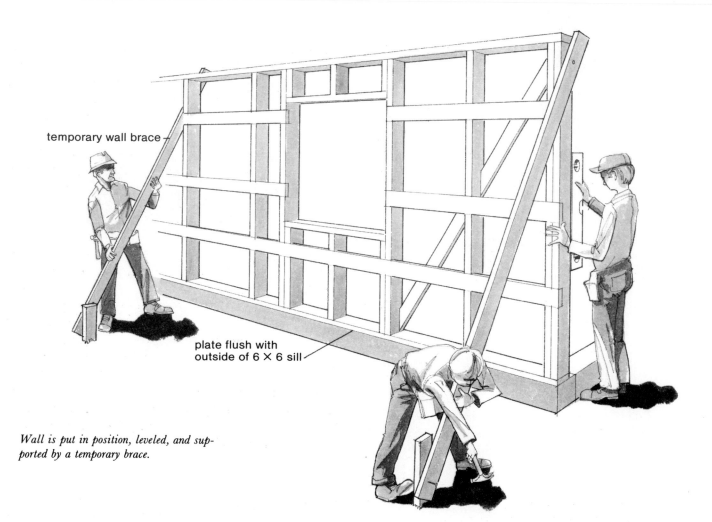

temporary wall brace

plate flush with
outside of 6 × 6 sill

*Wall is put in position, leveled, and supported by a temporary brace.*

# Setting
# the Rafters

Cutting and setting rafters is the most difficult part of framing. It is fairly complicated, and you are working high off the ground. It is important to take your time, have the proper ladders and scaffolding, and be sure you have one hand free to catch yourself when working in an awkward position.

First, a pattern rafter must be made and tested in place. This is then used to mark off the cuts on the other rafters. A framing square is used to do this by a method called "stepping off." This technique is described in handbooks on squares and in general carpentry texts, and will enable you to calculate the length of the rafter and also the angle of the cuts. There are three special cuts on a rafter, the *plumb* cut at the top which rests against the ridge plate, the *bird's mouth* which enables the rafter to fit over the top of the wall plate, and the *tail* cut which forms the outside edge of the eaves.

Once the pattern has been cut and tested, all the other rafters are cut from it. When lining up the pattern with the rafter to be marked, remember that the dimensions of the green lumber may be slightly different and that you will be able to line

up only one edge flush with the pattern. This should always be the top edge of the rafter. By lining up the top edges, the rafters will form a smooth, even surface for the roof deck. The inside of the rafters will be slightly uneven, but, like the studs, because they will not be covered or finished, this doesn't matter.

The next step is to cut the first 2 x 8 ridge plate, long enough to span half the length of the building. When the ridge plate has been cut to length, mark the locations of the rafters on it and on the top of the wall plate.

Working on the ground, nail the end set of rafters onto the ridge plate. This is the set that will be flush with the outside wall. The ridge plate can then be tilted up and the whole assembly hauled on top of the wall. With one person holding the ridge plate fairly level by means of a long 2 x 6, two others can nail the first set of rafters onto the top plate. Two more rafters can then be set at the other end of the ridge plate and everything will be self-supporting. Three people should set those first rafters, though it can be done with two or even one person with a lot of temporary bracing and supports.

After the rafters have been set for half the building, a second ridge plate should be cut and the remaining rafters set by the same method. Where the ridge plates butt against each other in the center of the building, two pieces of wood can be scabbed, one on either side, to hold the plates together.

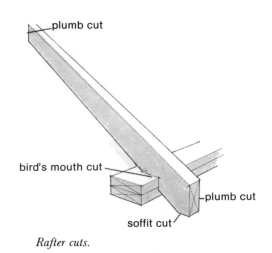

*Rafter cuts.*

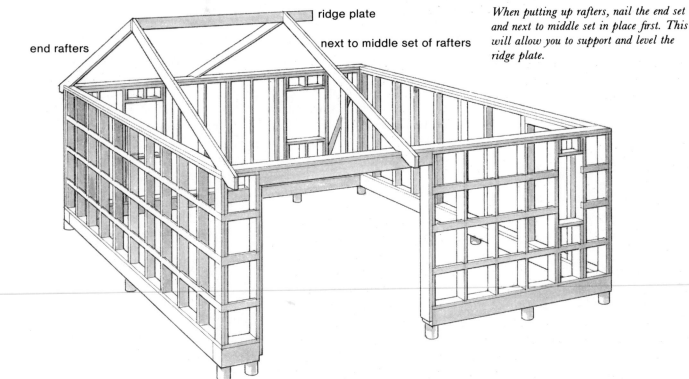

*When putting up rafters, nail the end set and next to middle set in place first. This will allow you to support and level the ridge plate.*

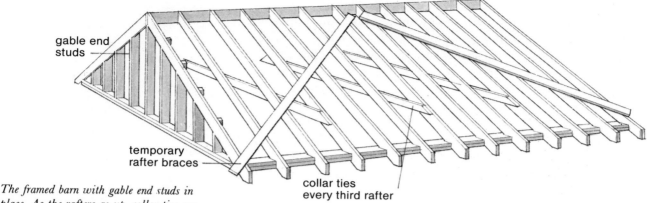

gable end studs

temporary rafter braces

collar ties every third rafter

*The framed barn with gable end studs in place. As the rafters go up, collar ties are put on to prevent spreading. Temporary braces tacked on to the top of the rafters prevent them from blowing over.*

## Collar Ties

When setting rafters, remember that their weight will tend to force the middle of both side walls to bow out. To avoid this, nail on collar ties when the second set of rafters is in place in the middle of the building. Collar ties should be set on the lower third of the rafter, and placed every third to fourth set of rafters. The collar ties in the Skinner barn are 16-foot 2 x 6s nailed about 10 feet off the ground. Because of their span and their use as storage racks, they were reinforced with a vertical center support that runs down from the roof ridge.

When all the rafters have been nailed in place, temporary bracing should be put up to keep the rafters from collapsing to the side. Scraps of lumber, such as long pieces of 1 x 3 or furring strips, should be nailed diagonally over the rafters, tying them together and making them into a stiff assembly. Before you set the strips and lock the rafters in place, make sure the outside rafters are plumb with the outside wall.

With the rafters braced, the gable ends of the building can be studded in. Studs are cut to length and notched to fit under the outside rafter. The easiest way to make the notch cut is to cut the stud a little longer than is needed, hold it in place with a level against the rafter, and mark the angle cut with a pencil. When all the gable studs have been put in, you have finished the rough framing.

# Decking and Shingling the Roof

You can now start to close in the barn. A roof deck either of plywood or rough boards goes on first. Sheets of ½-inch plywood are the standard decking material because of their strength and ease of application. They are expensive, however. Rough-cut green wood boards make an inexpensive substitute, but they take much more time to put on and are not as strong. If a galvanized metal roof is to be put on, rough-cut boards spaced 12 inches apart are used.

On the Skinner barn ½-inch plywood decking was used to get a smooth surface for asphalt shingles and to cut down labor time. Plywood sheathing is put on with the outer grain running horizontally. On the gable ends of the building, the plywood should overhang the last rafter by 2 feet. A typical overhang that looks good and is wide enough to protect the siding from dripping water is about 12 to 16 inches wide. Later the eaves will be boxed in with an outside rafter and supports, and the plywood will be cut to the width of the eaves.

Use two ladders to set the first row of plywood along the bottom edge of the rafters. Once the bottom pieces have been nailed in place, 2 x 4s can be laid horizontally on top of the plywood, nailed onto the rafters, and used as cleats so you can stand on the roof without slipping. With the cleats in place, get up on the roof and put the next row of plywood in place. As you work up the roof, stagger the joints between the pieces of plywood so they all don't line up on one rafter. This will strengthen the deck and its ability to brace the rafters.

## Frame the Gable Eaves

When the sheathing has been applied to both sides of the roof, the gable eaves should be framed in. First, two rafters must be cut. They are like the main rafters but do not have the bird's mouth cut on them, are cut from 2 x 6s instead of 2 x 8s, and are slightly longer, since they will butt against each other, not the ridgepole. Putting these in place takes two people, one on a ladder and the other on the roof. The person on the ladder holds these *fly rafters* up under the edge of the roof decking. The other person nails them in place by driving 12d nails into them through the plywood decking.

Make certain the fly rafters are straight and positioned the correct distance out from the building so the eaves overhang

*How to install plywood roof decking with overlapping joints and overhang for eaves.*

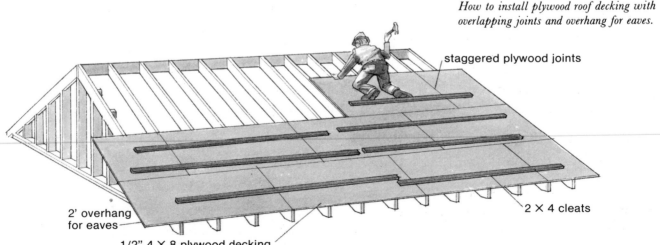

staggered plywood joints

2 X 4 cleats

2' overhang for eaves

1/2" 4 X 8 plywood decking

will be the same all around the building. On the Skinner barn, the eaves overhang was 12 inches from outside to outside of the rafters so that two 1 x 6 boards could be nailed up under the eaves to form the soffit.

With the fly rafters nailed in place and supported by the roof decking, 2 x 6 blocking, or *lookouts,* should be installed between the outside rafter and the fly rafter every 2 feet. These lookouts help support the fly rafter and also serve as nailers for the soffit boards. With the eaves framed the plywood roof decking can now be cut back to the outside edge of the fly rafter.

Before the roof can be tar papered and shingled, the eave *fascia* boards must be put on. These are the outside boards on the eaves which go on over the tail cuts of the rafters and on to the side of the fly rafter. The fascia boards must extend from the top of the roof deck down at least ½ inch over the soffit boards, so 1 x 8s were used on the Skinner barn. The fascia is put on with 8d galvanized nails and butted with 45° lap joints where they come together.

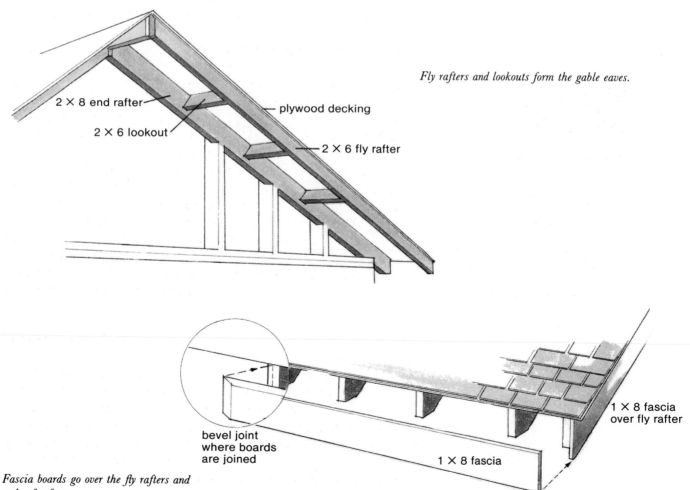

*Fly rafters and lookouts form the gable eaves.*

2 × 8 end rafter

2 × 6 lookout

plywood decking

2 × 6 fly rafter

bevel joint where boards are joined

1 × 8 fascia

1 × 8 fascia over fly rafter

*Fascia boards go over the fly rafters and ends of rafters.*

**LOW-COST GREEN LUMBER CONSTRUCTION**

## Working on Roof

Put metal drip edge and tar paper on the roof deck in preparation for shingling. Metal drip edge comes in 10-foot lengths and 3- to 5-inch widths. It is nailed to the edge of the plywood decking and keeps water off the fascia boards and also gives a straight edge for laying the shingles.

When the metal drip edge has been nailed in place, the plywood deck should be covered with fifteen-pound roofing felt or tar paper, as it is commonly called. Take several rolls up on the roof and set them on the cleats.

It's a good idea to make sure the rolls are secure and won't roll off while you are working on the roof. While working in the middle of a city on a roof four stories high, I once lost a full roll of tar paper over the edge. It seemingly hurled itself down to the sidewalk, hitting the pavement with a tremendous boom, and barely missing several pedestrians. It then proceeded to unroll majestically down the middle of the street for several hundred feet, bringing traffic to a halt. Since then I have been a bit more careful how I handle materials up on a roof.

Roll out the tar paper at the *top* of the roof, starting at one end of the ridge. Staple it down on top and in the middle but not on the bottom, since you will have to slip the next row up under the first. As you work down the roof, overlap the top and bottom joints by at least 2 inches and any side joints by 4 inches. Pull off the 2 x 4 cleats as you no longer need them.

With the roof tar papered and all the cleats removed, it is ready to be shingled. Asphalt shingles should be installed according to the manufacturer's directions using 1¼-inch galvanized roofing nails. If the roof is to be left unshingled for any length of time, the tar paper should be secured by nailing on

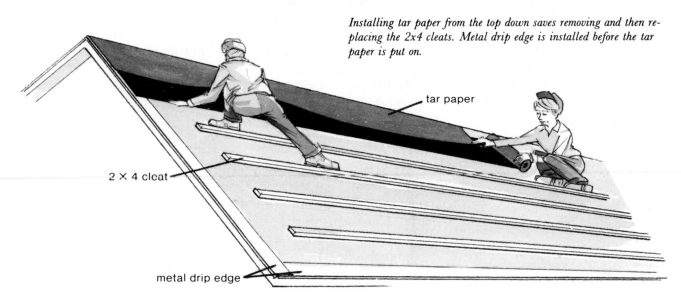

*Installing tar paper from the top down saves removing and then replacing the 2x4 cleats. Metal drip edge is installed before the tar paper is put on.*

tar paper

2 × 4 cleat

metal drip edge

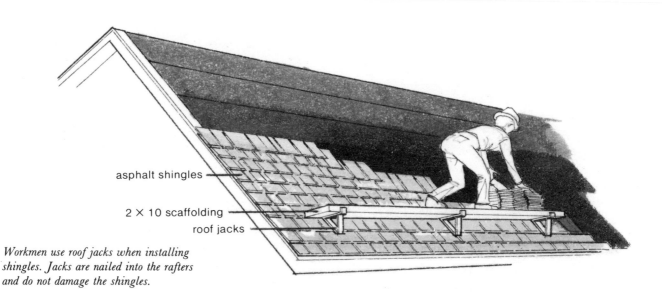

asphalt shingles

2 × 10 scaffolding

roof jacks

*Workmen use roof jacks when installing shingles. Jacks are nailed into the rafters and do not damage the shingles.*

vertical battens that will keep the wind from ripping the tar paper off the roof. Asphalt shingles are put on starting at the bottom of the roof and working up, each row overlapping the one under it. The first few rows are put on from a ladder, and then *roofing jacks* are used to hold scaffolding boards that allow you to work on the roof without damaging the shingles you have already put on. Jacks can usually be bought from a lumberyard or rented from a rental business that carries construction equipment.

# Installing Siding and Soffits

With the roof finished and the building protected from rain, the siding boards can be put on. The siding boards, usually 1 x 8s 8 feet long, are nailed vertically into the 1 x 3 nailers in the walls, running from the top of the wall plate to about 1 inch below the bottom of the 6 x 6 sill. Because the top of the siding will be covered by the soffit boards underneath the eaves, the top line of the siding boards does not have to be even and can run down 1 or 2 inches from the top of the plate. The bottom of the boards, however, must be exactly even and level.

To get an even bottom line on the siding boards, run a string the length of the wall section, tied to two stakes and set an inch below the sill. The siding boards can then be set just a hair above the string, forming a straight, even line across the building.

When nailing the boards in place, start at one corner, putting in two 8d galvanized nails at each nailer, and work across the building. When butting the boards against each other, use a level to keep the edges running straight up and down. Because the boards will vary in width from one end to the other, if you butted the boards together without checking with the level, you would soon find that the boards were not going on verti-

**LOW-COST GREEN LUMBER CONSTRUCTION**

cally. Don't worry about the small gaps between them. These will be covered by the battens.

Because the siding of your barn will determine its ultimate appearance, it is important to put it on carefully. Try to match the color and grain of the boards as you put them up. By having five to ten boards cut and ready to be nailed at any one time, you can choose among them, matching adjacent boards to achieve a unified, mosaic effect with the siding.

## Siding on Gable Ends

At the gable ends of the building the siding must extend much higher to cover the triangle formed by the rafters and top wall plate. First, nailers must be put in the gable studs as was done with the lower wall sections to hold the siding boards. There are two ways to put on the siding so the boards will extend to cover the upper triangle. One method is to join all the siding boards at one level, usually in the middle of the upper wall plate, using a drip cap that runs horizontally to form the joint between the upper and lower boards. Another method is to join the boards individually with 45° bevel joints at different

1 X 8 hemlock siding

1" x 1 1/2" battens

string guide

*A string guide and level are used in installing siding boards. Battens are put on after the eave and window trim have been added.*

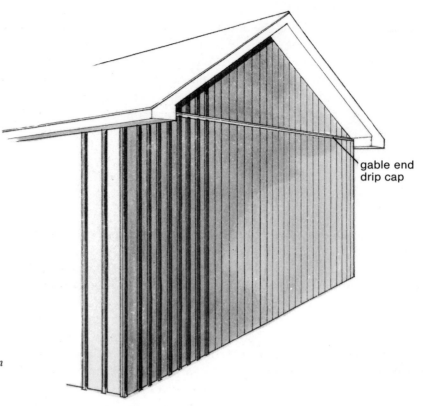

gable end
drip cap

*A drip cap joins upper and lower boards on the gable end.*

heights but always on a nailer so that the joint can be securely nailed together.

With the siding boards on, the soffit can be closed in, using 1 x 6 boards. Because the barn is an unheated building, the roof does not have to be vented as in a house, saving the time of installing soffit and ridge vents. First, lookouts made from short pieces of 2 x 4 must be nailed onto the end of the rafters. The soffit boards will be nailed against these pieces. The lookouts are nailed onto the side of the rafters running level back against the top plate. Put the outside soffit board on first, tight against the fascia board. The inside soffit board should be fitted tight against the outside board, and tight against the siding, using a plane if necessary to fit the board over irregularities in the wall surface.

## Building the Return

The trickiest part of eaves construction is the *return* which joins the gable-end eaves with the eaves on the front and back of the building. Returns can be built in many different ways, ranging from elaborate Victorian designs which almost require a blueprint all their own in order to be built, to very simple modern designs. The returns on the Skinner barn are very simple and require only a few extra pieces of trim.

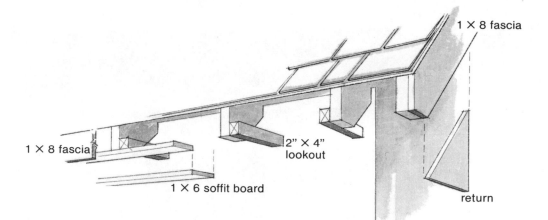

1 × 8 fascia

2" × 4" lookout

1 × 8 fascia

1 × 6 soffit board

return

*Soffit boards are nailed to the lookouts to form the underside of the eaves. A small return piece is used to finish eave corners.*

The additions to the Skinner barn were then built. The 8 x 10 woodshed was framed like the rest of the barn and covered with a gable roof that matched into the front of the main roof. The 8 x 10 breezeway roof was framed differently. Rather than running the rafters vertically, they were run horizontally between the two buildings and supported with joist hangers at each end. This simplified the framing and allowed the rafters to double as nailers for ceiling boards that were put on the underside of the breezeway.

## Putting on Battens

Once the additions were finished, the battens were put on. On the Skinner barn, the battens are 1½ inches wide, allowing five to be cut from a 1 x 8 board. Because of large knots and other defects, the battens will sometimes fall apart as they come off the table saw. When ordering boards for batten material, count on losing at least 10 percent due to knots.

In applying the battens, use 8d galvanized nails and a level to keep them plumb.

## Recycled Windows, Doors

All the windows and doors on the Skinner barn were recycled from other buildings. New window frames were made of green wood with 2 x 8 sills, and the old window tracks were placed inside the frames.

When you are making your own window frames, make sure the sill is wide enough to overhang the battens by at least an inch and is beveled to drain water. Drip caps over the windows should also be provided. An alternative is a large bead of caulk run on top of the window trim. Either will keep water from getting behind the trim and into the window and wall.

A used door was hung in a green wood frame for the breezeway entrance to the barn. The 6 x 6 sill of the barn serves as the

*Window trim cut from green 1x6.*

door sill, and a large piece of fieldstone was placed on each side of the door as a step, making it easier to get over the 6 x 6 beam.

Windows and doors can also be bought new as complete units, with frames that are placed in the rough openings, leveled and squared, and nailed in place.

## Green Wood Garage Door

The sliding garage door on the Skinner barn was made out of green 1 x 8s with a frame of 2 x 6s. It has wheels bolted to its top that slide in a metal track mounted on the inside of the barn. While such a wheel and track system is fairly expensive if bought new, a green wood sliding door can be built for a fraction of the cost of a conventional overhead garage door.

The first step in assembling a sliding door is to build a frame that is strong enough to hold the whole thing together. Green 2 x 6s were used for the Skinner door, with metal plates to tie all the joints together. The frame should be built to provide a

*This sliding door is 10 feet wide.*

nailing surface for the ends of all the boards and also rough openings for windows. The 1 x 8 boards can then be nailed onto the outside in any pattern that is desired. A diagonal pattern not only makes the door more interesting, but also helps brace the door frame, making it quite a bit stronger.

With the wheels bolted onto the top of the door and three or four strong people to help lift, the sliding door can be put on its track. The Skinner barn door, which measures approximately 8 feet high and 10 feet long, must have weighed close to 300 or 400 pounds. Lifting it is definitely not something you want to tackle alone.

## The Finishing Touches

The barn is now almost complete. With all the windows and doors in place, the barn is weathertight except for a 6-inch gap between the ground and the bottom of the sill. This can be closed in using bricks, fieldstones, or strips of water-resistant composition board. Using fieldstones with a backing of mortar

to fill any gaps is definitely the best-looking method, but it also takes the longest. Composition board nailed onto the inside of the sill will do just fine and will go on in an hour. The main point is to stop air flow under the sill while making sure the earth level stays at least 6 inches below the sill. The greatest destroyer of wooden buildings is earth that has climbed up over the sills and started the fatal process of wood rot. Soil naturally builds up at the edges of a building as leaves and other organic matter are trapped, so it is important to keep an eye on sills and make sure they are always high and dry.

The final finishing touch on the barn is to oil the siding and trim boards. I prefer to use linseed oil because it is non-toxic, doesn't darken the siding too much, and gives a beautiful protective finish to rough wood. By oiling the siding you will help preserve the wood from the degradations of the weather, and minimize splitting and cracking as the wood dries.

Think twice before painting your barn. The rough wood will soak up gallon after gallon, and in a harsh northern climate such as New England's you'll have to repaint every four years; in short, you'll have created a maintenance nightmare. If you're dead set on having some color on your barn, use oil-based stains that will give the effect of paint without all the headaches.

The barn is now ready to use. If you are going to insulate the walls and roof, wait a few weeks to let the framing dry out. In a month's time, the barn should have lost at least 50 percent of its moisture and can be insulated without hindering further drying.

# Attention to Detail

*Care and craftsmanship, not experience, are what count*

Green wood houses are always a direct reflection of their owners and builders. Because each green wood house is a unique conception and experiment, their style, size, and details invariably mirror their owners' outlook on life, their work, and imagination.

Eric and Carolyn Bauer's house in Fayston, Vermont, is no exception to this rule. Their green wood house is an open and friendly structure that displays the care and craftsmanship of its owners throughout.

Eric and Carolyn have built four green wood buildings on their property. These include the main house where they live with their two children, a three-bay garage, a woodworking shop, and a large blacksmith shop.

Eric and Carolyn are both self-employed craftspeople. Eric makes his living at woodworking and blacksmithing and Carolyn works in stained glass. While Eric professes that blacksmithing is his real love, he admits that woodworking supports the family.

## High Ceiling

Eric and Carolyn built the main house in 1971. It is a large and open building that was designed to serve as their home and as a shop and studio. For this reason, the first floor has no partitions, a 10-foot high ceiling, and a front door you can actually drive a truck through.

After the house had been built, Eric learned that the local building codes wouldn't allow a blacksmith and woodworking shop together on the first floor. Thus the first floor now serves as a combination living room, office, and studio.

The real living area of the house is on the second floor where there

**Right,** *standard door is built into a larger hinged door. Both sides of the large door swing open wide enough for a truck to enter the first floor area which was designed as a shop.* **Below,** *one of the many handmade windows.* **Bottom,** *the three-bay green wood garage has an attic storage area and a small shed.*

**LOW-COST GREEN LUMBER CONSTRUCTION**

are a dining room/kitchen area, bath, master bedroom, children's bedroom, and two large lofts. Off the dining room is a small porch area that is built into the house and affords an unobstructed view of the Mad River Valley and Green Mountains. This small porch area is beautifully trimmed with old recycled and stained glass windows.

---

**The first floor has ... a 10-foot high ceiling, and a front door you can actually drive a truck through.**

---

### Bought Wood in Canada

Eric and Carolyn built their house entirely out of green wood that was purchased from a Canadian sawmill. The wood was cut and delivered to their property in Fayston for only twelve cents a board foot.

The framing of the house consists of 2 x 6s placed 16 inches on center and doubled on the west wall because of the large two-story stained glass window made by Carolyn that takes up much of the wall.

The interior walls are covered with tongue-and-groove hemlock boards, while the exterior siding is shiplapped hemlock boards. The use of shiplapped boards, which are nailed onto blocks set between the studs, eliminated the need for battens to cover the vertical joints between boards.

### Wanted the View

According to Eric, the house is south-facing "more by accident than by design." Built before rising energy costs, the house was oriented to the south to capture the views, not the sun.

Despite the use of 2 x 6 studs,

the walls are insulated with only 3½ inches of fiberglass, and the ceilings with only 6 inches, since this was the standard practice at the time the house was built. The window units, which are all recycled or hand built by Eric and Carolyn, are also not as energy-efficient as they would like them.

Despite these drawbacks, its high ceilings, and large size, the house with its southern orientation is easily heated by a central wood furnace at a reasonable cost.

### Watched Home Age

Over the years, as Eric and Carolyn have worked on their house and watched it age, they have learned a lot about green wood and its peculiarities.

"One thing I'd do differently if I were building it all over again," Eric told me, "is not use hemlock for the siding. It just doesn't weather very well."

Eric showed me the south side of the house where the hemlock was particularly weathered due to the constant changes in temperature and moisture. Several of the boards had split, others were peeling, and many were cupped. This degradation was even more noticeable under the second-floor porch which sheds its water directly onto the siding and had stained it almost black.

### Will Add Clapboards

While the other sides of the house were holding up well, Eric plans eventually to clapboard the entire house in order to eliminate this problem and also make the house more airtight. If the siding had originally been protected with linseed oil and the water from the porch kept off the siding, I suspect the hemlock would have weathered just fine.

Another problem the Bauers encountered was Sheetrocking the

*The bedroom loft is above the living room. The ceiling fan helps circulate heat that rises into the cathedral ceiling area.*

loft area and cathedral ceilings. As many other green wood builders have discovered, applying Sheetrock over uneven green studs and rafters can be a painstaking and challenging process.

After recently completing the cathedral ceilings, Eric vowed he would be more careful where he used green wood on his next house.

Aside from these minor problems, the Bauers have experienced no major difficulties with their green wood house in the decade since it was built. It is the first house that either Eric or Carolyn had built, but you would never know it wasn't built by a master carpenter. While experience counts for a lot in the realm of building, it is attention to detail and pride in craftsmanship that really make the difference.

# Appendix

# Manufacturers of Portable Sawmills

## Portable Sawmills

Mobile Dimension Sawmill
Mobile Manufacturing Co.
Rt. 2 Box 22A
Sundial Road
Troutdale, OR    97218

Mighty Mite
International Enterprises of
    America, Inc.
PO Box 20066
Portland, OR    97220

Belsaw Machinery Co.
3679 Field Building
Kansas City, MO

## Chain Saw Mills

Mark III Alaskan
Grandberg Industries, Inc.
200 S. Garrard Boulevard
Richmond, CA    94804

Sperber Chain Saw Mill
Sperber Tool Works, Inc.
Box 1224
West Caldwell, NJ    07006

CLC Nordic Prince
CLC, Inc.
Box 189
LaGrande, OR    97850

George's 36″ Mill
George Prube
14135 Olde Hwy. 80
El Cajon, CA    92021

# Lumber from Logs

This table, furnished by Granberg Industries, Inc., gives the approximate units of dimensional lumber possible from logs of various sizes. Calculations are estimates only, and are based on a kerf of ½ inch.

| CUT LUMBER SIZE | DIAMETER OF LOG | | | | |
|---|---|---|---|---|---|
| | 6″ | 12″ | 30″ | 42″ | 54″ |
| 1 x 4 | 3 | 33 | 95 | 196 | 324 |
| 1 x 6 | — | 22 | 57 | 112 | 216 |
| 1 x 8 | — | 11 | 38 | 84 | 144 |
| 1 x 12 | — | 11 | 20 | 56 | 108 |
| 2 x 4 | 2 | 15 | 50 | 98 | 162 |
| 2 x 6 | — | 11 | 30 | 56 | 108 |
| 2 x 8 | — | 5 | 20 | 42 | 72 |
| 2 x 12 | — | 5 | 10 | 28 | 54 |
| 4 x 4 | 1 | 7 | 25 | 49 | 81 |
| 4 x 6 | — | 6 | 15 | 42 | 54 |
| 4 x 8 | — | 2 | 10 | 21 | 36 |
| 4 x 12 | — | 2 | 5 | 14 | 27 |

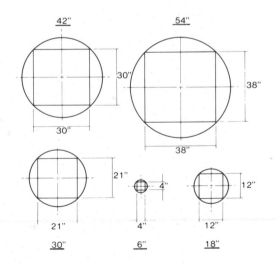

# Wood Characteristics

## Common Wood Characteristics

| SPECIES | WORK-ABILITY | SHRINK-AGE | STRENGTH[a] (BENDING STRESS AT PROP. LIMIT) | WEIGHT[b] (LBS.PER CU. FT.) | DECAY RESIS-TANCE | INSULA-TION[c] (R-FACTOR PER INCH) | USES |
|---|---|---|---|---|---|---|---|
| Balsam Poplar | easy | low | very weak (5000–6000 psi) | 26 | low | 1.33 | walls |
| Northern White Cedar | easy | very low | very weak | 22 | high | 1.41 | walls, posts |
| Hemlock | mod. | low | weak | 28 | low | 1.16 | walls |
| Black Spruce | mod. | low | weak | 28 | low | 1.16 | walls |
| Basswood | easy | high | weak | 26 | low | 1.24 | walls |
| Red Cedar (east) | easy | very low | weak | 33 | high | 1.03 | walls, shingles |
| Red Cedar (west) | easy | very low | weak | 23 | high | 1.09 | walls, shingles |
| Redwood | easy | very low | weak | 28 | high | 1. | walls, shingles, trim |
| Cypress | mod. | low | weak | 32 | high | 1.04 | walls, posts |
| Aspen | mod. | low | weak (6000–7000 psi) | 26 | low | 1.22 | walls |
| Cottonwoods | mod. | med. | weak | 24–28 | low | 1.23 | walls |
| Balsam Fir | mod. | med. | weak | 25 | low | 1.27 | walls |
| White Pine | easy | very low | fair (7000–9000 psi) | 25 | mod. | 1.32 | general, trim |
| Ponderosa Pine | easy | low | fair | 28 | mod. | 1.16 | walls, trim |
| Jack Pine | easy | low | fair | 27 | mod. | 1.20 | walls |
| Red Pine | easy | low | fair | 34 | low | 1.04 | walls, joists |
| Tamarack | fair | med. | fair | 36 | mod. | 0.93 | general |
| Yellow Poplar | easy | med. | fair | 28 | low | 1.13 | general |
| Elm, soft | hard | high | fair | 37 | low | 0.97 | fuel, floors |

*Continued*

[a] Stress at which timber will recover without any injury or permanent deformation.
[b] At 12 percent moisture content.
[c] Calculation for 12 percent moisture. Value *varies* greatly with moisture: variation is 43 percent for softwoods, and 53 percent for hardwoods (see USDA FPL handbook No. 72) for moisture ranging from 0–30 percent. Values given *per inch* of thickness in direction of heat flow; normal to grain.

## Common Wood Characteristics

| SPECIES | WORK-ABILITY | SHRINK-AGE | STRENGTH[a] (BENDING STRESS AT PROP. LIMIT) | WEIGHT[b] (LBS.PER CU. FT.) | DECAY RESIS-TANCE | INSULA-TION[c] (R-FACTOR PER INCH) | USES |
|---|---|---|---|---|---|---|---|
| Maple, Soft | hard | med. high | fair | 38 | low | 0.94 | fuel, floors |
| White Birch | hard | high | fair | 34 | low | 0.90 | fuel, floors |
| Black Ash | hard | high | fair | 44 | low | 0.98 | fuel, floors, furn. |
| Douglas Fir | mod. | med. | strong (9000–11,000 psi) | 34 | mod. | 0.99 | general |
| Yellow Pines | hard | med. low | strong | 36–41 | mod. | 0.91 | floors, joists |
| White Ashes | hard | med. | strong | 38–41 | low | 0.83 | fuel, furn. |
| Beech | hard | very high | strong | 45 | low | 0.79 | fuel, furn. |
| Rock Elm | hard | high | strong | 44 | low | 0.80 | fuel |
| White Oaks | hard | high | strong | 47 | high | 0.75 | fuel, floors |
| Red Oaks | hard | very high | strong | 44 | low | 0.79 | fuel, floors |
| Sugar Maple | hard | high | strong | 44 | low | 0.80 | fuel, floors |
| Black Locust | hard | low | very strong (11,000–13,000 psi) | 48 | high | 0.74 | fuel, posts |
| Yellow Birch | hard | high | very strong | 44 | low | 0.81 | fuel, floors, furn. |
| White Ash (2nd growth) | hard | high | very strong | 41 | low | 0.83 | fuel, floors, furn. |
| Hickory, Shag | hard | very high | very strong | 51 | low | 0.71 | fuel, floors, furn. |

# Calculating Shrinkage

Shrinkage in wood begins at the fiber saturation point (normally about 30 percent moisture content) and continues until all moisture is removed. While it is not possible to predict how much an individual board will shrink, it is possible to predict average shrinkage values for a species of wood. Using the following formula and the data in the shrinkage table, you can calculate the average shrinkage in inches of any species of wood.

$$S = \frac{(M_i - M_f)D}{\left(\dfrac{30}{S_t \text{ or } S_r} - 30\right) + M_i}$$

Where S is shrinkage or swelling in inches, $M_i$ is initial moisture content in percent, $M_f$ is final moisture content in percent, D is dimension at initial moisture content, 30 is the fiber saturation point, $S_t$ is total tangential shrinkage to 0 percent, and $S_r$ is total radial shrinkage to 0 percent. Both $S_t$ and $S_r$ are expressed as a percentage divided by 100.

For example, if you wished to figure the shrinkage in a piece of eastern hemlock that is 6 inches wide and drying to 12 percent moisture content, you would use the formula as follows:

$$S = \frac{(30 - 12)6}{\left(\dfrac{30}{0.068} - 30\right) + 30} = .24 \text{ inches or approximately } \tfrac{1}{4} \text{ inch}$$

## Total Shrinkage Values of Domestic Woods[1]

| | SHRINKAGE TO 0 PERCENT MOISTURE CONTENT | |
| | RADIAL | TANGENTIAL |
| --- | --- | --- |
| Softwoods | Percent | Percent |
| Baldcypress | 3.8 | 6.2 |
| Cedar: | | |
| Alaska | 2.8 | 6.0 |
| Atlantic-white | 2.9 | 5.4 |
| Eastern redcedar | 3.1 | 4.7 |
| Incense | 3.3 | 5.2 |
| Northern white | 2.2 | 4.9 |
| Port-Orford | 4.6 | 6.9 |
| Western redcedar | 2.4 | 5.0 |
| Douglas-fir: | | |
| Coast | 4.8 | 7.6 |
| Interior north | 3.8 | 6.9 |
| Interior south | — | — |
| Interior west | 4.8 | 7.5 |

[1] Expressed as a percentage of the green dimension.

From: Air Drying of Lumber, Agriculture Handbook No. 402

# Total Shrinkage Values of Domestic Woods

| | SHRINKAGE TO 0 PERCENT MOISTURE CONTENT | |
|---|---|---|
| | RADIAL | TANGENTIAL |
| **Softwoods** | Percent | Percent |
| Fir: | | |
| Balsam | 2.9 | 6.9 |
| California red | 4.5 | 7.9 |
| Grand | 3.4 | 7.5 |
| Noble | 4.3 | 8.3 |
| Pacific silver | 4.4 | 9.2 |
| Subalpine | 2.6 | 7.4 |
| White | 3.3 | 7.0 |
| Hemlock: | | |
| Eastern | 3.0 | 6.8 |
| Western | 4.2 | 7.8 |
| Larch, western | 4.5 | 9.1 |
| Pine: | | |
| Eastern pine | 2.1 | 6.1 |
| Jack | 3.7 | 6.6 |
| Lodgepole | 4.3 | 6.7 |
| Ponderosa | 3.9 | 6.2 |
| Pine: | | |
| Red | 3.8 | 7.2 |
| Southern: | | |
| Loblolly | 4.8 | 7.4 |
| Longleaf | 5.1 | 7.5 |
| Shortleaf | 4.6 | 7.7 |
| Slash | 5.4 | 7.6 |
| Sugar | 2.9 | 5.6 |
| Western white | 4.1 | 7.4 |
| Redwood: | | |
| Old-growth | 2.6 | 4.4 |
| Young-growth | 2.2 | 4.9 |
| Spruce: | | |
| Englemann | 3.8 | 7.1 |
| Red | 3.8 | 7.8 |
| Sitka | 4.3 | 7.5 |
| White | 4.7 | 8.2 |
| **Hardwoods** | | |
| Alder, red | 4.4 | 7.3 |
| Ash: | | |
| Black | 5.0 | 7.8 |
| Green | 4.6 | 7.1 |
| White | 4.9 | 7.8 |

*Continued*

# Total Shrinkage Values of Domestic Woods

| | SHRINKAGE TO 0 PERCENT MOISTURE CONTENT | |
| --- | --- | --- |
| | RADIAL | TANGENTIAL |
| Hardwoods | Percent | Percent |
| Aspen: | | |
|    Bigtooth | 3.3 | 7.9 |
|    Quaking | 3.5 | 6.7 |
| Basswood, American | 6.6 | 9.3 |
| Beech, American | 5.5 | 11.9 |
| Birch: | | |
|    Paper | 6.3 | 8.6 |
|    Sweet | 6.5 | 9.0 |
|    Yellow | 7.3 | 9.5 |
| Butternut | 3.4 | 6.4 |
| Cherry, black | 3.7 | 7.1 |
| Cottonwood: | | |
|    Black | 3.6 | 8.6 |
|    Eastern | 3.9 | 9.2 |
| Elm: | | |
|    American | 4.2 | 9.5 |
|    Rock | 4.8 | 8.1 |
| Hackberry | 4.8 | 8.9 |
| Hickory | 7.4 | 11.4 |
| Magnolia, southern | 5.4 | 6.6 |
| Maple: | | |
|    Bigleaf | 3.7 | 7.1 |
|    Red | 4.0 | 8.2 |
|    Silver | 3.0 | 7.2 |
|    Sugar | 4.8 | 9.9 |
| Oak: | | |
|    Northern red | 4.0 | 8.6 |
|    Northern white | 5.6 | 10.5 |
|    Southern red | 4.7 | 11.3 |
|    Southern white (chestnut) | 5.3 | 10.8 |
| Pecan | 4.9 | 8.9 |
| Sweetgum | 5.3 | 10.2 |
| Sycamore, American | 5.0 | 8.4 |
| Tanoak | 4.9 | 11.7 |
| Tupelo: | | |
|    Black | 5.1 | 8.7 |
|    Water | 4.2 | 7.6 |
| Walnut, black | 5.5 | 7.8 |
| Willow, black | 3.3 | 8.7 |
| Yellow-poplar | 4.6 | 8.2 |

## Average Moisture Content of Green Wood, by Species

| | | MOISTURE CONTENT[1] | | |
| | SPECIES | | | |
| Common Name | Botanical Name | Heartwood | Sapwood | Mixed Heartwood and Sapwood |
| --- | --- | --- | --- | --- |
| Hardwoods | | Percent | Percent | Percent |
| Alder, red | Alnus rubra | — | 97 | — |
| Ash: | | | | |
|   Black | Fraxinus nigra | 95 | — | — |
|   Green | F. pennsylvanica | — | 58 | — |
|   White | F. americana | 46 | 44 | — |
| Aspen: | | | | |
|   Bigtooth | Populus grandidentata | 95 | 113 | — |
|   Quaking | P. temuloides | 95 | 113 | — |
| Basswood, American | Tilia americana | 81 | 133 | — |
| Beech, American | Fagus grandifolia | 55 | 72 | — |
| Birch: | | | | |
|   Paper | Betula papyrifera | 89 | 72 | — |
|   Sweet | B. lenta | 75 | 70 | — |
|   Yellow | B. alleghaniensis | 74 | 72 | |
| Butternut | Juglans cinerea | — | — | 104 |
| Cherry, black | Prunus serotina | 58 | — | 65 |
| Cottonwood: | | | | |
|   Black | Populus trichocarpa | 162 | 146 | — |
|   Eastern | P. deltoides | 160 | 145 | — |
| Elm: | | | | |
|   American | Ulmus americana | 95 | 92 | — |
|   Rock | U. thomasii | 44 | 57 | — |
| Hackberry | Celtis occidentalis | 61 | 65 | — |
| Hickory | Carya spp | 71 | 51 | — |
| Magnolia, southern | Magnolia grandiflora | 80 | 104 | — |
| Maple: | | | | |
|   Bigleaf | Acer macrophyllum | 77 | 138 | — |
|   Red | A. rubrum | — | — | 70 |
|   Silver | A. saccharinum | 58 | 97 | — |
|   Sugar | A. saccharum | 65 | 72 | — |

*Continued*

[1] Based on oven-dry weight.

From: Air Drying of Lumber, Agriculture Handbook No. 402.

# Average Moisture Content of Green Wood, by Species

| SPECIES | | MOISTURE CONTENT | | |
| Common Name | Botanical Name | Heartwood | Sapwood | Mixed Heartwood and Sapwood |
| Hardwoods | | Percent | Percent | Percent |
| Oak: | | | | |
| Northern red | Quercus rubra | 80 | 69 | — |
| Northern white | Q. alba | 64 | 78 | — |
| Southern red | Q. falcata | 83 | 75 | — |
| Southern white (chestnut) | Q. prinus | 72 | — | — |
| Pecan | Carya illinoensis | 71 | 62 | — |
| Sweetgum | Liquidambar styraciflua | 79 | 137 | — |
| Sycamore, American | Platanus occidentalis | 114 | 130 | — |
| Tanoak | Lithocarpus densiflorus | — | — | 89 |
| Tupelo: | | | | |
| Black | Nyssa sylvatica | 87 | 115 | — |
| Water | N. aquatica | 150 | 116 | — |
| Walnut, black | Juglans nigra | 90 | 73 | — |
| Willow, black | Salix nigra | — | — | 139 |
| Yellow-poplar | Liriodendron tulipifera | 83 | 106 | — |
| | | | | |
| Softwoods | | | | |
| Baldcypress | Taxodium distichum | 121 | 171 | — |
| Cedar: | | | | |
| Alaska | Chamaecyparis nootkatensis | 32 | 166 | — |
| Atlantic white | Chamaecyparis thyoides | — | — | 35 |
| Eastern redcedar | Juniperus virginiana | 33 | — | — |
| Incense | Libocedrus decurrens | 40 | 213 | — |
| Northern white | Thuja occidentalis | — | — | 55 |
| Port-Orford | Chamaecyparis lawsoniana | 50 | 98 | — |
| Western redcedar | Thuja plicata | 58 | 249 | — |

*Continued*

## Average Moisture Content of Green Wood, by Species

| | SPECIES | MOISTURE CONTENT | | |
|---|---|---|---|---|
| Common Name | Botanical Name | Heartwood | Sapwood | Mixed Heartwood and Sapwood |
| Softwoods | | Percent | Percent | Percent |
| Douglas fir:[2] | | | | |
| Coast | Pseudotsuga menziesii | 37 | 115 | — |
| Interior north | P. menziesii | 37 | 130 | — |
| Interior south | P. menziesii | 30 | 130 | — |
| Interior west | P. menziesii | 30 | 140 | — |
| Fir: | | | | |
| Balsam | Abies balsamea | 120 | 140 | — |
| California red | A. magnifica | — | — | 108 |
| Grand | A. grandis | 91 | 136 | — |
| Noble | A. procera | 34 | 115 | — |
| Pacific silver | A. amabilis | 55 | 164 | — |
| Subalpine | A. lasiocarpa | — | — | 47 |
| White | A. concolor | 98 | 160 | — |
| Hemlock: | | | | |
| Eastern | Tsuga canadensis | 97 | 119 | — |
| Western | T. heterophylla | 85 | 170 | — |
| Larch, western | Larix occidentalis | 54 | 119 | — |
| Pine: | | | | |
| Eastern white | Pinus strobus | — | — | 68 |
| Jack | P. banksiana | — | — | 70 |
| Lodgepole | P. contorta | 41 | 120 | — |
| Ponderosa | P. ponderosa | 40 | 148 | — |
| Red | P. resinosa | 32 | 134 | — |

*Continued*

[2] Coast Douglas fir is defined as Douglas fir growing in the states of Oregon and Washington west of the summit of the Cascade Mountains. Interior West includes California and all counties in Oregon and Washington east of but adjacent to the Cascade summit. Interior North includes the remainder of Oregon and Washington and the states of Idaho, Montana, and Wyoming. Interior South is made up of Utah, Colorado, Arizona, and New Mexico.

## Average Moisture Content of Green Wood, by Species

| SPECIES | | MOISTURE CONTENT | | |
| Common Name | Botanical Name | Heartwood | Sapwood | Mixed Heartwood and Sapwood |
|---|---|---|---|---|
| Pine: | | | | |
|   Southern: | | | | |
|     Loblolly | P. taeda | 33 | 110 | — |
|     Longleaf | P. palustris | 31 | 106 | — |
|     Shortleaf | P. echinata | 32 | 105 | — |
|     Slash | P. elliottii | 30 | 100 | — |
|   Sugar | P. lambertiania | 98 | 219 | — |
|   Western white | P. monticola | 62 | 148 | — |
| Redwood: | | | | |
|   Old-growth | Sequoia sempervirens | 86 | 210 | — |
|   Young-growth | S. sempervirens | 100 | 200 | — |
| Spruce: | | | | |
|   Englemann | Picea engelmannii | 51 | 173 | — |
|   Red | P. rubens | — | — | 55 |
|   Sitka | P. sitchensis | 41 | 142 | — |
|   White | P. glauca | — | — | 55 |

# Building for Independence

*A green wood and stone gambrel*

The directions to Ron Bower's house in West Danville, Vermont, were as intimidating as they were accurate. After a myriad of left and right turns, forks and bends in the road, I finally found myself at an old abandoned farm where Ron had said his driveway started.

Not seeing any driveway, but noting an abundance of snow and several parked cars, I packed up my notebook and camera and set off on foot. After a half-mile or so, walking through the forest on what seemed to be more of a logging road than a driveway, I began to wonder just what I had gotten myself into.

Crossing a small wooden bridge over a stream, the road suddenly jogged to the right and I got my first glimpse of Ron Bower's homestead.

### Cabin in Clearing

The thick spruce forest had been cleared away, making room for a small wood cabin, a main house built of stone and native pine, and a large pottery studio and wood-fired kiln behind it. In front of the house, replacing the traditional front lawn, was a large vegetable garden, and to the right of that at the edge of the property were a small waterfall and stream. Picnic tables and chairs stood outside the pottery by the waterfall, vestiges of summer lunch hours and now covered with snow.

As I approached the house, a strange whirring noise caught my ear, and looking down by the edge of the stream I found its source, a small hydroelectric generator.

Ron Bower greeted me in his pottery studio and introduced me to the other potters who live and

work there, Sylvia Bumgarner, Karen Karns, and Ann Stannard. Setting aside his work for a moment, he gave me a tour of his property and the green wood buildings he had put up over the years.

---

**"The neighbors hee-hawed at almost everything I did. Now that's all changed, of course."**

---

Ron, his wife, and young daughter moved to West Danville in the fall of 1972. That first fall he built a small green wood cabin to spend the winter in and to live in while the main house was under construction. The next spring he started on the main house, a gambrel roof structure built entirely out of native materials, stone and green wood.

### Poured Foundations

The first job was to pour the foundation walls which he made 14 inches thick in order to support the massive stone walls of the house. Using a small cement mixer hooked up to the PTO drive shaft of a tractor, Ron mixed and poured all the concrete himself.

By the time he had his foundation in place and had built the root cellar, he had run out of money. He added another two rooms to the cabin so the family would have a little more room for the coming winter, and then went out and found a teaching job to pay the bills.

The next spring he started work on the house again and by fall had it closed in.

### Used Nearing Method

The stone work on the house was done using wooden forms, a method pioneered by Helen and Scott Nearing and described in their famous book, *Living The Good Life.*

The house is beautifully constructed and very efficiently designed. It faces south to catch the sun's heat, utilizes massive stone fireplaces which add thermal mass, and is bermed on the north by a hillside that deflects the cold north wind.

A large root cellar was also built into the northern hillside, so fruit and vegetable crops can be kept year-round in cool but not freezing temperatures.

### Insulated Stone Walls

On the interior of the stone walls, Ron framed 2 x 6 green wood walls to hold 6 inches of fiberglass insulation and serve as nailers for the paneling and Sheetrock. In the second floor ceiling Ron put 10 inches of fiberglass insulation. "I got chided for using so much insulation," Ron told me. "The neighbors hee-hawed at almost everything I did. Now that's all changed, of course."

All the wood in the house, except for the flooring, came from local sawmills. The white pine siding on the gable ends of the house, an amazing 18 inches wide, cost Ron only thirteen cents a board foot. "I hauled all the boards in my pickup. I'd make a run down to the mill every day, pick up a load, and nail the boards in place, sometimes within an hour of when they were taken off a tree," Ron told me with a smile.

### Dark Cherry Paneling

The interior paneling is dark cherry that was bought for twenty cents a board foot. Ron bought it green and then air-dried it in the house in stickered piles. When it came time to lay the finished floor, Ron cut 1,500 feet of hardwood trees from his property and took them down to the local mill to be sawed.

By the time he got the boards back, he realized he was tired of having drying piles of lumber all over his house, so he sold the hardwood he had cut and bought kiln-

*Construction of two massive fieldstone chimneys was an early step when this house was built.*

**LOW-COST GREEN LUMBER CONSTRUCTION**

*Ron Bower at work in his pottery studio.*

dried oak flooring that could be put down right away.

### Beautiful, Practical

The finished house with its cherry paneling, cabinets, and doors, oak floors, and massive stone fireplaces is as beautiful as it is practical. Since this was Ron's first building attempt, I asked him where he had run into the most problems.

His worst problem (and a pretty minor one at that) was the twisting of the 6 x 6 beams that support the second floor. As it dried, one of the main carrying beams twisted fairly badly, driving up the second story floor and playing havoc with the bedroom doors. This problem could have been avoided by making beam joints that would resist the twisting. Now the only way it could be remedied would be to use steel plates and bolts to force the beam back into position.

Another problem Ron encountered, which was aesthetic not structural, was the darkening effect of the cherry paneling. Because of the dark color of the paneling, doors, and cabinets, the house tended to be rather dark and gloomy. To offset this, Ron painted the ceiling beams and boards white, put down light colored oak flooring, and covered some of the walls with painted Sheetrock.

---

**Through hard work and his own two hands, Ron has gained a measure of true independence, a commodity very few people can claim in this day and age.**

---

A final problem Ron had to deal with was Sheetrocking. As so many other green wood builders have discovered, Sheetrocking over uneven green studs can be the ultimate test of one's patience and endurance. "When you mix modern building materials such as Sheetrock with green wood and traditional building methods, that's when you run into trouble," declared Ron.

### Hydro Power

For the first five years, Ron lived on his West Danville property with no electricity. He used a hand saw and chain saw to cut his wood, a kick wheel for throwing his pots, and a gravity spring to supply his water. Three years ago, he decided to tap the small stream that flows beside his house for hydroelectric power. His generator now produces 720 kilowatt hours of electricity a month. This is stored in batteries that line a wall of the pottery studio. The electricity is used to power lights and one pottery wheel which has been converted to run on direct current.

"I'm glad I lived here for five years without electricity," Ron told me. "I built my house around using a root cellar, kerosene lamps, a gravity spring, and wood heat. Now I'm not dependent on having electricity even though I have it and enjoy it."

## True Independence

As I walked back through the woods to my car, back to the world of resource shortages, inflation, and uncertainty, I thought about Ron Bower's demanding but secure life in the Vermont woods. Through hard work and with his own two hands, Ron has gained a measure of true independence, a commodity very few people can claim in this day and age. ❧

*A homey corner of the kitchen.*

# Index

# Other Garden Way Books You Will Enjoy

The owner/builder and the home-owner concerned about energy conservation and alternate construction methods will find an up-to-date library essential.

**Home Energy for the Eighties**
Newest devices now on the market to cut fuel costs without high investment: thermostat timers, insulating window shades, etc. Plus source catalog for each energy alternative – solar, wind, water, wood.
272 pp.   Order #84   $10.95

**Heating with Coal**
This just-published 192-page sourcebook can help you decide whether or not to burn coal. Includes differences between wood & coal, how to install and operate a coal stove, plus coal bin plans and complete source catalog.
Order #6   $6.95

**Wood Energy: A Practical Guide to Heating with Wood**
Includes woodstove and wood furnace evaluation, best types of wood, chimney and stove care and cleaning. Plus, a thorough source catalog of stoves and manufacturers.
170 pp.   Order #12   $7.95

**At Home in the Sun: An Open-House Tour of Solar Homes in the United States**
Benefit from the positive lessons (and some pitfalls) of people living in 31 varied solar homes around the nation. Solid answers to: How much did it cost? How much extra for solar? What changes in life-style? Plus floor plans and extensive photos.
248 pp.   Order #2   $10.95

**Wood Heat Safety**
The best "insurance" any woodburner can buy against unsafe equipment, improper installation, and unforeseen disaster. Answers questions on safe distances between wall and stove, installing stoves in fireplaces, burning other fuels like coal and paper in your woodstove and *more*!
192 pp.   Order #85   $9.95

**Designing & Building a Solar House: Your Place in the Sun**
A real breakthrough for the homeowner covering every aspect of planning and building passive and active solar-heated homes. Outstanding diagrams, illustrations, and photos.
288 pp.   Order #46   $10.95

**Be Your Own Chimney Sweep**
Don't waste costly heat or endanger your home with chimneys and stoves thick with soot and creosote. Best book on how and when to clean your chimney.
112 pp.   Order #35   $4.95

These Garden Way Books are available at your bookstore, or may be ordered directly from Garden Way Publishing, Dept. 171X, Charlotte, VT 05445. If your order is less than $10, please add 60¢ postage & handling.